Islamic Liberalism

Islamic Liberalism:

A Critique of Development Ideologies

Leonard Binder

The University of Chicago Press
Chicago & London

Leonard Binder is professor of political science at the University of California, Los Angeles. He is the author of many books on the Middle East, including *In a Moment of Enthusiasm: Political Power and the Second Stratum in Egypt,* also published by the University of Chicago Press.

The University of Chicago Press, Chicago, 60637
The University of Chicago Press, Ltd., London

Printed in the United States of America

97 96 95 94 93 92 91 90 89 88 5 4 3 2 1

Library of Congress Cataloging in Publication Data

Binder, Leonard.
Islamic liberalism : a critique of development ideologies / Leonard Binder.
p. cm.
Bibliography: p.
Includes index.
1. Islam—Arab countries. 2. Islam—20th century. 3. Islam and politics. 4. Political science—Arab countries—History. 5. Arab countries—Intellectual life. 6. Liberalism—Islamic countries.
I. Title
BP63.A4A723 1988 88-5455
909'.097671—dc19 CIP
ISBN 0-226-05146-3 (cloth); 0-226-05147-1 (paper)

O my dove
That art in the clefts of the rock
In the secret places on the terraced slope
Let me see thy countenance
Let me hear thy voice:
For sweet is thy voice
And thy countenance is comely

Who is she that appears like the dawn
Fair as the moon
Clear as the sun
And awesome as an army bedecked with banners?

Return, return, O Shulamith
Return, return, that we may look upon thee.
What will ye see in the Shulamith?
As it were the dance of the two camps.

Contents

Acknowledgments

The ideas upon which this book is based originated in a research project of which I was co-director, along with my colleague, Professor Fazlur Rahman. That project, based at the University of Chicago, and ambitiously entitled "Islam and Social Change," was generously supported by the Ford Foundation during the years 1974–1978. The plan of the project encouraged the collaboration of American and indigenous scholars. It also sought to overcome the isolation of field research by providing for each researcher's return to Chicago to participate in an interdisciplinary seminar attended by the project directors, other faculty, and a group of pre-doctoral students. Anticipating, if only briefly, what has become generally recognized during the course of the "Islamic resurgence," the project sought to find an alternative to the prevailing paradigm which predicted that an increase in social change necessarily caused a decrease in Islamic religious commitment.

Even though our program was impossibly ambitious, a great deal of it was actually achieved. Our relatively speculative and academic efforts were soon overtaken by events, and the immediate relevance of our work became only too apparent. Consequently, the scholarly contributions of Fazlur Rahman, Shahrough Akhavi, Donna Lee Bowen, Asim al-Dasuqi, Chris Eccel, Michael Fischer, Nur Cholish Majid, Amin Rais, Mumtaz Ahmad, Ahmad Rhazaoui, and some others, have become significant parts of the collective international effort to understand the meaning and consequences of recent developments in Islam.

A great many people are to be thanked for the support and encouragement received by our group at the University of Chicago, in Iran, Egypt, Pakistan, and Morocco; but not—let's face it—in Indonesia or Turkey. My own special thanks are extended to Fazlur Rahman for his unfailing friendship and to Reuben Frodin of the Ford Foundation for his guidance, interest, and support throughout the years of the project.

Although I administered the project, selected the research teams, negotiated with the Foundation, helped prepare the groundwork with some of the political authorities in the field, visited with some of the researchers in the field, and led the seminar at Chicago (and even wrote a few pieces), I did not really begin to think through the issues in a fundamental way until the project was formally ended and the accounts closed. Only after the administrative responsibilities of running such a complex project were set aside was I able to get the time to do my own thing.

The University of Chicago and the Department of Political Science at that unique institution are to be thanked for many generosities, but none so important or so simple as their readiness to grant time for research at full salary or to supplement external research grants. It was this sound policy of placing the primary emphasis upon the research and scholarly development of the faculty that allowed me to accept a six-month appointment as a fellow of the Institute of Advanced Studies at the Hebrew University in 1978–79, and a three-month appointment in 1980 as Albert Einstein visiting professor at the Haifa University department of Middle East History, then a one-month appointment as distinguished visiting professor at the American University in Cairo in 1982, and most important of all, a six-month NEH research fellowship at the American Research Center in Egypt (ARCE) in Cairo in 1983. During each of these research periods I was at least partly supported by the host institution. I was given ample opportunity to present my work to seminars and at public lectures for the criticism of my peers, and I was given excellent support by the administrative staffs at each establishment. I would especially like to express my gratitude to the late professor Gabriel Baer who invited me to participate in his seminar at the Institute for Advanced Study, to Professor Gadi Gilbar and his colleagues at Haifa University, and in particular to the faculty, staff, and administrative officers of the American University in Cairo who literally took me under their wing. In Cairo, where I did extensive interviewing of members of the religious classes, I was the beneficiary of considerable hospitality and friendship going far beyond the minimal civilities extended to persistent foreign scholars. Among those who were particularly helpful and even sympathetic are Muhammad Abd al-Quddus, Father G. C. Anawati, Dr. Hamid Ansari, Professor Sarwat Badawi, Professor Robert Bianchi, Professor Ali al-Hilal Desuqi, the late Shaykh Suad al-Galal, Professor Hasan Hanafi, Professor Sa'd al-Din Ibrahim, Dr. Muhammad Imara, Professor Mahmoud Isma'il, Gilles Kepel, Dr. Muhammad Khalafallah, Ms. Suheir Lutfi, Professor Zaki Naguib Mahmud, Dr. Fouad Mersi, Professor Amr Muhi al-Din, Dr. Ali Mukhtar, and last, but by no means least, Professor Muhammad Shama.

It is doubtful that the work of those five years would yet have seen the light of day, and certainly not in its present form, were it not for the timely and flexible grant which I received from the National Science Foundation (#SES-8218401). I don't know how many NSF grants are given for foreign area study, especially for those that are concerned with the religious, cultural, and literary aspects of politics as well as the social aspects. I don't think that any of the reviewers or the administrators concerned were under the illusion that this study would be in the "mainstream" of contemporary political science. I think that the NSF is to be commended for its willingness to take a chance on the unusual; and I hope that the result justifies the risk.

Though the Joint Committee on the Near and Middle East of the Social Science Research Council and the American Council of Learned Societies has not directly supported the research upon which this book is based, my participation in the deliberations of that committee over the last five years has contributed indirectly to the final product. The committee failed to agree upon an agenda that was as well defined as the program of the Comparative Politics committee, but it did provide a forum for the discussion of opposed views and alternative approaches. There was also a kind of concrescent evolution to our disagreements, first expressed in the remarkable, if brief, consensus achieved at our meeting in Muhammadiyya in 1984, and partially retrieved in the committee's conference on "Retreating States and Expanding Societies," held at Aix-en-Provence in March of 1988.

This book has been greatly improved by the criticisms and suggestions of three readers of various revisions of the manuscript. Typing, retyping, urgent retyping, emergency retyping, and typing to and from disk were all achieved with her usual frantic but persistent optimism and resignation by Ms. Sherifa Zuhur, graduate assistant and coordinator for the Halqat al-Dirasat al-Duwwaliyya at UCLA.

The revised drafts, entailing much more rethinking, rereading and revising than is comfortable to remember, were accomplished after I moved to UCLA. Though some parts of the book have been published earlier and some were presented as lectures, every part of the book has been extensively revised. In particular chapter two, part of which appeared in *Comparative Studies in Society and History,* volume 28, number 1, January 1986, and chapter four, part of which appeared in *Asian and African Studies,* volume 16, number 1, have been substantially changed and new material has been added. The original material that has been retained is republished here with permission.

My son, Guyora, who is now a professor of Law, introduced me to the subject of literary criticism, and guided my reading in that area. He also read parts of the manuscript and made useful suggestions for improving it. My wife, Yona, who has been pursuing a full-time career in electronic banking since the emptying of our nest, found the time to read much of the early drafts, to comment thereupon and to make helpful suggestions for the revision of, especially, chapters 1, 3, and 8. She has also, relatively cheerfully, agreed to coordinate her limited vacations with my trips to the field. But these much appreciated editorial improvements to the book hardly indicate the extent and depth of the assistance I have received from them and other members of my family.

Los Angeles, February 25, 1988

Note on Translation and Transliteration

Except where otherwise indicated, all the translations in this book are by the author. Words from the original text in transliteration and alternate translations are included in parentheses. The author's interpolations are included in brackets. In some cases, passages are quoted in the original French where I thought that the cost of losing the subtle nuance of the author's expression was greater than the benefit of facilitating the reader's task. Specialized Arabic terminology is usually defined in the text. Occasionally, a simple definition is added for those less familiar with such terms, or where singular or plural forms are likely to be unfamiliar.

A rudimentary system of transliteration from the Arabic has been used. All diacriticals, except for the *ʿain*, have been omitted. Otherwise, the system used by the *International Journal of Middle East Studies* is employed. The first use of each Arabic word is italicized except for words that are widely used in English, such as ulama or Qur'an, Names are also transliterated according to the same system unless they are widely used in English, such as Khomeini or Nasser, or have been transliterated by the named individual in some relevant context.

1

Introduction

Liberalism: Cognition and Belief

Phenomenological theory proposes that scientific inquiry begin without presupposition. It is tempting to try to begin thus from the very beginning, urging the reader to forget everything he or she believes, and pretending that I have suppressed all that I believe. It is, however, difficult in practice, and probably impossible in theory, to build up the entire world out of nothing. It is easier, and possibly more candid, to start with what one thinks one believes, and then to proceed to engage the reader in a dialogue which will examine the warrant for these beliefs. Let us then begin with the presuppositions upon which I believe this book has been constructed:

1. Liberal government is the product of a continuous process of rational discourse.
2. Rational discourse is possible even among those who do not share the same culture nor the same consciousness.
3. Rational discourse can produce mutual understanding and cultural consensus, as well as agreement on particulars.
4. Consensus permits stable political arrangements, and is the rational basis of the choice of coherent political strategies.
5. Rational strategic choice is the basis of improving the human condition through collective action.
6. Political liberalism, in this sense, is indivisible. It will either prevail worldwide, or it will have to be defended by nondiscursive action.

7. The rejection of liberalism in the Middle East or elsewhere is not a matter of moral or political indifference.

8. Political liberalism can exist only where and when its social and intellectual prerequisites exist.

9. These preconditions already exist in some parts of the Islamic Middle East.

10. By engaging in rational discourse with those whose consciousness has been shaped by Islamic culture it is possible to enhance the prospects for political liberalism in that region and others where it is not indigenous.

The hallmark and the paradox of liberalism is that, though it is founded upon the distinction between knowledge and opinion, and the separation of the spheres of the applicability of both, it legitimates a diversity of opinions about opinion. At any given time, some opinion prevails and determines both politics and culture, power and social truth. The essential point, from the liberal perspective, is that it must be possible for that opinion which has become hegemonic to change. It is, perhaps equally essential that at any given time there is some determinable opinion which actually does prevail.

At any given moment, some opinion may carry the legitimacy of truth or knowledge. At a later time, another opinion may come to prevail. Yet it is not possible to believe that everything that we think we know can turn out to be false without destroying the material and technical base of the societies we live in. Neither can a liberal society permit the conjunctural equilibrium to be transformed into an historical absolute.

The traditional position is that knowledge is given either by revelation or reason, and that opinion is not knowledge. Knowledge means the correct representation of the world, free of error and without the distortion of perspective, intentionality, or physical frailty. Knowledge is of things as they truly are, in themselves, and not as we would see them or as we may find them in particular situations. Faith is not opinion to a true believer. Islam cannot be a matter of opinion. There can be no opinion regarding the theoretical absolute or the revealed truth, though differences may be unavoidable in practice. But even this contrast between theory and practice is to be distinguished from the liberal justification of the diversity of opinion. Liberalism treats religion as opinion and, therefore tolerates diversity in precisely those realms that traditional belief insists upon without equivocation. Islam and liberalism appear to be in contradiction.

Tolerance has nowhere more exceeded its own scope than in the contemporary liberal attitude toward religion. In the belief that the separation of religious affiliation from political faction is desirable, liberal tolerance eschews the expression of any judgment on the content of specific religious doctrines. So long as religion and politics are kept apart, the particularities of religious doctrine need not be matters of public interest.

There is, in Western societies, a rather vague approval of religion in general; but that ill-defined position merely affirms that the separation of religion and politics is not meant to disapprove of religion or, worse yet, to approve of atheism. The tolerance of atheism follows the tolerance of other religions which follows the tolerance of other Christian sects. One starts with the problem of Christians of different denominations living together and quite naturally one finds political discrimination among Christians to be quite unchristian.

This tolerance is based upon the familiarity of one group of Christians with the doctrinal positions of other groups, and not upon the impenetrable mysteriousness and utter subjectivity of an alien system of belief. Insofar as it is based on the common belief in Christianity, tolerance should not be problematic. It is rather intolerance among members of the same religious community that must raise questions, and the answers have to do with matters of politics.

Political authority often enjoyed religious justification because rulers believed that social control was possible only under conditions where the rulers and the ruled were of the same religious persuasion. From the priestly point of view, there was a similar conviction that correct doctrine would not long prevail without the protection of the political authorities. Tolerance became possible only when the political authorities refused to compromise their legitimacy further by enforcing priestly policies, and when the priesthood refused to compromise their ministry by insisting on the political legitimacy of a ruler simply because he professed the faith according to their views. This parting of the ways has hardly been complete and there are many places where it has not occurred. Nevertheless, the principle of the separation of church and state has come to be accepted in word if not in practice in the Christian West. The political meaning of this principle is that the legitimacy of the regime and the divine ordination of the priesthood are no longer linked in mutual justification.

Because its scriptural or exegetical basis is weak, the separation of church and state, and the related liberal doctrine of tolerance, have been given a philosophical explanation. From the philosophical point of view, the doctrine of tolerance is founded on the epistemological heterogeneity of religion and politics, rather than upon any clearly argued ontological or ethical heterogeneity. Religion and politics may not belong to two different realms of being, but they cannot both be known in the same way. Presumably religion is known via the consciousness and political things may be known cognitively. It follows according to this point of view, that anything which cannot be known cognitively ought to be excluded from rational political discourse.

The basis of liberal political doctrine is that agreement on the common good for any historical group may be arrived at by means of rational discourse. The liberal doctrine assumes a heterogeneous political community, the membership of which is not fixed, and is concerned with the determination of the common good for a randomly compounded collection of interests and identities. The problem of determining the common good for a community which is made up of essentially similar individuals is very different. If, in addition, the political community is thought to be transhistorical, then the liberal doctrine becomes even more problematical.

If the political community is conceived of as a divinely ordained absolute, then it may follow that the good of that absolute community is to be derived from its essence as revealed in the divine word and not from the historical determinations of rational discourse constrained by praxis. Liberal politics are incompatible with, or unecessary in, an absolute community unless it is further believed that the individual members of the absolute community have been endowed with reason and free will by their Creator and that they have no certain knowledge of what were/are the Creator's intentions. But even in the latter case it need not be argued that there are transcendant moral implications of a given identity in order to diminish the relevance of liberalism. It is sufficient to argue that certain policies are obligatory because they will result in the perpetuation of the absolute community in the two senses of sheer survival and maintenance of its essential or authentic characteristics. That it can be known that a given community is an absolute community without at the same time knowing what is absolutely obligatory on that community appears paradoxical, yet that precarious position is the logical prerequisite of Islamic liberalism.

Liberalism and Islam

For Islamic traditionalists, the language of the Qur'an is the basis for absolute knowledge of the world. For Islamic liberals, the language of the Qur'an is coordinate with the essence of revelation, but the content and meaning of revelation is not essentially verbal. Since the words of the Qur'an do not exhaust the meaning of revelation, there is a need for an effort at understanding which is based on the words, but which goes beyond them, seeking that which is represented or revealed by language.

Rational discourse in Islam seeks to bring practice into accord with some norm of revelation, of history, of reason, or of exegesis, whereas the liberal notion of rational discourse aims primarily at agreement based on good will. Western liberal thought does not predict that rational discourse will always lead to agreement on the same set of institutions—the ideal democratic state—but it has held that the political-cultural continuities of Western civilization are due to the continuous effort to apply rational discourse, despite the heterogeneity of historical experience.

This conviction has gradually crumbled under the influence of pragmatism, epistemological behaviorism, and ontological existentialism, with the result that tolerance has assumed the form of agnosticism and moral neutrality—especially where religion and religious identity are concerned. So long as the West was convinced that its moral superiority rested upon the confluence of rational discourse and its own political practice, the practical example of the liberal West encouraged the liberal interpretation of Islam. But when the West began to doubt its own moral superiority, then the norm of Western liberal rationality no longer served as a plausible explanation of political experience in the world. As a consequence, it is no longer imperative that certain traditional Islamic practices be explained away, or even simply explained. Their difference from Western practice is no less than an anticipated expression of Islamic authenticity.

The question raised by this change of perspective is whether the discourse of the Islamic liberals has not been a form of false consciousness, an abject submission to the hegemonic discourse of the dominant secular Western capitalist and imperialist societies, an oriental orientalism, or whether it was and is practical, rational, and emancipatory.

The reduction of Western cultural pressure has left liberal Islam more than ever subject to pressures from Muslim traditionalists and fundamentalists. The removal of the liberal Islamic commitment to various aspects of Western liberalism has also facilitated a reconciliation with the traditionals and the fundamentalists. Consequently, the outstanding characteristic of the Islamic political revival of the 1980s is its rejection of Western liberal pretensions and practices and its sense of a heady freedom in reaching back into the history of Islam for authentic political and cultural inspiration that may have nothing whatsoever to do with the West. The outstanding characteristic of the contemporary Islamic political revival is that it points toward the end of a dialogue. It remains to be seen whether it is practically feasible to deny the significance of a dialogue which has gone on for so long.

6 Consciousness and Dialogue

There is no sense engaging in a dialogue if it cannot lead either to mutual understanding or to an improved self-understanding. This is the problem that lies at the root of the controversy over orientalism. The question that has been raised by Edward Said is not merely or strictly a matter of literary criticism, nor is it identical with the apologetic efforts of the would-be defenders of Islam.

Edward Said has pointed to the profoundly complex philosophical issues involved in the interpretation of another culture. That Said, following Foucault, describes orientalism as a *discursive formation* rather than a *dialogue* is of capital importance in understanding his argument. A discursive formation sustains a power relationship in addition to whatever else it does, while a dialogue is supposed to produce agreement among equals. Said argues that, in fact, dialogue leads to the establishment of hegemonic or repressive forms of discourse, rather than consensual agreement.

There are at least three distinct issues involved in the controversy over the virtues of dialogue or *conversation* among those who are presumed to "have" different consciousnesses. The first issue is whether consciousness is subjective or objective, individual or collective, biographical or historical. The second issue is whether those whose consciousnesses are different can understand one another. The third issue is whether such a conversation leads to mutual benefit or not.

All three issues are linked in a single system of logical transitivity. If consciousness is solipsistic, conversation will be meaningless. If it is individual, subjective, and biological, then any external attempt at intervention in the process of consciousness formation imposes alterity in place of authenticity. If it is objective, collective, and historical, it is accessible via discourse, but it may be locked in its own experience.

While there are many exponents of the exclusivity of the collective authenticity of consciousness, most thinkers are inclined toward the view that all collective consciousnesses are social and hence essentially open to external influence and accommodation. So the central issue is whether a universal political community is possible, or only partitive communities based upon the forms of discourse which are produced by a common consciousness which has, in turn, been formed by history, culture, and the material basis of life.

While most political philosophers agree that political community is both necessary and good in an ideal sense, they recognize that in practice political community, often, if not always, entails a degree of inequality, exploitation, and coercion. Insofar as exploitation is systematically integrated into the structure of the community, it is sustained by consciousness or "hegemonic" forms of discourse. The question is, how much inequality or exploitation is the community willing to suffer in order to gain the benefits of an orderly political life? The answer clearly depends upon the quantity and quality of those benefits. When they are deemed insufficient, the aggrieved may opt for either a smaller or a larger community. The option of the formation of a larger community is possible only if one admits the possibility of a wider conversation leading to a new cultural and ideological consensus—a new consciousness.

The more optimistic philosophers will argue that under certain conditions it is possible to form wider communities, overcoming the differences between divergent consciousnesses and diminishing alienation, hatred, fear, and inequality. Paradoxically, however, political pragmatists (such as Dewey and Habermas) set such ideal preconditions upon the situation within which a benign conversation can take place, that they virtually deny such a possibility. If freedom is the precondition of equality and equality is the precondition of freedom, can either ever be attained by means of discourse alone? Manifestly, the concept of the ideal speech situation can be no more than a methodological device to guide us toward an understanding of the nature of actual speech situations.[1] Actual speech situations are always characterized by dominance and subordination—by the legitimation of some forms of consciousness and the rejection of others.

Since dialogue can be coercive, there is good reason to consider whether the opening of a conversation with the exponents of an alternate form of consciousness is always going to be of mutual benefit. The risks involved may be found not only in the coercive character of hegemonic discourse, but even in some apparently optimistic theories. Hans-Georg Gadamer, for example, recognizes no limit to the capacity of conversation to generate new and wider communities of understanding and belief. His conception of the hermeneutic process is that the reader engages the text in an interactive conversation, similar to that of two persons who wish to understand one another. Ultimately, the *act* of understanding which creates a common consciousness occurs like an event which creates conviction by the very force of its affect upon the individual consciousness—an event which Gadamer describes as an aesthetic experience.[2]

The idea that conversation can transform one, even if qualified by insisting upon the need for a transcending aesthetic experience, can be frightening in its suggestion of an involuntary process. It is even more frightening if one confronts a culture and an aesthetic which appears to be more sophisticated and more powerfully sustained by material wealth. Gadamer seems to believe that the transformation of consciousness via aesthetic experience is always benign, and never coercive or exploitative, because of the self-justifying or self-affirming character of aesthetic experience: truth is beauty and beauty is truth. But Gadamer, it seems to me, is more concerned with justifying religious faith than in elaborating the ground of the possibility of a free and equal political society.

Richard Rorty stands somewhere between the pessimism of Foucault and the optimism of Gadamer, and it is this sort of middle position that most accords with the logical prerequisites of political liberalism. Rorty does not deny the "facticity" of consciousness or of mental events, nor does he deny that we have priviledged access to such mental events. He rather denies the Cartesian-Kantian assertion that consciousness is the ground of determining whether something is true or not. Rorty distinguishes between the subjective experience of "raw feels," or pain, or "patches of color," and the social experience whereby conversation forms consciousness. In contrast to those who argue, without convincing evidence, that consciousness is both non-cognitive and self-validating, Rorty argues that all forms of consciousness are socially repressive, that they are vulnerable to critique by means of rational discourse, and that the critique of extant forms of consciousness is liberating.[3]

A religious tolerance which is based upon the opposite assumption must either erect a barrier between religion on the one hand and ethics and politics on the other, or it must deny the compatibility of religion and political liberalism. If religion makes claims upon the liberal state, then it must itself be open to the dialectic of critical, rational, discourse, raising the question of the degree to which certain forms of religious consciousness are themselves repressive.

Self-Criticism

The same critical and reflexive question can be raised regarding the disciplined forms of academic discourse which come to prevail at any given time in any given place. Consequently, it is apposite to raise this question regarding the currently widely prevalent, if not dominant, *neo-liberal development paradigm*. The origins and the emergence of this recent academic orientation will be traced in chapter two, where it will be claimed that it represents not only a new (but not unanimous) intellectual consensus, but that it expresses a widespread cognitive convergence among liberals and Marxists regarding the meaning of the recent historical experience of many of the developing countries.

The mere fact that an academic paradigm has emerged as a

dominant discursive form, or has attained a hegemonic position within its own cultural sector, does not validate it. In fact, in the eyes of some of the philosophers introduced, the hegemonic character of an academic paradigm immediately and unequivocally identifies it as repressive. Others, however, take exactly the opposite position, as we have seen, holding that convergence and prevalence are evidence of the successful unfolding of a dialogue.

It may nevertheless be questioned whether any sort of exchange between Western scholarship and the current Islamic movement is actually taking place, since the development specialists seem to be talking to one another while the leading exponents of the Islamic revival have decided to break off the dialogue. In point of fact, the dialogue has not yet been broken off, and most of the present work is devoted to an analysis and critique of some of the more interesting texts in which this cultural conversation is still being pursued. This is not a completely open and reciprocal form of discursive interaction, if only because Western intellectuals read very little of what Muslim intellectuals write. Still, insofar as these thinkers explore Western ideas and confront them with the hegemonic forms of Muslim thought, they carry out the dialogue in their own works. I believe that the further strengthening of Islamic liberalism and the possibility for the emergence of liberal regimes in the Middle East is directly linked to the invigoration and wider diffusion of this dialogue. This belief defines the purpose of this book.

In chapter two, the complex intellectual path by which the neoliberal consensus has come into being is discussed. There, the exposition is very much influenced by Foucault's notion of the *archaeology* of knowledge, except that it employs the similar notion of the natural history of ideas.[4] Foucault's usage emphasizes the fact that certain earlier forms of discourse remain imbedded in, and determinative of the meaning of, some current forms of discourse. I would rather emphasize the related fact that prevalent forms of discourse have emerged dialectically and pragmatically, taking account of circumstances, political interests, and strategic considerations. While the original ideas and usages are important in understanding later forms of discourse, it may also be helpful to pay attention to the conjunctural settings in which discursive formations are adapted to new events or challenges.

The path by which a new paradigm becomes dominant is not the same as the reason or reasons why a new paradigm becomes dominant, though the two are related and sometimes conflated. One can be relatively more certain about discursive events and sequences than one can be about nondiscursive events, so it is possible to be more confident of conclusions regarding descriptions of the path than explanations of the cause. These two types of explanation or description are related in that events shape discourse, just as discourse shapes events. Some philosophers are inclined to believe that discourse, or language, is far more efficient in shaping events than the other way around, but it is difficult to prove such assertions regarding circular relationships. Nevertheless, insofar as a consensus emerged regarding the meaning of salient events of world significance, that consensus is often invested with the legitimacy of effective historical truth, in the formulation of Gadamer, or the validity of empirical truth, in the view of Talcott Parsons.

Even for those thinkers who would deny the constitutive character of consensus, the explanation of how things came to be the way they are depends upon the constitutive effect of the natural history of society in the sense of the random walk of power relationships. Moreover, even if the structure of power relationships is determined randomly, in the nature of prices in the free market, they are ultimately determined by the subjective, individual interest in the rational maximization of personal gratification. It seems, then, that no matter how critically we look upon the validity claims of a hegemonic paradigm, we cannot lightly disregard its consensual and natural historical foundations. In a pragmatic sense, the hegemonic paradigm is a political fact that cannot merely be wished away. It must be acknowledged and confronted on its own ground.

This is not to argue that every and any dominant paradigm ought to be accepted until it is no longer dominant. It is rather to argue that the pragmatic theory of the validation of dominant forms of discourse proposes a political logic, and hence allows for the construction of rational strategies for either the reproduction or change or existing societies. The alternative is to argue that there can be no explanation of the emergence of liberal government in the West that can be of any use to those who aspire to the enjoyment of liberal government elsewhere in the world.

The natural history of the emergence of a hegemonic paradigm must offer good reasons for the conjunctural dominance of a form of intellectual discourse, as well as an explication of the path by which it arrived at its present state. This book is primarily concerned with the emergence of a liberal Islamic discursive formation which poses a challenge to the existing scripturalist and fundamentalist alternatives. The liberal Islamic paradigm can hardly be said to be dominant in the Middle East at the present time, so our inquiry must be limited to an examination of the discursive shaping of that paradigm and the conditions under which it may become dominant. These two forms of explanation are assumed to be related in the same manner in which they are related in the natural history of the new development paradigm. We start with an explication of the natural history of development theory because that natural history suggests the conditions under which the liberal Islamic paradigm can become dominant and, therefore, the ideological constraints which are likely to attend upon the further shaping of that paradigm.

The New Development Paradigm

The new development paradigm is the consequence of the convergence between neo-Marxian theory and the previously established liberal theory. The neo-Marxian theory reaffirms the view that Marx's most important scientific contribution is to be found in his analysis of capitalism, a view shared by many liberal thinkers. On this common ground it has been possible to construct a consensual explanation of the rise of capitalist states, of the peculiarities of representative government, and of the capacity of capitalist states to reproduce themselves (or to achieve long-term stability). This convergence is based upon the agreement between liberal development theorists and Marxists that the emergence of bourgeois states is historically determined or at least predictable in general if not in particular cases. The Marxist conviction that the demise of capitalist states is equally predictable has not prevented this theoretical convergence, because the Marxists are at a loss to explain why capitalist states have not only persisted, but in some cases have come back from beyond the brink.

Liberal theory was clearly incapable of explaining the rise of capitalism without democracy in several newly industrializing countries, just as it failed to explain the persistence of authoritarian government in countries which had experienced "modernizing" revolutions. The neoliberal theory has borrowed heavily from Marxian thought in order to explain such phenomena, and in so doing has laid the groundwork for a new explanation of the way in which democratic government arises. This new explanation postulates the disjunction of capitalism and democracy, or, more hyperbolically, of economics and politics. The link between capitalism and democracy is historical and pragmatic rather than necessary or ontological. Neoliberal theory accepts the Marxist view that bourgeois class domination is unstable, but it proceeds to draw the conclusion that bourgeois domination cannot therefore explain the ability of capitalist democracies to reproduce themselves. The explanation of democratic stability must have recourse to a new, nonreductionist, conception of the state, to a nonreductionist conception of ideology and culture, to a more sophisticated conception of class conflict, and to a new understanding of the role of the educated "middle class." In all of these regards, the liberal theory had been insufficient while orthodox

Marxist theory deployed its elaborate conceptual apparatus to prove the imminent demise, rather than explain the persistence of capitalist states.

In this sense the natural history of development theory links the present historical conjuncture with the present state of theory, and the resultant provides us with a context of contemporary historical reality over against which Islamic thought may be understood or may seek to understand itself. At the present time that reality is constituted by the apparent failure of socialist economic development and the limited success of both capitalist development and political democratization. The combination of experiences of some newly industrializing countries, and several Latin American and south European countries which have undergone a sort of redemocratization, has led to the hope that at least some of the developing countries of the Third World will enjoy an extended period of economic growth followed by a similar period of political liberalism. Dare we hope for such an evolution in the Middle East? In which countries, and under what conditions can we expect such cautious hopes to be fulfilled? At the moment, the Islamic resurgence and the rise of capitalism appear about to converge or clash. The question is whether their confluence can lead to the establishment of liberal government, or whether it is more likely to lead to an anticapitalist authoritarianism of the state, to an obscurantist rejection of modernity and capitalism, or to the emergence of a repressive, authoritarian, capitalist state.

Applications to the Islamic Middle East

There have been at least four important recent developments in the politics of the largest Middle Eastern states. Most observers have focused attention on one or another of these secular trends while neglecting the significance of the others or failing to consider how these trends interact, reinforce, or counterbalance one another.

The most widely acknowledged of the trends has been the Islamic resurgence, but this general phenomenon has not always been analyzed in terms of the differences between movements led by the clergy, those led by petit bourgeois intellectuals (or members of the educated middle class), and those strategies employed by governments or even by leftist opposition movements, to affirm or deny the legitimacy of existing regimes.

The second most generally recognized trend has been the increased concentration of the power of the state. Sometimes described as either increased "stateness" or as an increase in the relative autonomy of the state, the central aspect of this phenomenon is expressed in the stabilization of regimes which are similar to those Latin American regimes which have been described as bureaucratic-authoritarian. The distinctive feature of these regimes is the dominance of the apparatus of the state in both the political and the economic spheres.

The third, and virtually unnoticed, trend has been the emergence of a haute bourgeoisie. The members of this small class of influential and aggressive entrepreneurs have excellent connections with multinational corporations, as well as with the key economic ministries in their own countries. They dispose of great wealth and frequently are involved in large scale industrial and agricultural development projects. In some cases it is possible to discern the beginnings of a vigorous rivalry between this highest capitalist stratum and the elite of the apparatus of the state.

The least noticed trend has been the gradual maturation of serious leftist movements of opposition in the largest Middle East countries. In some cases this trend has been manifested in the development of a more autonomous and assertive labor movement emphasizing economic and political demands which are well short of revolutionary in nature. In others we find variant forms of Marxist parties which emphasize ideology and revolutionary strategies of achieving cultural hegemony (not excluding the exploitation of Islamic movements). These movements are largely ignored because they have either lost some recent battles, as in Turkey and Iran, or because they have failed to develop a coherent strategy, as in Egypt or Algeria. It is, however, likely that we will find such movements soon again at center stage.

Since most political analysis of Middle East events concentrates on one country or on one of the four phenomena identified as secular trends, it follows that these may often be interpreted as autonomous developments. There has, in fact, been a strong and growing tendency to deny the significance of both economic and social structural influences, and to assert the autonomy of the state and of ideology (including religion and culture).

Assertions of this kind are unfalsifiable, even if their precise meaning could be specified or the operational boundaries between the state and civil society stipulated. The purpose of insisting upon such conceptual distinctions when they cannot possibly have a valid empirical ground appears to be ideological—part of a polemic against "liberalism" at home and against Marxism abroad, especially where one wishes to support the legitimacy of authoritarian states which are, for the moment, pro-American. Paradoxically, this conservative inclination, reflecting the continued dominance of the paradigm which sets state authority against popular participation (and against Islamic movements) has led to the neglect of the significance of the rise of the bourgeoisie in many Middle Eastern states. It is questionable whether the bourgeoisie "dominates" or holds "hegemonic" power in any Middle Eastern Muslim country, but some of those regimes may be fairly described as "bourgeois states" or at least emergent or embryonic bourgeois states.

The words bourgeois state do not correspond to some universally understood and immediately apprehended phenomenon. The meaning of the term, like so many others in this discourse, is dependent upon a context of theory and polemic and historical narrative, some of which will be explored in the deconstructionist critique and reconstructive hermeneutic which is undertaken in the following chapters. For the moment it may be sufficient to note that a number of scholars, not all of them of the same ideological persuasion, have come to doubt that there is any such thing as a bourgeois revolution. There is far more agreement, however, that there is such a thing as a bourgeois state, or a state in which the capitalist mode of production prevails, and in which the propertied classes, and especially the owners of the means of production, constitute the most influential political elite, and in which what is vaguely referred to as bourgeois culture and ideology predominate. The question, then, is how and when does such a bourgeois state come into being? Both revisionist development theorists and neo-Marxist theorists have given considerable attention to this question, asking in particular whether it may be the "function" of a Bonapartist state, a bureaucratic authoritarian state, or of a state capitalist regime, or even of an Islamic state, to pave the way for the emergence of the bourgeois state in the Middle East.

The dominance of the apparatus of the state does not, therefore, necessarily preclude the analysis of Middle East politics from the perspective of the problem of the emergence of the bourgeois state. In fact, the prevalence of bureaucratic authoritarianism fairly begs the question. Hence, these two trends, the strengthening of the state and the emergence of the haute bourgeoisie, may readily be seen, or at least investigated, as a single process. It is not difficult to understand how the recent reverses of leftist movements are related to these two trends, but the diverse ideological inclinations and strategic orientations of various components of the left indicate that the issue of class conflict is likely to continue to influence Middle Eastern politics. Hence, it does not appear that the emergent big bourgeoisie can dispense with the protective domination of a very powerful state apparatus.

The most outstanding, if ambiguous examples of bourgeois assertiveness can be found in the Egyptian *infitah* (Sadat's policy of economic liberalization), the economic policies of the Ozal government and even the very establishment of that government in Turkey, the destruction of the left wing of the Iranian revolutionary coalition, the intervention of the government in the *Suk al-Manakh* crash in Kuwait, and the reversal of the socialist policies identified with Ahmad Ben Salah in Tunisia beginning in 1969. Some parallel developments have occurred in Iraq and Syria, though they have not been punctuated by dramatic events. In both of those countries the extreme socialists within the Ba'th have lost out to more pragmatic leaders who have been responsive to the interests of the bourgeoisie in spite of, or perhaps because of, their very restricted numbers. And in Lebanon, of course, the demise of Shihabism can be read in the same light, even though it contributed to such tragic consequences that it may be interpreted as a self-destructive policy on the part of the Lebanese bourgeoisie.

From the Lebanese and the Iranian cases one learns readily of the risks involved for the bourgeoisie when the masses are encouraged to attack the apparatus of the state. The underlying problem was that of the balance of power and the structural relationship between the bourgeois class and the apparatus of the state where capitalism was weak and still struggling to develop an indigenous base. Under such circumstances the strategic dimensions of the rivalry between the bourgeoisie and the apparatus of the state resembles the prisoner's dilemma more than it does a simple two-person zero-sum game, in the sense that the failure of the two to cooperate may bring about a consequence which is far worse for both than the alternatives of mutual cooperation or the acquiescence in the domination of either. The game is not the same as the classic prisoner's dilemma, however, in that each may choose other allies, such as the petite bourgeoisie, usually considered to be the "natural" allies of the state elite, or the ulama (sing., ʿalim,) usually considered the natural allies of the bourgeoisie.

The political processes which have produced this non-zero-sum power game among the bourgeoisie and the petite bourgeoisie, the clergy and the bureaucracy, do not necessarily involve direct confrontation or overt conflict. It is only in those Middle Eastern countries that enjoy a degree of party political life that we can see these class-based differences expressed through rational and self-conscious strategies. In most countries that is not possible. The structures of the state are still the realm of the petit bourgeois interests and, as a consequence, they are objectively still better organized to protect their interests than are the members of the bourgeoisie. But the political power of the petite bourgeoisie (or that power which is being wielded in their name) is being progressively undermined by a constant redivision of economic resources, which are not growing at a sufficient pace to keep up with the constant growth of demands and expectations. The legitimacy of the "national state" (i.e., the Nasserist model) has been founded upon the promise of the continued expansion of the state clientele, and it is precisely this shaky basis of legitimacy which has limited the "relative autonomy" of the state, and rendered it vulnerable to mass disobedience and religious protest. The food and price riots in Cairo, Tunis, and Casablanca are all recent cases in point.

The growing alienation of the petite bourgeoisie parallels the impatience of the bourgeoisie with the jealous suspiciousness of the apparatus of the state, but there is neither an organizational basis nor a community of interests which can serve to routinize the cooperation of these two classes. Since both sets of interests are arrayed against those of the state elite, there are few overt struggles between the petite bourgeoisie and the bourgeoisie, but there are also few opportunities for rational compromise and cooperation. Instead, the situational contradictions lead to an ideological process in which antagonistic and conciliatory impulses alternate with one another.

The national state and its particular form of nationalist ideology served the bourgeoisie in freeing it from the domination of the monarchy and of monarchical bureaucracy in Egypt and in Iran, though not (yet) in Morocco. Only where the bourgeoisie is weakest does it seem content to accept the hegemony of the apparatus of the state without reluctance. In Syria and Iraq, the bourgeoisie may generally believe that they have worked out a suitable modus vivendi with the bureaucratic authoritarian elite. In Turkey, Iran, Egypt, and Algeria there is more tension, while in Morocco, the frequent intimidation of the bourgeoisie is reminiscent of prerevolutionary Iran. Obviously, the various segments of the Middle East bourgeoisie are uncertain about how far they should assert direct dominance, and where they should rely on powerful protectors or popular allies, religious, or petit bourgeois or both. We can also expect that they will not always make prudent choices.

The Muslim bourgeoisie has, to a considerable extent, abandoned nationalism in its earlier form. The bureaucratic-authoritarian state, identified with the Ba'th, Nasser, Ataturk, Reza Shah, and Boumedienne, transformed liberal nationalism and used it to strengthen the state. But the inadequacy of the capacity and the resources of the national state, its cultural alterity, and its overextension in international affairs, all led to limited achievement and growing opposition. In time, this opposition was sustained by a coalition of traditional regimes (led by Saudi Arabia) and some Western powers (led by the United States).

In a sense, the rise of Islam is an ideological dimension of the movement to restrict the power of the state—a movement constituted of a loose coalition of bourgeois fractions, some rural agrarian capitalists, notables and estate owners, and the virtually proletarianized members of the state-employed petite bourgeoisie, the underemployed intelligentsia, and the large student population. The interests that these segments appear to have in weakening the state apparatus, or in gaining a larger share of influence within it, are not compatible, so one of the purposes of the contemporary ideological process is to mask the divergence of these interests. This may be one of the functions of new Islamic ideological formulations.

Maxime Rodinson has argued that there is no necessary contradiction between Islam and modern capitalism. If there are any doctrinal obstacles to the development of capitalism, they may be dealt with by creative reinterpretation of scripture, as they were in the past. The resurgence of Islam is both a threat and a promise, so the task of the moment is to appropriate religion as part of the new bourgeois ideology before it is appropriated by some rival social force.

The problem is not a new one, but there is a new urgency that challenges the bourgeois elite to devise an effective ideological strategy. In the recent past, in Egypt and in Iran, the political subordination of compliant clerical establishments and the religious protest of "fundamentalists," both within and without the religious institution, split the ranks of the religionists themselves. Exponents of modernizing religious reforms reaped the benefits of the decline of traditional religious authority. But more recently, in these two countries, and in Turkey as well, it became evident that one might go too far in the other direction, that is, in the shaping of a militant and extremist Islam with violent and/or Jacobinist tendencies. If the bourgeois elite is uneasy with the rise of Islamic extremism, it has been even more cautious in implementing a preemptive strategy. It cannot afford to alienate the forces of militant Islam, lest it suffer the political decline of the Iranian bourgeoisie. But neither can it afford to take chances on the arbitrary fortunes of doctrinaire exegesis. It is in such a context that the professional intellectuals may play a significant ideological role.

It is the consensual view of all those who insist upon the relative autonomy of the ideological that there is no one-to-one relationship between given works of political thought and the interests or political strategies of those they are thought to serve. It may be assumed that cultural elites serve their own interests first and foremost, but they do so in complex ways, because they are complex people, and because the rewards they seek can only be won by the most indirect and uncertain paths. It is often safest to present one's ideas as though they merely reaffirm an existing, if inarticulate, consensus. And while that does not prevent some from seeking to shock or to overthrow, a great many have bought respectability by demonstrating how dangerous they might be if they *chose* to unmask the hypocrisy of the system.

The liberal intellectual elite is only one among several possible allies of the private economic sector, and each of these potential alliances implies an ideological as well as a political strategy. Moreover, political liberalism, freedom of intellectual expression, and the rule of law describe only one kind of bourgeois hegemony, and it is not clear that the bourgeoisie of any of the Muslim countries of the Middle East has made the necessary commitment. It is too early in the game, and there are too many uncertainties to allow us to predict the victory of the Middle Eastern bourgeoisie in the construction of liberal capitalist states in the region, but it seems likely, as that struggle continues, that the liberal intellectual elite will have a role to play.

The problem of understanding the political consequences of the Islamic resurgence remains, therefore, and that problem has two dimensions, at least. The first of these is whether the Islamic resurgence will foster or hinder the emergence of the bourgeois state in the Middle East. Should the Islamic movement be analyzed as might any other petit bourgeois movement, now opposing and then serving the interests of the bourgeoisie? Or will the Islamic movement seize the state, strengthen its hold on the masses even more, and decisively block the effort of the bourgeoisie to capture hegemonic power?

The second question is, what impact will the Islamic resurgence have on the quality of political life in the Middle East? We take it for granted, perhaps too easily, that the emergence of an influential and politically organized bourgeoisie is a necessary but not a sufficient condition for the achievement of a liberal, pluralist, democratic, participatory, and competitive regime. This is the type of regime found in many countries in the western hemisphere and in western Europe. It is widely held that such regimes have existed only where there is a bourgeois state, although one might not preclude the future possibility of a liberal regime in an institutional and cultural context which might no longer be recognized as bourgeois. It may be possible to establish a recognizable form of social democracy without first consolidating the bourgeois state, but there do not appear to be any actual cases. If, therefore, the bourgeois state is not a sufficient condition for the achievement of a liberal regime, then it is reasonable to ask whether the Islamic movement will increase the probability of the development of liberal democracies in the Middle East.

This last question is a very complicated one with many dimensions, some of which are already invoked in the prior question. But if we assume that the Islamic movement does not prevent the further development of the bourgeois state, two branching possibilities follow. The first and less likely of these is that the Islamic movement will decline and be replaced by other equally ephemeral expressions of lower middle class alienation—as some would argue was the case with pan-Arabism. The second, and more likely, is that the Islamic movement will remain vigorous, and that it will become increasingly central to the political restructuring of power in these countries. In this second case, where the Islamic movement may actually facilitate, or at least not prevent, the emergence of the bourgeois state, it is likely to have a profound influence on whether that state will be liberal or authoritarian.

The Plan of the Book

The central focus of this book is on the relationship of Islamic liberalism to political liberalism. It considers the opinion that, at the present time, secularism is declining in acceptability and is unlikely to serve as an ideological basis for political liberalism in the Middle East. It asks whether an Islamic liberalism is possible, and it concludes that, without a vigorous Islamic liberalism, political liberalism will not succeed in the Middle East, despite the emergence of bourgeois states.

Following the assumption that facts never exist outside of some intellectual and intentional context, the purpose of this book is to construct a framework, or paradigm, for the proper study of the Islamic resurgence. I shall not ignore the still opaque events that are frequently referred to as the facts of the case, but I shall question whether there are not other, more important, if less dramatic, events to which attention should be paid. Thus, the central purpose of this book is to question the intellectual ground of the currently dominant interpretive paradigm employed in both the public and the academic explanations of Middle East politics.

Principally, I wish to refute the idea that some sort of esoteric knowledge or intersubjective understanding is essential to an explanation of the dismaying developments of the last decade or so. Middle East specialists have the obligation to try to render the experience of the Middle East intelligible in terms of their own experience. This does not mean the blind application of some Western paradigm. It means, exactly, the dialectical application of a hermeneutic to the cultural expression of the experience for both Islam and the West.

It is this perspective which has led to the conclusion that the central phenomenon of contemporary Middle East history has been the emergence of the bourgeois state and the gradual growth of capitalism. This central transformation continues to have enormous implications for international politics, and it has been relatively well understood in this context. The internal political implications of this lengthy process have been misconstrued because of the "false consciousness" of liberal development theory, and because of the cultural confusion surrounding the question of orientalism. Among the most important consequences of the resultant ideological distortion of our perspective have been the twin dogmas that the state is superior to civil society and that cultural authenticity is superior to cosmopolitanism.

In the simplest terms, the dominant paradigm diminishes our commitment to political liberalism at home and abroad, and it discourages those few but influential exponents of Islamic liberalism who are steadfastly trying to keep the movement alive in the Middle East. The emergence of liberal states in the Middle East is neither assured nor even highly likely. But if the emergence of bourgeois states is already upon us in many cases, then it is important to show how one can be the precondition of the other.

It seems to me that much of the contemporary discussion of Middle East politics has diffused a rhetorical fog which obscures the historical opportunity for a major improvement in the quality of political life in the Middle East. It is, consequently, a major assumption of this book that we live in a single world of political meaning and experience, and that the recognition of this (ontological and epistemological) unity is the foundation of political liberalism. The central thesis of the book will be examined in an ideological and critical context made up of elements of both Western and Islamic thought. I shall deliberately try to pass from cultural context to cultural context, from the methodology of the social sciences to the problematics of culture and consciousness, from political to academic polemics. The method employed is both self-conscious and eclectic, borrowing from a number of thinkers who have been concerned with the limits of what can be known and what can be said. In moving from chapter to chapter, the ideological perspective will change abruptly, even though the central issue remains the same throughout. This approach may be readily recognized as dialectical, and though it forces the reader (and the author) to submit to the demystifying experience of a *coupure,* it should affirm that the conclusion reached is not the product of a functional teleology or an historicist eschatology.

Though I have tried hard to submerge myself in ideological contexts which have been collectively constituted, this remains a highly personal work. It is tied together by my personal quest for an understanding of great events and by my own role as a professional scholar who is called upon to explain these events. I have proceeded by the traditional method of reading what others have to say, but I have thought of these others as alter egos, my own intellectual and professional counterparts. The choice of these authors followed the sequence with which certain theoretical questions arose in my mind, and the authors chosen appeared to me to be the right ones for dealing with the question at hand: orientalism, secularism, Marxism, fundamentalism, nationalism, pragmatism and, finally, the critique of the bourgeois state.

For reasons which will become apparent in the course of exposition, I decided to use the technique of analyzing only a few texts in great depth. Each text is treated as the creation of an individual consciousness, rather than as the cultural product of a class. Other works and other writers might have been chosen, and the results would inevitably have been somewhat different. But given the particularistic method employed, one might always argue that the result lacks generality. The counterargument is that the general does not exist as an empirical reality, so that one is as well served by developing the larger implications of a significant particular as in surveying a large number of relatively insignificant cases. Both types of analysis are widely used and abused in the social sciences, and I cannot say that I am fully at ease with either one of them. Nor do I believe that the adherence to one or another is a matter of faith or identity. One should adapt the method to the problem to be researched, so it should be remembered that the goal is to frame a paradigm rather than to survey various categories of political thought.

Chapter two presents a critical interpretation of the natural history of development theory. It begins with the argument that development theory originated in an intellectual rather than a political context, but that it soon fell prey to the exigencies of national policy. Politicization of the field invoked a counterpoliticization, which all but discredited the whole thing. Fortunately, the parallel critique of orthodox Marxist theory by various Marxist revisionist thinkers produced some ideas which allowed for a vigorous revival of the field. Unfortunately, this promising intellectual turn has not yet seriously affected Middle East political studies, and our question is why not?

Part of the answer is given in chapter three, which is devoted to a critique of the critique of orientalism. While crediting the major complaint of the anti-orientalist polemic, it is argued that the political aspects of scholarship explain but do not validate the epistemological claims of area specialists who argue that culture areas are unique and therefore beyond the reach of any general paradigm. In the course of this chapter I try to show that there is considerable confusion about the notion of a benign or sympathetic portrayal of an alien culture.

Chapter four revisits the notorious work of ʿAli ʿAbd al-Raziq which called for the separation of religion and the state in Islam. ʿAbd al-Raziq's book is still widely read and debated, but it seems clear that the secularist position has lost political support. Our analysis concentrates on what appear to be the scriptural limits beyond which any liberal doctrine cannot go. His exposition is, in fact, scripturalist, though he emphasizes what the Qur'an does *not* say. ʿAbd al-Raziq's failure defines the need for an Islamic liberalism which accommodates the traditional scripturalist conception of Islamic government, but which adds an interpretive framework, the function of which is to link liberal political practices to an acceptably authentic hermeneutic of the Islamic tradition.

Chapter five investigates the ideological and rhetorical possibilities for the coexistence of fundamentalism and liberalism through the analysis of the most famous and presumably most radical work of Sayyid Qutb. While my reading draws heavily on the work of others, it finds that it is misleading to say that Qutb is a scripturalist and a traditional. His work is to be read as a dialectical response to secularism and to westernization. Its central themes of aesthetics and consciousness indicate that it is anything but a scripturalist reflex. Qutb's work provides wide scope for a profound change in emphasis in the popular as well as the intellectual understanding of Islam. There is considerable room for a rhetorical convergence between fundamentalism and Islamic liberalism. Given the wide appeal of Qutb's interpretation of the Islamic *idea* or the Islamic *consciousness*, his work may be helpful in altering the popular conception of the balance between scriptural and nonscriptural elements in Islam.

Chapter six examines a number of Marxian interpretations of Islam, and the related problems of economic development and class conflict. These works are similarly nationalist, romantic, and accommodationist, emphasizing authenticity and cultural emancipation rather than socialism. These Marxian theorists are no more secularists than are the Islamic liberals, but, like ʿAbd al-Raziq, their arguments for the compatibility of Islam and socialism depend upon what the *Shariʿa* does not say. It follows that the intellectual structure of these (nonorthodox) Marxian critiques of Islam is similar to that of the liberal critique in that both justify the need for an historical and cultural interpretation of Islam that will supplement the scriptural minimum, and yet provide an Islamic justification for democratic government. In the light of the discussion of neo-Marxist theories of development in chapter two, these interpretations reflect the process of theoretical convergence, and affirm the plausibility of the new paradigm.

Chapter seven surveys the historical analyses of Tariq al-Bishri, a liberal nationalist who has attained considerable influence in Egypt in the last decade. Al-Bishri attempts to synthesize fundamentalism, liberalism, socialism, and even aspects of Islamic scripturalism by means of a revisionist interpretation of Egyptian history. His work, too, emphasizes authenticity, but his great influence appears to be due more to his effort to reconcile the conflicting groups than to his production of a workable formula. There are strong pluralist implications in his reformulation of the Islamic *turath* (heritage) as Egyptian authenticity.

Chapter eight presents two interpretations of contemporary Arab ideology, or of the turath, one pragmatic and the other *Marxisant*. Each favors a liberal regime, but each would reconcile it with its own interpretation of the Islamic turath. Zaki Nagib Mahmud proceeds by means of a pragmatic critique of reason, and Abdallah Laroui proceeds by means of a Marxian critique of the Nasserist state. Mahmud proposes a dualistic symbiosis of Islamic culture and liberal politics in a skillful restatement of the classic liberal position. Laroui offers a monistic solution, arguing that a liberal bourgeois state is the necessary historical precondition for the creation of a culture which is at once modern and Islamic. In this complex argument, Laroui expresses the interest of the intellectual class in freedom of expression while affirming the neo-Marxian (Gramscian) theory of the necessary role of the intellectuals in transcending the limits of bourgeois liberalism. Laroui's analysis is dialectical and pragmatic, and his "solution" is, as expected, circular. Nevertheless, he poses the questions that have to be resolved by any empirical analysis of politics in the Middle East, or, indeed, the Third World. In this sense, Laroui brings us back to the theoretical exposition of Chapter two, and suggests the ways in which the study of contemporary Middle East politics may overcome the obscurantist limits of both orientalism and anti-orientalism.

The concluding chapter returns to the theme of the role of the intellectuals with which Laraoui's work concluded. It considers the present developmental conjuncture in Egypt, Turkey, and Iran, and examines the positions of the key actors, inquiring particularly into whether there is any political incentive for the further elaboration of liberal Islamic ideas.

2

The Natural History of Development Theory, with a Discordant Note on the Middle East

The Origin of Modernization Theory

Modernization theory is an academic transfer of the dominant, and ideologically significant, paradigm employed in research on the American political system. Despite increasing criticism and revisionism, the still-dominant paradigm is the pragmatic-pluralist conception of the political process, which links democratic legitimacy with high levels of participation and with egalitarian distributive outcomes. While this paradigm has been criticized as either scientifically inadequate or normatively skewed (toward freedom, against order), its vigor as a legitimating explanation is largely undiminished. The pluralist legitimation of the American political system is based upon a relatively simple, dualist conception of political movement (freedom) and political structure (order). The hiatus between the two produces a formal contradiction which is resolved by means of the concept of time (or process). Just as Martin Heidegger used the idea of temporality to resolve the apparent contradiction between Being and existence, so the temporality of the pragmatic-pluralist political process resolves the apparent contradiction between the structured inequality of the American system at any given time and the legitimating idea of equality. Temporality justifies inequality by subordinating it to the freedom to restructure the system through unfettered, self-motivated mobility.

In the American context, the political utility of that paradigm is well established, but it is not clear whether its application to the study of political development is meant to justify policies directed at less-developed countries, or whether it is an example of how quasi-scientific discourse becomes functionally autonomous, or whether its geographical extension is meant to provide a methodological validation for both pluralist theory and modernization theory as a single set of non-situated propositions. There is probably some truth to each of the three hypotheses, but the last is the most relevant in the academic context.

Neither the origination of modernization theory in pluralist theory nor its application in "alien" cultures automatically invalidates it. In fact, the relevance of the theory to some extant historical conditions is precisely the prerequisite for any sort of empirical or historical validation. On the other hand, if it is only related to the first world and not the third world, and even then only as ideology, then its relevance as development theory is open to question.

Pluralism and the State

The original, if not the chief, problem of politics, is whether the state is necessary. If the answer seems obvious to most of us, that has not prevented the repeated proposal of the anti-Aristotelian alternative as either a blessing of primitive man or a final reward of virtue, or both, for those enamored of closed circles. It is possible for us to conceive of politics without the state, as it is possible to think of the state without politics, and each conception has its appeal to some. Now the desirability of the state is not the same thing as the necessity of the state, so that it may be possible to get at the question by means of the presumably factual observation that some societies "have" no state.[1] But as we might expect, this empirical approach is immediately refuted by a more idealistic metaphysical orientation which asserts that stateness is a quality which may be discerned to prevail in greater or lesser quantity or intensity in all human communities.[2] The task of comparative government is, therefore, to find ways and means of determining the degree of stateness which exists, and to find out what difference it makes.[3] Normally, if one is more concerned with the values of security, material well-being, social order, risk-sharing, sociability and culture, then one concludes that more stateness is better than less stateness.[4] On the other hand, when one is more concerned with equality, freedom, justice, and self-esteem, one concludes that less stateness is better than more stateness.[5] But none of these values can be discussed intelligibly without the assumption of some degree of stateness.

There are two, usually implicit, simple definitions of political development, then. The first defines it as an increase in stateness and the second as a decrease in stateness. It might be possible to define political development in yet a third way, that is, as the increase in the objective prevalence of all the values mentioned: equality, freedom, justice, security, material well-being, risk sharing, and so forth. To take this latter definition simply restates the dilemma as an internal contradiction, transforming an issue of value preference into a logical problem.

The central logical question is whether a practical increase in one set of values necessarily diminishes the other at all stages of development, or whether, at certain stages, freedom and order are necessary and mutual complements. If the two sets of values are not opposites and/or contradictories, it may be possible to conceive of special configurations which maximize the sum total value by means of a kind of asymmetrical aggregation of them all. Such an aggregation may, nevertheless, dissatisfy many because it implies the transferability of preferences among a set of substitutable values, or the applicability of some pragmatic principle of measurement such as marginal utility or pareto optimality.

Scholars seem to prefer logical problems to political problems, probably because they make their living off the former while their jobs are often threatened by the latter. Consequently the problem of political development, like the problem of politics itself, has been summed up as the problem of resolving the contradiction between the benefits of stateness and the maleficences (or, if you will, *dysfunctions*) of stateness.

Logical problems such as this are the lifeblood of ancient philosophy and theology as well, but some modern philosophies have found a satisfying answer by means of converting the logical issue into an ontological issue. Instead of referring the issue to the "natural" tension between theory and practice, they have instead argued that this epistemological dualism (and its resultant moral dilemmas) masks a philosophically absolutely unacceptable ontological dualism. Ontological monism is insisted upon, not alone for religious reasons but for epistemological reasons as well, since it is deemed impossible to found science on any other basis.[6]

In its application to political analysis, ontological monism asks not whether the state is necessary or desirable but whether it is *real* or not. Of course real and unreal, being and nothingness, represent an insidious dualism just as much as do theory and practice, reality and appearance, and all the rest. Still, in a metaphysical sense it seems to answer a logical problem, and in an ideological sense it has proven useful, indeed. In an ideological sense all of these issues are of primary interest to the advocates of democracy, because it is possible to argue, as Marx does, that a democratic state is a contradiction in terms. Marxism does envision the possibility of a total absence of stateness according to its own definition of that quality. Some liberal democratic theorists have countered this eschatological view with the pragmatic conception that the state is not "real" but only apparent, or rather that the state is a process, and hence constantly changing and always in flux. The state is thus not a thing, and it cannot be described except as it was, and then only fleetingly. What is real, according to this pragmatic theory of democracy, is the observable activity of human beings.

This is, of course, the theory of Arthur Bentley, which has been either explicitly or implicitly restated, modified, and adapted to the ideological needs of liberal democrats, primarily in the United States.[7] The major reflections of this perspective are to be found especially in the work of Talcott Parsons, but also in that of Harold Lasswell, David Easton, Karl Deutsch and, of course, David Truman and a host of other group theorists.[8] Bentley seems to be laying a foundation for a science of politics by reducing all of politics to observable behavior.[9] It is this scientistic orientation which apparently accounts for the absolute, even passionate rejection of both psychological factors and beliefs—the other half of the Kantian mind. This insistence upon the obvious is what accounts for his selection of *groups* as the basic unit of analysis, even though groups themselves are products of changing human interaction as much as is the state or a social class, according to the pragmatic definition. This strategic choice does, however, allow Bentley to assume that the motive of political action is both rational and material, otherwise it could not be either expressed or shared with others.

Bentley's rhetoric is not only impassioned and urgent; it also asserts that the author is revealing something which others have not seen and as a consequence, these others have been misled. It is suggested that many citizens in our democracy have not freely and pragmatically pursued their own interests because psychological and ideological "spooks" have been used to mislead them into believing that political institutions, laws and values are "real" in the sense of being fixed, constant, and permanent. There is thus an implicit urging of the democratic citizen to open his eyes and to act vigorously to pursue his interests by changing himself freely to accommodate the changing political circumstances around him. This implicit democratic ideology is made more explicit, though not fully, in David Truman's work—especially in the much-criticized discussion of latent interest groups—and in the work of other group theorists.[10]

The Ideological Critique of Pluralism

The ideological point is as follows: according to the pragmatic perspective, no political or social structure is permanent or real. What is real is human activity, which constantly produces ever-changing configurations of power, privilege, welfare, et cetera. Political freedom is defined as this capacity to constantly change, just as political development is defined as the willingness and enlightenment to want to change continuously. The reason why one ought to want to change continuously is because the world, nature, all of creation is changing continuously. Not to change continuously is to be submerged in ignorance and to be condemned to struggle against, rather than with, the world of ordered creation. Well-being can be attained only by changing. Alienation from the world can be overcome only by constantly adapting to a constantly changing world. Democracy is the only political system which permits this constant, adaptive, random change and the freedom of individual political action that it requires. Democracy therefore accords with nature and philosophic truth in its commitment to process itself, rather than to particular, temporal, outcomes. If it turns out that the particular allocations of political values in a particular time and place are not exactly egalitarian or just by some other criterion, then wait, those allocations or the configuration of groups or something else will change. It is, therefore, not the allocation of political values by the state among groups, classes, or other structures which determines legitimacy, but rather whether the system accords with the metaphysical truth of pragmatic being—that is, whether it allows constant change. Hence it is not the actuality, but rather the potential for freedom, equality, justice, security, risk sharing, material well-being, self-esteem, and so forth, which legitimates American democracy.[11]

The contradiction between Bentley's insistence upon constant social flux and the methodological requirement of social scientific analysis for fixed and relatively unchanging objects of observation or units of analysis, has been noticed by several scholars, especially Paul Kress and David Greenstone among contemporary political scientists. Each, however, was inclined to treat Bentley's position as excessively rigid and even compulsively metaphysical to the point that his "paradigm" virtually precluded the development of a normal science. Kress is, therefore, primarily concerned to describe the academic "domestication" of the process idea so that it could be related to fixed observables. Greenstone's concern is more the contradiction between the conceptions of process as flux and as institution which is found in the work of the important group theorists analyzing American politics. He sought a resolution of that contradiction in the notion of class, but the addition of another concept or an intervening variable, in the eclectic spirit of normal science, cannot reconcile fundamental conceptual and ideological differences. Greenstone's question was posed as a problem of accounting for political behavioral phenomena which were not accounted for by means of the pragmatic group process theory. The addition of a concept which is to lead to the production of additional and more complex propositions and branching possibilities (dulling Occam's razor) produces another pigeonhole but loses the ideological point. Despite the inclination to modify, and thus preserve, the established pluralist paradigm by arguing the practical utility of certain Marxist categories, Greenstone did note Bentley's defense of American democracy as pragmatic, and thus signalled, if he did not pursue, the ideological motive to be found in the Bentleyan gestalt.[12]

The ideological critique of pluralism, because it justifies what is at any given time, and often for quite a long time, an inequitable distribution of power and wealth and self-esteem, is not to be confused with the objectivist critique of its "inability to account for the facts." Pluralism may be a good thing, but not a practical program. It is also possible to argue that pluralist doctrine does not set up an unattainable norm so much as justify the status quo. Inattention to the distinction leads some critics of pluralism to conflate arguments denying the value of pluralism with arguments denying either the existence or future possibility of pluralism.

The pluralist-as-empirical-scientist describes the U.S. polity in quasi-Bentleyan terms, but the anti-pluralist argues that the rigidities of the system are manifested in the acquisition of control over areas of the public interest by pressure groups, often by means of what appears to be a form of government regulation. Conservatives may then argue that good sense requires that we face the "scientific" facts of the necessary or "natural" role of the state and *bring the state back in*, in both a paradigmatic and a normative sense, combining the two, perhaps, in advocating an autonomous regulatory role for the state. Libertarians, by contrast, accepting the values sought via pragmatism, are rather more inclined to see the state and groups, both, as enemies of individual freedom. These devices are attacked as leading to the rigidification of systems and hence rendering them antagonistic to nature, to science, to modernity, and to democracy. There is yet another discourse which is concerned with the best way of dealing with the political consequences of a pluralism which, according to some observers, does not work as it should.[13]

It can be argued that, if the pragmatic perspective is converted from an ontological position to a normative one, then we have to be able to distinguish between political systems which accord with nature's pragmatism and those which do not. We also have to be able to account for continuing political rigidities such as those identified with corporatism, consociationalism, domination by the state apparatus, military domination, class domination which may be related to the mode of production, or forms of domination which are sustained by such superstructural elements as ecclesiastical formations. For the pragmatic theory of democracy to make any sense, that is for it to avoid our drawing the conclusion that in the long run every system is democratic, political systems have to be judged over time and not merely in an instant. The mere fact of change, while giving hope, does not prove either the potentiality of democracy or its pragmatic reality as a manifold of experience over time.

But just as this metaphysical theory of democracy can be used to legitimate non-democracy, so can it be used to argue for the destruction of constitutional and legal guarantees for the protection of the interests of groups who find themselves in precarious positions. The Bentleyan perspective is pragmatic precisely in that it considers movement real and stability or fixity an illusion. But movement is also invested with positive normative value, while stability is negated in both metaphysical and ethical terms. Movement is described in two basic ways. The first is the pursuit of individual interests, and the second is the temporal aggregation of individuals into groups. Though the first is the basis of the second, Bentley employs the more complex unit as the basis of his political science, admitting of no theoretical reason why it might be impossible in principle that, at any given moment, individuals might aggregate to form a plurality, a majority, or even a unanimity. Other pragmatic theorists find a logical contradiction in Bentley's easy if impermanent movement from individual interest to collective action.

It is virtually axiomatic for many social scientists that individual human behavior is determined by the rational pursuit of self-interest, while collective outcomes may (frequently) lead to results which are detrimental to the interests of the majority. This is the contradiction which is given logical form in Arrow's theorem, according to Amartya Sen, in the assertion that no summation of individual preferences will yield a collective choice that is universally acceptable.[14] The same contradiction serves as the ground for Jon Elster's interpretation of Marx—an interpretation which links individual rational choice with collective consequences that are unintended.[15] The difference between the two approaches is that the free-market theorists conceive of collective outcomes as essentially unpredictable in that they are produced by the market, while the point of Marxist rational choice is that collective outcomes are predictable because it is possible to predict individual choice by class membership or other material criteria.

If it is possible to predict collective behavior, then it is also possible to modify the strategic assumptions of individual rational choice to accord with the rational expectations of this new kind of Marxist theory. But if it is possible to predict, it may also be possible to control, and so it may be expected that political authorities will be tempted to apply this sort of reason to achieve their own ends. In either case, predictability eliminates the possibility of unintended consequences and makes it logically possible, if politically improbable, to determine which of several alternatives might produce the greatest good for the greatest number.

Free-market rationality also has certain political implications, for while it appears to argue against arbitrary methods of determining the collective goal by various aggregative devices, it nevertheless recognizes that collective outcomes may be harmful to the long-term interest of the collectivity—even if that interest is defined only in terms of maintaining the capitalist system. Although this sort of reasoning may be used to justify a minimalist state, it is possible to argue that if one can discover the general interest in some cases (threat of war, conservation of resources) why not in all cases? Is there a set of cases in which we might prefer not to achieve some collective good in order to allow many individuals to achieve their own preferences? But then the collective outcome is surely invidious, in that some individuals will be harmed while others will be benefited. Besides, insofar as the preservation or the "reproduction" of the system is deemed necessary and desirable, it is likely to be achieved by political devices which so structure expectations as to induce rational individual choices that will sustain the system—or which it is believed will sustain the system.

If government is presumed to act in order to compensate for the self-destructive or collectively irrational consequences of individual rational choice, then, obviously, it cannot be controlled, nor can policy be determined by individual rational choice. Insofar as liberalism is defined in terms of free-market rationality, liberal government must also be determined by principles which are logically consistent. In other words, the limits upon individual rational choice must be self-imposed rather than imposed by means of an alien and contradictory principle. If not, then it follows that setting the legitimate bounds between individual and collective choice will be a matter of disagreement and even conflict. If the determination of the bounds of individual rational choice is a function of the state, then the state is not a liberal polity.

According to the reasoning which has been presented, we should expect to see the eventual breakdown of liberal politics because of the inherent contradiction between individual and collective choice. Liberal government will break down either because the government imposes a collective choice which satisfies no one, or because a sufficient number of individuals fail to agree on a limit to their pursuit of their own interests. We might also expect that authoritarian governments would successfully reproduce themselves. Obviously, not all liberal governments have broken down, and a number of authoritarian governments have become more liberal, at least. Moreover, insofar as any theoretical pretensions have been expressed on the matter, there is a rather stronger body of literature predicting that liberal governments will replace authoritarian governments—in the long run.

The question of the relative autonomy of the state, which will be dealt with at greater length below, is linked to the preceding in that free market liberals need to hypothesize the existence of a state which has no interest of its own and whose sole function is to overule market decisions which may be very detrimental to the collective interest. Without such a minimalist state, liberal government must sooner or later fail. The denial of the relative autonomy of the state implies one of at least three alternatives: that the state is actually the instrument of a class or some similar group; that the state is a set of activities or decisions which are the outcome of a pragmatic process in which a plurality of interests are engaged; or that the state, or the apparatus of the state, or the state bureaucracy, has interests of its own which it pursues either alone or by means of alliances with various segments of "civil society."

It will be readily recognized that the third alternative is ambiguous in that if the state bureaucracy has interests of its own, that fact would seem to affirm its autonomy. On the other hand, insofar as those interests are pursued by means of an alliance with a class or group, then the state may be seen as the instrument of that group. It is, however, difficult to be sure whether the bureaucrats are manipulating groups or groups are manipulating bureaucrats, and given the complex nature of politics, it is never clear that a bureaucratic elite is ever acting without any "societal" allies whatever.

Mancur Olson has argued along these lines in explaining "stagflation" in the United States, and Michael Hudson has done the same, relying more explicitly on Deutsch, in calling for an end to confessionalism in Lebanon.[16] Those who are acquainted with Olson's theory of the logic of collective action will note that it suggests that Bentley's theory of the randomness of the group process is quite incorrect empirically, because group processes are in fact structured and predictable.[17] Hence Olson argues the need for a periodic cleaning out of the channels of collective action lest there be a violent revolution. Olson believes that it is up to government, acting in the collective interest, to restore movement and change to the political system whenever groups have succeeded in establishing their own interests as the public interest. Groups are the villains, the individual is the victim, and the state is the hero of this drama.

Hudson subscribes to the pragmatic mythology that if all things are free to move at will they will adjust to one another in a benign equilibrium. If, however, objects are confined and regulated so that their freedom of movement is restricted, the result will be a dangerous disequilibrium, or contradiction, which will result in an upheaval. Hudson argued against maintaining traditional (consociational) barriers preventing collective action among persons of different religious persuasions, thus providing for a degree of political change that will accord with the level of modernization attained by Lebanese society. Lebanese democracy was a sham—a contrivance which prevented the realization of a truer democracy which was already foreshadowed by the level of social mobilization of the Lebanese people. Hudson argued that minority guarantees and the consociational formulas prevented change and precluded the equilibration of the political and the institutional, and thus produced contradiction and strife. If he was right, then one may wonder whether the natural pragmatic equilibrium is always superior to the artificial construction of a social ideal.

In both cases there is an implied distinction between the natural, which is the atomic-pragmatic, and the unnatural, which is the regulated, institutionalized, or the aggregated. Nevertheless, one cannot avoid the feeling that those who advocate such changes are well aware of who is likely to benefit in the short run. If the short run changes are then institutionalized, or fixed in a new set of regulations, or a new interconfessional agreement, then, of course, short run gains will be converted once again into long run distortions of the natural process of social development.

Pluralism and Development Theory

The pragmatic-pluralist doctrine may still be the dominant paradigm in American political science, but it surely was the dominant one in the Political Behavior Committee of the Social Science Research Council (SSRC).[18] The Comparative Politics Committee was set up as a consequence of some of the discussions in the Political Behavior Committee, so it was natural that the same paradigm should be strongly represented, at least in the beginning. Many critics of the liberal theory of development have argued that it can best be understood as an ideological reflection of American capitalist and imperialist interests in the Third World. While that is not entirely incorrect, I submit that the origin of the liberal development theory is to be found in a quite natural extension of the dominant (ideological, of course) paradigm to the new field because of the aspiration, if not the conviction, that pragmatic-pluralism could be the basis of a universal science of politics as well as an explanation and justification of the American political system.[19]

The liberal approach to development, or modernization, theory is composed of two theoretical elements, the first of which is the Parsonian theory linking the cultural pragmatic with the conception of a modern culture.[20] The second theoretical element is the Bentleyan metaphysic of process. The idea of the cultural pragmatic is the core of Parson's action system, in which intentionally motivated interpersonal relations are deemed to be determined by an existing culture and, at the same time, determine how that culture will adapt and change to accord with new social circumstances. The concept of a modern culture, like the "Deweyan" idea of a democratic society, is one which values change itself and, hence, changes more readily than traditional cultures, in accordance with the changing intentionalities of participant individuals. By combining the thesis of culture with the antithesis of experience, Parsons produced a dialectic of development which has been made even more explicit by Habermas, who holds the view that the modernization of belief systems is a "rational" and a natural process.[21]

The combination of the cultural pragmatic and the process metaphysic account for the fundamentally optimistic view of liberal development theory, even though the process necessarily starts with a characterization of the politics of underdevelopment as the epitome of the traditional pattern variables. This characterization is especially evident in the "path-breaking" formulation produced by Kahin, Pauker, and Pye—which was used as the rationale for founding the Comparative Politics Committee.[22] The optimism could not be based upon the virtually absolute traditionalism of the politics of the developing areas, but had to rest upon the idea of constant change, even evolutionary change, and the addition of special theories, such as those of Deutsch or Lerner, that explain how traditional culture is transformed into modern culture.[23]

The liberal theory of development argues that political development, modernization, and hence democracy, would result in the short or long run, so long as change was introduced into any part of the social system, and people were allowed, pragmatically, to pursue their own interests. Obviously, urbanization, education, media exposure, political participation, and economic change would massively alter the traditional system.[24] The pressures for egalitarian change would eventually force the opening of the political system, and then permanent change would prevail. Shmuel Eisenstadt, following Parsons, sums up the position by defining modernity as the capacity to sustain change; but the paradigmatic concept which summed up the liberal theory better than any other was Deutsch's social mobilization, which attributed the processes of change for the most part to nongovernmental social forces.[25]

This liberal theory of development was virtually ubiquitous in the late 1950s and early 1960s. Its defect is not in that it subordinates the interests of developing nations to the ruling class in the United States, but that it extends an image of ourselves as some liberals would like us to be to the potentiality of other, quite different countries. In fact the liberal development theory is a radical call for virtually unlimited expansion of political participation in developing countries, and it is a radical assault on all established institutions, traditional elite and religious structures, corporate arrangements, distributive coalitions and the like. As such it was a gross distortion of what the United States was actually like, and it was viewed increasingly as an irresponsible academic construction. The policy product of this theory was, and still is, being administered as part of our Agency for International Development (AID) program, but it is easy to see why it is being resisted by recipients of our largesse, and it is also easy to see why it aroused considerable opposition among conservative scholars long before the Marxist opposition got its act together.

The Critique of Liberal Development Theory

The seminal importance of Parson's contribution to development theory, or the "sociology of development," may have been generally recognized, but no one has done as thorough a job of showing how much liberal development theory owes to the Parsonian oeuvre as has John Taylor.[26] Taylor's critique is in many respects brilliant, demonstrating the connection between the central conceptions of development theory and the idea of the action system, the pattern variables, and the functional requisites. But Taylor's critique falls short in a number of important respects.

Taylor chooses to treat Parsonian development theory as a variant of bourgeois intellectualist discourse. In so doing, he denies both the philosophical and ideological dimensions of this form of discourse, and instead insists on its empirical and nontheoretical character, arguing that Parsonian empiricism sustains the reality claims of the dominant bourgeois superstructure. Taylor accuses all liberal development theorists of failing to *theorize* their arguments, and he characterizes liberal development theory in accordance with certain apparent empirical features of its discursive formation, without regard to its philosophical and ideological aspects.[27] The most important intellectual losses resulting from this critical shortfall are, first, the failure to distinguish the ideological function of Parsonian theory in the context of democratic-capitalist politics, and, second, the failure to properly identify the ideological position of those who hold what might be called "non-antagonistic" contradictory views of development, and who oppose the Parsonian position.

Taylor criticizes Parsonian theory specifically for its failure to "theorize" the sources of disturbances to the equilibria of social systems (i.e., changes in the mode of production) and for its failure to similarly theorize extant patterns of social action (class struggle).[28] This nontheoreticization of sources of change and end points of change processes is not explained by reference to the pragmatic philosophy which is the foundation of Parsonian theory, and which rejects the significance of starting points and end points. Taylor's failure to grasp both the philosophical and the ideological significance of Parson's work is due to his acceptance of Althusser's idea of theory, and to his inability to recognize the ideological character of Althusserian theory itself.

Philosophic pragmatism dispenses with the need to explain the origin of system disturbances, because it postulates a constantly changing or evolving world. The same sort of beginning in medias res is found in Easton's conception of the environment of the political system, and in Deutsch's steering metaphor. There are no starting points and no end points in the pragmatic system, only apparent, temporary configurations that are intelligible within the context of prevailing forms of discourse. The fact that Bentley and Parsons stand on common ideological ground, that they are conscious of the ideological challenge of historical materialism, and that their discourse is not merely a reflex of the dominant intellectual paradigm of the bourgeois class, is evidently not discerned by Taylor.

Despite the availability of T. S. Kuhn's critique of the scientific method and his important distinction between ordinary science and the origination of paradigms, Taylor fails to distinguish between these two types of activity in Parson's work.[29] *The Structure of Social Action* lays down a powerful paradigm which has had, as Taylor rightly points out, an extraordinary influence in the elaboration of development theory. But Parsons' work on the pattern variables and on the four functional subsystems lacks originality, and illustrates how he was unable to resist the temptation to be drawn into the routinizing work of those who would turn him into an "ordinary scientist." It is inevitable that the transformation of the paradigmatic vision of pragmatic social process into a framework for ordinary science must lead to the denaturing of the idea of eternal flux, to the structuring of process, and to the substitution of empiricism and/or positivism for the mystery of pragmatism.[30] It is also the case that the ideological function of such ordinary science differs from that of the pragmatic action system, for whereas the latter is based on a vision of an open-ended democratic process of communicative accommodation, the former justifies the status quo, and employs the rhetoric of relativism to support order and stability.

Taylor quite correctly focuses on the key concept of differentiation as the foundation of the explanatory theory of the sociology of development.[31] He points out that the liberal theorists of development hold the view that societies adapt to the challenge of change by becoming more complex via a process of differentiation. He cannot account for this sort of theory because he neglects the initial pragmatic premise that change is always present. It follows that adaptation is constantly present and, if felicitous, then a kind of equilibrium results. Accordingly, Taylor argues that the whole notion of differentiation is "untheorized," and is treated only in an ad hoc or empirical manner, drawing on the experience of European countries, and resulting in an ungrounded projection of a narrow historical experience.

The main point of the structural-Marxist critique of development theory is that it would employ a description of the European experience as a schema for predicting the path of development in the underdeveloped countries without taking into account the different historical conditions under which those countries are attempting to achieve modernization. Since, for Taylor, the most important difference is that a powerful international capitalist system already exists, he reads Parsons as diverting attention from underlying causes to superficial effects. He is consequently able to recognize that Parsons was extremely influential, but he cannot explain why he should have been more influential than any other bourgeois scholar. The answer is to be found in the difference between the carly Parsons and the late Parsons, or between the liberal Parsons and the conservative Parsons.

The Conservative Theory of Development

While the conservative attack on development theory has often focused on the epistemologically unacceptable use of the two concepts of modernity and tradition as universals representing mutually exclusive principles, the real thrust of the critique is opposition to the idea that pragmatic change which holds nothing sacred is beneficial. The conservative interpretation of the genius of American politics and its legitimation is quite different. Far from arguing the pragmatic position, Huntington declares that the American system is a mixture of modernity and tradition, that the highest political value is effective government, that political organization (parties) and administration (bureaucracy) are the indispensable means of creating political order, and that without political structure of that kind, extension of the franchise will lead to political decay and chaos.[32]

It is true that both the liberals and the conservatives emphasize culture, rather than class or political institutions, but the liberals do so under the pragmatic influence of Parson's concept of the action system while Huntington, Shils, Bendix, the Rudolphs, and Nisbet are really talking about traditional cultural institutions and not cultural processes of change.[33] Moreover the growing apprehension that was the consequence of the breakdown of order in newly independent countries, and the difficulty of building new structures of order in places such as the Congo and South Viet Nam led to a new conservative emphasis on the centrality of the role of the state in political development. Political development was now defined in a quite different manner emphasizing control, planning, technology, and of course, stability. The works of J. P. Nettl, Aristide Zolberg, Myron Weiner, Morris Janowitz, Joseph LaPalombara, and many others reflect this shift in emphasis, but nowhere was the shift more complete than within the SSRC Committee on Comparative Politics.[34] The long-delayed volume on the crises of political development indicated the shift in emphasis, although there is considerable internal evidence of dissension and noncoordination in the book.[35] Another book, edited by Charles Tilly, and including a polemical essay by Tilly criticizing the earlier work of the committee, represented the new orthodoxy in full regalia.[36] Subsequent works by Gabriel Almond and G. Bingham Powell, Huntington and Joan Nelson, and others consolidated the trend and now began to evoke a diffuse and scattershot response from a new generation of liberals and leftists.[37]

The decline of the first formulation of the liberal theory of development is but one dimension of the general retreat of the liberalism of the 1950s and early 1960s. There are major intellectual defects to be found in the liberal-democratic paradigms, yet the largest difficulty arose in trying to combine a liberal domestic program, which was meant to encourage change, with a foreign military involvement that was frankly meant to resist change abroad. The civil rights movement, the opposition to the Vietnam War, and the adoption of various political techniques associated with the Chinese Cultural Revolution added up to a general assault on the authority and legitimacy of the state and of many public and private institutions. The reaction to this diffuse effort to achieve rapid and profound political change was not long in coming, even though its greatest successes are relatively recent. One dimension of the ensuing political conflict was an intensification of the ideological struggle for the cultural soul of America. Insofar as this *kulturkampf* was pursued within academic political science, the two major fields of conflict were those of American politics and the comparative politics of the developing areas. In both cases, the first phase entailed attacks on the established paradigms. In American politics the point of attack has been centered on the reductionist conception of the state which characterizes the pragmatic-pluralist paradigm. In comparative development politics the point of attack has been the hostility to traditional culture which characterizes the liberal (Parsonian) development paradigm.

Thus political realities contrived to strengthen the conservative political paradigm as the antipluralists and rational-choice theorists began the attack on the pragmatic-pluralistic paradigm. Olson, Lowi, McConnell and others have argued that the American interest system has not worked according to the Bentley-Truman model, but has instead resulted in a dangerous stagnation that is the consequence of interest groups capturing control of regulatory arenas. Their solutions run the gamut from libertarianism to neopluralism to *dirigisme,* but all are critical of the received tradition of pragmatic-pluralist liberalism.[38] These, and other critics believe that solutions have to be found by strengthening authority, discipline, order, and technological efficiency. In general they believe in strengthening the state rather than increasing popular participation. The prime value which they seek, and which sums up their position, is the enhancement of the collective rationality of the political community.

If the contradiction of individual rational choice and social choice is taken as axiomatic, it is to be expected that some theorists will prefer social choice, and vice versa. It is, nevertheless, important to bear in mind that both groups of theorists admit the ontological priority of individual choice, and both deny the possibility of deriving rational collective choice from rational individual choice. Conservatives and libertarians may then conclude that collective choice, as expressed through political institutions, is bound to be irrational. The central question of political theory is, then, how to render social choice rational. The answer proposed by some theorists requires the separation of the state from civil society, so that the state may become the rational agent of society, determining the strategies for the collectivity in the light of the centrifugal preferences of partitive groups and the challenges of external groups or other states. This solution confuses the logical contradiction between existing ways of defining individual and collective choice with the empirical process by which social choice or public policy is determined. The political relevancy of this confusion depends upon whether one wishes to defend or attack the existing political order. If one wishes to defend the existing order, then one might be inclined to argue that its virtue lies precisely in the degree to which it is not responsive to the contradictory influences of individual choice, especially as those influences may be expressed through systematic attempts to aggregate individual choice in the form of interest groups.

Logically, however, government depends upon the possibility of attributing collective interest to the political community as a whole. There are those consistent libertarians who simply reject the validity of any such attribution, but, for the most part, theorists attempt to bridge the gap between individual and collectivity by means of the notion of culture. Liberal development theory emphasizes the dynamic, pragmatic, and adaptive aspects of culture as a product of what Parsons called the action system. Conservative development theorists rather emphasize traditional culture, its ability to reproduce itself under changing conditions, and its contribution to the formation of a collective consciousness. When this question is raised in the debate on American politics, the liberal tradition in America is itself the subject of cultural analysis. When the question is raised regarding many if not most underdeveloped countries, it is rather religion and its political consequences that is the subject of cultural analysis. Rorty, for example, refers the Western political tradition of liberalism to culture rather than to reason. By contrast, Foucault expresses his radical individualism in a general suspicion of culture as even more repressive than government. Edward Said would defend Islamic culture against the intrusiveness of Western, Christian culture, or so it seems.

The belated "establishment" of the new conservative tendency in development theory and in American political science may have been achieved in the appointment, ten years after the demise of the Comparative Politics Committee, of a new Social Science Research Council Committee on States and Social Structures.[39] The rational choice theorists have asserted that the Bentley-Truman conception does not conform to the way the world is, not because of the phenomena of class, as Greenstone proposes, but because of the contradictions between individual interests and the public interest, and because of the rigidities of actual groups and other organizations. The mission of the new Committee on States and Social Structures has been explicitly thematized as compensating for, if not correcting, the excesses of group theory, which treated the state as no more than a legal fiction, or as a misleading reification of the idea of political obligation.

The new committee seeks "to bring the state back in," but it goes no further toward defining this state than to cite some suggestive passages from the work of Weber and Hintze.[40] Despite this invocation of the notion of the cultural norms influencing the historical ideal type, the rhetoric of justification of the new committee emphasizes the objectivist analysis of the political role of organizations (bureaucracies) identified with the state. In fact, the political significance of the state is not "theorized," nor is a new paradigm consciously put forward. Instead, the proponents of this new direction point to the inadequacy of prevailing approaches. The state is described as an actor, which is self-motivated and which has interests and power of its own. The ability of the state to act on its own is described as "state autonomy," in a phrase reminiscent of Huntington's elaboration of the idea of the autonomy of the political and the role of institutions in determining the public interest. On the other hand, state autonomy is also explicated as "instances . . . in which non-constitutionally ruling strategic elites have used the state as a whole to redirect and restructure society and politics."[41] Although Almond's concern with the question of capacity (of states) is not directly cited, Tilly's edited volume in the Political Development series does receive favorable mention in regard to this subject—although emphasis again is placed on recruiting able administrators.

Implicitly, this new orientation conceives of political actors as of two sorts, state actors and societal actors, thus denying the metaphysical monism of the pragmatic pluralists.[42] While the normative or ideological orientation of the new approach is nowhere made explicit in the flow of scientistic and empiricist rhetoric, it is, perhaps, noteworthy that in all the examples of state action cited in the conference report, the bureaucrats are the good guys and the societal actors are the bad guys.

The notion of the autonomy of the state is ambiguous depending upon whether we are considering Western, "developed," states, or "underdeveloped" states. In the case of advanced capitalist states, the autonomy of the state is employed to explain and to justify the resistance to pluralist demands. The court system, the party system, the bureaucratic structure, and the important cultural institutions connected to the state, represent a public interest and an historical-cultural consensus which lend stability and continuity to what would otherwise be a chaotic, characterless system which is always in flux. In contrast, the autonomy of the state, when applied to developing systems, is used to explain the arbitrariness of government, the apparent absence of a ruling class, the irrelevance of social structure, or economic structure, or even culture, to the explanation of politics.

It is difficult to follow the reasoning whereby the autonomy of the state is transformed into the autonomy of the ruling elite or the ruling autocrat. One of the characteristic implications of the use of the term autonomy of the state is that while the state is thereby declared *not* to be the instrument of some class or unofficial elite, neither is it merely the instrument of office-holders or of the military-bureaucratic elite. Just as the contextual structure of classes, the organization of production, and the complex of language *cum* culture cannot be taken as totally given to transformation at any single moment in time, so is it the case that the state is a similar context or structure, or set of rules, or cultural patterns, or institutions that constrain those acting in its name. If the state is not such a context, then it is nothing. If it is such a context, then it is possible and reasonable to speak of the autonomy of the state, insofar as the structure of meaning and behavior and rational action which is the state is, in fact, uninfluenced by other similar non-state structures.

The identification of the autonomy of the state with extreme forms of autocracy, whether of a Nasser, a Qadhafi, or even especially a Khomeini, represents a lamentable confusion, because it suggests that the autonomy of the state is not a way of looking at the state—a statement of its ontological independence from other social entities—but a reference to the arbitrary use of power.

Logically and empirically the concepts state, government, bureaucracy, apparatus of the state, political institutions, and so forth, ought not be treated in a reductionist manner, whether in a Marxist frame of reference or a pluralist frame of reference. But neither should one go to the opposite extreme of reification and personification, as was the case with the neo-idealists such as Bluntschli or Bernard Bosanquet. This reification is not merely a methodological error, but has had enormously important, and sometimes devastating, practical political consequences. Even if one finds a way to avoid reification of the state while still using the ideologically questionable term *autonomy of the state,* the explanatory result is likely to be circular, because the clear implication of the term is that the state determines itself.

The phrase "bringing the state back in," and the concept of the autonomy of the state, are both parts of the current attack on pluralism as a value and as a scientific explanation of democratic politics. Doubtlessly, the two aspects of this attack are linked, but the latter has more merit than the former when applied to the analysis of the politics of developed countries. When applied to the politics of the developing areas, it seems to me that it is not the autonomy of the state which is the fact to be explained, but the centrality of the apparatus of the state as manifested in the power of bureaucratic, centrality of state is important.

military, clerical, technocratic and party elites. Concentration upon the autonomy of the state as description and as explanation diverts attention from the possibility that these elites are likely to transform the very conditions of their own hegemony, leading to the creation of competitive forces that may not be as closely identified with the state apparatus. While the strategic choices of the hegemonic elites are not absolutely constrained, it is possible to achieve an understanding of the logic of their circumstances and to draw conclusions regarding the limited choices available.

* State action can have centrifugal forces — can result in changing conditions of hegemony.

The argument for the renewed interest in the state has been presented in the framework of normal science, in a language that obscures as well as eschews ideological commitment. This circumstance, which is all but obligatory if one is to receive institutional and financial support in a system which believes itself to be pluralist, naturally facilitates the recruitment of scholars of diverse ideological positions to the support of the new paradigm. Some of these recruits may be governed by false consciousness, but the fact is that among those who have become interested in studying the state are some who consider themselves, respectively, liberal, radical, and conservative. It is virtually impossible, and not very interesting, to try to account for the ideological motivation of each and every scholar who thinks that the state ought to be brought back in. Nevertheless, one can account for a good many by noting that radicals and conservatives sometimes converge on the importance of the state, not on empirical grounds, but because they see the state as possibly providing some of the conditions the lack of which renders their own theories irrelevant or inoperative. Of particular significance in this regard are those who believe that it is possible to establish a bourgeois state without a bourgeoisie and those who believe that it is possible to establish a socialist state without a proletariat. In both cases the belief prevails that the state can somehow perform the function that has been attributed to the missing or deficient social class. Insofar as this view of the state is sound, individuals holding quite diverse ideological positions appear to converge in their scientific positions. Insofar as both radicals and conservatives would substitute state action for "social" participation, both take an antiliberal position. It is this sort of consideration that has led me to the conclusion that the ideological significance of bringing the state back in is largely conservative, given the institutional setting of this scientific activity, regardless of the self understanding of those engaged in the retrieval effort. It must take a special sort of ideological naiveté to persist in the belief that strengthening the state in a developing system will lead, in general, to increasing political freedom.

Neo-Marxist Development Theory

Liberal development theory was blamed for apparent errors in Cuba, Chile, Vietnam, Iran, and now in Central America. Moreover, there has been a strongly conservative cultural and intellectual, as well as economic, reaction to the strange culmination of the Civil Rights movement of the 60s in a "cultural revolution." This apparently irrational response to political disappointment and frustration (caused by the Vietnam War) seemed to validate the concept of political decay and the identification of pragmatic pluralism with irrational sentimentality. Liberalism has not been driven from the field, but it has had to rethink its position, and in so doing it has depended very much on the contributions and the failures of the Marxist critique of the conservative development theory. As for the conservative theory, it has forgotten one of the major functions of the liberal theory, and that is to demonstrate that development—or an affluent, cultured, egalitarian democracy—could be achieved without revolution. Conservative theory was more concerned to show that the liberal theory itself led to revolution without leading to development.

The whole point of Marxist theory is to show the necessity and the beneficence of revolution, so even when no explicit reference is made to Marxism, development theory, whether liberal or conservative, is also debating Marxism. But for a long time, Marxists seemed to take little notice of development theory, as though it simply did not fit their intellectual schemes, or did not appear to offer any ideological gain. Surely, there might be little benefit in debating Western theorists unless it could be established that some Third World intellectuals were listening, or that it mattered at all what Third World elites were thinking. Moreover, Marxism had long since developed some quite sophisticated ideas about underdevelopment, even if it might be argued that there was no comprehensive Marxist or Marxist-Leninist theory of the thing. The basic points of reference are well known: Marx's theory of the "progressive" consequences of the spread of world capitalism and his conception of the Asiatic mode of production (AMP), and Lenin's theory of imperialism as finance capitalism, the highest and final stage of capitalism preceding world revolution.[43] Aside from these points of theoretical reference, one may also wish to take account of a number of ad hoc and fairly inconsistent statements and policies such as the resolutions adopted at the Baku conference of the Peoples of the East in 1920, or the Sixth Comintern in 1928, or Stalin's nationality theories, or the policy of benign neglect of the Third World identified with Andrei Zhdanov, or the use of the concept of the noncapitalist path with reference, at least, to Egypt and Algeria in the 1960s, and others still that highly motivated scholars have been able to collect. All of these together have not reassured most observers that there is a single, dominant, integrated, Soviet theory of development. This body of material looks rather more like some sort of practical adaptation of ideological pronouncements to the short-run tactical needs of Soviet policy. The adaptive tactical use further suggests that the issue is not one of primary ideological concern, even though there is some argument about the extent of capitalistic development in Russia before the revolution. Still, as far as the Soviets are concerned, the question of when, how, and where revolution might occur in the Third World is a matter of Soviet foreign policy and the interests of the entire socialist bloc rather than a matter to be left to scholars.

Dependency Theory

Marxist intellectuals who happen to be interested in the Third World may be pardoned if they have nevertheless sought to work these matters out for themselves, and so we might expect that the positions they come up with will not accord with Soviet preferences, just as their concentration on the matter itself is not something that the Soviets have desired. For this reason it is not so surprising that the key contribution in this new Marxist paradigm is that of Andre Gunder Frank, who works from a Western economic point of view, and who specifically targeted economic development theory.[44] The main point of Frank's argument for our purpose is that international economic relations of exchange between the capitalist states and underdeveloped states either cause or perpetuate underdevelopment. He argues that underdeveloped countries have no way out of this situation except to sever economic relations with the world capitalist system, and that this sort of policy can only be achieved by means of a revolution. Frank is therefore seen as calling for a socialist revolution in each Third World country; these countries would then cut all economic relations with the capitalist systems, regardless of the state of development, or class structure, or political institutions prevailing in the particular country. Criticism of Frank's views has concentrated on his unMarxian disregard for class structure, and his faith in autarchic development for all. Despite Frank's attempts to cope with these criticisms, he seems to have been treated by more sophisticated Marxist theorists like some sort of country bumpkin who has marched into the living room without removing his muddy galoshes.

For Marxist theorists there are at least two separable issues here, one, the explanation of underdevelopment, and, two, the determination of those circumstances in which Third World socialist revolution is possible or even likely. The first issue is concerned with why capitalist development has not taken place in the Third World in spite of the belief that capitalism has reached its highest stage—that is, we are now in the age of "late capitalism." As far as I can tell, there are three major approaches to this question. The first argues that underdevelopment is caused by unequal exchange, because the law of comparative advantage does not work as it should.[45] The second argues that underdevelopment is caused by the differential in surplus value (lower in advanced capitalist countries and higher in underdeveloped countries, usually) which is in turn caused by the relations of production (sociopolitical factors) and results in a structurally determined lower return to labor in the Third World. The third argues that permanent or prolonged underdevelopment is caused by the articulation of the capitalist mode of production with the indigenous (AMP or feudal) mode of production in such a way as to create a symbiosis rather than to cause the collapse of the indigenous mode.[46]

The classic Marxist position is that, in AMP countries, some outside force must intrude in order to set the wheels of historical materialism going. Explanations of continued underdevelopment appear to be modifications of AMP theory which can give only the most pessimistic answers to the questions of Third World Marxists. Without capitalist development, revolution is unlikely, unless one begins to look to the national bourgeoisie or to some nonmaterial force, or unless one theorizes that some part of the society can function as the equivalent of an industrial proletariat.[47] China and Vietnam are the usual examples chosen when arguing that peasants or even landless agricultural labor can provide an adequate social base for a revolution. This was the explicit argument of the book on Egypt by Mahmoud Husain.[48] Either we have to have a theory which explains the possibility of Third World revolution where development is not occurring, or we have to show that development is actually occurring, or else we have to tell Third World Marxists that there is nothing they can do until the world capitalist system collapses.

One of the attendant problems seems to be that "late capitalism" does not appear to be growing weaker and more precarious. Of course this may only be an illusion which can be explained away by a variety of arguments such as those of Ralph Miliband, Ernst Mandel, and even Habermas.[49] In an interesting variation on these themes, Geoffrey Kay has written a book purporting to prove that the prolongation of the agony of late capitalism is due to an articulation of modes of production in the underdeveloped countries which, in fact, results in higher surplus values being produced in the metropolitan countries.[50] This superexploitation of the capitalist working class is not immediately discerned because the relative productivity of that labor is so high. But, in due course, the most exploited class will prove itself to be the revolutionary class, as Marx predicted. And even though the proletariat of the underdeveloped countries are absolutely less well off than the metropolitan working class, they are relatively less exploited, and hence less likely to rebel.

It is theories such as this, depriving Third World elites and masses alike of any significant world historical role, which encourage those more sympathetic to the Third World to find ways and means to affirm the possibility of Third World revolution; or if not that, then at least the possibility of autarchic development; or if not that, then the possibility of some absolutely original and culturally authentic economic system.[51] The ideological issue is simply whether the next revolutionary phase, leading to the collapse of capitalism, will be initiated in the Third World or in Europe. The persistence of "late capitalism" has had its effect on the growth of Eurocommunism, too, and that has further debased the ideological and political coinage of Third World revolution. As we might expect, this sort of argument has produced alternatives, one of which is to emphasize cultural factors and the role of the national bourgeoisie, another arguing that in fact development does occur under conditions of dependency, and another is to push the point further and to hold that such development confirms Marx's original theses and disconfirms Lenin's argument that the "proletarian nations" will have a role to play in world revolution.[52]

Marxist theory appears to have tied itself in a number of knots over the issues of late capitalism, AMP, the revolutionary role of the Third World states, the international economic system, the scientific status of Marxist economic theory, the articulation of modes of production, and the possibility of dependent development or autarchic development. This confusion has opened the way for some liberal theorists, now more influenced by Marxian thought than pragmatism, to propose a number of alternative approaches that have begun to take on the character of a new liberal (or not-so-conservative) paradigm. The components of this include the concept of associated dependent development, the theory of bureaucratic-authoritarianism, world systems theory, and a revisionist theory of social revolution.[53] Together, if not separately, these pieces of the new liberal paradigm support the belief in the possibility of advanced economic development in a stable, liberal political system, without the need for revolution. The pieces have not yet been put together in a smoothly working system, nor has it yet been put into an easily expressed political formula so that it might be sold to policy-makers, but there is some chance that all that will occur. It should be at least moderately interesting to trace the evolution of a new development paradigm.

The initial components of the emergent paradigm are not the

 elements of pragmatic-pluralist theory, but elements of Marxist theory dealing with peripheral capitalism and class formation, the contradictions inherent in capitalist development, and the preconditions for revolution.

The origins of a revisionist Marxist theory of political development may be traced back to the political and ideological crises identified with the critique of Stalinism and the suppression of the Hungarian uprising.[54] Two forms of revisionist Marxism arose, and attempts were made to appropriate the authority of Marx by amending or supplementing the received tradition in ways which rejected the constitutive character of Soviet experience and, in particular, the ideological and strategic contributions of Lenin and Stalin. The first of these has been referred to as humanist Marxism, and the second is known as structuralist Marxism. The most outstanding exponents of humanist Marxism were Maurice Merleau-Ponty and Jean-Paul Sartre in France, and Herbert Marcuse, Theodor Adorno, Max Horkheimer, and Jurgen Habermas, all of the Frankfurt school, in Germany.[55]

Humanist Marxism

Humanist Marxism is distinguished by its emphasis upon individual and collective emancipation, its adoption of aspects of psychoanalytic theory, and its reflection of the influence of Heidegger's existentialism, and his concept of authenticity.[56] Since the values of subjective freedom and individual gratification are central in humanist Marxism, Marxism itself was understood more as an ideology than a scientific theory or historical truth, and it was justified as an appropriate and effective means for the achievement of freedom under prevailing conditions. The most strikingly successful application of the Freudian reinterpretation of the critique of imperialism in the spirit of the early Heidegger may be found in Frantz Fanon's, *The Wretched of the Earth*.[57]

It may be further argued that humanist Marxism encouraged the growth and development of a number of revolutionary and/or violent movements, sometimes involving terror, throughout the Third World. In some cases these movements were controlled or captured by the communist party, but in many others, the Marxist doctrinal element was superficial or tactical at most. The Soviet response was ambivalent. Wherever it believed that it might gain an advantage in its competition with the capitalist powers, it supported these movements and encouraged the production of academic explanations of the relationship between Third World national movements and the revolution. But the vigor of the anti-Stalinist campaign, the criticism of Soviet policy in East Europe, the break with Maoist

China, and the failures of Soviet policy in Egypt and Algeria, tempered Soviet enthusiasm.

Structuralist Marxism: Althusser

Structuralist Marxism reflects an alternative impulse. Rejecting the subjectivist elements in the early Marx, it insists that Marxism is an emergent science, the fulfillment of which depends upon the completion of the task begun in *Das Kapital*. Louis Althusser is credited with inventing structuralist Marxism, in the adaptation of many of the elements of the structuralist epistemology identified with the work of Levi-Strauss in Anthropology and, especially, of DeSaussure in linguistics.[58] Althusser's Marxist scientism and rationalism was not so much directed at the question of extra-European political development as it was at the question of freedom and discipline within European communist parties. Althusser's particular target was Marxist humanism and those intellectuals who had left the Party (or had never joined it) and who presumed to appropriate Marxist theory. Althusser insisted that Marxism was not a humanism nor an historicism, but an aprioristic, logically ordered, and comprehensive theory.

Despite the idiosyncratic abstruseness of Althusser's language, he has had an enormous impact on Marxist studies in France and England. There have been few recognizable influences of his work on the politics of the Third World, but that does not mean that there have been no indirect political consequences of the rise of structural Marxism. Althusser has, however, aroused impassioned attacks among his European colleagues, who have accused him of both providing a theoretical justification of Stalinism, on the one hand, and of undoing Marxism by offering a functionalist theory in the form of a dogmatic Marxism, on the other.

It is this latter criticism that is of greatest interest to our present inquiry, because it is apparent that, whether intended or not, Althusser provided an intellectual ground for a significant theoretical convergence of functional theory and Marxism, and, as a consequence, for the surprising reinvigoration of the liberal theory of development. This remarkable intellectual cross-fertilization was actually accomplished through the work of Althusser's disciples (and by means of a partial adaptation of some of the perspectives of Antonio Gramsci).[59] To my mind, the two most suggestive contributions have been those of Nicos Poulantzas and John Taylor.[60]

Whether or not the critical accusations made by Althusser were justified, there do not seem to have been any serious intellectual consequences of his purported defense of Stalinism. Regarding his alleged functionalism, however, there have been important consequences, especially for academic thought in both the United Kingdom and the United States. Althusser's insistence that Marxism is not an historicism is linked to his position that each of the spheres of the political, the economic, the ideological, and the theoretical, are relatively autonomous of one another. His conception of theory was among the most unique aspects of his thought. For Althusser, scientific theory is a self-consistent, logical system, linking concepts and propositions. Theory is abstract and independent of historical or empirical determinations. Comprehensiveness, coherence, completeness, and self-consistency, are the indispensible characteristics of theory; so it follows that a truly scientific theory must break completely from all earlier theoretical efforts. But the break, or *coupure,* is only the starting point. Thereafter, the working out of the complete system of theory can only be accomplished by means of what Althusser called theoretical praxis: in effect, the work of professional intellectuals.

This position has been criticized because it separates the production of theory from the consciousness of the proletariat, as well as from the need to be grounded in history or experience.[61] While it may free Marxism from the need to explain away or justify Stalinism, it also dispenses with eschatological elements in Marxist thought. Althusser read *Capital* as a break from the earlier humanistic and historicist (Hegelian and Feuerbachian) tendencies of Marx, and as the preliminary construction of a new and absolutely separate and different scientific theory. Marx's work was not complete, though, and it was therefore the task of Marxist theoreticians to complete that work by means of their own theoretical praxis. Althusser's conception is far more radical than Kuhn's understanding of the genesis of scientific revolutions, because he held that the telos of theoretical praxis is the creation of a theory with its own epistemological foundations, rejecting the theory, method, problematic, nomenclature, concepts, and everything else connected with earlier theory.[62]

Manifestly such a theory cannot be invalidated by experience or refuted by any reference to consciousness, so long as it is self-consistent. Ideology represents merely the present condition or the historical circumstance of the consciousness, but not the potential. Althusserian theory poses a challenge to both historical conditions and to ideological consciousness, reversing the relationship between existential being and knowing. Scientific theory is, therefore, an arbitrary, idealist, intellectual construction, that may express an ethical system, a religious consciousness, a class consciousness, or any preferred pattern of substructural-superstructural relationships. Althusser does not attempt to justify Marxism as a theoretical expression of the ideological consciousness of the proletariat under capitalism.

Political praxis and theoretical praxis are two relatively autonomous activities, just as are the economic and the ideological. In the real world, as opposed to the theoretical, the various forms of praxis are more or less integrated, with certain forms or structures predominating in certain societies, but never to the exclusion of all others. Thus, modern capitalism, as described by Marx, is a structure in dominance, an arrangement of substructure and superstructure, or of politics, economics, ideology, and science, that is dominated to a considerable degree by bourgeois theoretical praxis. The goal of Marxist political praxis is to replace bourgeois theoretical praxis with Marxist theoretical praxis, especially with regard to its superstructural function or its role as a hegemonic political culture. Apparently, Althusser would have communist political praxis directed by Marxist theoretical praxis rather than the other way around. It is his implicit argument for the intellectual autonomy of Marxist scholars, based on his notion of the autonomy and totality of scientific theory rather than on any conception of the value of intellectual freedom and individualism, that justified some critics in affirming his anti-Stalinism.[63]

In some ways this amoral, agnostic, positivistic, and intellectualist doctrine, by its insistence on the *coupure,* seems to cut off the possibility of dialogue between Marxist and bourgeois scholarship. But this apparently logical consequence was more than made up for by the contrary influences of intellectual freedom, the relative autonomy of various forms of praxis, and the special use that was made of the concept of the mode of production. This concept, which was used loosely in the classical texts, was to be rigorously defined to refer to a fully integrated system of politics, economics, and ideology, as determined by means of theoretical abstraction. The full elaboration of the concept would resolve the problem of the relationship between substructure and superstructure and fix the meaning of the *eventual* determination of the latter by the former.

In practice, pure modes of production might never exist, but their nature could be understood in terms of their dominant tendencies. It is also the case that the most fully worked-out part of Marxist scientific theory that we have is Marx's theory of the capitalist mode of production. When linked to the problematic of late capitalism and the debates within the French Communist Party (PCF) regarding the proper political strategy to be followed in the present conjuncture, this theoretical orientation led to a concern with the theory of the modern or late capitalist state in the light of the intellectual understanding of the capitalist mode of production as the reification of a self-consistent, self-reproducing, integrated, and adaptive theoretical conception. Historical breakdown and self-contradiction were excluded by the epistemological independence of theory itself. If Marxist theory is independent of Marxist political praxis, so is capitalist theory independent of capitalist political praxis. The result is a theoretical conception explaining the stability of bourgeois democracies that has many similarities with the pragmatic, pluralist, functionalist, and idealist paradigm which dominates liberal or bourgeois social science.

Despite the connection between the rise of structural Marxism and the struggle within the PCF and the debates within Eurocommunism after the Twentieth Party Congress, the long term consequences of Althusser's efforts have been more academic than political. The academicization of structural Marxism led to the transformation of Marxist theory from a tool of party leadership to an area of debate over definitions, logical consistency, the critique of forms of literary expression, problems of method, and even of empirical testing. In effect, structural Marxism was made over into a properly bourgeois form of intellectual discourse in which the central or critical question is, what would have to be true in order for historical materialism to be a really universal science?

Many of Althusser's followers were unconcerned with his political motivation, and they turned enthusiastically to the task of theoretical praxis, concentrating on explaining the realities of late capitalism. Instead of isolating themselves from a dialogue with bourgeois scholarship, some found areas of convergence with contemporary social science, not only because liberal theory is a guide to the functioning of the Capitalist Mode of Production (CMP), but because bourgeois social science has been made self-conscious by the challenge of Marxist humanism, by the apparent inapplicability of pluralist theory to the developing world, by the successes of the Chinese and the Vietnamese revolutions, and by the rise of neoconservative theories of development which have lost interest in the role of the bourgeoisie, and have turned toward the role of traditional and bureaucratic elite factions. As a result of the slow opening of this dialogue, a neo-liberal theory of development has begun to take shape. This neo-liberal theory has adapted some of the concepts of structural Marxism, and it has been encouraged by the several incidents of redemocratization which have occured in Latin America, in southern Europe, and to a more limited extent in the Middle East. One suspects, but it is more difficult to establish, that this neo-liberal orientation is partly influenced by revulsion at the realization of the connections that can obtain between "humanism and terror."

From the perspective of the critique of development theory and a concern with the politics of the Third World, it seems to me that the work of Nicos Poulantzas and John Taylor, among the structural

Marxists, is the most relevant; and of the two, certainly, Poulantzas has been the more influential.

Nicos Poulantzas

For Nicos Poulantzas, as for Barrington Moore and so many theorists of political development, the problematic is defined by Marx's *Eighteenth Brumaire*, and the paradigmatic case to be explained is the Bonapartist state. The key question is that of the relationship of the bourgeois class to the apparatus of the state in the light of the Marxist conception of the state in the CMP. Influenced by the experience of Third World countries, Poulantzas argues for the relative autonomy of the state *as a characteristic feature of the CMP*, but he also holds that Bonapartism was the consequence of the incompleteness of the bourgeois revolution in France.[64] It follows that the dominance of the apparatus of the state, or of bureaucratic-authoritarianism in the Third World, is due to the partial success of the bourgeois revolution and the autonomy of the state in the CMP. But the resultant situation is not a stable one, because it is one where the CMP is a "structure in dominance" but where the bourgeoisie is not actually hegemonic. Such situations may be understood in terms of the teleological consequences of the Althusserian concept of a structure in dominance, or in terms of the Gramscian notion of a disastrous equilibrium or stalemate between the traditional or feudal class and the emergent bourgeois class.[65] Poulantzas is inclined toward the view that Bonapartism, or Third World bureaucratic-authoritarianism, is a preliminary, or incomplete stage of the realization of the CMP.

Poulantzas makes it clear that he is seeking a Marxist political science, but he rejects the idea that there can be a bourgeois and a proletarian science. In fact he draws on what he calls contemporary social science quite frequently, and he asserts that he finds some convergence between recent tendencies in bourgeois social science and Marxist analysis.[66] His approach is often eclectic. He conflates theoretical issues and he seems to force a comprehensiveness where it does not exist, sometimes quoting nontheoretical Marxist sources, and sometimes misreading Western liberal sources. The biggest problem may be his misreading of liberal sources, especially in identifying functionalism as the foundation of liberal social theory, without at the same time grasping the ideological relevance of pragmatism to functionalism.

In spite of this theoretical confusion, Poulantzas defines class in pragmatic terms as the self-interested behavior of individuals (agents of production) who stand in differential relationships to the economy (ownership of means of production, method of surplus appropriation, relations of production, etc.), the polity, and the cultural system.[67] Social class is thus an abstraction which is manifested in the dispersed form of political, economic, and cultural behavior or in the form of the economic class struggle, the political class struggle, and the ideological class struggle. We don't have far to go to find Arthur Bentley and Talcott Parsons looming behind this conception.

Thus, Poulantzas treats social structure "dynamically," as class struggle, which is in turn conceived of as the class practices resulting from the effects of the other structures that distribute the "agents of production" among the various classes. As a consequence, agents of production become supporters of class interests and engage in class-oriented practices that bring them into conflict with others. But because no mode of production is "pure," the articulation of modes of production produces new classes, while still not eliminating the old. In addition, various groups, fractions, categories, and parts of classes reflect somewhat different interests, and may or may not be organized, self-conscious, and so forth. Among such groups we may find the apparatus of the state, the clergy, the intelligentsia, or subsections of the bourgeoisie, or various categories of landlords and peasants.

The upshot of all this is that the social-structural map is quite complicated, and further subdivided into "regional" conflicts, such as the economic class struggle and the political class struggle. Only at times does this struggle manifest itself as a contest for control of the state, and that is usually the case only where there are "mature" classes, which are organized politically, and which are the appropriate classes for the "mature" state of a relevant mode of production, that is, the bourgeoisie and the proletariat in an advanced capitalist state where there is a socialist party.[68]

Another consequence is that the pattern of class struggle reflects the complexity of the practices of the multiplicity of classes, fractions, segments, et cetera, and may or may not reveal that a given fraction has achieved political hegemony. The pluralist character of the political process obscures the perception of who is actually in charge: and that is precisely the point of the liberal state under the CMP. Since it is the purpose of the bourgeois class to mask its power, the bourgeois state must be relatively autonomous in political fact as well as in political theory. Hence, the relative autonomy of the state in the CMP is a scientific truth for structural Marxism.

Hegemony, thus, has both an ideological and a coalitional character, in the sense that bourgeois culture dominates ideologically, but bourgeois political dominance is achieved by means of a coalition with other social forces. Similarly, social structure is defined as a complex and changing pattern of class struggles, functionally determined by the structure of the political, economic, and ideological "regions," and not necessarily by self-conscious organization and pursuit of interest. Knowledge of class structure is achieved by a deductive summation based on the empirical examination of each separate region, that is, the relatively autonomous regions of politics, economics, and ideology. Hence, especially for those segments that play a secondary class role, such as the agrarian fractions under the CMP, their relevance is determined by what Poulantzas calls the "pertinent effects" of their existence on the regional structures.[69] This formulation leads to the a priori determination of which are the primary and which are the secondary classes and fractions, but it severely limits the independence of all classes.

In Poulantzas' treatment, the relative autonomy of the political, the economic, and the ideological, and his conception of social process, introduce an element of functionalism and a form of pluralism which well accord with liberal pluralist theory. His use of such terms as dislocation, decentration, levels, structures, practices, and the like, further stresses the adaptive and systematic character of the CMP, as well as its concomitant pragmatic and pluralist process. In place of the key concept of contradiction, which points to the demise of the CMP, structuralist Marxism emphasizes the *conjuncture,* or the immediate situation, which is to be contrasted with the teleological nature of the system.

But in spite of the pragmatism, pluralism, and functionalism which suffuses Poulantzas's exposition of the capitalist state, he argues that it is a class-dominated state over against the frequently reductionist conception of the state held by liberal theorists. It is consequently fascinating to witness the manner in which exponents of a more conservative theory, which emphasizes the autonomy of the state in the sense of its autonomy "from" class influence, have adopted the terminology of Poulantzas, and through him of Althusser. In the view of such theorists, the autonomy of the state is valued not because it is the condition of the possibility of bourgeois domination, but because it protects the dominant class from its own excesses or prevents the emergence of a hegemonic class.

John Taylor

Taylor's useful critique of liberal theory is matched by an equally stern critique of what he calls the sociology of underdevelopment, as found in the works of Frank, Paul Baran, Paul Sweezy et al.[70] His major argument is that theories which do not explain themselves in terms of class structure, the method of appropriation of surplus value, the method by which the ruling class reproduces the conditions of its dominance, and the ideological situation, do not explain anything. Implicitly, Taylor may be concerned with explaining why revolutions have not occurred in Third World countries, but more explicitly he offers an explanation of why capitalist development remains incomplete in these countries. If the conditions for revolution do not yet obtain, then it follows that revolutionary proposals for the solution of extant problems are aberrant from the Marxist point of view.

Taylor ignores the notion of dependency, and instead emphasizes the articulation of modes of production as the explanation of underdevelopment. By this he means not merely that both capitalist and precapitalist modes of production coexist in many if not all Third World countries, but that they are so structured that they have become interdependent with regard to one or more of the four essential aspects of any mode of production. Beyond this fundamental position Taylor does not or cannot go, arguing that the theoretical work has not been done.[71] At this time, all one can do is to describe the particular configurations, or conjunctural situations in accordance with which the capitalist and precapitalist modes are articulated in particular countries. Taylor denies that there is some sort of a law of nature by which economic systems tend toward homogeneity of mode of production, just as do some development theorists deny that cultural modernity necessarily drives out tradition. Taylor is certain that rational and material explanations will always be found for each configuration, but he does not argue that it will be possible to predict whether and by what path capitalist development will triumph, let alone revolution occur. Despite his sympathies for Althusser, he does not even describe the "complete science" to which he may aspire. Instead, and despite his criticism of bourgeois empiricism, he seems to be content to explain a great deal in terms of a profound conjuncturalism.[72] Notwithstanding Taylor's use of a particularly difficult neo-Marxist language, once translated into ordinary English, (or rather into the discourse of liberal development theory), most of what Taylor offers as description of conditions obtaining in Third World countries, or as the methods of imperialist penetration, would be found entirely acceptable as empirical description.[73]

The Resurgence of Liberal Theory

Out of the proliferation of neo-Marxian theory and the aspiration for a Marxian social science have come some new, bold, and attractive ideas, which, however much they may fail to inspire orthodox Marxists, have aroused a great deal of interest among liberal social scientists, and especially those dealing with Latin American affairs. The attractiveness of these new ideas has not merely drawn attention, but has encouraged their wider employment by a number of followers, and in some cases we find at least one relatively outstanding disciple, adapting the original ideas. There has been a kind of public appropriation of these concepts and partial theories, most notably in the case of O'Donnell's *Bureaucratic Authoritarianism*, to the extent that the originators have virtually lost proprietary control. In each case a major interpreter and adapter has begun the process of remaking the original idea in a manner more acceptable to liberal thinking, more amenable to empirical research, and more workable from the perspective of normal science. As logical and empirical anomalies are turned up, theoretical explanation is transformed into a proliferation of minute descriptions and the predictive orientation is dissolved in the objectivist rhetoric of unlimited pragmatic possibilities.

Nevertheless, despite the cautious eclecticism of the new literature, the implicit issue remains how far can we expect to realize the liberal, democratic affluent state in Latin America: to what extent can Latin American states move to the semi-periphery; will an autonomous and influential bourgeois class come into existence; will revolution be avoided in Mexico, Brazil, Argentina, and Venezuela? As the original creative ideas have been appropriated by the community of scholars, and as the literature has expanded, there has been less emphasis on a distinctive Marxist social science and more on the usual objective criteria of bourgeois social science. Marxists have been less attracted than liberals, because these new ideas are essentially glosses and refinements which explain why Marx's predictions (if so they may be truly called) have not been realized.

F. H. Cardoso and Enzo Falleto have been resoundingly successful in altering the direction of dependency theory from concern with unequal terms of trade to the possibility of development under conditions of dependency. Despite a fair degree of imprecision in the description of these preconditions, Cardoso and Falleto made it clear that indigenous development depended, among other things, upon the emergence of an entrepreneurial segment under conditions that were not predetermined by international economic relations. They argue that the nature of the bourgeois capitalist class in peripheral countries was not necessarily directly determined by the needs of metropolitan capitalism. They thus challenge the idea of the "tight fit" of world and peripheral capitalism that is the product of aprioristic deductive logic from "Frankian" premises, and which has inspired some of the discussion of the articulation of modes of production. As a result, Cardoso and Falleto have also drawn attention to the importance of class conflict and class formation in Latin America, the significance of which is, of course, related to the theory of the prerequisites of a proletarian revolution. Despite their close adherence to Marxist rhetorical forms, their argument has been read as a decisive refutation of Frank and his revolutionary solution to dependency.

Peter Evans, among many others who have appreciated the work of Cardoso and Falleto, has developed these ideas with empirical detail for Brazil, and he has emphasized, instead of class struggle, the struggle between the capitalist bourgeoisie and the military rulers, in a paradigmatic context borrowed from bureaucratic authoritarianism.[74] Not the least significant element of Evans' work has been a restatement of the development of the literature in the field which is no less than a cogent, if (liberal) ideological, shaping of the paradigm within which he then proposes his own research as normal science. It is worth noting, as well, that Evans is, for the most part, far more optimistic about the possibilities for the development of classical capitalism and a coordinate liberalized state than were Cardoso and Falleto. The pessimism of Cardoso and Falleto may have been due to the difference in the dates when each of these works was written, but I also believe that the heavier use of the Marxist idiom quite naturally led to a lower level of confidence in peripheral, dependent, capitalist development.[75]

Guillermo O'Donnell's theories of bureaucratic authoritarianism are the outstanding case of the collective appropriation and transformation of one scholar's creative thinking.[76] In its original version, O'Donnell's theory is derived from an analysis of the modern Latin American equivalent of the Bonapartist state. He sought to understand whether the most recent form of authoritarian government in Latin America, as exemplified by the Peron regime, was an obstacle to development or not. In his very influential book, O'Donnell explained the emergence of authoritarianism in Argentina. In a later article, however, O'Donnell confounded his colleagues by "extending" the theory (although calling this extension a mere gloss on the first stage of bureaucratic-authoritarianism) to predict the counter-emergence of democracy.[77] Perhaps this sort of elusiveness is the law of survival for creative scholars who, like Satchel Paige, have to keep moving and ought not look over their shoulders.

According to O'Donnell, agrarian oligarchy is supplanted by an early stage of capitalism, sustained by wide popular-nationalist support. The limits of easy capitalist development are reached, whereupon the bourgeois-proletarian alliance, formed in a moment of enthusiasm, is dissolved. The haute bourgeoisie allies with the technocracy and the military to stave off the economic crisis which comes with the end of import substitution and the effort to deepen capitalist development. Deepening capitalist development requires a reorientation toward an export economy, which, in turn, requires cutting consumer imports, reducing wages, increasing savings, and increased capital imports. Bureaucratic authoritarianism is brought into being to replace populist nationalist regimes by the clear, conscious choice of transnationally connected capitalists, who cannot otherwise get their economic policies implemented. The resultant situation is described as a contradiction of capitalist development.

But in a subsequent essay, O'Donnell argues that the aspect of the resolution of this class conflict that interests him is the restoration, or rather, the fuller achievement of democracy. The contradiction which leads to this outcome is not described as that between the interests of the capitalists and the interests of the proletariat, but rather the well-known idealist contradiction between a state which claims popular and national legitimacy and yet serves the interests of the least national and least popular class of all—the transnational capitalists.

There is a glaring theoretical inconsistency between the two contributions to the theory, despite O'Donnell's claims to the contrary. There is, in fact, nothing much in the second version that is incompatible with the liberal paradigm. The attraction of the first version is to be found in the way in which it employs a Marxist structure of analysis to explain how it was possible to achieve a high degree of political and economic cooperation among the state elites, the bourgeoisie, industrial labor, and the middle sectors. The key to understanding O'Donnell's argument is to bear in mind the long-term consequences of the beneficent aspects of the Peronist experience. To the extent that social harmony, economic prosperity, political participation, and national unity were even temporarily realized, that experience has shaped the political culture of Argentina. This is what O'Donnell alludes to in his use of the term *lo popular.* It is questionable whether this sort of development has occurred anywhere else, or whether it is even likely to occur elsewhere. It hardly appears to be a characteristic feature of Bonapartism, although populist nationalism and mass democracy are identified therewith.

In the hands of his followers, disciples, and colleagues, this scheme is picked apart until no single assertion stands unqualified in terms of space and time. Instead of predictive theory, it is transformed into an explanation of how the new authoritarianism arose in Latin America.[78] One critic asserts that O'Donnell explains nothing because the very same (exogenous) cause that gave rise to authoritarianism gave rise to democracy—and that is a severe economic crisis.[79] In place of O'Donnell's self-conscious haute bourgeoisie pursuing a rational and self-interested strategy, his critics see a collection of nervous transnational capitalists reacting in terms of often exaggerated (psychological) "perceptions" of threatened social disorder or upheaval.[80] The idea of the structure of capitalist production or something akin to a mode of production, is replaced with the notion of accumulated or available wealth to pay off the masses.[81]

The form of the collective critique is disaggregation, breaking down the general, and interesting holistic conception into a host of component parts which can then serve as the basis of future research. In this case the process of the creation of a paradigm and the appropriation of creative thought is overt and apparent. The ideological significance of O'Donnell's work is not wholly ignored, but it is given short shrift. With the messy ideological matter put off to one side, objectivist scholars can go on and pursue detailed information that will, of course, disconfirm the existence anywhere of an ideal-typical bureaucratic authoritarian state.

World Systems Theory

Immanuel Wallerstein, in contrast to O'Donnell, has taken his own substantial historical study and has successfully transformed it into a paradigm, and has been able to persuade a number of people to convert it into a framework for normal science.[82] It is apparent that in the process some new bells and whistles had to be added so that lesser scholars might rely more upon the elaboration of hypotheses and theoretical propositions growing out of the semiperiphery notion, and less upon their own searching insights into the history of European capitalism.

Most people seem to think that the main point of Wallerstein's World System theory are the conclusions he draws from the fact that markets and polities do not coincide geographically, from the greater importance he attaches to international stratification than to domestic stratification, and from the special role which he attributes to countries of the semiperiphery. The theory which is constituted of these and other elements appears to be a modification of Lenin's theory of imperialism, except that it does not look upon core-periphery relations as inevitably leading to the ultimate demise of capitalism as a consequence of its own contradictions. Nor does he argue that the international system will become a two-class system. He specifically provides that states can move from the periphery and others may drop out of the core. The dual nature of his system, transnational economic actors or units and national political actors or units, allows for shifts in the relative positions of national units without necessarily disturbing the economic structure of world capitalism. Wallerstein does not treat the economic units as real, and the political units as apparent; and since both are real, a logical as well as a practical problem arises in attempting to determine how they affect one another.

Insofar as the two subsystems do not articulate, or mesh, or fit together, it follows that changes in one will not directly affect changes in the other. It is this disarticulation of the political and economic world systems that has permitted capitalism to survive, and even prosper beyond the expectations of orthodox Marxist-Leninists. It is this same disarticulation which permits the Soviet Union to be a part of the world system, and which prevents it from realizing full socialism. It follows logically that the world capitalist system cannot be changed piecemeal, but only all at once, either by a total breakdown or perhaps by a worldwide revolutionary movement that would probably have to start in the semiperiphery. The semiperiphery is selected for this role because of a number of special functions which it performs on behalf of the core countries, but also, one suspects, because its political self and its economic self are least sundered of the three. Because of the closer integration of its economic and its political natures, it can act more effectively and with greater coordination, at least in its own sphere. Still, the temptations to try to move into the core or to exploit the periphery, and to compete with other semiperipheral states or to respond to the threats and blandishments of the core countries, are not likely to encourage a worldwide "third force" movement, while any attempt to realize socialism in one country is bound to fail.

The conclusions we draw, are that the prospects for world revolution are not very good, while the possibilities for the competitive improvement of individual states are real. A world socialist system might end the exploitation characteristic of the capitalist system, and thereby bring about greater worldwide equality, but it is not clear that it would increase the total wealth available.[83] Since Wallerstein insists that the capitalist system precludes the possibility of equal exchange, and attributes capital accumulation to this inequality, the attractiveness of a world socialist system must be diminished for those who want affluence rather than equality. Moreover, because the capitalist system is necessarily exploitative, semiperipheral states that move to the core while awaiting a worldwide socialist revolution need not feel uneasy about their new exploitative role.

Even though world systems theory emphasizes the significance of the early history of capitalism, there can be little doubt of its relevance to the question of late capitalism. The problem of late capitalism concerns how to explain the continued vigor of contemporary capitalism, and how to discern the obscure signs of the imminent collapse of capitalism if that vigor is only apparent. Presumably, the signs of that demise ought to be related in some way to the characteristic feature of late capitalism, that is, to the internationalization of capital as imperialism, finance capital, and the growth of multinational corporations. But continued increase of the stigmata of late capitalism is accompanied by little convincing evidence of increasing weakness. Wallerstein's argument is that under capitalism, the political and economic systems were separated *ab initio,* hence capitalism was international from the start. Leninist theory, therefore, points to a stable and not a dynamic feature of capitalism, even if the international character of capitalism was not sufficiently emphasized by Marx. Moreover, Wallerstein argues that the international character of capitalism militates against revolution. Consequently, for Wallerstein, what is stated as the problem of late capitalism in Marxist-Leninist theory is no more than a reference to a characteristic feature of capitalist economics that makes it enormously stable as a world system.

Wallerstein's history of the rise of European capitalism puts the answer to the question of "late capitalism" at the very origin of capitalism itself, in fact he makes it part of the nature of capitalism. Late capitalism is not late capitalism anymore, it is the original capitalism seen far more clearly than Marx did. Wallerstein's solution is ingenious, and probably deserves to be enshrined in a new normal science. It is also ingenious in that it uses a good deal of the Marxist-Leninist framework to refute that position, and to provide at least an interim justification for liberal development policies. In a more serious scholarly sense, Wallerstein has attempted to un-Marx Marx by means of "annalizing" the dialectic. The confusing discussion of the semiperiphery, and the nostalgic discussion of socialist revolution, strikes me as an expression of oedipal remorse, which the rest of us liberals and social democrats may be excused for not sharing.

Agrarian Patrimonialism and Revolution

In his review of "The Comparative and Historical Study of Revolutions" in the *Annual Review of Sociology,* J. A. Goldstone mentions both Barrington Moore and Theda Skocpol as having each contributed a nice additional consideration to the growing body of situationally unspecified propositions regarding revolution.[84] Moore, he writes, "demonstrated that variations in the relations between landlords and peasants were crucial in determining the course of political change."[85] Of Moore's student, if not disciple, Theda Skocpol, whom he confusingly mentions before Moore, he writes;

> . . . social scientists from both the Marxian and Weberian traditions were exploring the origins and growth of the state itself. . . . These studies were capped by Skocpol's (1979) demonstration that social revolutions have not arisen mainly from the

> acts of a powerful revolutionary opposition but from the internal breakdown and paralysis of state administrations, which rendered states incapable of managing normally routine problems of governance.[86]

Aside from reflecting the unfortunate Parsonian tendency to conflate Marxist and Weberian thought, and hence the failure to distinguish the extent to which Moore depends on Marx and Skocpol on Weber, Goldstone has also treated both works as normal scientific contributions amplifying the Brinton paradigm which Goldstone so brilliantly lays out at the start of his review.[87] There are thus two more things to "look at": the failures in the transformation of the agrarian mode of production (if there can be such a thing as a partitive mode) and the entropy of bureaucracies which are not wholly legal-rational or socially insulated. In the total scheme of the liberal theory of revolutions, these may be numbered as propositions 67 and 68, or even 167 and 168. You may place them wherever you please, because in a system of "empirical theory" you simply have to run your data against all the proposed configurations until you find the fit.

Goldstone is doing no evil in pursuing his own purposes in appropriating the work of Moore and Skocpol as though it comprised a couple of general propositions, but if one is not bent on constructing a pragmatic theory of political change in which democratic and authoritarian outcomes of revolution are equally to be expected, that is, have an equal probability, then one may see more in these works of historical sociology than the mere provision of two more types of breakdown that may lead to the generic revolutionary crisis. My point is not that Moore and Skocpol do not attribute equal probability to democratic and nondemocratic outcomes, because, implicitly they do.

Following Moore, insofar as revolution is caused by the failure to transform traditional agriculture, it may lead in the short run to authoritarianism, as in China; but where a bourgeois elite succeeds in integrating agriculture with the national and world markets, we get bourgeois parliamentarism, as in India, again in the short run. Both transformations are violent, both are modernizing, and both lead to increased production. It is uncertain whether the one or the other will be more beneficial to the masses over the long run, because the agrarian structure of the early stage of capitalist development leads to the creation of an oligarchic provincial gentry. Further development obviously depends on weakening the political position of this gentry, but parliamentary politics makes this progressive task more difficult.[88]

This strikes me as a theory of democratic development rather than one of revolution. It is not only that different revolutionary outcomes have an "initially" equal probability, but that revolution and nonrevolution have similar outcomes from the point of view of this development theory. Revolution is the consequence of the failure to perform a necessary task of economic modernization, that is, agrarian reform; but it is largely a case of "pay me now or pay me later," as the auto mechanic says, and it is not clear whether you pay more in preventive costs or in repairs after the breakdown. The argument's main thrust is that you arrive at the same place anyway, but I think that most of us would rather contemplate weakening the power of the Indian gentry than living through the Chinese revolution. Moore's is not merely an explanation of the etiology of revolution in a certain set of cases. It is an argument about how and why Marxist revolution is neither necessary nor beneficial, and how to avoid it both early and late. Moreover, if one prefers democracy in both the long run and the short, then he has marked the necessary path.

Skocpol's argument is a similar one, although she quite rightly notes that Moore grants virtually no theoretical significance to the international context (which Wallerstein treated as central).[89] But the linkage of the international and the national is essentially conjunctural in Skocpol's analysis—that is, the international forces are one more factor to be taken into consideration in explaining the revolutionary crisis. There is a more systematic link, or more of an "internal" relationship between her treatment of the bureaucratic crisis and Moore's agrarian crisis. The main connection is, of course, that in the prerevolutionary situation we have a neopatrimonial bureaucracy, segments of which are identified with feudal or latifundial landowner classes.[90] The same sort of reasons which lead to the failure to transform agrarian structure lead to the failure to perform other necessary modernizing transformations. The functional need is for a legal rational, technically proficient, professional and politically disinterested bureaucracy. It is a complicated matter to determine just how certain bourgeois intellectual segments come to see themselves as the agents of this requisite functional transformation, but somehow, sometimes they do, and it is at such critical junctures that we have a revolution. Or, more precisely, modernizing revolutions will often include this important pattern.

Once again, it follows from the logic of the argument, that revolution is not historically necessary, that it is not based on an inevitable class struggle. The key to Skocpol's position is in the assertion that the revolutionary crisis that grows out of administrative entropy is merely an interruption of a modernizing and centralizing trend, which has begun long before the revolution, and picks up again with renewed vigor thereafter.[91] Isn't it all a great waste? It is a particularly great waste if we attribute hegemonic power to the apparatus of the state over against social classes. If monarchs ally with the bourgeoisie in time to limit the damage that an aristocratic bureaucracy can do, then perhaps revolution can be avoided.[92] Some will regret that the Shah's advisors seem to have read Huntington rather than Skocpol.[93] But Skocpol's theory goes further in that it identifies bourgeois and socialist revolutions as having the same function, so that if neither is necessary and if both do the same thing, which would you choose? If we are so smart, why aren't we rich? If we know so much about revolutions why do we have them still? If not for the rivers of innocent blood shed in Iran, would not that revolution be farce rather than tragedy?

Skocpol's exposition may be compared to that of François Furet, who also denies the centrality of the idea of a bourgeois revolution and who is similarly concerned with the relative autonomy of the state.[94] But Furet's critical targets are the Leninist-Althusserian neo-Marxists, whose dogmatic interpretations of the French Revolution represent for him the perpetuation of the Jacobinist mythology which has distorted the scientific understanding of what actually happened.[95] Like Skocpol, Furet emphasizes the conjunctural, the diversity of interests, of class backgrounds, and of tactical preferences among the revolutionary activists, and the fact that much of what the Revolution was supposed to achieve had, in fact, already been achieved.[96]

Furet, with more than a little ambivalence, tells us that the French Revolution created the concept of the integrated, democratic, national community. "Augustin Cochin permet de comprendre comment la légitimité démocratique s'est substituée à l'ancienne légitimité de droit divin."[97] This, rather than the modern bourgeois state, is the yield of the Revolution, but Furet is careful to distinguish the actual events of 1789–93 from the long-term historical process, and he often cites Marx in his own support against those who would perpetuate the mythical idea of the Revolution in the light of the later experience of Russia and China. For Furet, the historical essence of the French revolution was ideological, not in the sense that it was caused by new ideas, but in that the changes which had already been wrought required new forms of discourse for their legitimation. The forms of discourse which triumphed are those of the Jacobinists, even though they no longer prevailed after Thermidor.

Skocpol, unlike Furet, does not enter into a direct dialogue with Marxism, neo or paleo. Instead she identifies herself as sympathetic to Marxism, and then argues that Marxist theory is of secondary importance in the analysis of social revolution.[98] This surprising position can be taken in at least two ways. Either it is an argument for the secondary importance of the processes of economic change which are central to Marxist theory, or it is an argument for the relative unimportance of social revolution.

Skocpol's social revolution is the consequence of a conjuncture of events, each of which is of relatively high probability. These events include external challenges, the development from traditional patrimonialism to pre-modern absolutism, increased social conflict, administrative breakdown, peasant revolution, urban disorders, the seizure of power by marginal elites preaching new doctrines, the reestablishment of state power, and the reshaping of society and economy by the modern bureaucratic state. The crucial element is the peasant revolution.[99] Peasants are always ready to rebel, but their rebellions will be crushed unless the state administrative apparatus has broken down, and unless they are effectively organized via either traditional (*gemeinschaftlich*) or modern structures. In the long run, the peasants will be crushed by the new state, led by the victorious marginal elites; but in the meantime a social revolution will have occurred, and a new and more powerful state apparatus will have been created.

This emphasis on the role of the peasant revolution serves many theoretical purposes. In the first place it is used as the common factor shared by the French, Russian, and Chinese revolutions. These revolutions, despite their conjunctural origins, are members of the same species, but not because class struggle causes revolution. Clearly, the wrong class rebels, and it does not emerge victorious. Moreover, peasant revolt is not the direct or clear consequence of a change in the mode of production: it is the consequence of exploitation and oppression. Where peasants are not well organized, marginal elites do not take over, and existing governments are able to reorganize themselves and restore order. England, Prussia and Japan are examples of the second species.

It follows that social revolution, despite the Jacobinist rhetoric, has nothing to do with liberal, parliamentary democracy. It is thus not only Marx who is refuted by Skocpol, but Barrington Moore as well, since he argued that the method by which the transformation of the mode of agricultural production was accomplished was the crucial social origin of democracy or dictatorship. Moore certainly separated democracy from revolution, and certainly identified modernization with the rise of capitalism, but he also asserted the link between democracy and the bourgeoisie. Skocpol all but ignores the problem of liberal democracy, implicitly arguing that where peasant rebellions fail, the elites of absolutist states, who are already well along into capitalist development, will manage to hold on to power.

This is not to argue, however, that the long-term processes described by Marx are not occurring, or that history has lost its meaning. It is rather to argue, as Furet does, that the romanticized conception of revolution is misleading, whether in the context of European absolutism or Third World nationalism. Revolution is the product of change and not the cause of change, except insofar as it may permit the further fulfillment of earlier transformations, albeit in a distorted fashion.

Furet struggles to explain how democracy, revolution, and class interests are linked in the French Revolution. There were in, in fact, two revolutions: an ideological revolution which led to the Terror, and a "revolution of interests" which was revealed only after the demise of Robespierre. The fall of Robespierre produced "le recouvrement par le société de son indépendence, à tous les niveaux, qu'il s'agisse de la vie quotidienne, des moeurs, des habitudes, des passions et des interêts. La liberté retrouvée en thermidor a comme contenu essentiel une revanche du social sur l'idéologie . . . la société a recouvré son autonomie par rapport au politique."[100]

According to Furet's interpretation, the bourgeoisie is not revolutionary, but neither does it support absolutism. Instead, the bourgeoisie pursues its partitive interests pragmatically, restoring society and commonsense realism over against the excesses of ideology. This restoration is the condition of the possibility of the Bonaparte regime, which could unite the revolution and the centralized state, the two Frances, in a way in which the bourgeoisie could not. So for Furet, the bourgeoisie seems to be the hero, while for Skocpol, the state is the hero. Bourgeois democracy is, therefore, the product of the confluence of two distinct cultural tributaries, neither one of which originates in the bourgeois experience. Democracy itself is rooted in the revolution. The bourgeois hegemony emerges after some time during which "society recovers its autonomy." But for Skocpol, as for Moore, revolution and democracy are separate.

Thus does the critique of the liberal theory of development refute the claim that modernization produces democratization, ignoring the ideological impact of the Jacobinist idea, and relegating democracy itself to the realm of the politically epiphenomenal. And there, surprisingly enough, has it remained, despite the rather impressive number of "peripheral" and "semiperipheral" states that have "returned" to some form of democratic government. The redemocratization of Argentina, Brazil, Spain, Portugal, Greece, Turkey, the Philippines, and possibly South Korea, has inspired a great deal of scholarly interest, but the major work so far produced reaffirms the view that democracy is essentially a "conjunctural" phenomenon, linked to the inadequacies of authoritarian regimes, and dependent upon the skillful bargaining tactics of the "liberals".[101]

Despite the failure of the Woodrow Wilson group to find some sort of unifying theoretical explanation of this remarkable series of redemocratizing events, there are both promising and puzzling consequences of this entropic conclusion. The more promising suggestion is that democratization is not precluded by its failure to emerge along with the emergence of the modern state, or the bourgeois state, or upon the collapse of the absolutist state. Democratization appears as an alternative solution to crises, and may even have a particularly important connection to international pressure.[102]

The more puzzling aspect of the conjuncturalist position is its consistent rejection or avoidance of the political significance of class in explaining, or failing to explain, democratization. It is, in fact, possible to distinguish between those neo-Marxist theorists such as Barrington Moore, Nicos Poulantzas, Cardozo and Falleto, and Perry Anderson, who perceive a class link between the bourgeoisie and the modern liberal democratic state, and those such as Theda Skocpol, Peter Evans, and Guillermo O'Donnell, who are willing to admit that the modern state produces conditions congenial to capitalist development, but who are more inclined to see the bourgeoisie as passive beneficiaries of the modernization of states. There is, in fact, a greater inclination to acknowledge the influence of bourgeois interests under absolutist, presumably feudal, states than under capitalist states. Above all there is a general reluctance to see the question of democratization and redemocratization as a problem of the role of the bourgeoisie in the modernization process.

Once it is concluded that there is no such thing as a bourgeois revolution, and once it is admitted that the bourgeois state serves the interests of many besides the bourgeoisie, then the concept of class is put aside in favor of state, elite, culture and ideology. The bourgeoisie, or the propertied sectors, then become no more than the subordinate allies of the bureaucratic elite or the military oligarchy, that is, the historical equivalent of the absolutist monarchy. From this perspective, it may be argued that there is no "real" difference between bourgeois democracies and bourgeois autocracies, only an apparent difference based upon which of the tactical alternatives is required by the situation.

This is the more usual Marxist position, and it calls into question the importance of differentiating between bourgeois or bureaucratic dominance of the alliance between the two, or the importance of cross-class alliances as achieved by bourgeois parties, or the protection and exercise of political and civil rights during the democratic interludes which alternate with periods of bureaucratic autocracy. Nor is it true that Marx himself discounted the value of bourgeois democracy, as any reader of *The Eighteenth Brumaire* knows. Marx was rather contemptuous of the various factions of the French bourgeoisie for their failure to assert themselves, for their inability to form a strong class alliance, and for their fear of working with other classes. Bonapartism was the result of the failures of the bourgeoisie, but these failures are not the expression of the inherent character of bourgeois politics. At least it is the contention of Nicos Poulantzas, Ralph Miliband, and Adam Przeworski that the liberal politics of contemporary bourgeois states is built upon overcoming the shortcomings that led to Bonapartism. And it is in this sense that the question of the relative autonomy of the state is to be pursued, for only if the state may be autonomous of class domination does it make any sense to investigate the degree to which bourgeois hegemony exists, and to explore the ways in which it is exercised. If the issue is an empirical one, and not a matter of definition, then the value of bourgeois democracy is a meaningful and not a false question.

Implicitly, the *Eighteenth Brumaire* has emerged as the sacred text of the new development paradigm, replacing Parsonian sociology, group politics and the functional theory of elites. Certainly this has been the case in recent studies of Latin American politics, where democratization and redemocratization have been interpreted in terms of the relations between the military-bureaucratic ruling circles and the big bourgeoise. Understandably, there has been some reluctance to argue that the capitalist elite is gaining power at the expense of the military. The episodic character of the shifts in the balance of power and the role of mass politics and international affairs make it difficult to draw reliable conclusions. A number of alternative hypotheses have, however, been proffered, and they represent alternative interpretations ranging from Cardozo and Faletto's discussion of the modernizing and liberalizing role of a truly indigenous (not comprador) bourgeoisie, whose wealth and influence is also the product of indigenous development, to Evan's doubts that the Brazilian bourgeoisie will ever gain hegemonic power, given the character of the military elite and the "ungovernability" of the Brazilian masses, to O'Donnell's ambivalent identification of the bureaucratic-authoritarian elite with the educated middle class and his rediscovery of the masses (*lo popular*) as the democratic force in Argentina.

But these alternatives were presented before the events of redemocratization that have inspired the new literature on tactical negotiation and compromise between the liberal bourgeois elites and the military elites. These alternatives were also presented when it was possible to argue that Brazil, Argentina, and Chile were all pretty much the same. The emphasis on the conjunctural origin of redemocratization reflects the continuing influence of Skocpol, and the justifiable apprehension that the future holds more military seizures of power in Latin America and elsewhere. But the greatest source of this reluctance to develop a systematic explanation based on class, is the belief that Marx's description of the political behavior of the French bourgeoisie is generally valid, and that the logic of class analysis leads to the dogmatic and mistaken conclusions of the Communist Manifesto rather than to the more ambiguous conclusions of Poulantzas, Przeworski, Schmitter, and O'Donnell.

Przeworski makes the interesting argument that redemocratization involves two processes rather than one: the breakdown of the authoritarian regime, and the "emergence of democratic institutions."[103] This position directly contradicts the view that military dictatorship and bourgeois parliamentarism are two faces of the same coin, but it also points out that authoritarian breakdowns are not themselves events of redemocratization. Yet the tactical conclusions reached by Schmitter and O'Donnell are based on the assumption that redemocratization is the result of a dialectic between *democraduros* and *dictablandas*. Their discussion, emphasizing situation-oriented political maneuvering, assumes that an original democratizing event (a revolution?) has already occurred (possibly in some other country?), which has so shaped the political culture of the country in question that bourgeois democracy exists as a practical alternative for effective governance in the case of a crisis.

There are, however, other situations in which bourgeois democracy is either not recognized as a legitimate and a useful alternative, or where it is imposed by elites (marginal or not) in a social context where few are motivated by self (or class) interest to play by the rules of the game. The central idea of the neo-Marxist theory of bourgeois democracy is that the role played by the bourgeoisie provides the rational incentive structure (pay-off schedule) which channels collective action in conformity with the rules of the game of parliamentary democracy. If parliamentary democracy is a rational alternative for the bourgeoise under the conditions described by Poulantzas, it might be argued that the alternatives of absolutism and bureaucratic authoritarianism are "suboptimal" even if the bourgeoisie would find both preferable to the disorder of a social revolution.

Crisis Theory

There are at least three types of theory focusing on the idea of crisis: the Comparative Politics Committee's multiple crises, Jurgen Habermas's legitimation crisis, and even O'Donnell's theory of bureaucratic authoritarianism.[104]

Crisis theory is primarily concerned with the consequences of the contradiction (disequilibrium or incongruence) between the demand for political participation and the need for administrative autonomy. While Huntington and those who would bring the state back in are mostly concerned about the breakdown of state institutions and the organizational instruments of political mobilization, the crisis theorists appear to be concerned about the interests of repressed majorities demanding participation. O'Donnell writes about the crisis of early capitalism, which leads the bureaucratic-authoritarian regime to suppress demands for participation and redistribution. In the longer run it is the reassertion of democratic aspirations and *lo popular* which will overthrow bureaucratic authoritarianism and establish democracy. Habermas is concerned with the crisis of late capitalism, but he, too, reads this as a crisis of promised democratization and egalitarian redistribution that is unfulfilled, leading to an explosion from the mass. For both, the solution is more democracy rather than more authoritarianism. The Comparative Politics group was rather more cautious.

Marxist theory postulates the inevitable breakdown of capitalism as a consequence of its internal contradictions, and it is this idea which sustains the notion that "late" capitalism will undergo one or more crises related to its final agony when those contradictions are most intensified. That there should be an equally anticipated crisis of early capitalism, even one restricted to the late developing countries, does not follow from orthodox Marxist theory, though it is not precluded either. O'Donnell appears to postulate such a crisis as a usual if not necessary occurrence, contributing to the rise and the institutionalization of bureaucratic authoritarianism. It is significant that this crisis of peripheral capitalism is a consequence of the premature success of early capitalism and the expectations to which that success gives rise. The development literature is already well acquainted with the idea of a revolution of rising expectations and the possibility of a subsequent revolution of rising frustrations. Nevertheless, O'Donnell's formulation is valuable, because it relates these ideas to the political experience of Argentina and to actual policies of restricting participation and reversing redistributional entitlements. Moreover, when referred to the complex multiple crisis scheme of the Comparative Politics Committee, O'Donnell's crisis has the virtue of simplifying the theory by denying the residual pragmatism by which the crises are treated as random occurrences. By hypothesizing a non-random historical process, manifesting itself in late developing "bourgeois" social formations, O'Donnell implicitly provides a theoretical framework which structures the relationships among the crises.

But there is clearly a great difference between a situation in which absolutism is challenged by a traditional parliament, and one in which a military and bureaucratic dictatorship is challenged to restore modern pluralizing institutions. It is, perhaps, one of the greatest difficulties of the literature on the crises of political development that it fails to distinguish between the crises of absolutism and the crises of modern bourgeois states. The major reason for this failure is, again, the interest in avoiding the use of Marxist terminology and the rejection of "stagist" conceptions. The issue is brought out most clearly by Perry Anderson's unequivocal insistence that there *is* such a thing as a bourgeois revolution, and that European absolutism represented the highest development of feudalism.[105] Of course the highest stage of feudalism, or any mode of production, is the point where it is closest to its replacement by the succeeding mode. The absolutist state was already pregnant with bourgeois capitalism, and its crises led to bourgeois revolution; but the absolutist state was not, for Anderson, a bourgeois state. It was a feudal state.

Many might be inclined to reject the class characterization of the state, insisting that such a characterization denies the relative autonomy of the state, even though Poulantzas argues that it actually affirms the relative autonomy of the state. However that may be, the theoretical consequence of Anderson's position is that the political crises of the absolutist state are likely to be different from the political crisis of the bourgeois state. This distinction was neglected by the crisis theory proposed by the Comparative Politics group, which was influenced by Almond and Easton in seeking a transhistorical functional theory of politics. That group was also convinced of the importance of the modernity-tradition distinction, in accordance with the Parsonian school, so it did not entirely neglect the idea that the five crises might take on a special form in the transition to modernity. The group struggled with the idea of alternate sequences of the five crises, but never seriously considered that sequence might be related to the class basis of the regime rather than to culture.

There was, also, a tendency to confuse noninstitutionalized (primitive, tribal, segmentary) systems with highly elaborated monarchical-patrimonial systems, a confusion which is paralleled by the Marxist use of the Asiatic Mode of Production (AMP) to describe the absence of capitalism under absolutism, as well as the stagnation of primitive, classless societies.

Anderson also argues that there was a profound difference between western European and eastern European absolutism. In the east, the perfecting of the feudal regime was accelerated by the threat of external conquest. Hence absolutism developed more rapidly than did capitalism, and it was accompanied by a more complete concentration of authority and power. The nobility was bureaucratized, and in return the peasantry was crushed and bound in service to the nobility. Anderson goes on to reject the idea of the AMP, specifically as it applies to the Ottoman Empire and the Islamic world. The Ottoman empire had many of the characteristics of the Asiatic mode, but it was neither classless nor unchanging.[106] In fact, Ottoman absolutism shared many characteristics with eastern European absolutism, except that it was even less favorable to the emergence of capitalism and the growth of an indigenous bourgeoisie than was eastern Europe. If one of the major consequences of the absence of an enterprising nobility and a propertied bourgeoisie was the greater possibility for the long-term success of marginal elites in capturing the leadership of social revolutions, then one might expect the relevant probabilities to increase the further east one travels. In Turkey, Egypt, and Iran, though, it seems as if the old regime collapsed under the burdens of external challenges and internal strains, only to be taken over by Bonapartist leaders without the chaotic interlude of social revolution. Iran, alone among the Muslim countries, reproduced something like an absolutist regime, and it alone has undergone a full-scale social revolution.

Skocpol, though succumbing to the Parsonian temptation to exaggerate the martyric culture of Shiʿism, compares the Iranian revolution to the French model, and to her own analysis of social revolution.[107] In a very useful summary of her own theoretical position, Skocpol fills out the balance sheet of the Iranian revolution, finding it deficient in certain of the anticipated prerequisites. Like Furet, however, Skocpol's analysis shifts uneasily from long-term historical and cultural factors to short-term factors, and even events, during the actual upheaval. One is uncertain about whether this is a theory of the dialectics of revolutionary violence or whether it is a broad historical-sociological analysis of how the postrevolutionary situation came about. This uneasiness appears to be an effort to show that violent revolution is historically epiphenomenal at best and, at worst, might allow the longer-term historical process to be diverted from its developmental goal.

Skocpol finds the Iranian revolution deviant in three particulars: (1) it was the product of rapid modernization and disruption of the traditional society and culture; (2) the security forces of the state were "rendered ineffective . . . without the occurrence of military defeat . . . and without pressures from abroad . . . or . . . contradictory conflicts between the regime and the dominant classes"; and (3) the revolution was "deliberately 'made' by a mass based social movement."[108] But these are only "apparent difficulties" which are accounted for when one considers the significance of Shiʿite ideology within the context of Iranian culture and society.

Despite the fact that peasants and landowners played a minor role in the Iranian revolution, the popular urban classes, many of them recent migrants from the countryside, lived within vital, integrated, largely traditional communities linked by clerics, merchants and artisans. These communities could perform the revolutionary function performed by integrated peasant communities in France and Russia. Moreover, Shiʿite Islam provided the organization, the leadership, and the ideological justification which permitted it to overcome the lack of formal organization, the questionable loyalty of the security forces, and the inertial obstacles to the mobilization of the popular masses.

The shifting historical focus of Skocpol's brief analysis is manifested in the questionable conclusion that the Iranian revolution "was 'made'"—but not, everyone will note, "by any of the modern revolutionary parties . . . not by the Islamic guerillas nor by the Marxist guerillas, nor by the Communist (Tudeh) Party, nor by the secular National Front."[109] And in a startling statement, calling into question the meaning of the relative autonomy of the state, Skocpol writes that "the State did not rule through or in alliance with, any independent social class."[110] Typically, the meaning of this statement is obscured by the word "independent," but we are not told what happened to the expropriated landowners, or of the social origins of the members of the bureaucracy, the military, and the revolutionary and reformist parties. Mosaddeq was overthrown in 1953, but the revolution began in 1977.

Skocpol gives no political or ideological credit at all to the "Western-oriented liberals, the liberals of the National Front, the modern-educated intellectuals, technically trained modern officials."[111] Though Western observers put their faith in these groups, Skocpol reminds them that "In the classic social revolutions, liberals and democratic socialists—people who want to limit or to decentralize state power—invariably lost out to political leaderships able and willing . . . to use unlimited coercive means to establish vanguard control in the name of the whole revolutionary people."[112] Those elites turn out to be the radical clerical supporters of Khomeini and their technocratic allies. This Shiʿite leadership is described as at once radical and authentically representing the prevailing cultural ethos. In fact, ignoring or disregarding the radical ideologies of the Mujahidin and the Fidayan, Skocpol chooses to compare the clerical elite with the Jacobins, and to speculate on their eventual, even inevitable demise: "These Islamic Jacobins may well endure quite a bit longer than their eighteenth-century French predecessors. Nevertheless, they cannot last indefinitely. For when the oil runs out . . ."[113]

Skocpol's ambivalence toward Islam, which is evident in this contradictory analysis of the cultural role of the orthodox Shiʿite clergy, is further expressed in her insistence that Shiʿism somehow makes Iranians more willing to get themselves killed in confronting the security forces of the repressive regime. This theme, repeated and emphasized in the brief article, stands out as the only unresolved anomaly distinguishing the Iranian revolution from the three classic ones, but it is questionable whether Iranians were more willing to sacrifice life than are Filipinos, or South Koreans, or Panamanians. The number and severity of such confrontations before the flight of the Shah seems greatly exaggerated, and the actual character of revolutionary confrontations seems to have been misunderstood. It is evident that much of what has happened after the revolution has been attributed to Iranian national character rather than to the ruthless exploitation of Islam by the new revolutionary "state builders."

There are many useful and unusual insights in this piece, not the least of which is the emphasis on the role of the Iranian revolutionary elite as state builders. But the greatest defect of this analysis lies in the myopic concentration on the two years of actual struggle to the neglect of the lengthy processes which alienated the educated and the propertied classes from the regime. In his analysis of the French Revolution, Furet argues that the main thing about that revolution was not its bourgeois character, as argued by the vulgar Marxists, and not the consolidation of the centralized state, as argued by de Tocqueville (and Skocpol), but its transformation of French political culture. He tells us that both of these characteristics of modernity have emerged elsewhere in Europe without the accompanying revolution, and they would have come to France as well.

> Ce qui fait l'originalité de la France contemporaine n'est pas qu'elle soit passée de la monarchie absolue au régime representatif, ou du monde nobiliaire a la société bourgeoise: l'Europe a parvenu le même chemin sans révolutions et sans Jacobins—même si les évènements français ont pu, ici et là, accélerer l'évolution et fabriquer des imitateurs. Or la Révolution Française n'est pas une transition, c'est une origine, et un fantasme d'origine. C'est ce qu'il y a d'unique en elle qui fait son intérêt historique, et c'est d'aillieurs cet «unique» qui est devenu universel: la première experience de la démocratie.[114]

Furet is inclined to attribute the postrevolutionary centralization of the French state to the way in which traditional French culture was transformed (rather than rejected) by the Jacobinist ideology. Hence, the French Revolution was not a bourgeois revolution. It was a *French* revolution, and it shaped the cultural and institutional context in which a bourgeois hegemony over a centralized state would emerge.

> Ainsi, l'idéologie révolutionnaire, qui est en 1792–1793, sous sa forme chimiquement pure, à l'origine de la guerre et de la Terreur, reste-t-elle en 1799, sous une forme degradée, semi-opinion, semi-legitimité, la clé du nouveau pouvoir qui s'installe. La bourgeoisie brumairienne cherchait un militaire libéral pour coiffer un système représentatif. Le sentiment populaire pousse un général victorieux à instaurer un état absolu. Comme l'explique Marx, c'est une version administrative de la Terreur qui clôt la Révolution française. . . .
>
> . . . Or c'est le triomphe de cette culture, et d'une administration centralisée dont elle est la cause et l'effet, qui constitue le sens de la Révolution française, en réunissant Louis XIV et Napoléon.[115]

One suspects that the Iranian revolution will have a similar impact, setting the cultural and ideological "structure" within which the Iranian elites of the future will rule, whether they turn out to be bourgeois or not. But in contemplating the way in which the Iranian revolution will reshape the political culture of that country it is well to remember that the Islamic revolution has not been based upon a revolutionary concept of Islam.

A Discordant Note on the Middle East

The influence of events in Portugal, Spain, Brazil, Argentina, Greece, Turkey, and even Chile and the Philippines, more recently, has further encouraged inquiry into the sort of crisis or situation which eventuates in the reassertion of parliamentary participation by the middle sectors. The study of democratic "restorations" has great relevance for the ideological critique of development theory, but it is obvious that it will not have universal applicability. The biggest question that will have to be answered in determining the scope of the relevance of new information regarding these (possible) democratic restorations will be whether they rest on a cultural-historical foundation that can only be randomly duplicated, or whether they provide examples for the course of development to be followed in other countries now also thought to be lost to democracy and liberal government. Is there, for example, any reason to expect an expanding reassertion of the liberal faith in parliamentary democracy in such countries as post-coup Turkey, post-revolutionary Iran, and post-Sadat Egypt?

I think it is of more than ordinary interest that Latin American scholars, as well as scholarship on Latin America, have played so large a part in the reassertion of liberal development theory. This is not only a case of how specific situations and events can influence our general perspective, but also of the exercise of an intellectual initiative which is supposed to be absent under conditions of dependency and peripherality (is there any such word?). This important intellectual contribution is all the more remarkable because no other region, it seems to me, has made a similar contribution. Why this should be the case, I am not sure. It may be due to the special circumstances of some Latin American countries, or to the Marxist exposure of Latin American intellectual elites, or to the fact that Latin culture is either European or so close that there is really no significant communications gap. Whatever it may be, Latin American scholars may be said not only to have made original contributions, but also to have eschewed cultural defensiveness as the inevitable debate over their ideas has ensued.

It is surprising that the two central ideas, that is, dependency and bureaucratic authoritarianism, do not seem to travel well, especially to the Middle East where some reasonable facsimiles of both phenomena may readily be found. Books by Adil Husain and Galal Amin, as well as a newspaper article by Isma^cil Sabri Abdallah, employ the Arabic term *tabi^ca* (from the root to follow) as a near equivalent of dependency, but that word emphasizes the idea of political subordination rather more than does the Latin American term.[116] Bureaucratic authoritarianism by that and other names may also be found (again in a largely nontheoretical form) in the work of Marnia Lazreg on Algeria, and the pluralism-corporatism issue is dealt with by Robert Bianchi in his book on Turkey, and his forthcoming study of labor organization in Egypt.[117] There may well be a good deal of Latin American–inspired literature on Turkey by Turks that I am not acquainted with, since there are many Turkish scholars who are well acquainted with the literature we have been discussing. But for the Arab countries of North Africa and the Middle East, for Israel, Iran, and Pakistan, there has been little application of Latin American ideas.[118]

An apparent exception is John Waterbury's book on Egypt, but his use of the paradigm is little more than a grasp at an analytical straw which is hardly adequate to sustain the interpretive ambivalence which persists throughout the book.[119] Despite some explication of the theory in the introduction and some parting shots in the conclusion, Waterbury never really tests the validity of the paradigm in this one Middle Eastern setting. Instead, his effort remains essentially within the confines of the "political cultural" analysis of competing elites. Substantively, the work is a retrospective gloss on the classic interpretation of Halpern, emphasizing a more general recent consensus on the autonomy of the state and the insulation of the personnel of the apparatus of the state from external social influence.[120] Classic development theory considers the military to be the vanguard of the modernizing middle class and, therefore, justifies its seizure of the state as an effective means of transforming the social order according to its preferences.[121] Bureaucratic authoritarianism links these ideas with the Marxian model of class structure, class conflict, and regime change. But in this study of Egypt, as opposed to studies on Latin America, it is assumed that the bureaucratic authoritarian elite has little or no need for coalition-formation strategies in dealing with classes, economic sectors, corporate groups, associations, regions, ethnic groups, and religious groups.

It is, of course, one thing to argue that the state is an autonomous, non-class, actor. It is quite another thing to argue that it is the only actor.[122] This classic political mobilization model is pushed to a further extreme when it is argued that, ultimately, the strategic development decisions of the Egyptian political elite under Nasser were expressions of Nasser's personal preference, and were neither ideologically determined nor the resultant of some political process.[123] The ultimate reduction of politics to particularistic psychological properties, especially as applied to the explanation of political underdevelopment in the Islamic world, has ideological implications which are by this time so well understood that they hardly need further repetition here.[124] Suffice it to say that Middle Eastern political studies, despite some superficial change in terminology, remain remarkably impervious to scientific revolution. Twenty years from now we shall probably still be discussing the Nasserist period under the rubric of charismatic leadership.[125]

The earliest and most influential studies, especially those of Daniel Lerner and Manfred Halpern, and both of them taking on the whole region, applied the liberal theory with its pluralist pragmatics, its Weberian developmental ethos, and its emphasis on "political culture."[126] They found that urbanization, education, media exposure, and Western economic and cultural influences were breaking down the traditional society, creating a new middle class, and a new willingness to change.[127] The new middle class would build the new state and then make it, eventually, democratic.[128] Islam was not considered a formidable barrier to this projected developmental path, because religion would be personalized, relegated to a narrow sphere of life, or be largely replaced by modern ideologies such as nationalism, socialism, secular liberalism or combinations thereof. No one predicted the demise of Islam, but rather the continuation of a process of reform and apparent contraction of scope that had begun around the turn of the last century. The paradigmatic case was Turkey, as described by Bernard Lewis in his magisterial *The Emergence of Modern Turkey;* but a similar liberalist optimism can be discerned in discussions of Nasserist Egypt by Halpern, Wheelock, and Safran, in works by Upton, Cottam, and Wilber on Iran, in Rustow's treatment of the Middle East in the *Politics of the Developing Areas,* and in Clement Henry Moore's analysis of *Political Development in Tunisia.*[129]

One might have thought that the emergence of the very interesting phenomenon of Nasserist authoritarianism would have stimulated the development of new analytical tools to deal with apparently new forms of authoritarianism; but for the most part the existing categories of charismatic leadership and military "interventionism" were used to reassure us that these were only transitional events, still leading to our rendezvous with development.[130] Even the challenging persistence of monarchy in Iran, in Morocco, in Jordan, and in Saudi Arabia, failed to evoke original conceptions. The existing category of the political culture of elites, whether masked in abstraction or buried in empirical detail, was used instead of explaining the central phenomenon of royal autocracy.[131] Nothing that occurred in the politics of the Middle East was perceived to have revealed so great an anomaly that Middle East specialists were induced to look for a new explanatory paradigm.

The possible emergence of an assertive and influential bourgeoisie or capitalist class, was either ignored, or assumed to be either impossible or a profound threat to modernization and democratization. The central political conflict was thought to be between the modernized intelligentsia and the traditional strata of landowners, rentiers, merchants, and clerics. Now, of course, the new middle class is so closely identified with the state that it is questionable whether the new state-centered development theory has negated or affirmed the earlier development orthodoxy. But no one argues that a strong centralized state is a sufficient condition for liberal democracy, even if many consider it to be a necessary condition. It is rather the neo-Marxian theorists who make the connection between the notion of a strong state on the one hand and the rise of the bourgeoisie on the other. Possibly because of their opposition to the ideological orientation of the new middle class, the neo-Marxists insisted on the link between nationalist regimes of the Nasser type and the long-term interests of the bourgeoisie. That connection may have been illusory or merely conjunctural, but the unwillingness of liberal theorists to seriously consider the potential significance of the indigenous bourgeoisie is similarly doctrinaire.

Liberal development theory is to be condemned neither for its commitment to liberal democracy, nor for its insight into the culture and ideology of the new middle class. Liberal development theory was wrong in assuming that the world historical process was more determinative than the social process in individual countries, and it was wrong in assuming that the prospects for the emergence of an indigenous bourgeoisie in the Middle East were virtually nil. Whatever may be said of the political successes of the new middle class in gaining power, rather than in instituting democracy, it is now clear that such regimes have not been very successful in either stabilizing their authority, or, more significantly, in reproducing themselves. In Turkey, Egypt, Iran, and Algeria, the classic petit bourgeois or Bonapartist state is in the course of being transformed. The simple fact seems to be that bureaucratic authoritarian regimes are unable to reproduce themselves in either the Middle East or in Latin America, or even in southern Europe. The sorts of regime that might follow is still an open question.

If both new and old forms of authoritarianism produced no special intellectual response, the persistent significance of Islam in Middle East politics certainly did. Before the Egyptian defeat in 1967, there was widespread discussion of whether Islam could serve as a barrier to Communism.[132] There was a less obvious discussion of whether Islam could or would be a barrier to the spread of the "virulent" Nasserist form of Arab nationalism.[133] While some took the "hopeful" position that Islam, especially under the banner of Saudi Arabia, would limit the influence of both communism and Nasserism, or could be thus manipulated, others took the view that the encouragement of Islam, especially in its traditionally orthodox form, would lead to quite negative results. Traditional orthodoxy and the fundamentalist alternative, it was argued, are essentially antipathetic to liberal political development.[134] They were likely to lead to a rigidly authoritarian regime, which would be compelled to engage in political and military adventurism in order to maintain the popular support of its mass base. One may think of parallel situations in which a populist nationalism has been invoked to mobilize mass support for a weak regime, but it is more usual to find observers assuming that the masses are already devout traditional Muslims and that the political invocation of Islam is a manifestation of mass politics—making the government too accessible to the mob—rather than an attempt at political mobilization.

The question is whether Islam is the primary explanation of any political matter at all, or whether it enters into the analytical picture only after we have understood the situation in terms which are not at all so parochial, or exotic, or culturally unique. Considerable question may be raised regarding whether such general references to Islam as a holistic entity is an adequate statement of the political culture of any Middle Eastern country—I am certain that it is wholly misleading to equate Islam and culture in general in any Middle Eastern country, and not only in the most westernized of them. Islam in its various forms, and categories, and applications, is only a part of

Middle East culture, and by itself accounts for little. It is often far more accurate to see various Islamic symbols as instruments wielded by those who have power. Of course, this has nothing to do with what Muslims call "real Islam," but it has everything to do with the study of political development.

Still the worst fears and the wildest hopes of many regarding Islam seem to have been realized in the Iranian revolution. Non-Shiʿites are somewhat hesitant to see the Iranian Revolution as a full expression of an Islamic alternative, but a great many acknowledge it as proof of the ability of the spiritual force of Islam to defy social structure, military power, and great wealth. For others, the Iranian Revolution seems to confirm the ominous analyses of Ernest Gellner and Bernard Lewis.

Gellner proposes that throughout the history of Islam there has been a pendulum-like swing of dominance from the emotional Islam of the unlettered tribesman to the pharisaic Islam of the urban ulama.[135] In modern times, however, the pendulum has stopped swinging, because of the overwhelming power of the urban-based central government. While this is an example of high culture supplanting low culture, Gellner makes it clear that it is also authority replacing freedom and spontaneity. This development might also be seen as a manifestation of increased statism, and still greater control of the periphery by the center.

Lewis argues that the centralization of state authority and the search for popular support will lead Middle Eastern regimes to become more Islamic.[136] Islam and populism are closely linked in his analysis and the consequences, he finds, are disturbing: "Islam is a very powerful but still an undirected force in politics. As a possible factor in international politics, the present prognosis is not very favorable. . . . the lack of an educated modern leadership has so far restricted the scope of Islam and inhibited religious movements from being serious contenders for power. But . . ."[137]

Neither Gellner nor Lewis intended these insights to stand as comprehensive analyses of the development process in the Middle East, yet both draw upon the liberal paradigm in order to express their apprehension that a traditional form of pluralism may be lost only to be replaced by a weak form of authoritarian rule that may be driven to rely upon demagogic appeals to Islam. In the context of Middle East politics, it isn't obvious whether they are appealing for the preservation of traditional society and culture in the manner of the conservative development theorists, or whether they propose the achievement of both secularization and pluralism in the manner of the liberal theorists, or whether they disagree with one another. Their critics see them as simultaneously opposing Islamic reform or modernization and attacking traditional Islamic culture. If it is correct to conclude that they prefer a secular, westernized, and pluralist regime, then it is appropriate to say that they have applied the liberal development theory in their critique of contemporary Islam.

The Iranian revolution, both as it appears to many outside Iran and as the leadership of that revolution wishes it to appear, seems to confirm the validity of these insights. In his attempt to explain why the Iranian revolution does not conform to the extant theories of revolution ("The regime that it toppled had not been crippled by insolvency or by a lost war: it had more money than it knew what to do with, and its enormous army was still intact."[138]) Ernest Gellner points to those characteristics of Shiʿi Islam which distinguish it from Sunnism; and first and foremost among these is a symbology of martyrdom and revenge: "So Shiʿites internalize, at each annual passion play, the idea that a Moslem ruler may be the paradigm of evil and deserve to be violently overthrown, that to achieve this requires willingness to undergo martyrdom, and that the job must be completed with bloody thoroughness."[139]

Sunni Islam, being more "protestant" than "Catholic," lacks structures and symbols which would facilitate arousing mass fanaticism, so he doubts that the Iranian events will be repeated elsewhere. In spite of these doubts, he concludes with a firm reassertion of his view that the scripturalist and formalist reforms which have made the most recent pharisaic and textualist reform movement in Islam "definitive," have rendered Islam a normative unity. This particular form of Sunni Islam, he argues, carries with it a systematic doctrine of textual interpretation consisting "of elements that are on the whole congruent with modern conditions and viable. It is this that makes Islam into such an unusually powerful political force."[140]

Doubtlessly Gellner has something here, but I think his point is unusually exaggerated. In point of fact, the combination of an elaborately formal intellectual structure for determining what Islamic Law is, together with the absence of a clear definition of the interpretive authority, makes for quite lively controversy with very little political force behind it. In itself, the normative structure of Islam is unusually open to adaptation to the political and cultural needs of a liberal bourgeoisie in maintaining social peace, protecting private property, and attaining a measure of freedom of choice. It would be surprising if the trend toward the organization of middle-class religious movements does not continue in several Middle Eastern countries. But Gellner does not predict the emergence of strong states in the Middle East, nor does Lewis. It is Islam rather than the state which is described as a powerful force, but it is difficult to separate Gellner's concern with the empowerment of scripturalism, or his use of the words "congruent with modern conditions and viable," from the idea of a powerful state. Perhaps the reason why we have not seen the proposal of a liberal developmental paradigm for the Middle East is because we have assumed that it must somehow counter the Islamic trend.

When we look for alternative ideas, reflecting, perhaps, the special experience of the region, the most distinctive contribution of scholarship on the Middle East is an insistence upon the otherness of the Islamic world. If Latin America is concerned about economic exploitation, the Middle East is most concerned about protecting its cultural heritage. I think it correct to say that no other cultural region is so deeply anxious about the threat of cultural penetration and westernization. And the central symbol of this anxiety is Islam, with which authenticity, identity, dignity, and even manhood are associated.[141] The primary defense of personality in so many situations seems to be the assertion and reassertion of Islamic belief—even when apparently unsupported by deep faith or exceptional piety or orthodoxy.

Elite Latin American society is an intrusive, or colonial society, which shares dominant religious identitive characteristics with Europe and North America, and harbors few misgivings about the benefits of "modernization." For the Islamic world, not only are all of these things reversed—, the elites are indigenous, religious identity is differentiated, and "modernization" has alienative cultural as well as economic connotations—but Western colonialists have on numerous occasions referred to Islam as an enemy, as a barrier to be penetrated, as a mystery to be fathomed, as a unity to be sundered, and as an explosive entity to be dealt with preventively.[142] But Muslims have not simply reacted reflexively to Western attacks and Western intellectual formulations. The history of that *kulturkampf* is much too long and varied to put all of the responsibility on one side. It would hardly be possible to account for the intensity of this attachment to Islamic symbols were we to ascribe it to a mere reaction.

Development theory, whether liberal or Marxian, postulates the need for the penetration of either or both Western culture or Western capitalism to change those who cannot change themselves, whether because of Islam's hostility to capitalism or because of the erstwhile prevalence of the Asiatic mode of production.[143] There have been three important responses to these alternative theses of development theory. The first is the intellectual attack on development theory as culturally parochial, ideologically imperialist, and intellectually unsophisticated. The second has been the systematic refutation of the two theories themselves, that is, the Weberian dictum that Islam, unlike Protestantism, is infertile ground for the growth of capitalism, and the argument which asserts that the AMP prevailed throughout Islamic history.[144] The third is the assertion that there is an alternative form of development which is not only compatible with Islam, but which may even be the fullest expression of Islam under modern conditions.[145]

This third argument goes on to say that, in order to realize a form of development defined by the Islamic heritage, many long-established distortions and confusions regarding the self-understanding of Islam, which are the consequence of imperialist penetrations, must first be cleared away. Hence, to succeed in defining the Islamic alternative, it is necessary to take the precaution of excluding or minimizing alien cultural, economic, and political influence.[146] This is particularly important regarding the field of orientalist scholarship, which has assertively defined the Islamic essence for Muslims.

There is a certain tendency, not yet or perhaps ever to become the major tendency, to withdraw the process of development under Islam from scholarly (and concomitantly, political) scrutiny. The defensiveness of this tendency is manifest, and possibly understandable, but it is doubtful that this recourse to intellectual and cultural autarky will be any more beneficial than has been the recourse to economic autarky in a similarly inspired desire to cope with the intrusiveness of imperialism. The argument for offering a blank check to those who would produce an Islamic alternative, is an argument for allowing the present array of political forces to continue to run things as they have. This explains why the question of Islam, of Islamic reform, and of orientalism and foreign intellectual imperialism is so relevant to development theory, and to the fact that Middle Eastern scholarship has produced no alternative paradigm. It is, moreover, unlikely that Middle Eastern scholarship will produce such an alternative until a somewhat higher degree of intellectual freedom is allowed to prevail in Muslim countries.[147]

3

Deconstructing Orientalism

The Question of the Validation of a Cultural Tradition

A recurring if not dominant theme in contemporary Western philosophy is a profound despair, not only of being able to give a complete and satisfying account of human being and of society, but even of being able to given an intelligible account of itself.[1] Though it may be widely believed that there is much of value in the long philosophical heritage of the West which began in ancient Greece, we cannot offer an absolute justification for this cultural complex upon which our civilization is based; nor can we be sure that there is no better way of organizing human life. It is not even clear that we have had or now have any choice in the matter, either. Nevertheless, we cling to our culture and society, and we search, with diminishing confidence for some solid ground of reason or revelation upon which to construct a justification of the way things are or might be.

Those who would preserve the cultural benefits identified as part of Western civilization have been constrained to argue that less than absolute justifications are adequate to warrant the belief that our inherited values are the right ones. Kantian reason, Hegelian history, Marxian materialism, Husserlian phenomenology, and Heideggerian existentialism all argue that the world is intelligible, and that man can find his proper place in it, even though knowledge of essences, or of things in themselves, is denied us. These views are all founded upon a justifiably modest assessment of human epistemological capabilities. In this sense they ought not scandalize traditional religious opinion regarding the limits of possible human knowledge of the divinely created world. Traditional Semitic religion postulates revelation, or some accessibility of divine knowledge, as providing the grounding or justification of inherited values. Modern epistemology is agnostic, however, and modern ontology denies ever hearing of the tree of knowledge.

Epistemology is concerned with various kinds of knowing, but principally with science and religion and the difference between the two. At times, a single theory has been proffered, asserting the identity of these two kinds of knowing. For the most part, though, the two have been considered quite separate. There have been occasions when the revelational evidence for Semitic religions has been treated as an empirical proof, and at other times nature itself is taken as evidence of religious truth. There are, however, many who doubt that evidence has anything at all to do with it. At least they deny the significance of empirical evidence which is based upon observation and interpersonal agreement. The evidence which might rather be accepted is the evidence of consciousness, or the subjective evidence of mental events.

The Analytic of Finitude

Philosophy, like religion, may aspire to a justification based upon external evidence, but it must rely upon an account of cognition which is either bound by Cartesian subjectivity or must admit its circular dependence upon a cultural milieu. The efforts of modern philosophy to offer adequate but not absolute justifications for received ideas of justice, truth, goodness, beauty, equality and freedom, have not been convincing, or at least satisfying. This dissatisfaction is well expressed in Foucault's description of these philosophical efforts, from Kant to our day, as the "analytic of finitude," by which, paradoxically, the philosopher builds a system of understanding the world upon the postulated limits of human understanding.[2] That is to say, to all intents and purposes, the way we know the world is the only way we can know it because that is the only way that human beings are capable of knowing.

Foucault points out that the analytic of finitude builds an epistemological system based upon the idea that the very possibility of knowing is founded upon the finiteness of man. The point is not that man, created in the image of God, has a little less knowledge or makes more mistakes. It is rather that the whole idea of knowing is a human phenomenon that can work only in accordance with the mental apparatus with which evolution has endowed humanity. When compared with the skeptics, the nihilists, and the mere cynics, the philosophers of human finitude are the more optimistic of modern philosophers regarding the human condition. Among the philosophers of human finitude are relativists, pragmatists, structuralists, existentialists, historicists, and a variety of philosophers who are enthralled by the idea that all philosophical discourse is necessarily structured by, or mediated via, language. For the linguistic philosophers, language itself is the essential aspect of human finitude, so that an understanding of how language works is the key to understanding the limits of human knowledge—but since their philosophical discourse cannot avoid language either, their attempts to define the notion of linguistic finitude must be defeated by the very limits of their medium of investigation.

Phenomenology is the study of the world as it is available to the human consciousness. Phenomenology does not usually aim at gaining a knowledge of the world as it actually is or as it is, say, for God. Edmund Husserl attempted a transcendental phenomenology aimed at an understanding of the world which is not conditioned by the circumstances of the knower, and in that sense, is not characterized by finitude.[3] Critics of Husserl, and there are many, would argue that his extreme subjectivism leads him into solipsism and hence the ultimate finitude of the isolated ego.

Husserl's last desperate effort to reestablish the idealist tradition of absolute knowledge[4] was soon overwhelmed by the existential phenomenology of his most famous student, Martin Heidegger. Heidegger subordinated epistemology to ontology, summing up his position in the paradoxical statement that the being (or essence) of man is existence.[5] Since the essence of *Dasein* (or human existence) is his or her particular situation and circumstances, the most important thing to know is those circumstances. To understand one's ownmost, particular, and unshared circumstances, and to live one's life in acknowledgment thereof, is the most important kind of knowing, a kind of knowing and living, or more generally being, which Heidegger called authenticity.

The Aesthetic Hermeneutic of Heidegger

Heidegger comes to virtually the same kind of extreme finitude of the individual as does Husserl, but on diametrically opposed grounds. Where Husserl chose essence, Heidegger chose existence. Where Husserl chose theory, Heidegger chose practice. Where Husserl chose cognition, Heidegger chose consciousness. Nevertheless, the central epistemological problem in both systems is how to bridge the gap between subjective experience and objective knowledge. Husserl thought it possible to universalize the *ego cogitans*. Heidegger, denying the universal, postulated an authenticity that was both historical and collective.[6] Where Husserl proposed a method of speculative analysis, Heidegger proposed an aesthetic hermeneutic as a method of understanding collective authenticities.[7]

Heidegger has had a profound effect on modern literary criticism, as well as on contemporary philosophy.[8] Heidegger's aesthetic method reflects the influence of Nietzsche and, therewith, a revision of the linkage of academic history and the hermeneutic method in Germany. Hans Georg Gadamer is perhaps the leading hermeneutical philosopher in Germany, and a Heidegger disciple. Gadamer's influence ranges from philosophy to history to the social sciences and to theology. His profoundly religious orientation has quite naturally influenced him to seek to restore the universal to its rightful place within the Heideggerian philosophy. He expounds the view that both aesthetic and historical hermeneutical methods may be combined and "rationalized," to produce a coherent interpretation.[9] It is not, however, the coherence of the hermeneutic which is crucial for Gadamer; it is rather the enlightenment and the consequent conviction which results from the experience of coherence which produces knowledge. The truth which thus becomes known is universal, and its consequence transforms the individual consciousness, changing doubt into belief. Gadamer thus employs Heidegger's method of justifying a cultural tradition in order to justify a religious tradition.

Still, the essence of the hermeneutic method is coherence. The hermeneutic circle links the part and the whole in a form of wholistic interpretation which is sometimes called "totalizing." Jean-Paul Sartre, for example, argued that it was possible to derive a totalizing interpretation of a given historical period, and he tried to do so in his *Critique de la Raison Dialectique*.[10] One can further imagine totalizing interpretations of "nonhistorical" phenomena such as Islam or the Qur'an. The two principal intellectual problems that emerge from this pretension to be able to perform a totalizing hermeneutic are, whether the culture or era under study is in fact unitary and capable of being given a singular characterization, and, whether the relevant cultural "essence" can be accessible to those who are not indigenous to that culture.

Structuralism, Post-Structuralism, and Deconstruction

There are a great many scholars who do not give a damn about the claims of totalizing hermeneutics, but of those who do and who are still skeptical of those claims, three divergent positions may be specified: the first is the structuralist, often identified with Lévi-Strauss; the second is the post-structuralist, of which Michel Foucault is the best known; and the third is the deconstructionist, expounded by Jacques Derrida.

Foucault was actually closely identified with structuralism, and his disclaimers were unconvincing except, perhaps, in his very late writings. In particular, Foucault's notion of the archaeology of knowledge was strongly influenced by structuralist thinking. Derrida's critique of Foucault includes both direct and indirect attacks on structuralism.[11] His disagreements with Lévi-Strauss appear in many places, but we shall be particularly interested in the way in which he employs a deconstruction of the work of Emmanuel Levinas to criticize the particularism of both structuralism and post-structuralism.

The major structuralist thesis is that the world is intelligible insofar as we can discover some sort of order, or structure, or systematic patterning of things, or events or words, or indeed any phenomena. It is the case that phenomena can be perceived as structured, but there is apparently no preordained set of structural patterns or any law of the structuring of types of phenomena, nor is the structure obvious to an observer. Structuring renders phenomena intelligible, and thus human cultures and knowledge are built up around structuring ideas and structured phenomena both consciously and unconsciously.

Derrida is explicitly critical of structuralism, especially that of Lévi-Strauss. Though he is not an orthodox structuralist, Edward Said has been, implicitly, critical of Derrida. The link between the two is Foucault, with whom Derrida studied, and upon whom Said relies in his critique of orientalism. Said's argument is developed out of the structuralist-deconstructionist context, and is, in fact, a part of that controversial discursive formation. Hence, by bringing about a confrontation between Derrida and Said, it may be possible to gain a better understanding of Said's views on the limits of the knowledge that non-Muslims can have of Islam.

There are two major points on which Derrida has criticized structuralism. The first of these is on the distinction which Lévi-Strauss makes between speech and writing. Lévi-Strauss describes writing as repressive, violent, and authoritarian, while speech is seen as natural, original, naive, spontaneous, creative, free, and, of course, good. Derrida argues against this dichotomy, claiming that it perpetuates an ancient Greek prejudice and a Rousseauian romanticization of the primitive, the savage, and the uninstructed or unsophisticated. Christopher Norris elaborates as follows: "Moreover, as Derrida argues, this suggests that writing is always already a part of social existence, and cannot be dated from the moment when the anthropologist, that guilty spectator, introduced its merely graphic conventions. In truth, there is no such pure 'authenticity' as Lévi-

 Strauss (like Rousseau) imagines to have been destroyed by the advent of writing in this narrow senses."[12]

Derrida does not deny what Norris refers to as the inherent violence of writing, but he does challenge the notions of a lost innocence, and of writing "as a means of *colonizing* the primitive mind."[13] Lévi-Strauss sees primitive social organization and culture as structured, formed, or patterned, and, hence, "saying something" about the society, even though that something is articulated only in names and ordinary speech. Writing violates that order, and alters it violently, even if it does so by enhancing the capacities of the members of the society. Derrida argues, according to Norris, that "on the contrary writing emerges both within the very *theme* of speech and within the text which strives to realize and authenticate that theme. Deconstruction is in this sense the active accomplice of a repressed but already articulate writing."[14] Speech conceals the unwritten writing which is no less violent, though it is repressed. As a consequence, Lévi-Strauss's presuppositions lead him to misread his own evidence regarding the nature of the society he is studying and, in particular, to minimize the extent to which coercive violence already exists, while exaggerating the presence of naive and benign cooperation, especially that which is the consequence of not saying certain things, or not using certain tabu names (i.e. ways in which speech is repressed).

The second major point in Derrida's critique of structuralist thought is that, far from discovering structure by a purely empirical-inductive and external process of observation, structural analyses will be found, upon deconstructive inspection, to be based upon some metaphor which functions as an a priori organizing principle for the structuralist observer. Derrida claims that the observer brings the structural metaphor with him, possibly as culture, ideology, or repressed desire. Since the origin of the metaphor is displaced upon the object observed, its meaning and purpose are denied or ignored by the observer. The typical aporia of structuralist writing is to be found in the supressed organizing metaphor. Properly understood, that metaphor contradicts the structuralist claim that the existent structural form is arbitrary and meaningless—that it says nothing to us—that it is mute, silent, or simply there.

Foucault's theory of discursive formations argues, unlike Wittgenstein's relating of "language games" to "forms of life," that such formations can become quite autonomous of "background" conditions, and their development can follow a discursive logic of their own.[15] Language and life influence one another, but they are not the same thing, nor can we predict one on the basis of knowledge of the other. The link between the two cannot serve as the ground of a social science, as some seekers after an "alternative" methodology would wish. Foucault specifically includes the intellectual disciplines as discursive formations, but their relationship to empirical reality is at least open to doubt.[16] Insofar as some nondiscursive organizing element is influential, it is likely to be a political element which uses existing discursive formations to perpetuate domination.[17]

Edward Said made this political interpretation of the academic disciplines more explicit in his *Orientalism,* and in so doing he thoroughly subordinated the autonomy of the discursive formation and its institutional practitioners to the political motivation of the patrons of learning.[18] There are some passages in which he acknowledges the autonomous cultural role that orientalist thought plays in the West, but for the most part he seems concerned to treat orientalist writing as a clearly intelligible, unproblematic, ideologically dependent variable.[19]

For Derrida, there is no existential difference among different types of literature. Poetry, travelogues, political science, and Egyptological hermeneutics are all similarly texts in which there is a fundamental ambiguity that is the consequence of the nature of language itself. Language necessarily employs concepts which presuppose a structure of the world and a reality which are essentially ungrounded. Moreover, language necessarily involves the use of metaphors (many of which we do not recognize) thus rendering all texts fundamentally ambiguous. Derrida holds that there are many possible ways to read and understand a text, that a text outruns the intentions of its author, and that a full account of a text must offer multiple understandings at the same time.[20]

In a suggestive phrase, Derrida's goal is said to be to "liberate the text." I understand this to mean that the text is to be liberated from a singular official meaning which may be given to it by the hegemonic culture or the institutional structures that define discursive formations. Sophisticated authors understand that conforming to the strictures of such formations is the condition of being understood and rewarded. For Derrida, conforming to such strictures is possible only by means of suppressing some contradictory element, or by eliminating some ambiguity, or in some way presenting the world as more intelligible and less differentiated than it is.

Derrida writes of liberation, but specifically of liberation of the text in the sense of its openness to possible meaning. But this openness does not mean that the text is accessible via interpretation and hermeneutic. Derrida rather insists on the essential and historical ambiguity of the text. Hence, the text is liberated when we are able to take more than a single meaning from it. Foucault's idea that a text may be approached by an archaeological method which discovers the origins of its elements in historically and culturally established discursive formations, is incompatible with Derrida's position, as is the rationalist notion that the successful interpretation of a text will reveal its one and only real meaning.

The task of deconstruction is to liberate the text, to deliberately develop its ambiguity, to uncover its suppressed ambiguity, to reveal its self-contradiction, and to identify the flaw, which is the condition of the possibility of every text. This flaw, which Derrida refers to as an "aporia," is not an explicit contradiction, but a kind of paradox, or gap in intelligibility, which emerges from the text, and beyond which the text cannot go. Derrida's purpose is not to show how it is possible to produce a coherent and logically sound text, because his view is that ambiguity, metaphor, shifts in meaning, and semiotic gaps—the sort of thing which he seems to sum up in the word *différance*—are the very character of all texts.

Said's position is somewhat ambiguous. On the one hand, he is quite emphatic that all texts are political. On the other, and unlike Derrida and the philosophers of language, he seems to believe that it is possible to escape from the tyranny of speech. Norris sums up Said's positions as follows:

> Texts are irreducibly "worldly" in the sense that they take on a circumstantial setting and lead a varied afterlife of meaning and *uses* which place them squarely in the public domain. . . . Texts are in and of the world because they lend themselves to strategies of reading whose intent is always a struggle for interpretative power. . . . The control may indeed be illusory, a wishful projection of authorial power, but it reflects an awareness that texts exist from the outset as ground to be competed for by various strategies of self-promoting knowledge.[21]

Derrida would not disagree with this statement as far as it goes, but it does not go far enough from the deconstructionist point of view. Said credits the intention of the author with too much control over the outcome of his literary effort, and gives too little attention to the dynamics of the writing process itself, and to the metaphorical foundation of language. Said subordinates the emotional and psychological motives of the author to the political motives of the author.[22] The result is a rather well-worn restatement of the concept of ideology linked loosely to the idea of the sociology of knowledge, applied to imperialist politics, and pursued by the methods of textual criticism which here seem to have granted a license to assemble only that exemplary evidence which supports the writer's theme, without defining the field of evidence in advance.

Mannheim, Habermas, Lukács, Sartre and Merleau-Ponty, to

name only a few, have all struggled with the problem of distinguishing political truth from political error in a world which is at once pan-ideological and Wittgensteinian. Given the philosophical context, we do not wonder that the problem has not been resolved, but it may at least be said that what Edward Said is arguing is attempted much more clearly and systematically and self-consciously in the social sciences, where the problematic assumptions of the epistemological ground of ideological analysis are more clearly brought into question. The major issue of such epistemological and methodological problems is, of course, the objectivity of the investigator himself—a matter which Said never seriously addresses in his *Orientalism,* but one with which Derrida is obviously concerned (to the point of deliberately playing games with his own texts so as to simultaneously demystify while deliberately and obviously mystifying, doubtlessly in order to induce a more critical attitude on the part of the reader).

The Deconstruction of Revealed Texts

It seems to me to be impossible to consider these ideas without referring them to the fundamental idea in our own culture from which these are most certainly derived, and that is the idea of a sacred, revealed text which is either the word of God or inspired by divine will. The speech of God and the writing down of his divine message are inseparable in the Islamic doctrine of revelation. Moreover, there cannot be a more authoritative text than one which is (claimed to be) the word of God. Judaism, Christianity, and Islam are all three based upon revealed texts, the authority of which cannot be questioned by a believer. If one insists thereupon, such texts may be considered authoritarian and even repressive, in that they establish the nature of the worldly order, and determine how human beings shall think. They fix the fundamental concepts of discourse, and thus constitute the very conditions of meaningful or intelligible discourse. These texts determine, as well, who shall speak and who shall listen, who shall have power and who will submit.

If one insists that the political order is necessarily violent, then we must be prepared to go the whole way with both the structuralists and the deconstructionists who equate authoritative written texts with violence. I do not doubt for a moment that Lévi-Strauss and Derrida are implicitly critical of the authoritarian repressiveness that they believe is a concomitant of religion based upon a revealed text. Derrida certainly believes that liberating the text liberates man, while Lévi-Strauss seems to hold the view that liberating man requires the suppression of the text.

Against Derrida, it may be argued that to give an intelligible conception of the world is, in fact, liberating, as opposed to the idea that the world is essentially unintelligible, or, at least, not given to explication in any possible human language. Since, in any case we cannot determine which conception is correct, some coherent conception of the world is better than none. But Derrida does not say that the world is unintelligible. He is critical of a particular method of reading (sacred) texts which makes them violently repressive, rather than liberating. It is, then, not the world which is incomprehensible, but the text which has a superfluity of meaning. And it is not only, or even primarily, sacred texts that Derrida has in mind, but the Western philosophical heritage as well.[23]

Derrida's attack on structuralism is not only an attack on an incorrect critical method, but an attack on the violence, repressiveness, and authoritarian character of structure itself. In order for such an attack to succeed, it is necessary to describe the structure—to show how it is constructed—so that the demonstration of the aporia, or the autolimitation of the text, will really have the consequence of deconstructing that particular structure rather than all possible structures. To deconstruct all possible structures would require an abstract statement of the theory and method of deconstruction, or a sinking into the very form of theoretism from which Derrida wishes to be liberated.

Islam and Orientalism

Some kind of structural analysis, or a specification of the meaning of the text, is necessary before any effective deconstruction is possible. The question is, which construction of Islam or of the Islamic tradition is it that Said wishes to attack and perhaps replace? Orthodox Muslim critics of orientalism have no doubt about what it is they are defending, and they see the conflict as a two-sided struggle between unbelievers and the faithful, complicated by the fact that the motives of the unbelievers are multilayered, religious, political, and cultural. While this agonistic perspective has been exaggerated, and even distorted, it reflects the original "worldliness" of Islam. Exponents of the Islamic tradition are generally aware of the fact that Islam has not viewed itself as an isolated, self-contained, nonhistorical, and subjective experience. Islam arises in an historical context defined by the temporalization of divine revelation, and Islam has understood itself in relation to other faiths as well as to events in the world.

It follows that Islamic discourse, or the canonical texts, also have the form of a dialogue with other religious systems, the other side of which is, in part, orientalism itself. Muhammad ʿImara may go further than the standard historical structuring of this identification of Islam in terms of its relations to the two preceding monotheisms when he asserts that all three religions are the same. He writes

> Thus, that which Muhammad announced was not a Muhammadan religion . . . rather from the legislative point of view and in terms of the liberation of man and his social and political situation, we are faced with a new Muhammadan legislation (or Shariʿa) because even though the religion of Allah is one, his shariʿas (or legal systems)—in the sense of the methods and ways which lead to the realization of the goals of the one religion—are many in accordance with the plurality of the prophets and messengers, as were they numerous in accordance with the differences existing among the societies of those messengers and prophets and in their times.[24]

Merely to negate one side in this dialogue, to turn it into a monologue, is to produce a systematically misleading understanding of the traditional construction of Islam. The result is not so much a defense of the Islamic tradition as a distortion of it by transforming it into the object of a solipsistic consciousness. Negating the dialogue negates a particular construction of Islam and, dialectically, promotes one or more alternatives; and, in such a way contributes to the ongoing process whereby Muslims (and others) are engaged in determining what Islam is at any given time. This selfsame process can be understood as a struggle for discursive hegemony or an ideological conflict which is part of the more general, if mundane, struggle for power in Muslim lands.

Orientalism, in its broadest sense, and including many diverse forms of discourse, is essentially an attempt to articulate an interpretation of Islam. Even were we to agree with non-Muslim critics of orientalism, and argue that Islam is not singular or universal, and therefore cannot be given a singular interpretation, it does not follow that nothing can be said about Islam. Despite the possibility of disagreement, and despite the apparent impossibility of achieving universal agreement, Islam is not nothing. If it is something, let alone the final and complete divine revelation, then we must be able to say something about it: either to describe it in some objectivist language, or even in some Nietzschean, Heideggerian, Derrida-esque mystical play of poetic, aesthetic, thematization of antithetical themes.

The deconstruction of orientalism, insofar as it says nothing whatsoever about Islam, declares orientalism to be an autonomous discursive formation, at best related to Western culture and society but having nothing to do with Islam. This claim is, naturally, denied by orientalism, or by orientalists, because they argue that, in their various ways, they are explaining, or describing, or explicating an objective reality. The refutation of this claim by referring only to Western society, or only to selected orientalist texts, and not to Islam (or Islamic society, or Islamic history, or Islamic texts), begs the question of whether, after all, the orientalists, or some of them, may not yet be correct, or whether some may not be correct some of the time. But, of course, Said is not merely silent about Islam. He does state that the most important formal defect of orientalism is its imputation of a universal character to Islam. This he sees as a violent attack on Islam and Muslims, an attack to coerce them into conforming to roles imposed by Western imperialism.

Now it can be argued that the issue raised by the question of orientalism is whether the orientalist critique of Islam (and other non-Western religions) is inimical to Islam precisely because its interpretations have the effect of imprisoning the text of the Qur'an rather than liberating it. The insistence upon the essential, or orthodox, version of Islam in the critique of heterodox, or modernist, or fundamentalist Islam, is based on the notion that there is one authoritative meaning to the text. Consequently, there emerges a kind of double repression and violence of the original text and of the orientalist critique. Presumably the result of this combination of rigidities produces an unnatural ideological alliance between the orientalist and the traditional ulama,[25] not because they have similar imperial interests, but because they have similar knowledge-interests (as Habermas following Kant might put it) in the same text.[26] The text may be worldly in diverse ways.

The liberation of the text of the Qur'an for quite new and varied interpretations may then be seen as the prerequisite to the ending of a dual repression of the "rabbis" and of the unbelievers.[27] It is interesting to note, however, that only a few of those who call for an interpretive reform in Islam seek to liberate the text by means of a deconstructive *tafsir* (commentary). Such widely divergent theorists as Fazlur Rahman and Sayyid Qutb have both emphasized the importance of establishing an integrated and self-consistent hermeneutic framework to be applied to all parts of the text.[28]

A deconstructive critique of a divinely revealed text implies the possibly sacrilegious; and insofar as it entails an explicit attack on the tradition, it may arouse more heated opposition than simply ignoring or minimizing the importance of the text. Belittling the text does not liberate the text. Its goal is to weaken the text in order to reduce its worldliness and its power, or, in this case, to liberate Muslims from the text. But the encouragement of diversity within Islam, in the name of nationalism, or authenticity, or Anthropology, is itself a highly political form of discourse.

Good Orientalism: *Islam Observed*

Said praises Geertz because he denies that Islam is a single, transhistorical phenomenon, forever fixed in the text of the Qur'an.[29] Instead, Geertz argues that Islam has taken on distinctive forms and emphases which vary with historical (and cultural, economic, etc.) circumstances. Geertz argues that his method is inductive and empirical, but in fact he pursues an interesting combination of French structuralism and Parsonian functionalism. The structuralist elements are evident in his description of religion (and ideology) as an arbitrary and circular doctrine linking a description of the world with a system of moral imperatives.

> This is circular. But religion, considered as a human phenomenon, is always like that. It draws its persuasiveness out of a reality it itself defines.[30]
>
> The world view is believable because the ethos, which grows out of it, is felt to be authoritative; the ethos is justifiable because the world view, upon which it rests, is held to be true.[31]

From these passages in *Islam Observed* it would appear that a religious or some alternate world view need have no necessary or fixed relationship to "empirical reality" in order to "work." Apparently any number of circular creeds might do equally well in interpreting the world or in picturing "the ultimate structure of existence in such a way that the events of everyday life seem repeatedly to confirm it" (p. 39). How, then do we account for the differences in world views, especially when we find the same religious system given widely divergent interpretations in different historical and geographical settings. This question is the central one in Geertz's book, and it is crucial to his effort to sustain the scientific character of the discipline of Anthropology. Geertz flatly rejects the idea "that the first step toward a scientific comprehension of religious phenomena is to reduce their diversity by assimilating them to a limited number of general types" (p. 24).

> So far as religion is concerned, the problem becomes one of a particular sort of perspective, a particular manner of interpreting experience. . . . The aim of the comparative study of religion is (or anyway, ought to be) the scientific characterization of this perspective: the description of the wide variety of forms in which it appears; the uncovering of the forces which bring these forms into existence, alter them, or destroy them; and the assessment of their influences, also various, upon the behavior of men in everyday life. (p. 96)

The functional aspect of Geertz's approach is in the assumption, implicit in this book, that some sort of coherent world view prevails always and everywhere except during times of crisis and change, and that some sort of widely shared world view is necessary for human communal life. In other words, there is a kind of natural law that requires the production or reproduction of culturally shared interpretations of the *lebenswelt*. In the introduction to this book, Geertz makes it clear that he believes that material or historical circumstances have something to do with both the specific content of the world view and the reason why it changes (pp. 1–2):

> It is a matter of discovering just what sorts of beliefs and practices support what sorts of faith under what sorts of conditions.
>
> But the aim of the systematic study of religion is . . . to determine just how and in what way particular ideas, acts, and institutions sustain, fail to sustain, or even inhibit religious faith.
>
> . . . we must distinguish between a religious attitude toward experience and the sorts of social apparatus which have, over time and space, customarily been associated with such an attitude.
>
> [faith] is sustained in this world by symbolic forms and social arrangements. . . . But such a religion's career—its historical course—rests in turn upon the institutions which render these images and metaphors available to those who thus employ them.

The operative term in Geertz's search for a science of comparative religion is association rather than causation. Nevertheless, Geertz's discourse leaves little doubt that he believes that world views change as a consequence of material or historical change. But such material change seems to have only the negative affect of breaking down the viability of an existing world view. Geertz does not argue that material forces determine the character of the succeeding world view, only that it must somehow satisfy the requirement of giving a plausible explanation of events in the world of everyday experience, while also providing a guide to living in a world thus defined.

Islam, seen from this perspective, is not the selfsame phenomenon in every historical context. Historical circumstances contrive to lead human beings to understand the Islamic world view in significantly different ways. Historically, Geertz argues, Muslims have not been bound by the text of the Qur'an, but neither have they freely interpreted the text in accordance with individual inclination. While Islam has not, in fact, been a single religious phenomenon as some orientalists would have it, neither has it varied so as to defy the tyranny of the disciplined discourse of Anthropology.

Geertz's text does not look like a didactic text. It takes the form of a narrative, or a depiction of the conversion and subsequent religious careers of two legendary medieval figures. These two, one Moroccan and one Indonesian, are meant to exemplify the particular cultural adaptations of Islam in each of these antipodal contexts. The narrative images are intended as aesthetic rather than textual presentations, and are meant to sustain more than a single interpretation. But the use of these two personalities as metaphors does not succeed in liberating the text so much as, initially, masking its authoritative judgments. In employing this strategy, Geertz appears to be cognizant of Lévi-Strauss's preference for speech above writing. First implicitly and then explicitly, Geertz demeans writing, text, and what he calls (Islamic) scripturalism.[32] Each of these two personalities is taken as a metaphorical representation of an authentic or aboriginal, preliterate or nonliterate, regional culture.

Far from taking religion, and Islam in particular, as pure *différance,* Geertz describes Morrocan Islam in terms of the personality of Sidi Lahsen Lyusi: ". . . extraordinary physical courage, absolute personal loyalty, ecstatic moral intensity, and the almost physical transmission of sanctity from one man to another" (p. 33). The spirit of Indonesian Islam is similarly exemplified in the personality and career of Sunan Kalidjaga: steadfast, forebearing, personally willing his own spiritual transformation, and seeking a balance between two opposed cultures by means of achieving an equipoise within his own consciousness.[33] Geertz describes the Indonesian way as "essentially aesthetic; it portrays its ideal. The second [the Moroccan] is essentially moral; it commands it" (p. 30). Can one doubt of which he approves more?

Indonesian culture is described as a form of exemplarism which never became fully integrated with the elements of medieval Islam and the folk religion of the countryside.[34] Indonesian religious culture "was less a synthesis than a sort of balance of power" (p. 43). Clearly, the Indonesian balance was something less than the complete integration of a self-sustaining and circular cultural system. One might contrast the idea of such an unintegrated balance with the earlier use of the term "magic circle" to describe the traditional Indonesian culture. Kalidjaga is a metaphor for balance and diversity—for an attenuated *différance.*

Lyusi, by contrast, did not submerge himself in the larger religious idea. Instead he personified it to the point where Geertz refers to him as *homme fetiche,* and to Moroccan culture as anthropolatrous.[35] Where Indonesia failed to achieve an integrated world view, the Moroccan counterpart became consolidated. "In fact, surprising as it may seem, the two principles—that charisma was an individual talent and that it was a family patrimony—actually fused. . . . And as with literature and the scholar, so, more gradually and less completely, with the society as a whole. The views of different sorts of men . . . concerning the nature of ultimate reality and true morality did not separate into distinct streams" (p. 47). Certainly, Indonesian culture appears to have been more fragile than Moroccan, but the author remains curiously ambivalent regarding the respective values of balance vs. integration.

Geertz recognizes that there are aporetic elements in both of the biographical metaphors he employs.[36]

> That the story of Kalidjaga's confrontation with the new should end with intransigence in the guise of accommodation—Indicism maintained beneath an Islamic veneer—and that of Lyusi's with a capitulation in the guise of rebellion—the sherifian principle of religious legitimacy accepted in the course of a moral collision with its quintessential representative—is again superbly diagnostic. At the same time that Indonesia was moving toward spiritual cleavage, Morocco was moving, no less haltingly, toward spiritual consolidation. (p. 48)

Kalidjaga, he points out, became a devout Muslim without ever reading the Qur'an; while Lyusi demanded a royal rescript confirming his descent from the house of the Prophet. The contradictions in these two stories are presented as characteristic reassertions of the underlying cultural character of the two countries. These personalities are exemplary representatives of their respective cultural traditions, but they are even more obviously idealized examples of true Muslim believers who have committed themselves to live their lives completely within Islam. The aporetic element in both cases arises not from the conflict between Islam and pre-Islamic cultures, but from the fact that both stories are used to support rather than to weaken the established political authorities of the day. Those political authorities are identified with the pre-Islamic social order. Though Geertz is well aware of the important role institutions play in sustaining world views, he seems less cognizant of the role world views play in sustaining ruling institutions.

The traditional cultural systems of Morocco and Indonesia broke down under the impact of the imperialist intrusion of the West, and in the search for a new "magic circle," a new Islamic scripturalism and doctrines legitimating a new nation-building state have been adumbrated. The intrusion of the capitalist-Christian West weakened both the political authorities and the traditional world view, allowing the rise of new social elements bearing the ideology of Islamic scripturalism. After a good deal of confusion—a time of troubled transition—traditionally oriented political authorities have begun to reassert their control, invoking the legitimacy of a modernized version of the original and indigenous world view. The traditional rulers seemed willing, at first, to cooperate with the social and cultural forces of Islamic scripturalism. If the exponents of traditional, pre-Islamic, legitimacy succeed in dominating those forces, the indigenous culture will ultimately prevail.

It is scripturalism, with all of its implications of a violent writing which would forcefully transform a traditional culture, which is most strongly criticized by Geertz. It is identified with merchants, schoolteachers, and the ulama. It is "scholastic, legalistic, and doctrinal" (p. 62). And more pointedly: "Stepping backward in order better to leap is an established principle in cultural change; our own Reformation was made that way. But in the Islamic case the stepping backward seems often to have been taken for the leap itself, and what began as a rediscovery of the scriptures ended as a kind of deification of them" (p. 69).

Despite Geertz's antipathy for scripturalism, and despite his surprisingly stereotypical identification of scripturalism with intellectual stagnation, he does credit scripturalism with the provision of "an ideological stance for Islam in the modern world" (p. 107). But even scripturalism has its diverse emphases in the two countries compared. In Indonesia, he believes that the indigenous syncretistic tendencies encouraged the view that Islam comprehends modern science, while, in Morocco, scripturalism is supposed to have sought to distinguish sharply between the realms of religion and of science.[37]

The struggle of scripturalism to define a modern Islamic world view, despite a degree of success, has not led to a decisive outcome. Geertz carefully avoids predicting the demise of scripturalism, and in the light of the Iranian revolution and related developments elsewhere in the Muslim world it certainly appears that the career of modern scripturalism has hardly begun. Nevertheless, Geertz does treat it as a cultural movement which has run its course. It has produced three results of dubious value. The first of these is what he calls the national movement. The second is a substitution of a formal creed for religious consciousness. And the third is the ideologization of religion.

By the national movement Geertz means the effort to construct a modern nation-state. In Geertz's scheme, the modern-day leaders, Muhammad V of Morocco and Sukarno of Indonesia, appropriated and benefited from the scripturalist doctrine, but they also acted as the spiritual descendants of, respectively, Lyusi and Kalidjaga. In the assertion of Moroccan and Indonesian nation-statehood, there are important reassertions of the prescripturalist cultures of the two countries. The modern state is the institution which sustains the plausibility of the new world view which seeks to synthesize the authentic and prescriptural with the neoscriptural and with what Geertz refers to as "practical reason" or "common sense."

In developing this threefold structure which is the basis of the political ideologies legitimating the Moroccan and the Indonesian states, Geertz expresses grave doubts regarding the value of the contribution made by scripturalism. The contributions of modernist scripturalism were more effective "in the service of the classical religious styles against which its reforms were primarily directed. As nationalism grew out of scripturalism, it also grew away from it and turned for its spiritual roots back toward the more established patterns of belief of the two countries. But . . . it adopted the strategies that scripturalism had already developed . . . it carried the process of the ideologization of religion . . . to its final stages" (p. 107).

This passage seems to me to argue that, had the national political authorities, relied on the "more established" cultural patterns of the two countries and on practical reason alone, they would have done better in providing a modern world view and a modern ethos than they have done by relying in part upon the scriptural Islam of Muhammad Abduh and his rationalist disciples. It also seems to argue that scripturalist Islam is somehow a distortion of an authentic culture, and perhaps even of religion itself. The phrase "ideologization of religion" clearly differentiates between the two, and implies the denaturing of religion, despite the widespread belief that Islam makes no distinction between religion and politics. This invites one to ponder the differences and similarities in Geertz's treatment of religion and of ideology as cultural systems.

Geertz has no thought that religious consciousness can be replaced by a secular nationalist ideology drawing on original and authentic preliterate symbols. Nor does he envision the full development of a secular, "commonsensical," world view for a long time to come. Consequently, he falls back on the well-worn orientalist theme that the modernist scripturalist reform must be pushed further to completion if credible political and ideological solutions are to be found in the proximate future.

> For scripturalism to become a living religious tradition rather than merely a collection of strained apologies, its adherents would have to undertake a serious theological rethinking of the scholastic tradition they can, apparently, neither live with nor live without. But since Abduh, who, for all his hesitations and incoherencies, made a valiant attempt at such theological rethinking, virtually nothing has been done; certainly not in Indonesia and Morocco, where, a few marginal and not very impressive exceptions aside, critical reexamination of Islamic doctrine has never been even begun. (P. 115)

Despite his scientific inclination and his search for objective and empirical referrents of religion, Geertz's antipathy toward scripturalism leads him back to the study of religion as the study of internal (i.e., mental) events. His text in developing this subject is Schutz's differentiation between the immediate experience in the stream of consciousness and reflexive experience.[38] Put quite simply, Schutz's conception of the stream of consciousness is a mystification, because he argues that it is simply unrecoverable in its original, unrationalized immediacy.[39] Any thetic formulation of experience must transform it from feeling into text, from speech into writing. Geertz accepts this conception, arguing that this virtually inaccessible and highly transitory character of religious experience makes it "extremely difficult to get phenomenologically accurate descriptions of religious experience."[40]

So Geertz, who starts out by questioning the use of definitions and classifications, and who announces that Anthropology has transformed the study of religion from the study of inner experience to the study of systems of public symbols, reverts to the very positions from which he sought to liberate himself, positions shared in part by traditional ethnologists, and in part by traditional orientalists. Speech is more authentic and democratic than writing. Folk culture is better than urban intellectual culture. Practical wisdom is better than revealed religion. Authoritarian and paternalistic leadership is more efficient than movements of the middle class intelligentsia. In all of these views or prejudices, Geertz may be right, but it is difficult to read his text as a new and liberating approach to the comparative study of the orient.

Bad Orientalism: *Hagarism*

Most of those who have called for a thorough modernist and rationalist reform of the scholastic tradition have had in mind some parallel to the development of modern religion in the West, allowing for a range of psychological and emotional religious experiences which do not impinge upon the purposeful commitment to practical affairs. Others have had liberal political reforms in mind. But there are also those who, while criticizing aspects of Islamic religion, call for no reform, rather insisting that Islam can by its very nature never change, and that its defects are neither historical nor ideological but inherent.

There is, perhaps no more outrageously antagonistic critique of Islam than that which calls it Hagarism. Patricia Crone and Michael Cook, the inventors of Hagarism, employ a twofold paradigm: a fixed and unchanging Qur'an, and a model political society against which Islamic society is compared. Geertz's model of an ideally integrated society and culture is drawn from the dynamic ideal of Parsonian functionalism, while the metaphoric ideal of Crone and Cook is none other than ancient Israel.

The authors of *Hagarism* conceive of the world as composed of communities, differentiated from one another by ethnicity and culture, each striving to maintain and enhance their identity in an Hobbesian arena of cultural and military conflict. The struggle for identity and independence is carried out within a framework of strategic logic, which requires that socially integrative and culturally distinguishing mores be nicely balanced against the benefits of universal civilization and a universal political order. The relevant alternatives are almost always presented as binary options: particularism vs. universalism, priesthood vs. prophecy, pharisaism vs. sadduceeism, Shi'ism vs. Kharijism, uniformity vs. diversity, barbarism vs. civilization, and so forth.

The highest value in this system is integrated, self consistent, self-ruling community; and the world is divided between communities that have identity and integrity and those that do not. It is apparent that this central value is pretty much the same as the Parsonian "magic circle" of which Geertz was writing. The most complete example of such a community is that of ancient Israel, united in ethnicity, religion, polity, priesthood, and culture. But the perfection of ancient Israeli identity and integrity poses a problem to the rest of the world in the sense that, either, other communities must emulate Israel, or the whole world must be capable of achieving the equivalent on a universal scale. Christianity made this alternative possible by synthesizing Judaism, Hellenism, and Roman imperialism, and thus presents Judaic religion to the world in a universalist mode. Hellenism offered an alternative to the principle of the ethnic foundation of the community; and Rome supplied the universal polity. But the full potential of this alternative was never realized, in part because of the imperfections in Christianity, Hellenism, and Roman imperialism, and in part because of the Islamic conquest.

The Arabs were one of many poorly integrated communities, lacking in any but the most "barbaric" form of identity: the ethnic. The conversion of some Arabs to a form of Judaic monotheism posed the fundamental question of how the Arabs could at once become civilized and still retain their identity. According to Crone and Cook, the history of this Arab effort is one continuous tissue of failure, error, and distortion. The Arabs managed always to make the wrong choice at the wrong time, thus bringing disastrous results upon themselves and upon the civilized peoples that they conquered.

Early Arab Islam, or Hagarism, is described as the unity of barbarism and Judaism, in which barbarism always leads to the selection of the wrong Judaic alternative: Samaritanism instead of orthodoxy, a priestly policy instead of the separation of prophecy and kingship, pharisaism instead of sadduceeism, military force instead of accommodation. The Hagarists chose universalism as in Christianity, but they wished to retain their identity as in Judaism. They might have adapted the pluralist civilization of Christian and Hellenist Rome, but their barbaric Samaritan cultural intransigence led them to reject much of the civilization they conquered. Nevertheless, in those countries like Egypt and Iran, which were characterized by strong communal cultural identities, the pre-Islamic civilization persisted (as it did briefly under the Umayyads in Syria and under the influence of the Shuʿubiyya in Iraq and eastern Iran). Heterodoxy, rebellion, and political fragmentation were the consequence of the failed strategic choices of Arab Islam. 105

It was virtually only in Syria, in which there survived no strongly integrated and culturally differentiated community, that the idea of an Arab-Islamic identity was able to penetrate and flourish. And even today, it is only in the Fertile Crescent that such an identity is still strong. Moreover, if one but removes the Islamic, that is, the Judaic, element, even today, one is left with the barbarism which is Arab nationalism.

> The Syrian messiah is not the king of Baalbek, but the Sufyani who will restore Muʿawiya's Syrian Empire. . . . Hence, if the fate of the Syrian Muslims was to become pan-Arabists, the fate of the Christians could only be to beat the Muslims at Arabism as the Muslims had beaten them at the beginning. Islam purged of its monotheist accretions thus became Arab culture to Jurji Zaidan, Arab nationalism to Nejib Azoury, Arab socialism to Michel ʿAflaq and Arab defense to George Habash. The Copts and the Nestorians are Zionists who have lost their claim to the lands they once possessed, but the Syrians have joined the Palestinians.[41]

So the Christians of old who became Arab Muslims are unworthy mongrels as are the Christian Arab nationalists of today, compared with the virtuous Copts, Nestorians, and Jews who have retained their authentic traditional cultures and creeds, and, thereby, their identities. Arabism is barbarism and inauthenticity. After the conquest of the region, the Islamic assimilation of Middle Eastern civilization took the form of a violent collision followed by a relentless and systematic plucking of discrete items from their cultural, philosophical, and theoretical contexts: science, law, and philosophy were thus forced into the Hagaristic mold.

> Against the discouraging background of this persistent religious hostility, the history of Islamic philosophy was long and unim-

> pressive. But if the erosion of its status was slow, it was also relentless. The sciences of the ancients were progressively reduced to a sort of intellectual pornography, and the elite which had cultivated them, to a harrassed and disreputable subculture. . . . The fates of Roman law and Greek philosophy were thus in the last resort symmetrical . . . the conceptual shape was fully removed so that the formless mass of details could be repackaged as indigenous products through attribution to the Prophet. (p. 101)
>
> The Hagarenes were thus precluded by their faith from any direct inheritance of the traditions of the world they had conquered. (Pp. 78–79)

The consistent theme of the work is that Islam is deeply flawed both as a religion and a civilization. Virtually no conceivable aspect of Islam is left without direct or indirect critique. Hagarism is described as primitive (p. 12), pagan (p. 13), inconsistent (p. 15), parvenu (p. 16), and barbarian (p. 73). The Qur'an is described as "frequently obscure and inconsequential in both language and content" (p. 18). The significance of Mecca is described as "secondary" (p. 24). The traditional date of the prophet's death, as well as the orthodox conception of the role of ʿUmar and the historicity of Hasan and Husain are all doubted (pp. 28 et passim). Both Judaism and Islam are dominated by rabbinic legalism and the pharisaic spirit, but "in Judaism the other side of the coin is messianic hope, in Islam it is Sufi resignation" (p. 34). The synthesis of Judaic values and Arab barbarism is described as a "conspiracy" (p. 77), which permitted the "long term survival" of Hagarene doctrine and the "consolidation of the conquest society."

Since neither the Judaic nor the Christian solution to the tension between religion and ethnicity was possible for Islam, "Hagarism . . . fell firmly and irredeemably between two stools" (p. 123). Nor could Islam find a way to reconcile the values of the Hebrews and the Greeks; instead the Muslims "inherited the worst of both universes" (p. 127) by adopting "monotheism . . . in its most intransigent rabbinic form," together with a theology of "doctrinaire obscurantism" (p. 128).

"The incoherence of Islamic civilization in the dimensions of ethnicity, polity, and world-view in thus a strikingly uniform one" (p. 129) is the conclusion of Crone and Cook, disallowing, as usual, any third alternative in their rhetorical binarism. Even the early Islamic military success is criticized for having been too rapid and too complete, thus preventing a prudent and culturally beneficent compromise with the infidel elites.[42]

In their concluding blows, the authors declare Islam to be "austerely unitary" and governed by a fundamentalist certainty which, in contrast to the contribution of Protestant fundamentalism, produced an "ethical vacuum" in the political realm and discouraged both science and nationalism. "The hetrogeneity of the Muslim world was real enough; but it was not till the reception of nationalism from Europe that it became possible to construe this Islamic vice as a western virtue" (p. 145). Islam, therefore, and despite the commitment of Christian Arabs to Arab nationalism, remains hostile to nationalism, and hence incapable of providing the basis of modern states.

Why, then, does anyone believe in Islam? The appeal of Islam seems "puzzling," write Crone and Cook, in what must be the most astonishing passage in this astonishing book. The answer they give is that, despite its numerous inadequacies, Islam has great appeal in "the world of men in their families" (p. 147). "The public order of Islamic society collapsed long ago . . . but the Muslim house contains its *qibla* within itself" (p. 148). Thus do Crone and Cook deny what most others see as the essential and persistent aspect of Islam, and declare its public and political aspects to be mere illusion. Islamic civilization is, then, absolute *différance,* a jumble of unrelated atomic particles with no ordered, structured form.

Pragmatic Orientalism: *The Venture of Islam*

Over against the relatively benign and the extremely hostile historicist reductions of Islam we may contrast the position of the late Marshall Hodgson. In his *Venture of Islam,* Hodgson is bound to describe his subject matter as a unified whole.[43] But that which renders it a unity is not the historical realization of the Islamic ideal. It is the continuous search and struggle to achieve the Islamic ideal in practice. Hodgson ignores the formal juxtaposition of theory and practice, preferring instead the concept of Islamic civilization, which he conceives of as a core of religious doctrine surrounded by a series of ever widening concentric circles of cultural practice of ever diminishing religious relevance and legitimacy. Nevertheless, the Islamic ideal of a completely integrated human cultural and social order is continuously invoked in the face of the perception of anomalies linked to time and place and human diversity. Islam has never everywhere been the same, but some Muslims have always tried to make it the same, and all true believers are united in what Hodgson calls the venture of Islam, that is the commitment to "winning through to the best that is open to mankind."[44]

The unity of Islamic civilization is thus an ideal which has guided the action of many Muslims of all walks of life, but particularly that of members of the Islamic intellectual elite in every age.

Thus, for Hogdson, the cultural unity of Islam is real, even if only a matter of belief, elusive but not illusory, and a subject of general consensus, even though never approached in historical practice.

> At any given time, in any pious mind, Islam could thus seem a timelessly integral ideal whole. . . . Such a viewpoint is not purely a subjective illusion. . . . On occasion, what comes to be lived as Islam, in particular cases, does violate the integrality of Islamic life: that is, it proves inconsistent with more fundamental cultural presuppositions of Islam, as Islam has been developed (P. 78)

> When we look at Islam historically, then, the integral unity of life it seemed to display when we looked at it as a working out of the act of islam almost vanishes (P. 85)

> What then is Islam? Can we study it as a meaningful whole? Is it more than the name for a hope, and a few common symbols? Clearly, yes: but only in the way that any cultural tradition, whatever its internal contradictions, is a whole. However diversely it develops, or however rapidly, a tradition does not lend itself indifferently to every possible opinion or practice. It imposes limits which are none the less enduringly effective for being impossible to formulate in advance. . . . For to the extent that the dialogue is cumulative, every later comer having to reckon both with the point of departure and with later debate, there will needs be a common vocabulary of ideas (or of art forms or institutional principles or whatever). . . . It is this integrality of dialogue that can provide an intelligible framework for historical study. (Pp. 86–87)

> Such a cultural heritage has been carried not only by all of the upper, educated classes, but even, to a lesser degree, by still wider sections which have absorbed something of its outlook, down to the ordinary peasants. But within this mass, a much smaller group has played a special role: those who have taken the more articulate and far-reaching ideals of the heritage as a personal responsibility, which they themselves must realize. This concerned minority . . . are not usually the men of immediate power . . . they are the men of cultural initiative. (P. 93)

For some people there may seem to be little to choose from between an orientalism which describes Islam as an historical epiphenomenon, and a structural anthropology which demonstrates the naturalization of Islam—that is, its *différance,* which is the consequence of its dissemination. The two interpretations are similar in structure, even if they are very far apart in moral purpose, because Crone and Cook treat Islam as an Arabization of Judaism, parallel to the cultural incorporation of Moroccan and Indonesian Islam. Of course, Geertz is not criticizing Islam; he simply takes no account of the sort of claims which the orthodox scripturalists make for a universal Islam. His definition of religion, though influenced by structuralism, requires the "dispersion" or the "dissolution" of Islam in the sense of a univocal moral and cultural force. The only part of religion that is not epiphenomenal is that which expresses symbols that are regionally indigenous, and specific in their reference to time, place, and persons. Moreover, this conception of culture makes virtually no attempt to work out the influence of class differences, rural-urban differences, and ethnic differences in the development of a religious-cultural system.

There is no doubt that modernization has strengthened scripturalism, but it is not clear why that is considered lamentable. Is it because the growth of scripturalism strengthens the state and weakens rural authorities, or becauses it strengthens the bourgeoisie and weakens the westernized intellectuals, or because it stultifies social life and restricts artistic creativity? All of these arguments have been made, but the most important point to be made is that the rise of scripturalism coincides with the demise of an era wherein a restricted, privileged, and cosmopolitan elite enjoyed a cultural, political, and social liberalism which was usually expressed in private circumstances and in an idiom that barely concealed its contempt for the traditional masses.

That it may be possible to retain the idea of a universal Islam, and at the same time take an objectivist and neutral position regarding its future development, is demonstrated by the pragmatic position taken by Marshall Hodgson. But Hodgson was too ready to accept (implicitly) the functionalist interpretation of the role of specialized elites in ideological matters, and less ready to assimilate the ideological process to both the social and political processes. The virtue of Hodgson's exposition is that it denies that the only alternatives are a universalist scripturalism or a dispersionist cultural authenticity.

Following Foucault

In his critique of orientalism, Edward Said's major argument is that the West has imposed a singular, essential, unchanging identity on all of the Orient, that this cultural characterization is false; that it reflects the cultural characteristics and needs of the West itself; and that it has served certain western political interests, including the justification of imperialism and the reaffirmation of Christianity. This image of the Islamic "cultural synthesis" conforms to the "paradigm" of academic orientalism, and it has been taken into European culture by means of both the imaginative and descriptive works of literary geniuses and some lesser lights. Eventually, the whole complex of prejudice has become popularized and has been made a part of mass culture in the West.

Throughout most of his work, Said treats this literature as an ideological phenomenon in which representation, text, and trope are the major vehicles of expression. At other times, Said suggests that the issue is mainly epistemological in the sense that it is a question of the validation of research findings and the proper designation of a discipline or a field of inquiry.[45] In treating these aspects of orientalism, Said follows Foucault rather than Marx or Mannheim.

In *The Order of Things,* a work devoted to the exposition of the discursive foundation of the human sciences in the modern age, Foucault contrasts the modern episteme with that of the classical age. The classical episteme, which prevailed from the middle of the seventeenth century to the beginning of the nineteenth, was founded on the principle of representation and classification in which the act of representing the order of the world was not itself brought into question. The modern episteme is characterized by the temporal and the historical, by the genetic or developmental analysis of the object of inquiry. The human sciences, which arise only in modern times, are dominated by the self-conscious concern with man himself as the performer of the act of representation, and therefore with the question of how the contingent particularity of a given human being, his historicity, his culture, his personality, his experience, "his" gender, his sexuality, et cetera, might impinge on the validity of his representation.

The epistemological model that has dominated this period is derived from the Kantian philosophy that embraced the limits of man's ability to know as the foundation of the possibility of knowing man. Man cannot know the infinite without being, himself, infinite. Knowledge of man is, therefore, knowledge of his limitations. This perspective, which has inspired a series of similarly formulated epistemological anthropologies, is as we have seen, called the "analytic of finitude" by Foucault. Finitude, rather than leading to the denial of the possibility of the knowledge of man is, paradoxically, taken as the very condition of the possibility of such knowledge.

Foucault holds that the intellectual and discursive development of the last 150 years was the inevitable consequence of the epistemic change that occurred at the end of the classic period. Moreover, the changed conception of man, for all its political significance, was the consequence of the change in the episteme, and not the other way around. But if modern economics is a subject about which one may remain complacently neutral, despite its ideological dimensions, Foucault is anything but neutral regarding the human sciences.

Foucault is critical of the human sciences, which are based on the analytic of finitude. He does not deny that man is finite. He denies that a valid epistemology of science can be built on such a notion, and he particularly condemns the philosophical anthropologies and historicist doctrines that have been constructed on the foundation of the analytic of finitude. The human sciences which are thus constructed contradict themselves and their own episteme by daring to define the human essence. This definition seeks to overcome the limits of human finitude by defining man as a knowable finitude whose limits are accessible to himself. In this way, knowing finitely leads to a universal conception of generic humanity.

Foucault fervently wishes for the early demise of the human sciences, so much so that he anticipates the replacement of the modern episteme, or its profound revision, in the near future.[46] He would like to see "the end of man" or the "death of man" or the ultimate "dispersion of man."[47] In such strong language, he condemns the idea of a general theory of man—a theory which would resolve the tension between difference and sameness in favor of "the Same."[48] But Foucault does not explain this intellectual development in terms of some political motive, some form of exploitation, or some ideological process. All of these are present, and, naturally, the dominant classes have used the prevailing forms of discourse to their own advantage.

Foucault does not suggest that the existing episteme and its array of human sciences will be defended by the dominant elites, or that changing the episteme requires a political revolution. In fact he tends to trivialize the modern formation of the human sciences as inadvertently derivative from the far more significant intellectual developments by which the classical episteme was surpassed. There is some ambiguity here, in the sense that Foucault appears at times to argue that we can only get rid of the concept *man* by getting rid of the episteme of the modern sciences which produced the idea of man. At other times he seems to argue that an alternative group of human sciences has been or can be developed within the framework of the existing episteme. These sciences are psychoanalysis, ethnology, and structural linguistics. The distinctive feature of these sciences is that they do not pretend to surpass the finitude of man. They are rather based on the idea of the particularity of individuals, cultures, and languages. These disciplines may lead to the "dispersion of man" which Foucault desires.

Foucault's idea of psychoanalysis is similar to that of Merleau-Ponty and Habermas in emphasizing the therapeutic praxis of communication, but, otherwise, he does not discuss political emancipation.[49] He has separated Marx and Freud quite decisively. Nor does he see ethnology as a kind of psychoanalysis of a society, even though it takes the same form, of a dialogue between Western culture and the culture of societies without histories. Psychoanalysis both defines the ultimate nature of finitude (as death, desire, and language-law) and its insuperability. Ethnology, or structural anthropology, mocks the historicist discourse, because it demonstrates the historicity of a form of scientific discourse that can never satisfactorily recover its own history, but still would understand societies that deny the idea of history. Hence psychoanalysis and ethnology are truer to the idea of the analytic of finitude than are those disciplines which would conjure away the limits of the analytic.

Nevertheless, "ethnology has its roots . . . in a possibility that properly belongs to the history of our culture."[50] And from this ethnocentric starting point, it seems to me that Foucault goes on to make a case for orientalism, and for the inevitability of a dialogue:

> . . . the history of our culture . . . enables it to link itself with other cultures in a mode of pure theory. . . . There is a certain position of the Western *ratio* that . . . provides a foundation for the relation it can have with all other societies. . . . Obviously, this does not mean that the colonizing situation is indispensible to ethnology: neither hypnosis, nor the patient's alienation within the fantasmic character of the doctor, is constitutive of psychoanalysis; but just as the latter can be deployed only in the calm violence of a particular relationship and the transference it produces, so ethnology can assume its proper dimensions only within the historical sovereignty—always restrained, but always present—of European thought and the relation that can bring it face to face with all other cultures as well as itself.[51]
>
> . . . ethnology, on the other hand, is situated within the particular relation that the Western *ratio* establishes with all other cultures; and from that starting point it avoids the representations that men in any civilization may give themselves of themselves . . . of the significations laid down in their language; and it sees behind those representations the norms by which men perform the functions of life. (P. 378)
>
> One can imagine what prestige and importance ethnology could possess if . . . it were deliberately to seek its object in the area of the unconscious processes that characterize the system of a given culture. (P. 379)

Foucault's discussion of the nexus between psychoanalysis and ethnology studiously avoids all the important political questions in deference to the goal of "dissolving man." He argues that the common development of the two fields would advance the formalization of both. The unconscious and culture would each be shown to have a formal structure, but these formal structures would be found, in fact, to intersect, in such a way as to explain the conjunctural constraints and the particular finitude of each.

Foucault turns to structural linguistics for what he hopes will be the development of the ideal formal structure that will comprehend the three "good" human sciences. Language, like the unconscious and culture, is a true expression of the impenetrability of man's finite givenness, and structural linguistics seem capable of providing us with a general theory that still refrains from imposing the concept of the "Same" on all mankind. Foucault sees in the rise of the new discipline the possibility of the fulfillment of the promise of the modern episteme. This formalism is not the herald of a new episteme so much as the continuation of a long struggle that has characterized the episteme of modernity: a struggle between man and God, symbolizing the tragedy of finitude on the one side, and the myth of the possibility of a return to innocence on the other.

> . . . is it not the last man who announces that he has killed God, thus situating his language, his thought, his laughter in the space of the already dead God . . . since he has killed God, it is he who must answer for his own finitude . . . his murder itself is doomed to die; new gods the same gods, are already swelling the Ocean; man will disappear. Rather than the death of God . . . what Nietzsche's thought heralds is the end of his murderer; it is the explosion of man's face in laughter, and the return of masks; it is the scattering of the profound stream of time by which he felt himself carried along and whose pressure he suspected in the very being of things; it is the identity of the Return of the Same with the absolute dispersion of man. (P. 385)

When viewed from the perspective of this conclusion, Foucault's call for the liberation of the individual personality, for the recognition of the diversity of cultures, and for the freedom of discursive expression, all seem to be obscured by the violence and irascibility of his attack on what he insists on calling man. The political implications of his position, given the two-edged meaning of the denial of human sameness, that is, of the universality and equality of human being, are not spelled out.

In his later work, *The Archaeology of Knowledge*,[52] Foucault moved from a fascination with structural linguistics to a concern with the pragmatics of linguistic philosophy. There, too, he is involved in the formalization of his own particular human science of psychoanalytic anthropology, and its method of the discursive analytic. He is much more explicit about the political implications of the evolution of dominant forms of discourse, but if there are any emancipatory interests expressed, they are, as in the earlier book, primarily concerned with freedom from politics.

In the *Archaeology,* Foucault defines discourse as a pragmatically shaped discursive nexus with duration and structure, and governed by immanent rules of contextually determined intelligibility. But, like any pragmatically determined unity shaped in dynamic process, it arises in time, constantly changes, and suffers—if not a total demise—a desuetude and a declining archival half-life, from which it may be retrieved only by procedures reminiscent of archaeological research. But as living discourse it is integrated with institutions, modes of behavior, social practice, and social structure. Scientific disciplines are not the only discursive formations; they are rather *also* discursive formations.

For Foucault, a discursive formation is to be examined like any observable object. It is an empirically sensible fragment which should be approached as are archaelogical fragments—without presupposition regarding the sweep of a unitary historical "geist" integrating all temporal worldly phenomena. Foucault explicitly differentiates his concerns, or the function of his archaeology, from the function of hermeneutic and ideological analysis. Kant, Husserl, Sartre, Merleau-Ponty, and Marx, are criticized because their doctrines provide for an a priori framework, or origin, or eidetic absolute, which determines or guides us to the unequivocal meaning of any fragment of discourse. Presumably, Foucault's archaeological discipline exists alongside other critical and analytical disciplines in a kind of mutual silence, if not unintelligibility. Nevertheless, insofar as any alternate disciplinary approach purports to explain anything, it is challenged by Foucault's archaeology, since he argues that the development of a discipline is not governed by its discovery of truth, but rather by the evolution of its special language in accordance with rules or a linguistic structure that may be understood along the lines of Wittgenstein's analysis of language. Furthermore, all disciplines share characteristic forms of discourse concerned with issues of epistemology, methodology, and the formal or logical ordering of propositions. Hence, orientalism is discourse. Islam as interpreted by Muslims is also discourse. And all of the social and human sciences are discourse.

Said's Critique of Orientalism

Said has chosen to analyze the discourse which he calls orientalism, and which some pretend has crossed some sort of disciplinary threshold to become Middle East studies in our day. But Said is not disinterested in the ideological issue. On the contrary, he is most concerned to show that orientalism was and remains ideological.[53] Said describes some of the major cultural themes contained in orientalism, and shows that they are not the result of events in the Middle

East, but that orientalism is, in fact, a fantastic Western discourse. This Western discourse is, for Said, factually wrong or erroneous. It is also, necessarily, different from Middle Eastern or Muslim discourse regarding Islamic culture. But Muslim discourse is not necessarily correct either. Said does not argue that Muslim discourse is correct, and he certainly never suggests that Islam is the true religion. In fact, Said says virtually nothing about Muslim discourse regarding Islam. Nor does he encourage us to study such discourse, let alone enter into it. Orientalism is, after all, the consequence of the Western study of such discourse.

Foucault would probably not be surprised at the notion that there may be two forms of discourse on Islam, one Western and one Muslim. He might even allow that *both* are ideological, in the sense that we can determine the social limits of each discourse. But it is not likely that he would suggest that the discourse of one group is somehow priviledged or authentic. Moreover, given the dialectical relationship of Islam and orientalism, I am not sure it is legitimate to separate the two in a structured critique.

Orientalism is, thus, a fragment of Western discourse which has undergone the process of transformation into a discipline. Its practitioners see themselves as employing a comprehensive system of interpretation of a total culture. That comprehensive system rests upon the epistemological ground of what Foucault criticizes as the notion of an interpretive key, a philosophically derived principle of distinguishing the real from the apparent, of the content from the form, of essence from accident. Orientalism further has developed a method of applying that principle, mainly by means of philological and historical analyses. Thirdly, orientalism has ordered such discourse according to formal rules of evidence, causality, sequence, and so forth, all based on the concept of a culture and its manifestation in history.

Said argued that orientalism is merely ideological discourse, and he set himself the task of undoing the process by which it came to be seen as a discipline—and, hence capable of distinguishing authoritatively between truth and error.[54] Said's method is to demonstrate how the earliest religiously prejudiced Western discourses on Islam constituted the foundation upon which later literary, political, and scientific discourse was built up.

But Said's critique, like Foucault's, must confront the problem that all such attempts at unmasking ideological discourse must face. How can Said's discourse be distinguished from ideology itself? What is the epistemological ground from which he begins? How does he distinguish truth from error? Said disregards the epistemological consequences of the linguistic pragmatics he has adopted from Foucault and Wittgenstein. Foucault's structural pragmatics of discourse allow description only. If one goes further and offers a systematic explanation of the development of discourse, if one purports to distinguish the real from the apparent meaning, or if one wishes to relate the structure of discourse to the structure of any nondiscursive arrangement, then one has abandoned the effort to use "facts" rather than theoretical beliefs, and one has crossed over into the discourse of speculative anthropology and neo-Marxian theories of culture.

These considerations are relevant in considering Said's argument because of his paradoxical invocation of the established disciplines in his concluding statements.[55] Said would not have turned to the disciplines of the human sciences did he not consider that there remained a problem of the objective study of the Middle East. Foucault does not reject the question of truth and error as beside the point, but as we have seen, he does not believe that the structure of scientific discourse can be explained primarily with reference to truth and error. On the other hand, Foucault demonstrates in his introduction to the history of sexuality that a particular kind of discourse, here the emergence of a discipline of sexology and another of psychoanalysis which is based on a theory of sexuality, have in fact had important consequences for human behavior.[56] Apparently, there is some kind of a circular relationship between knowledge and power. Not all discourse originates in political dominance, though all discourse is powerful.

Said's purpose is not transparent because it is impossible to be certain whether his conflation of discourse and ideology is deliberate, or whether his differentiation between orientalism and humanistic studies was self-conscious, or whether his reading of orientalism was too much affected by his feelings about Palestine. But none of this is of as much concern as whether he intended to urge Muslims to develop their own forms of discourse, renouncing the dialogue with the West, in order to define anew their own authenticity.[57] If this is the case, then we must credit him with a synthesis of Heidegger and Foucault which is unique and powerfully suggestive.

> Lastly, for readers in the so-called Third World, this study proposes itself as a step towards an understanding not so much of Western politics and of the non-Western world in those politics as of the *strength* of Western cultural discourse, a strength too often mistaken as merely decorative or "superstructural." My hope is to illustrate the formidable structure of cultural domination and, specifically for formerly colonized peoples, the dangers and temptations of employing this structure upon themselves or upon others.[58]

It isn't very clear whether Said is urging the Muslims to assert their difference or their sameness, or, indeed, both at once. But it is of particular interest, from our point of view, to consider whether Said would include, within the structure of that Western discourse which he describes as dangerous and tempting, the discourse of political liberalism which has been an integral component of the strength of the Western cultural influence on the Arab world.[59] If we sum up his admonition against the submission to Western cultural influences, and his denial of the alterity which the West would impose on Islam, we find that, if they do not cancel one another out, neither do they solve the problem of how one can be both modern and liberal without being westernized or dominated by the West.

The Dispersal of Man

Although Foucault insistently refers his call for the dispersal or the destruction of man to Nietzsche and to the anticipation of an historical renewal or return, the origin of the conceit for modern philosophy is in the dénouement of Hegel's *Phenomenology.*[60] Hegel is not usually interpreted as anticipating a return or a reenactment of the historical process which culminates in the self-consciousness of Absolute Spirit, but rather the opposite. That is to say that Nietzsche's notions of the eternal return, the will to power, and the superman, are all taken as diametric contradictions of the Hegelian idea of the ending of history in the complete knowledge and self-awareness of man, and in his reconciliation with the world. Hegel juxtaposes transhistorical man with historical man as one might contrast a solution with a problem. Nietzsche, Marx, and a number of humanist Marxists, in contrast, take the Hegelian solution, or something like it, and treat it as the problem. They take the Hegelian idea of the negation of negation, of a demystified man, as rendering life itself meaningless and endlessly the same. It is this conception, this post-Hegelian idea of modern man that Foucault finds to be the distorted product of the modern episteme.

Some conservative theorists have taken the idea of "the end of man" as the characteristic position of structuralism and the standard under which a new, nihilistic, movement in the human sciences is being arrayed.[61] It may well be a practical rhetorical strategy to group all of the structuralists together with the humanist Marxists and the existentialists if one wishes to promote an idealist alternative, but there is no such unified movement. Despite their common rejection of the Hegelian ideal, significant differences remain between the humanists and the structuralists, between Nietzsche and Marx, between Kojève and Althusser, and between Foucault and Lévi-Strauss regarding the meaning and the consequences of the dispersal of Man. One important aspect of these differences is to be found in Heidegger's unresolved ambivalence between ontological individualism and (collective) cultural authenticity. The question is whether "dispersed man" is consciously reconciled with his anxiety or transcends his anxiety in the sublimation of self in a cultural community. The question is whether authenticity is individual or collective. A second and related aspect of the problem is whether collective authenticity (which is neither universal nor individual) is essentially objective and conjunctural or subjective and cultural.

Hegel's definition of historical man was translated by Kojève as negation, that is, as the force which changes the world. Kojève held that the ultimate negation of negation, with the historical manifestation of Absolute Spirit, entailed the negation of man. With the end of history and the realization of Absolute Spirit, or the closing of the hiatus between the *an sich* and the *für sich,* man is no longer (existentially) negation. For Kojève, this means that man loses at once both his anxiety and his alienation and attains a state of *un*self-consciousness. This state of unself-consciousness is expressed as an animal-like state of happiness rather than as the happiness of Man. *Homo ludens* replaces Hegel's *homo sapiens.* In some passages Kojève seems to welcome this possibility; in others he states that it is already a reality and there is no mistaking his dismay.[62]

One way of sorting out all these subtle and/or obscure differences is to ask, what is the consequence of the negation of man? The answer to this question depends upon the system of concepts and arguments in which the problem arises. If man is described as time, then the consequence is to leave only space (i.e., three-dimensional, intuitive empiricism). If man is defined as *für sich,* then it leaves only the *an sich.* If man is defined as alienation, then his negation is reconciliation. If man is described as wage slavery, then his negation is emancipation. If man is defined as dominated by the subconscious, then his negation is the triumph of consciousness. If man is defined as alterity, then his negation is authenticity. And, of course, if man is defined as speech, reason, or wisdom, then his negation is animal, but, perhaps, a happy animal.

From all appearances it would seem that the position of Kojève, as exponent of humanist Marxism, and that of Lévi-Strauss, as exponent of anthropological structuralism, are the same. If the relevant contradiction for Lévi-Strauss was between the raw and the cooked, the spoken and the written, then the negation of man means the affirmation of the *sauvage.* But Lévi-Strauss and the structuralists do not call for the negation of man in the spirit and idiom of Nietzsche; they rather call for the dispersion of man. They call for the intellectual, methodological, and normative primacy of practice over theory, in the classical, Aristotelian, terminology. That is to say, they call for the epistemological priority of the particular over the general, of the parochial over the universal.

> It would be inaccurate, therefore, to say that on the road toward the understanding of man, which goes from the study of conscious content to that of unconscious forms, the historian and the anthropologist travel in opposite directions. . . . The fact that their journey together appears to each of them in a different light—to the historian, transition from the explicit to the implicit; to the anthropologist, transition from the particular to the universal—does not in the least alter the identical character of their fundamental approach. The anthropologist goes forward, seeking to attain, through the conscious, . . . more and more of the unconscious; whereas the historian advances, so to speak, backward.[63]

In contrast, Althusser's antihumanism is an attack on the attempt to emphasize consciousness, authenticity, and ideology in Western Marxism. And, as Benton points out, Althusser invokes the Marx of the *German Ideology* in his rejection of humanism.[64] He specifically negates the Feuerbachian notion of man as the subject of an historical teleology. Like Marx, his notion of the dispersed conception of man differs from that of the humanist Marxists. His conception of man is profoundly historical (situational, conjunctural, empirical) rather than historicist. Althusser's antihumanism is closer to Hegel than it is either to Marx or Kojève. If, for Hegel, the negation of man is the triumph of Absolute Spirit, or disembodied knowledge, or the reconciliation of the world with its Creator, for Althusser the negation of man removes an obstacle to the productive pursuit of theoretical practice. Althusser is not concerned with the liberation of existential man from essential man. Althusser would liberate the known from the knower, so that knowledge could change the world.

Foucault, it seems to me, has something else in mind. He wishes to liberate Dasein from the imposition of what is considered knowledge in any given society. If one permits, he would liberate the knower from knowledge. Consequently, it is correct to relate Foucault's position to that of Kojève but not that of Althusser. There is a further contradiction between Foucault's appeals to both Lévi-Strauss and Nietzsche, as though the former's concern with the structure of the collective unconscious were compatible with the latter's concern with the cultural alienation of the individual.

> The conclusion would be that the political, ethical, social, philosophical problem of our days is not to try to liberate the individual from the state, and from the state's institutions, but to liberate us both from the state and from the type of individualization which is linked to the state. We have to promote new forms of

subjectivity through the refusal of this kind of individuality which has been imposed on us for several centuries.[65]

Said's Application of Foucault

But what is, then, the connection between Foucault and Said; what is it that leads Said to seek the authority of Foucault in his critique of orientalism? Or, to put the matter in other words, what is the connection between Foucault's deconstructionist impulse and the negation of orientalism?

Foucault argues that the form and logic (and possibly the content) of the established disciplines is not the consequence of the objective character of the thing being studied. Hence it is possible that the discursive form of a discipline may be alien to the object of its study. Said shows that, at least some of the time, orientalism is hostile to Islam. But he does not argue that the negation of orientalism is the affirmation of Islam. In fact, he argues that Islam is the creation of orientalism in much the same way that Man is the creation of historicism, or of Aristotelianism, or of the unhappy consciousness, or of capitalism, or of structuralism. That is, of course, Islam in a certain sense of the term, but Islam, nevertheless, and the only Islam he describes.

Said makes no assertion that Islam is less guilty of "objectivizing the subject" (i.e., man) than is Christianity. Though he does call, in passing, for a "liberating interpretation" of Islam, it is clear that he is concerned with the struggle against Western intellectual imperialism and not some kind of Islamic reform. Hence, the negation of orientalism turns out to be the negation of Islam, because no other conception of Islam takes its place.

Foucault, for all of his vehement commitment to the explosion of man, invoked psychoanalysis, ethnology, and structural linguistics as alternative ways of signifying, if not defining, a dispersed man. Said similarly invokes structural anthropology and humanist Marxism as methods which have produced less oppressive and objectifying studies of Muslim peoples. Said negates Islam as the point of reference for the learned discourse on the peoples of the Middle East, and he would substitute ethnology, nationalism, and cultural authenticity therefor—in a word, what some theorists call *jahiliyya*. All of this suggests that Said is in constructive agreement with the positions of Gellner and Lewis as well as Geertz.

There are a number of reasons that might explain why Said says nothing about Islam. He might have intended to write only of the West. He might not know enough about Islam. He might have felt that it was sufficient instead to name those of whose work he approves. He might have felt it best to say nothing rather than to say some one thing. He might believe that it is inappropriate or impossible or even hostile for any outsider to speak of a belief system which he does not share. Whatever his reason, Said says nothing and says nothing about why he says nothing, and it is this double silence which suggests an anomaly, a kind of paradox, an aporia or the very condition which makes Said's critical discourse possible. Of course it may be true that if Said were to have written anything about Islam, he might have been able to write nothing about orientalism.

Said's failure to discuss Islam in the course of his critique of orientalism is an aporia in Derrida's sense; that is, not a contradiction, but a kind of paradox which emerges from the text, and beyond which the text cannot go. As a consequence of the discovery of this aporia, we are led to doubt whether he means what he says, and to wonder what else he might also have to say if the aporia were resolved.

Said does not prove that Islam is not a singular, unified, holistic phenomenon. He merely asserts this empiricalist position as a well-established philosophical truth, despite the fact that he argues that orientalism is a singular cultural phenomenon given to holistic characterization. For him, spiritual unities have no cognitive standing. It is in this sense that he denies the reality of Islam itself in a more extreme manner than the orientalists themselves. He does not speak of Islam because, apparently, there is nothing that one can say that will not similarly be an orientalism. The Divine Speech which Muslims believe is Islam, is, obviously, just another discursive formation with its own set of dominating metaphors, literary structures and interpretations of reason and order which are themselves textual and rhetorical. The critical method which Said employs against his select group of orientalists implicitly deconstructs Islam by deconstructing the definitive character of the Islamic text par excellence, the perfect text which renders all other texts intelligible, that is the Qur'an.

This conclusion is the logical consequence of following Foucault rather than invoking Heidegger or the structuralists or the Marxist humanists. Foucault's concept of the dispersal of Man leads to the dispersal of Islam, as well. Said is compelled to stop short of declaring this logical conclusion lest he defeat the political purpose of his own text. As we have seen, he makes a rather lame effort to suggest that new structuralist studies of Islam may transcend the limits of orientalism, but Said has either misread or misunderstood the examples he offers.

It may be asserted that Said's aproach is emancipating because it leaves the interpretation of Islam to Muslims—but this interpretation is vitiated by the fact that Said argues that a political interpretation of orientalism *is* possible, and that it transcends any other level of meaning, even the meaning of orientalism to orientalists themselves.

Reticence and Writing: The Alternative of Silence

The question that Said poses is whether orientalism is violence—a violence that we perpetrate against Muslims in our study of Islam, and possibly even a symbolic violence that we gratuitously impose on alien peoples and even extinct "civilizations." The violence of scholarly discourse might be justified in the interest of some theoretical ideal of truth, but if we deny the existence of such, or what is the same thing, if we affirm that each discipline defines its own truth, then one may question whether such violence can be justified. Is not silence preferable to the violence of academic discourse?

It may be possible for us to gain some insight into this problem from Derrida's essay, "Violence and Metaphysics."[66] This essay is devoted to a deconstruction of the writing of Emmanuel Levinas, and it holds a special interest for us because of the similarity of the positions of Levinas and Said.

Levinas argues that both Husserl and Heidegger deny the autonomy and integrity of "the other." Husserl commits this violence by his solipsistic description of the manner in which knowledge of the other is constituted in the consciousness of ego, seeming to reduce the other to a figment of ego's imagination. Alter is not really different for Husserl since he is essentially like me, but since I know alter only in my own consciousness, I am never really with alter, but always alone. Heidegger is accused of denying the authenticity of the other because of the abstract theoretism of his use of the concept "being," in which both ego and alter are found. The result is summed up in the concepts of the same and solitude: "Therefore, there is a soliloquy of reason and a solitude of light. Incapable of respecting the Being and meaning of the other, phenomenology [Husserl] and ontology [Heidegger] would be philosophies of violence. Through them the entire philosophical tradition, in its meaning and at bottom, would make common cause with oppression and with the totalitarianism of the same" (p. 91).

Levinas argues that the only moral approach to the problem of constituting, or rather, of knowing the other, is to postulate the absolute otherness of the other; and it is to this conclusion that Derrida objects. Levinas argues that we must exclude any philosophical anticipation of the nature of the other because such a theoretical conception brings us into relation with the Being of the other, and not with the existent other himself. "The neutral thought of Being neutralizes the Other as a being: 'Ontology as first philosophy is a philosophy of power,' a philosophy of the neutral, the tyranny of the state as an anonymous and inhuman universality" (p. 97). The moral way to know the other is rather by means of a philosophically unanticipated encounter:

> "What then is this encounter with the absolutely-other? Neither representation, nor limitation, nor conceptual relation to the same. . . . Therefore, there is no way to conceptualize the encounter: it is made by the other, the unforseeable. . . . Concepts suppose an anticipation, a horizon within which alterity is amortized as soon as it is announced precisely because it has let itself be foreseen. The infinitely-other cannot be bound by a concept." (P. 95)

Derrida proceeds toward the deconstruction of Levinas's critique by pressing the idea that the absolute other is in fact an infinitely other because we can have no concept of it and still have morality. Derrida writes: "Despite all appearances and habitual thinking, it must be acknowledged here that the dissociation of thought and language, and the subordination of the latter to the former, are proper to a philosophy of finitude . . . and seems to us to support the entirety of Levinas's thought: the other is the other only if his alterity is absolutely irreducible, that is, infinitely irreducible; and the infinitely Other can only be Infinity" (p. 104).

Both Other and Infinity in this last passage are capitalized, indicating in advance that, in Derrida's analysis, Levinas means no less than God by the absolute other—and that he is opposing both Buber and Gabriel Marcel in this argument.[67] Derrida argues that the insistence upon the absoluteness of otherness leads to the concept of the infinitely other, which, as infinite, cannot be described and cannot be related to in the moral sense that Levinas claims. Derrida argues that it is impossible to know the infinitely other, impossible to relate to the infinitely other, and impossible to have discourse with the infinitely other. He argues, with Husserl, that it is impossible for ego to entertain such a concept apart from his own consciousness of himself, which must be present in every such conceptualization. Even our conception of God must begin from the neo-Cartesian "I am." The only way in which such a conception of otherness can be maintained is by returning to a pre-Kantian philosophy of infiniteness in which it is argued that man's knowledge can transcend his own finitude either as consequence of revelation or by the miracle of contemplation. In point of fact, though, the conception of the infinitely other will have to be empty, just as is our conception of God, and the resultant silence, argues Derrida, constitutes an even greater violence than does discourse.

Having established that Levinas's apotheosis of the infinitely other leads to silence, Derrida moves in to the final attack in a couple of brilliant if brutal passages:

> In the last analysis, according to Levinas, nonviolent language would be a language which would do without the verb *to be*, that is without predication. Predication is the first violence. Since the verb to be and the predicative act are implied in every other verb, and in every common noun, nonviolent language, in the last analysis, would be a language of pure invocation, pure adoration, proffering only proper nouns in order to call to the other from afar. In effect, such a language would be purified of all rhetoric, which is what Levinas explicitly desires. . . . Is a language free from all rhetoric possible? (P. 147)

And then finally:

> [despite] The thousand-times-denounced circle of historicism, psychologism, relativism, etc. [in which denunciation Levinas has joined] . . . the true name of this inclination of thought to the Other, of this resigned acceptance of incoherent incoherence [a reference to Islamic thought?] inspired by a truth more profound than the "logic" of philosophical disourse, the true name of this renunciation of the concept, of the a prioris and transcendant horizons of language is empiricism. . . . It is the *dream* of a purely heterological thought at its source. A pure thought of pure difference. (P. 151)

For Derrida a pure thought of a pure difference is an impossibility, it is an attempt to conjoin the infinitely other which is the Judaic and Islamic conception of God with the Greek philosophical Logos—a task, the potential success of which he profoundly and maybe prejudiciously doubts. The failure to accomplish this "coupling"[68] has in fact led to the sort of silence or talking past one another that Derrida has described as an even greater violence than discourse—the failure to recognize the being of the other.

It is likely that Said has been led to this position of silence, violence, and philosophical self-contradiction by the logic of his task, which was to counter the powerful discourse of orientalism, and thereby reduce its impact on a group of societies which are part of a community of belief. Insofar as it is Islam and not simply Middle Eastern societies which Said set out to succor, it follows that he must either accept Islam as it presents itself or else he must remain silent, presenting Islam as emptiness, as form without content, or more precisely as authenticity whose only purpose is to be different.

The crucial fact is that Islam designates a community of believers, whose basic philosophical outlook rejects the philosophy of finitude upon which both structuralism and deconstruction are based. It is this presumed or believed access to the infinite which must dominate the relationship of Islam to any modern philosophy or critical method, even as it dominated and defined the relationship of classical Islam to the challenge of Greek philosophy. The result has about it much of the character of Levinas's yearning to put Judaism and Greek philosophy together—a task presumably achieved by Christianity—but which Derrida feels must lead to silence. Edward Said provides a defense for such a position without actually taking the position himself.

Derrida's critique of the concept of the Absolute Other argues that a noncognitive orientation toward the non-ego, or toward those who do not share my identity, leads to an attitude similar to that taken toward an unseen and inscrutable God. This, for Derrida, is an extreme form of mystification which leads, in the realm of terrestrial objects, to a heterology, an epistemology which permits only a meaningless external perception of others as robotic monads which he identifies with empiricism. For Derrida, empiricism as heterology is, therefore, impossible. Right or wrong, any study of the other must start from a conception of the other that I have, or from some constitution of the other in my consciousness, as the phenomenologists would say.

But neither transcendental nor psychological phenomenology argues that the original, intentional, constitution of the other in the natural attitude, can ever remain the same throughout the process of moving from preliminary or pre-predicative constitution, on toward what Husserl called a transcendental constitution of the other. That transcendental constitution requires the exercise of a virtually unattainable discipline of the suppression (or the eidetic reduction) of the ego of the inquiring scholar. Failing the eidetic reduction of the ego, transcendental phenomenology must fail to produce either an ideally objective characterization or, alternatively, an ideally authentic interpretation of any other. Still, between the extremes of the complete idealization of self and the complete identification with the other, there are some intermediate possibilities which are based on the assumption that ego will undergo some change while gaining some understanding of alter. Hence, a more modestly defined phenomenological project, claiming only to deepen our understanding of the relevant cultural and religious phenomena, may not be without merit, either practical or theoretical.

The possibilities of a benign dialogue between Islam and the West are limited even for the believers among us, because the gap in understanding is really constituted by the fact that ours is an unbelieving society, as Muslims clearly perceive, while theirs is a believing society. The very forms of the discourse of belief in our society are already embedded in the critique of finitude as a suppressed premise. The central question is "How is it possible to believe, given man's finite knowledge?" or "How it is possible to believe, given man's finite nature and the consequences thereof for what he can know?" Most Muslims think these questions are foolish, and that they are as much expressions of unbelief as any scepticism. Certainly the answers that are offered appear to be unnecessarily complex to Muslim believers. Their response, if they are at all interested, is to adopt the conclusion, without the disturbing premise, regarding their own faith and the doubts of non-Muslims as a confirmation of the practical as well as the spiritual efficacity of Islamic truth.

Yet it is clear that even in the context of mutual, if second-level, violence, Western thought has had an impact on Islamic thought. Ali Shariati was obviously fascinated by French phenomenology and Marxism, Fazlur Rahman has become interested in hermeneutics, Sayyid Qutb was interested in existentialism, Zaki Nagib Mahmud is the leading exponent of pragmatism in the Arab world, Muhammad ʿImara has used an historicist frame of reference even if not consistently, and Khalid Muhammad Khalid remains one of the leading exponents of liberal rationalism among the ulama.

Insofar as western philosophical styles are employed without the adoption of the principle of finitude, then it is only the appearance, and not the substance, of Western influence which is discerned. Western rhetorical forms may be the mark of the bourgeois intellectual in the Middle East, but where the political discourse of the bourgeoisie is adapted to Islam (rather than nationalism) it must deny the analytic of finitude, and hence the philosophical raison d'être of the discursive formations they employ. Theologies which are founded upon the analytic of finitude have little support in the Middle East. Many of the more recent philosophical and ideological developments in the West have a "post-bourgeois" character, while the situation in many Muslim countries is still "pre-bourgeois," a condition which may have something to do with the radicalization of religious ideologies.

From this perspective alone, it seems to me to be quite true that orientalist discourse and Western discourse in general are violent in their effect on the Islamic world, and so is the discourse of Islamic apologetics violent in its impact on the West. We have not yet gone beyond this stage of the limited violence of discourse toward some deeper understanding of the being of the other, but at least we have not yet drawn back to the greater violence of silence. As Derrida writes:

> Discourse, therefore, if it is originally violent, can only do itself violence, can only negate itself, in order to affirm itself, make war upon the war which institutes it without ever *being able* to reappropriate this negativity, to the extent that it is discourse. *Necessarily* without reappropriating it, for if it did so, the horizon of peace would disappear into the night. . . . This secondary war, as the avowal of violence, is the least possible violence, the only way to repress the worst violence, the violence of primitive and prelogical silence, of an unimaginable night which would not even be the opposite of day, an absolute violence which would not even be the opposite of nonviolence: nothingness or pure non-sense. Thus discourse chooses itself violently in opposition to nothingness or pure non-sense, and, in philosophy, against nihilism.[69]

4

ᶜAli ᶜAbd al-Raziq and Islamic Liberalism: The Rejected Alternative

The Umma as a Political Community

The Arabic term *umma* denotes a religious community, or all those who hold the same religious beliefs. The Jews constitute an umma, the Christians are an umma, and the Muslims are also an umma. An umma is not necessarily also a political community, as the earliest Christians were not, but it may be, as the Jews were under the earliest kings. Most, but not all Muslim scholars believe that the Muslims, in principle, constitute a political community. The belief that worldly Islam ought to take the form of a political community is not dependent upon a theory of the caliphate, or indeed any specific doctrine regarding the ideal form of Islamic government, even though many scholars have attempted to derive the ideal form of Islamic government from the idea of the umma as a political community.

It is well known that, in point of historical fact, Muslims have not been united in a single political community for much of their history. At certain times, and in the opinion of certain scholars, the existence of a plurality of Muslim states was thought to vitiate the legitimacy of the rulers of those states, or at least of the rulers of all but one of those states. At other times, and in other situations, scholars admitted that historical conditions precluded the unification of the umma in a single state. The weight of tradition is nevertheless in favor of unity, or *tawhid*, in sociopolitical matters as in theology. Tradition favors the political establishment of Islam, or as a respected shaykh put it, "The Islamic religion is based on the pursuit of domination and power."[1] Still, the actual historical plurality of Muslim states does not have the consequence of invalidating the acts of such states, so long as they conform to the Shariʿa. On the contrary, every government of Muslims is obligated to implement the law of Islam. The practical application of the doctrine that the Islamic umma is a political community has not been to insist upon the political unification of Islam so much as to insist that Islam and political power must be united because it is the task of the Islamic state to bring about obedience to the revealed law.

The distinction between the notions of political community and government, or regime, is of particular importance in understanding the nature of the intellectual challenge which ʿAli ʿAbd al-Raziq posed to the traditional shaykhs of al-Azhar in his book *al-Islam wa Usul al-Hukm* (Islam and the sources of political authority). This relatively short political tract has taken its place as a classic of modern Egyptian liberal thought, and as the basis of a cause célèbre. The book, and the official reaction to it, attracted much attention in 1925 when it was first published, and a number of historians of Egyptian thought have dealt with it, most notably, Albert Hourani in his *Arabic Thought in the Liberal Age, 1798–1939*, and Muhammad ʿImara in his *al-Islam wa Usul al-Hukm li-ʿAli ʿAbd al-Raziq*.

Both authors put the debate on the book in its historical context. The new Turkish nation-state, under Kemal Ataturk, formally abolished the Ottoman caliphate in 1924, and there ensued a restrained but determined competition among a number of Arab rulers to appropriate the title, or alternatively, to prevent its appropriation by anyone. The issue of the caliphate had emerged as a significant political matter toward the end of the Ottoman empire, because this symbol of the spiritual leadership of the Muslims served the interests of the Ottoman government, even as its power over territory inhabited by Muslims in eastern Europe waned. The issue was further invigorated by the organization of a movement among Indian Muslims to protect the caliphate against the hostile attacks of the allied powers in the First World War. The leaders of the Indian movement encouraged the efforts of those Arabs who were interested in the potential political benefits that might flow from the reassertion of an Arab caliphate. The ulama who were called upon for advice in the matter seem to have acted with great circumspection, although they were under some political pressure. King Fuad of Egypt was especially interested in gaining the title of caliph, and he was able to use the monarch's well-established leverage over al-Azhar to further his cause. Shaykh Rashid Rida, the disciple of Muhammad ʿAbduh, was similarly inspired to publish an article on the caliphate in *al-Manar* in the spring of 1925. According to ʿImara, ʿAli ʿAbd al-Raziq's work was politically motivated and intended to refute the arguments of Rida while damaging the candidacy of the King.

Hourani presents an excellent summary of ʿAbd al-Raziq's position. "Abd al-Raziq's book . . . raised in a vivid way the most fundamental question involved: is the caliphate really necessary? . . . is there such a thing as an Islamic system of government?" ʿAbd al-Raziq grants that "some sort of political authority is indeed necessary, but it need not be of a specific kind." And even more far-reaching: "It is not even necessary that the umma should be politically united." According to Hourani, ʿAbd al-Raziq's book was criticized so vehemently because "it propounded a new historical theory . . . and this theory was drawn more from non-Muslim writers on Islam." Nevertheless, Hourani concludes that ʿAbd al-Raziq lost a personal battle while contributing importantly to the long-term advance of liberal westernization. Citing Shaykh Bakhit's dictum that "The Islamic government headed by the caliph and universal Imam is a democratic, free, consultative, government, of which the constitution is God's Book and the *Sunna* of God's Prophet," Hourani concludes, rather too easily, that Shaykh Bakhit's identification of Islamic government with Western parliamentary institutions "has opened the door to that very invasion of Islam by the ideas of Western nationalism."[2]

The difficulty with Hourani's conclusion, is that it concentrates on the question of the proper form of Islamic government, or whether there are any properly Islamic political institutions, as opposed to the question of whether the umma is a democratic, political community. Rereading Hourani's quotation of what is taken as Shaykh Bakhit's concessionary statement, we see that while the caliph derives *his* authority from the umma, the umma is not the constituent power in the sense of originating the constitution. The constitution of a Government of Muslims is the Qur'an and the Sunna. Bakhit's position appears to be compatible with the contemporary Muslim consensus that an Islamic government is one which maintains the Shariʿa for any group of Muslims. While this position probably owes more to Ibn Khaldun than it does to al-Mawardi and the *fuqaha* (specialists in Islamic legal reasoning), it is still fundamentally different from the Western idea of liberal constitutional democracy. The legislative responsibilities of such a government are quite restricted, nor would the parliament replace the function of the ulama in interpreting the law. While the legitimacy of the rulers would depend upon some democratic process, it would also depend upon their implementation of the Shariʿa. There are, consequently, grounds for the assertion that concessions of the sort made by Shaykh Bakhit have contributed more to the rise of Islamic fundamentalism than to the strengthening of political liberalism in Egypt and elsewhere in the Muslim countries.

A key doctrinal precondition for the contemporary reassertion of Islamic fundamentalism is whether, under contemporary historical conditions, it is feasible to establish and maintain an ideal, Islamic government. An ideal Islamic government (the phrase is actually redundant) is one in which the law may be determined with absolute certainty, so that Muslims are left in no doubt about what they must do and what they must not do. Traditionally, orthodox Sunnis believe that an ideal Islamic government has been attainable when conditions are right, as was the case under the Rightly Guided Caliphs. Shiʿites believe that an Islamic government is attainable under the rule of the Imams. Fundamentalists hold that an ideal Islamic government is possible regardless of historical conditions. Indeed, among the purposes of Islamic government is the overcoming of historical conditions.

ʿAbd al-Raziq's Argument

On the day after the Council of the Greatest Ulama ruled against him, a reporter for the *Bourse Egyptienne* interviewed ʿAbd al-Raziq and asked him to summarize the main points of his book. ʿAbd al-Raziq replied: "The main point of the book, for which I have been condemned, is that Islam did not determine a specific regime, nor did it impose on the Muslims a particular system according to the requirements of which they must be governed; rather it has allowed us absolute freedom to organize the state in accordance with the intellectual, social and economic conditions in which we are found, taking into consideration our social development and the requirements of the times."[3]

From there the questioning turned specifically to the matter of the caliphate, and ʿAbd al-Raziq repeated his position that the caliphate is not a religious regime, that it is not required by Islam, and that, despite the pretensions of the caliphs, they could not possibly have been the successors or caliphs of the Prophet because the Prophet "was never a king, and he never tried to establish a government or a state; he was a messenger sent by Allah, and he was not a political leader."[4]

By insisting that the Prophet was not a political leader, and that the caliphs were not successors of the Prophet, ʿAbd al-Raziq denied that there was any transfer of political legitimacy from the Prophet to the caliph. It further appears that he believed that the religious community constituted of common belief by means of the Prophet's mission did not have a political dimension. His insistence that the

Prophet was not a political leader is, of course, hardly acceptable from the historical as well as the traditional point of view. The statement that the Prophet was never a king is more acceptable, so long as the word king is not taken as the equivalent of political leader of any sort. This usage is frequent and important in ʿAbd al-Raziq's argument, because it allows him to overstate the case for distinguishing religion and politics during the Prophet's time, and it also allows him to make a radical distinction between religious authority and the authority of King Fuad. He does not argue that King Fuad is unqualified for the caliphate, but rather that the caliphate is unworthy of Islam. The caliphate is no more than a kingship.

The Debate with Ibn Khaldun

ʿAbd al-Raziq's argument and its rhetorical form depend very much on Ibn Khaldun's discussion of the caliphate and kingship in the *Muqaddima*. This relatively complex doctrinal position has been written about by a number of scholars, but the most noteworthy for our purposes is Muhsin Mahdi's *Ibn Khaldun's Philosophy of History.* He sums up relevant aspects of Ibn Khaldun's doctrine as follows:

> In Islam, it is doctrinally essential that religion should not merely have an external concern with wordly affairs, define the conditions upon . . . which it may coexist with kingly power, or clearly distinguish between affairs of the spirit and affairs of the world. None of these would suffice. Religion itself must be politicized. This is the historical basis which led Muslim philosophers and Ibn Khaldun to reflect upon Islam and the Islamic community as a political regime. . . . It is politics and not religion which is the central theme of Ibn Khaldun's reflections on culture. . . . Politically, religion can be the source of a regime with a wider horizon of man's ends.[5]

The caliphate is, for Ibn Khaldun, the prototype of the regime of Law, a divinely ordained political system which takes into its purview both the earthly and the otherworldly needs of human beings: "It should not be concluded, however, that the regime of Law either eliminates or suppresses man's natural desires or the social institutions based on them. This would be impossible since man's desires are the necessary bases of all political regimes, including the regime of Law."[6]

Mahdi states that the regime of Law was known to Ibn Khaldun through only a single case, the caliphate. Nevertheless, Ibn Khaldun treated it theoretically, defining its essential characteristics, and distinguishing it from other types of regime within his classification scheme. This analytical method would seem to leave no doubt Ibn

Khaldun believed that the Prophet did have a political role, that he did establish a political community, that the caliphate was both a political and a religious institution, and that the umma is essentially a political community. Yet Mahdi is compelled to add, "Thus, when Ibn Khaldun says that the 'caliphate is religion and has nothing to do with a kingly regime,' he does not mean that it has nothing to do with politics because it *is* a political regime [*siyasa*] but that the ends of the regime are religious and not mundane."[7]

Ibn Khaldun does distinguish the caliphate from kingship or royal authority, and there is no doubt that he considers the caliphate to be far superior. Nevertheless, in practice, there is an important continuity between the two. Both depend upon *ʿasabiyya* (social solidarity), and both include the element of kingship; but in the caliphate, kingship is subordinate to religious ends. In the famous passage in which Ibn Khaldun describes the way in which the caliphate declined into kingship, he describes this continuity: "It is thus clear that the caliphate at first existed without royal authority. Then the characteristic traits of the caliphate became mixed up and confused. Finally, when its group feeling [*ʿasabiyya*] had separated from the group feeling of the caliphate, royal authority came to exist alone."[8]

Even though Ibn Khaldun asserts that the caliphate first existed without kingship, he also states that those natural social processes upon which kingship is based are never absent, even under the caliphate:

> . . . royal authority is the natural goal of group feeling. It results from group feeling, not by choice but through (inherent) necessity and the order of existence. . . . All religious laws and practices . . . require(s) group feeling. . . . Still we find that the Lawgiver (Muhammad) censured group feeling. . . . We also find that (he) censured royal authority . . . . . When the Lawgiver (Muhammad) forbids or censures certain human activities or urges their omission, he does not want them to be neglected altogether.[9]

The point is even more strongly made where Ibn Khaldun, speaking of the caliphate of the early Umayyads and the early Abbasids, declares that during an interim phase of the decline, "caliphate and royal authority existed side by side."[10] And again, in justifying the requirement that the caliph be drawn from the Quraysh tribe, Ibn Khaldun argues that this was necessary in order to allow the caliph to draw upon the ʿasabiyya of the Quraysh and the Mudar.[11]

The lack of a sharp break between the caliphate and kingship and the necessary dependence of both upon ʿasabiyya has a practical, political consequence in that it provides a logical basis for the legitimation of a government of Muslims which is not a caliphate. Referring to Muhammad's condemnation of royal authority, Ibn Khaldun asserts that this condemnation is far from absolute: "If royal authority would sincerely exercise its superiority over men for the sake of God and so as to cause those men to worship God and to wage war against his enemies, there would not be anything reprehensible in it."[12]

It is not unreasonble to draw the conclusion from this section of the *Prolegomena* that Ibn Khaldun believed that a regime of Law could be established through a combination of religion, ʿasabiyya, wrathfulness (martial spirit), and human desires properly directed; that is, a combination of revealed law and the prerequisites of kingship. Hence, it is possible to argue that Ibn Khaldun provided a framework for the legitimation of kingship in terms of its religious service to at least a part of the umma. Political power, if not directed at religious ends is censured by the Prophet; but if, as Mahdi puts it, the king succeeds in "politicizing religion" for a segment of the umma, then there is nothing reprehensible in such kingship.

It is apparent that ʿAbd al-Raziq does not agree with Ibn Khaldun. This disagreement is of interest, because Ibn Khaldun is one of the favorite authors among the liberal modernizers. While Ibn Khaldun does not have the virtually universal traditional approval that al-Ghazzali has gained, his own synthesis of Sunni doctrine, practical philosophy, and historical pragmatism has won wide approval, and he is generally accepted as being within the mainstream of orthodox Islam. This general approbation is significant because, as we have seen, Ibn Khaldun does not argue that the caliphate is the only possible Islamic form of government. He does state that the caliphate is "obligatory" in the sense that it is provided with *Sharʿi* justification as a consequence of the *ijmaʿ* (consensus) of the Companions, the *salaf* (early Muslims), and the umma; and it is "necessary" in the sense that it fulfills the natural requirement of all human communities for government. The decline of religious ʿasabiyya has determined, however, that the caliphate cannot exist under present conditions, and that the umma cannot be constituted as a unified political community. But neither of these conditions precludes the possibility of Islamic government and Islamic communities under prevailing historical conditions, so long as the government may be Islamized, and Islam politicized. It is this evidently reasonable compromise, so widely accepted among Muslim liberals, which ʿAbd al-Raziq rejected.

ʿAbd al-Raziq's work is in a way a dialogue with Ibn Khaldun. He starts by restating Ibn Khaldun's general definition of the caliphate as an Islamic form of government concerned with the welfare of Muslims in this world and the next. He cites Ibn Khaldun's distinction between the caliphate and kingship, and quotes him fully on the decline of the caliphate into kingship after a period in which the elements of the two were mixed.[13] He then states that the Muslims differ on whether the caliph derives his authority from God or from the umma. He takes the questionable position that the *generality* of the ulama and the generality of Muslims hold the view that the authority (*sultan*) of the caliph is derived from God, while only some of the ulama hold the view that the authority of the caliph is derived from the umma.[14] ʿAbd al-Raziq goes on to say that "the best explanation and justification of this (latter) point of view that I have found is the *Manifesto on the Caliphate and the Governance of the Umma* that was published by the government of the Grand National Assembly in Ankara and translated from the Turkish into Arabic by ʿAbd al-Ghani Suni Bek and printed by al-Hilal Printing House in Cairo in 1342 H.-A.D. 1924."[15]

Rejection of the Consensus Doctrine

In his discussion of the source of caliphal authority, ʿAbd al-Raziq appears to have exaggerated the degree to which Muslims accepted the claims of the caliphs regarding their own authority. As we have seen, Shaykh Bakhit found no difficulty in accepting the idea that caliphal authority is derived from the umma. It is also easily possible to reconcile the two views by arranging to have divine authority pass via the umma, by means of the *bayʿa* (contracting of allegiance) or by means of ijmaʿ, to the caliph. But it is just this sort of reconciliation which ʿAbd al-Raziq wishes to prevent by his exaggeration. The distinction between the two views is enhanced in a tendentious way by comparing the more general view to what is said to be Hobbes' theory of the divine right of kings(!), and the second view to the theory of Locke. It is however noteworthy that ʿAbd al-Raziq does not show that the divine right doctrine was ever justified by the Sunni fuqaha. He writes: "The spirit of that opinion [i.e., the divine source of caliphal authority] may be found current among the generality of the Muslims also. All of their statements and studies about the caliphate are of the same nature, and they indicate this belief."[16] ʿAbd al-Raziq thus cautiously avoids ever quite saying that the doctrine was explicitly held.

The question of the delegation of authority to the caliph never arose in this form within the juridical framework of medieval Sunni discourse on the caliphate. The classical works do not include a doctrinal discussion of the source of delegated authority, as they do include a litany of well-established disagreements regarding the scriptural basis of the caliphate. This section has been invented by ʿAbd al-Raziq, and his purpose here was to weaken the widely accepted view that the authority of the caliph is in fact derived from the umma, and that the umma is a political entity.

ʿAbd al-Raziq's purpose is to demolish the argument that the caliphate is required by the Shariʿa as determined by a consensus of the umma. Having argued that the notion of the umma as the source of caliphal authority was only a minority opinion, he then goes on to write that the question of ijmaʿ was a secondary one and a late one, derived from the more academic question of whether the caliphate was required by reason or divine law. Actually, the philosophers differed on the extent to which they were inclined to identify the Prophet and/or the caliph with the philosopher-king or with ordinary kingship. Al-Farabi wrote of the ruler of the Virtuous City: "He is the ruler who is not ruled by any other person at all, and he is the *imam*, and he is the *ra'is al-awwal* [lawgiver, in this case] of the Virtuous City, and he is the head of the virtuous umma.[17] But Mahdi writes that Ibn Khaldun's caliphate is "definitely inferior to the virtuous city . . . the Law is only an imperfect substitute for the government of the perfect ruler or living intelligence." Nevertheless, the regime of Law or the caliphate is superior to what Ibn Khaldun called rational systems which are unconcerned about man's soul and which do not employ moral or religious persuasion.[18]

It is, consequently, possible to distinguish three forms of government here: (1) that of the Prophet, which is similar to that of the philosopher-king, (2) that of the Law or the Shariʿa, and (3) that of (practical) reason based on natural law, or kingship. ʿAbd al-Raziq is either unconcerned with, or oblivious to, the Islamic philosophical relevance of the question of the rational or religious derivation of the caliphate. At any rate he will show, implicity, that the caliphate was in fact a "rational" regime. That is the consequence of denying that the juridical basis of the caliphate is ijmaʿ, because if it is not based on ijmaʿ then it is not based on divine law.

ʿAbd al-Raziq writes that the dispute over the obligatory foundation of the caliphate does not concern us here because "in any case [the fuqaha] did not differ on the issue of its obligatory character until Ibn Khaldun claimed that it was [derived] from the conclusion of an ijmaʿ on it."[19] This certainly appears to be a misleading statement, for we find, for example, the same issue discussed in the same manner by al-Baghdadi (d. 429 H.). Al-Baghdadi wrote:

> There are differences of opinion regarding the necessity of the seeking after the imam and installing him. Most of our colleagues among the *mutakallimun* and the *fuqaha* along with the *Shiʿa,* the *Khawarij* and most of the *Muʿtazila* hold the imamate to be obligatory . . . and it is necessary to obey the incumbent (*al-mansub*

> *lahu*). . . . Those who hold the opinion that the imamate is obligatory differ [among themselves] on the reason. . . . Abu al-Hasan said that the imamate is one of those laws of the Shariʿa that we know by reason that we may follow, and that are known by report (*bi'l-samaʿa*) to be obligatory. But the companions of the prophet have agreed on its obligatory character, and there is no significance to the opposition of al-Futa (Kharijite) and al-Asam (Muʿtazilite) in the matter of the ijmaʿ [of the Companions].[20]

Obviously the argument that the caliphate was founded on ijmaʿ was not invented by Ibn Khaldun. He was merely repeating the widely held Sunni view on the matter. The intensity of ʿAbd al-Raziq's subsequent attack on the doctrine of the consensual caliphate indicates that he believed that Ibn Khaldun came forward with a patently unacceptable device for justifying the traditional doctrine, and then could not give an acceptable account of how it was that an absolute requirement of religion had not in fact been adhered to by Muslims for centuries. Ibn Khaldun's "inconsistency" was linked to his willingness to legitimize noncaliphal government, while ʿAbd al-Raziq's logical inclination led him to seek consistency by rejecting the religious legitimation of even the Rightly Guided Caliphs. As it turned out of course, ʿAbd al-Raziq's logic was too rooted in Western idealism and dualism to have much influence among Muslims. Muslims have preferred to pursue the implications of Ibn Khaldun's views, and have sought to establish the nearest equivalent of the caliphate.

ʿAbd al-Raziq repeats the well-known argument that there is no textual support for the caliphate either in the Qur'an or in the Sunna. He also cites the weakness of the position of the "author of *al-Muwaqqaf*" who claims that it is not necessary that an ijmaʿ be supported like a *hadith** by means of a continuous chain of transmitters, because the conjuncture may have been one that could only be understood by those involved.[21] ʿAbd al-Raziq insists that there is no explicit, warranted, authority for the caliphate. Every reference in the Qur'an or hadith is used deductively to prove the logical requirement of the caliphate, but there is no canonical statement on the matter which is direct. ʿAbd al-Raziq argues that all such references to political authority are not meant to establish a legitimate successorship to the Prophet, but merely refer to the fact of political power, just as did Jesus in his statement about "rendering unto Caesar." Neither political power, nor polytheism, nor slavery, nor any of the other topics of qur'anic legislation is rendered obligatory simply because it is dis-

******Hadith* **are constituent elements of the Sunna, reports of the Prophet's speech or acts which are, after the Qu'ran, the major source of the Shariʿa.**

cussed in the Qur'an. Even the most famous qur'anic verse, "Obey God, and obey the Prophet, and obey those in authority among you," does not necessarily denote any new political authority.

But ʿAbd al-Raziq goes further in arguing that such verses are "over-loaded" when one draws the conclusion that "they prove that the Muslims constitute a *qawm* or a political community."[22] For the sake of argument, he grants that his opponents' references to certain *ahadith* are sound: "Let us say that the imams and the authorities and such like, when found in the language of the Shariʿa do refer to the caliphate and those incumbent in the supreme Imamate (*al-imama al-ʿuzma*) and that the bayʿa means loyalty to the caliph, and that the community (*jamaʿa*) of Muslims means the Islamic government of the Caliphate (*hukumat al-khilafa al-Islamiyya*)."[23]

But ʿAbd al-Raziq clearly does not agree that these are the correct understandings of the ahadith. It is also important to note the subtle differences in the way in which the word qawm is used and the way in which jamaʿa is used, as opposed to the word umma. Nevertheless, ʿAbd al-Raziq grants that there might have been such a thing as an Islamic political order based on the institution of the caliphate, but he denies that it is required by the Shariʿa or that it is a form of political organization which is religiously obligatory. For ʿAbd al-Raziq, even the hukumat al-khilafa al-Islamiyya is a purely historical phenomenon, which has a virtually secular (*la-dini*) character. He denies the religious legitimacy of the Islamic political community as well as the caliphate, and consequently any possible claim to religious legitimacy by any government over any segment of the umma.

In the course of his argument, ʿAbd al-Raziq makes a number of points, among which the most important are that the caliphate was nearly always based on force, that the Muslims have never been in a position to make the sort of free choice upon which ijmaʿ must be based, that the tacit ijmaʿ, regardless of the group to which it is attributed, evidences fear of violence and not free acquiescence, that love of power is such a strong motivation that the caliphs were willing to perpetrate any evil in order to maintain their power, and that one of the intellectual casualties of the resultant tyranny was the study of political science itself.

ʿAbd al-Raziq makes so much of the weakness of political science among the Muslims, despite the fact that he refers so frequently to the *Prolegomena* of Ibn Khaldun, that we cannot simply ignore these statements. He neither exempts Ibn Khaldun from this generalization, nor does he criticize his specialized political knowledge. Instead he quotes Ibn Khaldun's assertion that kingship is based on power, and the statement that the caliphate declined into kingship and came to be based entirely on Arab ʿasabiyya.

ʿAbd al-Raziq boldly asserts that the Khawarij (all of them?) and al-Asamm of the Muʿtazila were simply correct in denying the caliphal ijmaʿ despite the fact that Ibn Khaldun called them deviationists (*shawadh*). He further argues that every single caliph was actually opposed by some faction or segment of the Muslims. And he concludes:

> It doesn't matter to us a great deal to know the secret behind all this. It may be that the secret is what we have stated, or there may be some other reasons that we have not set down, but the only thing that interests us at this point is that the concentration of the caliphate upon power is an actual fact about which there is no doubt. Consequently, it is all the same to us whether that tangible fact is in accordance with the laws of the intellect or not; whether it accords with the rulings (*ahkam*) of religion or not.[24]

Bearing in mind that ʿAbd al-Raziq only grudgingly agrees that the first three caliphs might have assumed office without the use of force, his refusal to differentiate between the caliphate and kingship denies the very concept of the rightly guided caliphate. He is not only denying the historicity of the rightly guided caliphate, he is also denying the significance of the theory. The ijmaʿ theory is not quite as weak as ʿAbd al-Raziq makes it, so long as it is restricted to the Companions; but it seems to me that its real purpose is to protect the most vital principle, which is contained in the statement attributed to Abu Bakr: "This religion needs someone to lead it (*la budda li-hadha al-din miman yaqum bihi*)."

It is important to remember that Abu Bakr's statement used the word *din* rather than any reference to a human collectivity. In commenting on Abu Bakr's statement, ʿAbd al-Raziq writes that he merely confirms the natural need of all societies for government of some sort, and he confirms this by referring to the qur'anic verse, ". . . and we exalt some of them above others in degrees, that some may take others into subjection" (*al-Zakhraf*, 32). Of even greater relevance is ʿAbd al-Raziq's reference to *surah al-Ma'idah,* verse 48: "For each one of you we have made a law and a pathway; and had God pleased He would have made you one nation . . ." from which ʿAbd al-Raziq concludes:

> One can then say truthfully about the Muslims, if we consider them as a jamaʿa, separate unto themselves, that they were like all other communities (umam) in the world, needing a government to look after their affairs. . . . If the fuqaha meant the same thing by the *imama* as the savants of politics meant by government, then what they said is correct in that the upholding of religious sentiments and salutary guidance does depend on the ca-

> liphate in the sense of government (hukuma), whatever might be the form of that government, or of whatever kind.[25]

Needless to say, this interpretation of the qur'anic verse is questionable because the verse is not concerned with government, but discusses the differences among the three monotheistic communities, each with its own revealed law, and each an umma. Moreover, the religious functions of the government of an umma are treated as a logical consequence of power, and not as a religious consequence of divine will.

ʿAbd al-Raziq concludes this section by saying that he has now broken down the claims of others regarding the caliphate, and he will proceed to present his own views on the matter. We are left to assume that he will be guided in this project by his own conception of political science, because he has insisted that the topic is not a religious one. ʿAbd al-Raziq has not revealed what he means by political science, but he does show a strong commitment to political liberalism.

> For Islam is the religion that is not satisfied merely to teach its followers the idea of brotherhood and equality . . . it has legislated laws based upon brotherhood and equality. . . . It is natural that those Muslims who believe in freedom of thought . . . reject submission to any but Allah . . . and they whisper that belief to their Lord at least 17 times a day during their five prayer times . . . they scorn submission to any of their own people or to any other—that sort of submission which kings demand of their subjects—except when they must submit to force.[26]

Theoretical Analysis of the Political Practice of the Prophet

In the second part of the book, ʿAbd al-Raziq discusses the political functions of the Prophet. He questions whether the Prophet was also a king; whether Muhammad established a state; whether Islam requires that an Islamic state be established, or whether the Prophet's role in establishing an Islamic state was part of, or separate from, his role as Prophet. ʿAbd al-Raziq states that, while there is no explicit doctrine on the matter, most Muslims are inclined to believe that the Prophet was both prophet and king. It is this inclination which has misled Muslim scholars into elaborating the political and administrative institutions of the Prophetic period on the basis of very flimsy historical evidence.

Actually, the historical record leaves things vague and uncertain, so that we really have no idea of what the situation was like. This is not merely a problem for scholarship, because it raises the question of how it is possible to believe that an Islamic state is a religious necessity when the Prophet was silent on the matter. Tahtawi in particular, is taken to task for using his imagination to fill in the institutional gaps, and then justifying his position by arguing that much detailed information was lost in the transmission. Others argue that it is not necessary that a state have all the institutions that we identify with a modern state to be a state—that the Prophetic state, in keeping with the spirit of Islam, was a simple and natural sort of organization—and this explains why we don't have a lot of information about it and why it seems vaguely defined to us.

ʿAbd al-Raziq admits that the Prophetic government (*al-hukuma al-nabawiyya*) had about it some of the characteristics of kingship.[27] He is especially concerned with the anomaly of jihad because it appears to have only a political justification, since the Qur'an explicitly forbids force in matters of belief. Jihad must be given some nonpolitical interpretation, or else we will be forced to conclude that the Prophet had a dual role (i.e., apostle and king) which for ʿAbd al-Raziq was a self-contradiction. There is, according to ʿAbd al-Raziq, nothing heretical about such a position, but it is not necessary to hold that opinion either.[28] Ibn Khaldun is the only one, according to ʿAbd al-Raziq, who has insisted that Islam requires both preaching and implementation, even though the latter may defeat the purpose of the former. Were Ibn Khaldun correct on the matter, we would have had a complete statement of the institutional requirements of the Islamic state from the Prophet. But we do not. The few statements we do have are so vague and incomplete that even the weaker argument for the simplicity and naturalness of the Islamic state cannot be sustained. ʿAbd al-Raziq concludes that the idea of an Islamic state is a self-contradiction, because Islam is religious only.

Having set up the problem, ʿAbd al-Raziq now proceeds to its solution by applying a rigid conceptual dualism to the institutional definition of the state and to the essential and inseparable differences between prophecy and kingship, between religion and the state, or between din and *dawla*. The only solution to the logical problem ʿAbd al-Raziq sets up, is to acknowledge that the Prophet had only the function of a prophetic mission and not that of a political ruler. ʿAbd al-Raziq describes the authority of the Prophet as far exceeding that of kings and other rulers, but prophetic authority is spiritual and not material. It is personal and charismatic, appealing directly to the heart and the consciousness.

Despite this essential distinction, ʿAbd al-Raziq states that a prophet must have power over his people if he is to succeed in his mission. Indeed, God does not send a messenger in vain. God intends such a messenger to suceed, so he is given "some sort of power which will prepare him to implement the word."[29] This seems to me to come quite close to the rejected position of Ibn Khaldun, regarding the dual function of those in authority in Islam. ʿAbd al-Raziq's position appears to be a quibble. The Prophet enjoyed tremendous, all-encompassing, power of a sort required in order to fulfill his mission. It was not political power in its essence, but in appearance, and in practice, it was very similar. ʿAbd al-Raziq even refers to the Prophetic government, and the *wilaya* (authority) of the Prophet. Nevertheless, this Prophetic regime did not have all of the institutional attributes which contemporary political scientists, according to ʿAbd al-Raziq, have determined to be necessary for a state to exist. This accounts for the vagueness or incompleteness of the reports regarding the organization of the government of the Prophet.

ʿAbd al-Raziq insists on a formal distinction between religion and the state. He then finds that the Prophetic regime was not a state as defined by political scientists, whose definition is invested with the same ontological validity as is the idea of Islamic religion. Hence, if the Prophetic regime was not a dawla, it must have been something else. Given the mission of the Prophet and the qur'anic encouragement of the Prophet when he met with serious political opposition, it is clear that the Prophetic regime was a pure Islamic religious essence, and not at all a political thing.

This line of reasoning is then further sustained by citing a long list of verses from the Qur'an, all of which call upon the Prophet to acknowledge that he is not a *wakil*, or has no *wikala* or political authority over those to whom he addresses the call. There seems to be some conflict between these verses and the most famous verse calling for obedience to the Prophet, but that does not detain ʿAbd al-Raziq. He is more concerned to establish that whatever power was enjoyed by the Prophet was derived from his prophetic mission. The logical consequence of this formal argument is that the caliphate cannot be a religious necessity because the caliph can only succeed the Prophet, who was the seal of prophecy, in his nonprophetic functions. Since the Prophet had no nonprophetic functions, the caliphate has no religious foundation.

At the end of this section of the book there is a further hint of the political purpose which may have animated ʿAbd al-Raziq's bold project. After describing Islam's universal summons to world brotherhood, ʿAbd al-Raziq is at pains to deny that Islam seeks to unify the whole world in a single Islamic state:

> It is reasonable for the whole world to have one religion, and for all of humanity to be organized in a religious unity, but for all of the world to be held by a single government and to be organized under a composite political unit, that would almost exceed human nature and would not accord with the will of God. That sort of thing is an earthly goal which Allah has left to our reason. He

has left humanity free to order their affairs according to whatever their reason and knowledge and interests and wishes and inclinations direct. The judgment of Allah is that mankind should remain diverse.[30]

It does not require much imagination to apply this view to the Muslim world as a whole, rather than to the rest of the world. It follows that ʿAbd al-Raziq did not believe that all of the Muslims should be joined in a single polity. The campaign to restore the caliphate did not necessarily entail the political unification of the Muslim countries, but it was related in an ideological sense, at least, to the declining pan-Islamic movement. In a more theoretical sense, however, ʿAbd al-Raziq is again insisting that Islam is not the legitimate basis of the state. The state can only have rational and natural grounds.

In the last section of the book ʿAbd al-Raziq is even more emphatic in rejecting the idea of pan-Arabism.

> Even though, the Islamic Shariʿa brought them together, the Arabs at that time did not cease in their erstwhile diversity in politics and in other spheres of civil, social, and economic life; which is to say that they constituted a multiplicity of states (*duwwalan shattan*) in accordance with the meaning that could be attributed to the notions of state and government, given [the nature of] Arab life at the time. . . . But the Arabs did not cease to be diverse nations (*umam*) . . . that was natural . . .[their diversity] lessened in intensity . . . but it is impossible to eliminate it in any way. . . . Arab unity, as we have seen, was Islamic and not political[31]

Since the Prophet did not die until his mission was complete, and since he said nothing regarding either an Islamic state or an Arab state, it follows that neither state can be understood as a religious necessity. The Prophet having had only a religious mission, could not be succeeded in that *risala diniyya;* hence he could not be succeeded in any way. Consequently—and here is the most scandalous conclusion—the caliphate was more or less secular [*naw'an la-dini*] and Abu Bakr was the first king in Islam. But somewhat more ambiguously: "The Arab state was established on the foundation of a religious appeal (*daʿwa*). Its ideal was the protection and the maintenance of that [religion]. Indeed, it had in actuality a great effect on matters having to do with that daʿwa. Its role in the development and transformation of that [daʿwa] was not negligible. Nevertheless, it did not surpass being (merely) an Arab state, supporting an Arab authority (sultan), and promoting Arab interests."[32]

The Reaction of the Ulama

The ulama ralized that they had much at stake in this issue precisely because it had become a political cause célèbre, and they could not let it pass in silence. Some of the ulama were also aware of the dangers of seeming merely to accommodate the wishes of the king, given the content of ʿAbd al-Raziq's book. Those who were responsible, therefore, were relatively cautious in the way in which they criticized the book, in order to avoid a sympathetic backlash which might obscure the doctrinal issues. The judgment of the Council of Higher Ulama concentrated on seven rather specific points of doctrine, and they avoided any more general criticisms that might be construed as political or even philosophical.

The seven points on which ʿAbd al-Raziq was mistaken according to the ulama were as follows:

1. Making of the Islamic Shariʿa a purely spiritual legislation, without any connection to governance or the administration of worldly affairs;
2. Holding that the Prophetic jihad was for the sake of kingly power and not to preach religion to all the world.
3. Holding that the organization of government during the time of the Prophet was unclear, confused, disturbed, incomplete, and that it caused perplexity (among those who tried to understand it);
4. Holding that the responsibility (*muhamma*) of the Prophet was only to promulgate the Shariʿa without governing or administering;
5. Negating the ijmaʿ of the Companions that the umma must have someone to manage its religious and worldly affairs, and regarding the obligatoriness of appointing an imam;
6. Denying that the *quda* [judgeship] is a Sharʿi function; and,
7. Holding the view that the government of Abu Bakr and of the Rightly Guided Caliphs after him was secular.

It will be readily noted that ʿAbd al-Raziq was not accused on any general theoretical grounds, but rather on what appear to be points of specific doctrine. ʿAbd al-Raziq was thrown on the defensive by these accusations, and he tried to minimize the deviationist impression he had made. He was not directly accused of denying that the Muslims necessarily constitute a political community, and in his reply he was content to state the permissive possibility of the jamaʿa establishing a state and setting a caliph over it. ʿAbd al-Raziq's defense pointed out that what he was accused of was not precisely what he said, or that in addition to saying these things, he also made some mitigating or explanatory statements.

ʿAbd al-Raziq straddled the issues of the political role of the

Prophet and the religious role of the Rightly Guided Caliphs, with an unsatisfactory result. Under pressure of the accusation, he emphasized what appeared to be common ground he shared with the ulama. Thus he repeats: "We do not doubt that Islam is a religious unit, and that the Muslims, as a consequence, are a single *jamaʿa,* and that the Prophet called for unity and that he achieved it before his death, and that he was at the head of the religious unit, its sole leader and singular *mudabbir* (administrator) and its lord whose word was not questioned."[33] And he continued: "And whoever wishes to call that religious unit a state, and to call the sultan (authority) of the Prophet—that absolute prophetic authority—a kingdom or a caliphate, and to call the Prophet a king or a caliph or a sultan, well, he may do so, because these are only names and there is no need to be detained by them."[34]

On the crucial fifth accusation, ʿAbd al-Raziq replied that it is not true that he denied the ijmaʿ of the Companions regarding the necessity of having someone in charge of the affairs of the umma. He does not similarly deny the charge that he negated the ijmaʿ regarding the appointment of an imam. He then quotes himself: "It is necessary that (any) organized umma, whatever might be its creed, and whatever might be its race, or color, or language, have a government to deal with its affairs. . . . Indeed, Abu Bakr, was only referring to that opinion when he said in his sermon . . ." this religion (din) needs someone to direct it."[35]

A somewhat more confusing exchange between ʿAbd al-Raziq and a group of ulama was published in *al-Siyasa* on 1 September 1925. In that exchange, the ulama quote a previous statement by ʿAbd al-Raziq in which he is purported to have said that Islam is a legislating (Sharʿi) religion, and that Muslims are obliged to establish the Shariʿa, that God charged them with such a task, and specifically commanded them to set up a government to carry out that work; but that He left it up to the Muslims to decide what sort of government it might be.

The ulama went on to ask his view of the legitimate claims of a government set up by "the Muslims" after consultation and after deciding to acknowledge (*yubayʿu*) someone as "entrusted with the affairs of the Muslims." This, of course was the traditionally legal method of appointing the caliph. ʿAbd al-Raziq answered:

> If the jamaʿa of the Muslims were of the opinion that it was in the interest of the Muslims that the government should be a caliphate, then in that case the caliphate would be Sharʿi and obedience to it in all matters not contrary to the Shariʿa would be obligatory; and if they thought some other form of government, not the caliphate, might accord with the interests of the Muslims, then that

> form . . . would be Sharʿi. . . . And as for the governments of the rightly guided caliphs and their bayʿa according to what we know from history, they were established and worked out in accordance with the approval of the generality of the Muslims, to take care of their religious and worldly interests, and therefore, obedience to them was properly obligatory.[36]

In this last statement, ʿAbd al-Raziq appears to be completely browbeaten. One wonders where the original quote was published, and whether the whole thing was not contrived by the editors of *al-Siyasa* to take the heat off ʿAbd al-Raziq. His new position is the standard orthodox position, in that it calls for the politicization of religion, for the religious determination of the political community, and defines the religious responsibilities of the head of state. The answer to the query regarding the authority of the Rightly Guided Caliphs represents a backing away from his refutation of the ijmaʿ upon which the caliphate was said to be based.

ʿImara's Analysis: Islamic Liberalism

The findings of the Court of Higher Ulama were cautiously directed at limiting the scope of the controversy to points of Islamic doctrine, but not so the critique of ʿImara. ʿImara has his own substantive views on the general question of Islamic government, views which reflect the preferences of the liberals who generally approve of the teachings of Muhammad ʿAbduh, and who are inclined to read Ibn Khaldun in the light of those teachings. ʿImara faults ʿAbd al-Raziq for deviating from that liberal position, but he does not seem to feel that ʿAbd al-Raziq has harmed the liberal cause. Quite the contrary, he seems to believe that ʿAbd al-Raziq has helped the liberals, because he has raised some questions that only they seem able to answer effectively, while apparently placing them in the position of moderates who remain within the Sunni mainstream.

ʿImara writes that ʿAbd al-Raziq was mistaken in some parts of his work, but he assumes that ʿAbd al-Raziq's theoretical intentions were the same as those of the mainstream liberals. Drawing on an article on the political theory of Muhammad ʿAbduh published in *al-Siyasa* (6 July 1925), he argues that the ideas of ʿAbd al-Raziq are a "developed extension of the ideas of ʿAbduh."[37] The most important citations which ʿImara has assembled from the works of ʿAbduh are that

> . . . the umma has the right of control over [the caliph], and it can remove him whenever it is in its interest, for he is a civil ruler from every point of view.[38]

> In the proper view, it is incorrect to confuse the caliphate according to the Muslims with what the Westerners call theocratic government.[39]
>
> It is not incumbent upon the Muslim to accept his creed or the principles of his behavior in that regard [i.e., the creed] from anyone, except from the Book of Allah and the *Sunna* of His Prophet . . . for there is nothing in Islam that might be called . . . a religious authority in any way. . . . The Shari'a does not provide for an explicit means of putting together a government nor for a given way of counselling the rulers, just as it does not prohibit any preferred way of expressing what is desired of [government]. Consultation is a *sharᶜi* requirement, but the manner of implementation is not restricted to a particular way. . . .
> . . . the incentive for those wars (*Khawarij* and *Qaramita*) [heretical groups] was not a disagreement over doctrines. They were kindled by political opinions regarding the way in which the *umma* should be governed; they did not fight the caliphs in order to gain victory for a creed, but in order to change the form of government. And the war between the Umayyads and Hashemites was not [over doctrine] it was rather over the caliphate, and that is similar to politics, or rather the very root of politics.[40]

I think that ᶜImara has made a very good case for the influence of ᶜAbduh on ᶜAbd al-Raziq in a very general way, but that does not mean that ᶜAbd al-Raziq was expressing ᶜAbduh's views. It is apparent that ᶜAbd al-Raziq went considerably beyond ᶜAbduh in rejecting the caliphate. Nevertheless, we note the emphasis upon individual conviction and interpretation of the Qur'an and Sunna and the even more questionable linkage between this formalist approach to the Shariᶜa and individual participation in the democratic political process. ᶜImara is probably reading ᶜAbduh correctly as seeking an Islamic ground for legitimating the liberal regime of parliamentary democracy as developed in western Europe.

ᶜAbd al-Raziq does not provide an Islamic legitimation of democracy at all. He argues that Islam has nothing to do with the state, and hence cannot legitimate any form of government. Since government is a matter of reason or human preference and not revelation, democracy or any other form of government can only be based on a natural ground. ᶜAbd al-Raziq may have been optimistic that, in the long run, human nature, human reason, and the natural condition of human beings might lead to democratic government; but his recitation of historical events leads to the opposite conclusion. He may have felt that the sorry history of politics in Islam was the consequence of mixing religion and the state, and that changing this condition was a crucial precondition for the emergence of the rational state. Nevertheless, it is clear that he departed from the other liberals in not offering an Islamic justification for democracy, and in denying that a political community of Muslims was the proper locus for the establishment of an Islamic democracy.

Though ʿImara reads ʿAbd al-Raziq's book with general approval as an extension of ʿAbduh, he has four major criticisms: (1) that ʿAbd al-Raziq fails to appreciate the degree to which the Prophet's achievements were political; (2) that he is confused and self-contradictory regarding the religious achievements of the first caliphs; (3) that he cites historical and poetic sources anachronistically, and that he draws incorrect conclusions from some qur'anic and hadith sources; and, (4) that he was inclined to overemphasize the oriental elements in Islamic thought and history, especially the image of oriental despotism. ʿImara's development of these criticisms is especially useful as an illustration of the views of at least one intelligent contemporary Islamic liberal:

> We believe that the author's evaluation of the experiment made by the Prophet is one of the weakest points in the book, because the unity of political authority and religious authority at the time of the Prophet is a matter which has become virtually certain through study after study; and that was due to many reasons, among the foremost of which are the unity of the being of the man who guided that unification, and the experience within the being of the man who received the inspiration from the heavens. . . . What probably motivated the author to fall into this contradiction, was his concern to deny that Islam established a "religious government," and we think that it must have seemed natural to deny [religious government] in Islam after the period of the Prophet . . . the connection here between religion and politics is one of "distinction" and not of "separation or detachment," just as it is not a relationship of "unity, congruence, or blending." The source of the mistake here, and the reason that caused him to fall into this contradiction, was his failure to elaborate the broad outlines, values, and general laws of the civic order, which Islam calls upon the people to establish in accordance with their interests, and in accordance with the broad outlines, values, and general laws of Islam. These two sets of conditions are brought into harmony by means of coordination (*al-tatabuq*) [i.e., an external relationship rather than an identity]. . . . This [mistake] is the result of the regretable hiatus that separates various conceptual and intellectual structures which . . .[are the] consequence of the prestige of that "idealist" thought which is contrary to the scientific thought and method.[41]

Quoting ʿAbd al-Raziq that Allah has given man a "free hand" to apply reason in matters of this world, ʿImara agrees in general but goes on to say that ʿAbd al-Raziq draws an inappropriate conclusion, "and that is that what is left to reason has no relationship to religion. . . . Nevertheless, no one has said, and no one will say that knowledge of God—because the way thereunto is reason only—has no connection to religion."[42] And ʿImara continues:

> The picture of the caliph and the *imam* which is scattered about the pages of the book . . . is alien to the spirit of Islam. [This distorted picture] came into the practical political Islamic life either by means of Shiʿite thought regarding the Imamate . . . and that thought is an extension of the feudal theories of the Persians . . . or by means of the government of the Umayyads which was impressed since the time of Muʿawiyya ibn Abi Sufyan with the imprint of the imperial throne of Byzantium, whose tradition prevailed in Damascus in Syria from before the time of Islam. . . . As for the intellectual tendency which correctly expresses the spirit of Islam and its general teachings and its general laws in this matter, that is the intellectual tendency of the Muʿtazila, and those of the Khawarij who agree with them. They are the ones who determined that the method of appointing the imam is the method of "selection, fealty, and contract" (*ikhtiyar wa'l-bayʿa wa'l-aqd*) of the imam by the umma . . . and the only legitimating support of the imam is the umma and not some absent authority; and that the removal of the imam is solely the responsibility of the umma and therefore this office is a political one, even though it is not devoid of all connection with the teachings of religion.[43]

These views of ʿImara have been translated and presented at length because they are intrinsically interesting as a statement of the liberal position, and because they may be contrasted with the emphases in the work of ʿAbd al-Raziq. Not every liberal will agree, for example, with ʿImara's flat statement that the Muʿtazila and the Khawarij were correct in their theories of the caliphate, but most would agree with the more general implication that there is such a thing as an Islamic political community, or at least a community, or several communities, which are to be governed by rulers who must take account of Islamic teachings. This implication is absent from the work of ʿAbd al-Raziq, and it is in this regard, it seems to me, that he has gone beyond the consensus of the Sunni community. This is by no means meant to condemn him, and certainly not to justify the judgment against him, but rather to point out what the nature of the minimal consensus is. ʿImara's emphasis on the generalities of the Islamic teaching touches on questions in dispute among those who apparently fall within the consensus—with those who insist that the mark of an Islamic state is the enforcement of the disembodied particularities of the Shariʿa being called fundamentalists, and those who believe that the umma has the right and duty to determine the particularities on the basis of a set of constructed generalities being called the liberals.

The Critique of Dr. Rayyis: An Attenuated Liberalism

The distinction between the Islamic liberal position and that of ʿAli ʿAbd al-Raziq is made even more apparent in the almost exasperated polemical critique of Dr. Muhammad Zia al-Din al-Rayyis, a professor of Islamic institutions (*al-nuzum*) at Cairo University.[45] Dr. al-Rayyis has no sympathy whatsoever for ʿAbd al-Raziq, and even less charity for his defenders. Dr. al-Rayyis is especially exercised over the defense of ʿAbd al-Raziq which appeared in the work, by the distinguished journalist Ahmad Baha al-Din, entitled *Ayyam laha tarikh* (Days which have a history). In that book, Baha al-Din has lionized ʿAbd al-Raziq as the courageous opponent of a collusive plot between the British and King Fuad to gain for the latter the dignity of the caliphate and to gain, thereby, for the former some influence over the entire Muslim world. Despite the "whodunnit" approach taken by al-Rayyis, and despite the lack of precise citation of sources, and despite the disconcerting self-serving elements in the book, Dr. al-Rayyis presents a serious case that ʿAbd al-Raziq was neither heroic defender of Egyptian independence nor very knowledgeable about the subject of the caliphate.

Al-Rayyis argues that, for both political and cultural reasons, it was entirely natural that Arab Muslims should seek to recapture and reestablish the caliphate after its shocking abolition by Ataturk. He credits the published statement of King Fuad that he was not particularly anxious to take on new burdens in addition to ruling Egypt. He praises the patriotism of those Egyptians who wished to see an Arab caliphate established in Egypt. He inclines toward the view that the ulama of al-Azhar were more enthusiastic than the king about the idea, but he concedes that the king had despotic ambitions, so he was easily tempted by the idea of becoming caliph. Hence, al-Rayyis argues that it was entirely plausible that patriotic Egyptians, motivated at once by visions of an Arab and an Islamic political renaissance of which Egypt would be the greatest beneficiary, should seek to return the caliphate to Egypt whence, according to some, it had been seized by the Ottomans in A.D. 1517.

Al-Rayyis admits that these patriots were quite willing to strengthen the authority of the monarch, and even to subvert the new Egyptian constitution, but he denies that the central issue was originally that of the constitutional struggle against authoritarianism. His argument on this point is based on the fact that, at the time, the court had succeeded in replacing Saʿd Zaghlul's Wafd-dominated "people's government" with a coalition of the Liberal Constitutionalists and the Unionist parties. The Liberal Constitutionalists, he argues, were long-standing allies of the British, having been derived from the prewar Ummah party. That party had been established, with British support, to oppose the Nationalist (Watani) Party of Mustapha Kamil, which sought to weaken British influence in Egypt by reaffirming the suzerainty of the Ottoman caliph-sultan. Hence al-Rayyis insists on the pro-British and secular-liberal position of the important personalities and notable families connected with the Ummah and Liberal Constitutional parties. Among those families was that of ʿAli ʿAbd al-Raziq.

According to al-Rayyis, the Liberal-Constitutionalists had no interest in weakening the governing coalition of which they were a part. On the other hand, the Liberal-Constitutionalist cabinet ministers could not acquiesce in the punishment of a member of one of their most prominent families. This dilemma was exploited by the Unionist Party, which wished to rule alone, and which was prepared to pander to the absolutist inclinations of Fuad. Hence, according to al-Rayyis, the ulama of al-Azhar, acting in good religious faith, did what was necessary to preserve sound religious doctrine. The constitutional guarantees were not breached in that the book was not banned, and still circulates. The formal act of denying ʿAbd al-Raziq's competence as a religious scholar required the signature of the minister of justice. The minister of justice, a member of the Liberal-Constitutionalists, refused to sign. He was dismissed. The rest of the Liberal-Constitutionalist cabinet members resigned in protest and left the coalition.

Despite his emphasis on the affinities between the British and the Liberal Constitutionalists, al-Rayyis does not argue that the British instigated the publication of the book, or that the leadership of the Liberal-Constitutionalists was behind it. He blames the publication on the simple-minded gullibility of ʿAbd al-Raziq, which at once justified the action of the ulama in withdrawing his *alimiyya* (religious degree) and opened him to the sinister influence of the British.

Through textual analysis, al-Rayyis tries to establish that important sections of the work were written during World War I, when the British were especially interested in discrediting the Ottoman caliph's call for a jihad against the Allies. During this period, British and German orientalists did engage in a propaganda-oriented polemic regarding the validity of the Ottoman caliphate, one of the products of which is the book by T. W. Arnold, *The Caliphate*.[46] Al-Rayyis believes that most of *al-Islam wa-Usul al-Hukm* was written during the war, and that much of it may have been written by a British orientalist—possibly D. S. Margoliouth or T. W. Arnold, or one of their students. He further believes that ʿAbd al-Raziq appropriated their work as his own, with or without their encouragement, and that he decided to publish this work during the crucial period following the abolition of the Ottoman caliphate in order to gain personal notoriety. Consequently those who have so lavishly praised ʿAbd al-Raziq, especially Baha al-Din and Muhammad ʿImara, have been taken in by a simple-minded fellow.

Far from being a hero who had opposed an absolutist monarch and the imperialist British, ʿAbd al-Raziq was an intellectual incompetent who had been suborned by a Jewish-Zionist, British orientalist who was bent on weakening the political solidarity of the Muslims. The medium of this ideologial subversion was, obviously, the Western liberal doctrine of the separation of church and state. Margoliouth, as is well known, was of Jewish origin, but a second-generation Christian and an ordained minister. He does not seem to have been a Zionist, though he was British. There is, however, the possibility that his views did influence ʿAbd al-Raziq in some instances, such as his statements that "Islam had till the nineteenth century no constitutional lawyers: and the works which are said to deal with constitutional law in the main consist of definitions" (p. 94); and "The principle of autocratic government may be said to have remained unquestioned in Islamic states until the nineteenth century" (p. 53); and "[Muhammad] established no hierarchy of officials. . . . He made no permanent appointments: the officials appointed by him were purely for the occasion" (p. 80).[47]

Nevertheless, al-Rayyis is least convincing when he suggests that the publication of the book was the result of an imperalist-Zionist conspiracy to divide and rule the Muslims by preventing the establishment of an Arab caliphate. Here his argument is based upon a far-fetched deduction, the foundation of which is the doctrinal and practical necessity of the caliphate. The hostility of imperialism and Zionism to the interests of the Muslims is axiomatic, while the association of a Muslim, Egyptian Arab educated at al-Azhar with such views is a manifest anomaly. Hence ʿAli ʿAbd al-Raziq could not have known what he was doing, and he cannot be credited with simply having a different view of the interests of Muslims or of Islamic values. Further evidence for this interpretation is found by al-Rayyis in certain "un-Arabic" phrasings in the text, and in the expression of some views regarding the Rightly Guided Caliphs of which no Muslim was capable.

Despite the fact that al-Rayyis utterly rejects the secular liberal position found in ʿAbd al-Raziq's book, he goes on to present his own theory of the caliphate in a manner which includes a number of liberal democratic elements. In fact it may be said that al-Rayyis's theory of the caliphate is typical of the apolegetic position of mainstream Islamic liberalism. As is appropriate, al-Rayyis totally rejects the idea that any substantial group of Muslims believed in the "divine right" of the caliphs.

> The source of authority is the choice by the umma of the khalifa, either by a valid acclamation (bayʿa) or by election. This is the position of the great majority of Muslims and it is the position of all the Sunnis, and the Muʿtazilis, and all the Murjiʿis, and all the Kharijis—and these constitute the great majority of the Islamic umma. Hence the position of the Muslims is that the umma is the basis, or as modern constitutions put it, it is the source of [constitutional] powers.[48]
>
> . . . the Caliph is only the executor of the Shariʿa under the supervision of the umma.[49]

Al-Rayyis argues similarly, in accordance with well established Sunni doctrine, that the canonical basis of the caliphate is in the ijmaʿ of the umma, all the members of which agreed upon the need to have someone replace the prophet "in preserving the religion, perpetuating it, in administering its Shariʿa, in protecting its *umma,* and in preaching its message to the remaining parts of the world" (p. 246). This doctrine of ijmaʿ is, in fact, a recognition by the Shariʿa of "the general will of the *umma* . . . as sacred" (p. 253). But ijmaʿ should not be taken as rigidifying the Shariʿa, for the sacred sources have only set down principles and have not specified how these principles are to be realized. These general principles include, especially, complete justice and the common good, to be achieved by means of discussion, deliberation and consensus. Thus we see that the Shariʿa "is, in the final analysis, a humane and social [not a theocratic] Shariʿa, based on reason, the virtues, and the common good of the *umma*" (p. 255).

Allah has called upon the Muslims to obey their rulers, which is to say the caliphs or their equivalents, but only on the condition that these political authorities rule with justice (*ʿadl*) "and justice means to rule according to what God has revealed as the Shariʿa of Islam" (p. 257). Obedience is thus conditional, and justice is grounded in the Qur'an and Sunna, even if it is applied by means of reason and consensus. The resultant arrangement is a state, and it is absolutely obligatory, according to al-Rayyis, that the Muslims establish such a state. The Muslim community, he says flatly, "is a community characterized by a political being" (p. 258).

It is true that Muhammad did not designate his successor (according to Sunni doctrine) but that does not prove that he never intended to establish a continuing political community. It is rather evidence of his desire to leave the umma free to choose, "thus recognizing the right of the umma. . . . So Islam established the . . . first principle of democracy and made it the basis upon which the Islamic state would stand" (p. 261). This Islamic state has but "one form and that is a democratic consultative state, bound by the Islamic constitution, or simply al-hukuma al-Islamiyya" (pp. 263–64).

The authoritative sources for this doctrine of the Islamic state are not only the Qur'an and Sunna and the consensus of the community in their usual jurisprudential senses, but include what al-Rayyis calls the practical Sunna of the Prophet, whence we derive the meaning of the Prophet's designation of Abu Bakr as his successor, and whence we can derive his intentions of establishing an Islamic state. But the very principle of the practical Sunna charges the Muslims with the need to adapt their explication of the Shariʿa to the prevailing historical circumstances—including the practical explication of the principles regarding the caliphate itself.

With this, al-Rayyis turns his attention to the refutation of what he considers to be ʿAbd al-Raziq's gross distortions of the history of the caliphate. As we have seen, the most objectionable of ʿAbd al-Raziq's statements were that the Prophet established only an imperfect state or no state in the political sense, that the regime of Abu Bakr was, in fact, virtually secular, that the caliphate was based on coercive force, that no caliph was ever legitimated by a true consensus, and that the caliphate became a form of tyranny, and hence was all but an unmitigated disaster for the Muslims.

ʿAbd al-Raziq's statements are certainly exaggerated, but they do reflect the influence of medieval historians who tended to judge both the Umayyads and the Abbasids quite harshly. While the critical assessment of the Rightly Guided Caliphs scandalized most Muslims, there is something to be said for a more balanced interpretation of the Wars of Apostacy as a test of the willingness of many Arabian tribes to perpetuate the political organization initiated by the Prophet. However this may be, al-Rayyis felt constrained to refute ʿAbd al-Raziq by outdoing him in hyperbole, and the result is an unrealistic and unhistorical legitimation of virtually all the caliphs up to A.D. 1924.

Al-Rayyis does distinguish the office from its incumbent, he does insist on the incorrectness of the view that religion and politics are essentially distinct, and he does allow for changing circumstances. But he does not accept Ibn Khaldun's position that the caliphate declined into kingship. The most that he is willing to conceed is that the Ottoman caliphate was somewhat tainted. Nevertheless, the function of the caliphate as a symbol of unity, as a source of political solidarity, and as defender of the faith was maintained throughout history, and the failure to maintain it at the present time is a source of the weakness of the Muslims and represents the successful policy of the enemies of Islam. The caliphate must be reestablished.

But the reestablishment of the caliphate in modern times is to be adapted to the political and intellectual standards of the times. Accordingly, we find his argument for the caliphate to be a translation of his functional analysis of the caliphate as a useful political institution insofar as the community of Muslims is concerned. Hence, the purposes of the Caliphate are to be achieved by institutions which are acceptable by contemporary standards. The title caliph itself is unimportant. The neo-caliphate should be collegial, elected, and periodically renewable. It should include an executive, a legislature, and a judiciary. It should concentrate on foreign affairs, and it should not supersede the governments of existing Muslim states or transnational groupings such as the Arab League. It should uphold the Shariʿa. It should deal with disputes among Muslim states and produce a permanent alliance against their external enemies. It should bear major responsibility for preaching the Islamic message worldwide toward the ultimate end of uniting all of mankind in a single political and religious entity. Thus, in his concluding chapter, al-Rayyis leaves the reader wondering about the seriousness of his praise of the caliphate as an exemplary political institution, since he now frankly borrows from the structure of the United Nations to propose a complex international organization devoted to the interests of Islam without, at the same time, indicating how this development might impinge on the other interests of Muslim states, nations, sects, and classes.

> The truth is that we have found that Islamic jurisprudence has proven to be flexible in its view of changing circumstances, and in the development of legislation so that it will accord with new things. Thus, in the past, when conditions changed, the *fiqh* (jurisprudence) recognized the theory of the delegation of political authority from the Caliph . . . to a *wazir* or to a cabinet of ministers; and the [legitimacy of a] plurality of Caliphs—or governments—if the regions [inhabited by Muslim communities] were distant [from one another], and the self-determination of regions (*ʿaqalim*) by either choice or force . . . so long as the unity (of Islam) was recognized and so long as there was someone to represent that unity. For all that the Islamic fiqh intends is that the Shariʿa be implemented, and that the Muslims, in the East and in the West, and in all the various regions, be joined together

> against . . . their enemies . . . and that there be discipline and cooperation and mutual assistance among them all. (Pp. 384–85)

> . . . it is indispensible that there be an office or an organization that represents the unity of the umma in general, and realizes the common interests of all the states of which the Islamic world is comprised, and that [the Muslims] should have a common leadership. Thus will be realized the great principle which Islam requires, and that is the unity of all the Muslims, as Allah, the exalted, said, "And hold fast together to the rope of God and do not separate." And this is the true essence of the caliphate, acting in place of the messenger, blessings upon him, in the leadership of his umma. . . . However—as we have explained—the caliphate must take a developed form in the modern period, conforming to the political and constitutional progress which has occured. (P. 358)

These two passages are not only illustrative of the style of Professor al-Rayyis, but also of the peculiar combination of traditional Islamic and modern European institutions which he desires to achieve. It is, however, primarily a combination of forms which he seeks. His historical analysis crudely correlates the glorious achievements of Muslims with the nominal existence of some caliphal institutions. The Shariʿa is flexible to the point where the caliphal obligation may be fulfilled in any manner deemed suitable by prevailing opinion. The essence of that obligation is, however, that the Muslims constitute a political community, though not an exclusive one. He is willing to accept several overlapping political communities, so long as none of them contradicts the essential principle that Muslims share common political interests. Once again, the centrality of the notion of political identity and community is manifest. The stigmata, which differentiate this group from others, are religious in one or more of several possible senses of the term. The liberal elements of his doctrine—democracy, individual rights, the legitimacy of opposition, the role of reason and deliberation, justice and the like—are brought into question because these liberal values are attributed to the Shariʿa virtually by definition. While the common opinion of modern times will affect the way in which these principles are understood, they are not otherwise referred to reason or nature or history.

Al-Rayyis's own condemnation of ʿAbd al-Raziq's "ignorance" and his manifest intellectual elitism, renders his doctrine vulnerable to exploitation by an authoritarian religious intellectual elite claiming superior knowledge of the content of the Shariʿa—as has occurred in Iran. The insistence that Islam unites religion and politics and that Islam is freedom, justice, and equality by definition, even if intended to break down the barriers between traditional Islamic political practice and the modern European political ideal, can result in an illiberal regime. The tension is not only between a literal and a flexible interpretation of the law, but between the idea that a given modern interpretation carries the sacred character of consensus itself and the alternative view (which al-Rayyis does convey) that it is important to distinguish between the sacredness of consensus itself and the contingency of particular rulings.

The gravest danger to liberal government arises when the application of a general Shariʿa rule to particular circumstances is given the sacred character of the word of God. The Iranian experience suggests that this is more likely to be the case where the state fears opposition and is anxious to consolidate power. Thus the apparent reasonableness of offering a modern functional interpretation of the Islamic state, in terms of the "emancipatory" interests of the Muslims, may subordinate liberal values, not to traditional dogma, but to the pursuit of the consolidation of state power.

The polemical tone of this last(?) work of professor al-Rayyis reflects his vexation that an issue which he himself had long since helped to lay aside should be revived by ignorant, ill-informed, secular liberals. His barely concealed irritation at their ignorance of his own work is matched by the implication that those who would revive the secularist doctrine of ʿAli ʿAbd al-Raziq are somehow serving the interests of foreign and hostile powers rather than advocating a form of political liberalism. Despite the severity of this implied accusation, the "objective" differences between the secularist and the scripturalist liberals seem minor. Both have in mind the same sort of regime and similar institutions. How these will work out in practice may be more a question of dominant classes and hegemonic cultural context in which either a form of political rationality or logical exegesis will be pursued. In some sense, or at least to some extent, the issue is one of a conflict between two factions of the intellectual elite, one of which purveys a secular reason and the other a scripturalist apologetic.

ʿAbd al-Raziq's departure from the rationalist exegetical position of ʿAbduh appears to have been an attack on his own class, or at least on his colleagues in the religious establishment. One of the reasons why his book was so bitterly rejected is because it would narrow the scope of the relevance of religious expertise and reduce the value of religious legitimacy. ʿAbd al-Raziq tried, but failed, to remove political reasoning from the scripturalist framework in which it was firmly fixed. In the face of such secularizing threats, many of the ulama joined the Islamic professoriate at the state universities in adopting the formula of Muhammad ʿAbduh, and thus entered into a tacit alliance with the emergent bourgeoisie and the parliamentary elites of the monarchist interlude.

But the liberal Islamic apologetic is systematically ambiguous, since it does not clearly distinguish between the two formulations: that Islam is democratic and that democracy is Islamic. It is this ambiguity which is the ground of the apparent agreement among the religious establishment, the fundamentalist movement, and the Islamic liberals. But the very idea of a religious establishment as a differentiated administrative organization devoted to the implementation of specified areas of public policy, is alien to the fundamentalist conception of Islam as a religion without a priesthood, and one in which religious structures are indistinguishable from state structures. The institutional interests of the ulama are clearly tied, not only to the other state structures of which they are a part, but also to the bourgeois parliamentary system, which sustains both institutional pluralism and the system of "positive" law. The parliamentary system offers the ulama the possibility of acquiring their own constituency, of forming alliances, of protecting the legally defined institutional integrity of their own administrative structures, and of putting a brake on arbitrary, sweeping, and possibly revolutionary reinterpretations or applications of the Shariʿa. There is a great deal of risk entailed in simply declaring the Shariʿa to be the law of the land rather than declaring that the Shariʿa will serve as the major source of legislation. Under present circumstances, in Egypt at any rate, it is the constitutional system itself which sustains the privileged role of the ulama in interpreting the Shariʿa, even if that function is shared with the parliament and "public opinion." Some ulama are doubtlessly willing to accept the extremist fundamentalist formula that Islam is neither democratic, nor constitutional, nor socialist, nor anything else but simply Islamic. Most, however, cannot conceive of themselves in the role of a Khomeini, and they fear the consequences of the emergence of a charismatic leader of a clandestine band of violent religious revolutionaries who would overthrow the present institutional amalgam and establish a millenial Islamic regime.

Shaykh Khalid Muhammad Khalid Recants

Nowhere is this fear and confusion better expressed than in the brief but embarrassing book in which Shaykh Khalid Muhammad Khalid retracts his earlier commitment to the separation of religion and state in Islam. Thirty-one years after the original publication of his sensational reformist book, *Min Huna Nabda'* (*From here we begin*), Khalid lamely admits his error and, in boldfaced type, declares that Islam is both religion and state.[50]

One recent commentator sees this change of heart as no more than a manifestation of the changed religious climate, a consequence of the Islamic resurgence.[51] Still, it is to be remembered that, among the many intellectuals who quietly submitted to the intimidating power and the permeating ideological influence of the Nasser regime, Khalid stood out as one who, at least on occasion, defended liberal democracy and criticized state policy publically and even to Nasser's face.

There is nothing very innovative in the alternative doctrine which Khalid now proposes. His new position is hardly to be distinguished from that of Professor al-Rayyis, from whose earlier writings he borrows freely. Islam is both religion and state. The Muslims constitute a political community, and it follows in nature as well as in doctrine that they must have a form of political organization. The Islamic state is democratic, constitutional, tolerant, committed to scientific and technological progress, and committed as well to engage only in defensive wars against powers that initiate hostilities. At the same time, Khalid recounts the long list of pre-Islamic Arab states and emirates and kingdoms, proudly affirming the political heritage of the Arabs in both the practical and theoretical realms. History, the natural order of creation, and revelation, all combine to affirm that Islam is at once *din wa dawla*.

But Khalid's swift restatement is not without some surprising, or at least interesting, echoes of fundamentalist themes. The most important of these is his repeated emphasis upon the idea that the Qur'an is the constitution of the Islamic state—a position mitigated only by a lesser emphasis on the Sunna and on ijmaʿ as supplementary constitutional elements.[52] Khalid also draws upon the little-used verses from Sura *al-Ma'ida*, which are the core of the fundamentalist claim that there is an explicit qur'anic textual requirement that an Islamic state be established. The same verses justified the extremists who declared that Sadat was killed in accordance with the qur'anic injunction that those who do not rule in accordance with God's law are heretics.[53] Khalid comes close to declaring the political sovereignty of God in the Islamic state, and he frequently quotes Ibn Taiymiyya (though not exclusively) who has become the preferred authority for some of the most extreme groups.

There are, however, other, contradictory themes in his exposition. The most striking of these is Khalid's high regard for the culture of the pre-Islamic Arabs, an opinion which stands in sharp contrast to the fundamentalist concept of the jahiliyya. Khalid does not hide his strong nationalist inclinations. In fact, he writes that "Wherever one finds an umma (community) comprised of a common language, ethnicity, and religion . . . and where there is a territory or a homeland (watan) inhabited by that umma . . . and where there is a 'higher sovereignty' (*sulta ʿaliya*) which orders the affairs of that community, there do we find a state."[54] Thus Khalid declares that the Prophetic community was in fact a state, in contrast to the view of ʿAbd al-Raziq, but his argument is historical and social rather than doctrinal and textual.

Khalid suggests that Islamic government is based on contract; in one place comparing the appointment of the caliph to a social contract, and in another suggesting that Islamic government entails a sort of contract between God and the rulers.[55]

On the matter of jihad, Khalid is clearly opposed to Mawdudi and Qutb and most fundamentalists in declaring that in Islam war is always defensive. He softens this statement, though, by asserting that Islam is not embarrassed to be a "religion of war" when the Muslims are attacked, and he adds that in such a case war is an obligation (*faridha*) echoing the title of the extremist tract of ʿAbd al-Salam al-Faraj.[56] Finally, Khalid insists, against the view of both the fundamentalists and of the reactionary Shaykh al-Sha'arawi, that it is not only incumbent upon the ruler to consult the representatives of the people, but that the majority view is binding on the caliph.[57]

There are too many easy explanations that can be suggested to account for Shaykh Khalid's inconsistency, so none can be readily validated. Nevertheless, it may be instructive to return to his recantation and the explanation he offers for it. Khalid excuses his earlier error by admitting that he was influenced by two matters, both of which are extraneous to the issue of the Islamic state. The first of these was his mistaken identification of the historical experience of Muslim authoritarianism with the Christian experience of the theocratic state. The second was his dismay upon learning of the terrorist activities of the "secret apparatus" of the Muslim Brotherhood during the 1940s.[58] Upon reflection, he has come to the conclusion that the unity of religion and government in Islam need not produce the same results as did Christian theocracy. That leaves the question of religious terrorism, doesn't it?

The two explanations or excuses offered by Shaykh Khalid neatly balance the two greatest contemporary challenges to Islamic liberalism: Western cultural influence and fundamentalist extremism. I am inclined to believe that Khalid's recantation was not an act of recreance, even though the atmosphere of the ongoing *kulturkampf* is often menacing. Doubtlessly, he was trying to draw attention to his position and to get an audience. He may also have chosen to express himself in a way that would draw the attention of those who were influenced by the fundamentalists. But dropping the idea of the separation of religion and the state in Islam was little more than sensationalizing his acceptance of what is now a broad consensual agreement. Liberalism can no longer be based on the argument of ʿAli ʿAbd al-Raziq if it is to succeed. What Shaykh Khalid was trying to do was to join his colleagues in seeking new and more effective ways of legitimating the idea of liberal government in Islam.

Mohammed Arkoun: Islamic Structuralism

Writing from Paris, Professor Mohammed Arkoun of the Sorbonne criticizes ʿAli ʿAbd al-Raziq and Taha Husain for their naiveté in believing that they might demystify two of the most significant cultural symbols of Islam: the political role of the Prophet and the divine origin of qur'anic rhetoric.[59] But, in spite of this criticism, Arkoun does not advocate compromise with the orthodox tradition or the prudent acquiescence in state policies of supporting established Islamic institutions.

Arkoun is a critic of both the orthodox tradition and of the objectivism and positivism which permeates not only Western science but also Western orientalism. He argues that the orientalist paradigm actually sustains the orthodox conceptions of "Islamic reason" by utilizing the same categories, the same symbols, and the same significations.[60] Orthodox Islam is dominated by *logocentrisme,* a deconstructionist variant of the Anglo-Saxon notion of scripturalism. The ulama and the fuqaha believe that they can seize and control the truth of revelation by means of grammatical and lexical analysis of the text, on the assumption that language is essentially a reflection of the world and that the foundation of the Qur'an is a set of facts. Instead, Arkoun refers to Islam itself and the Qur'an as facts, that is, as phenomena which have evolved historically to shape the understanding of the words despite the efforts of the ulama to capture and fix the meaning of holy writ.[61] The error of the ulama and the fuqaha resides in their belief that their knowledge of language gives them access to the text, whereas they ignore the deeper truth of the historicity of language itself.

> Tout l'effort pour connaître le vrai (al-haqq) consiste donc, en fait, en une soumission totale (taqlid) a l'autorité du texte coranique dont l'immanence linguistique est nécessairement confondue avec la transcendance de la Volonté de Dieu. . . . Par suite, l'usage correct des regles grammaticales et lexicologiques de l'arabe suffit a garantir la validité permanente des significations.[62]

Arkoun has been deeply influenced by recent trends in French academic thought, especially by structural linguistics and the attempt to reconstruct all of the social sciences and humanities in the structuralist image. He has also been influenced by more recent poststructuralist writings such as those of Foucault and the deconstructionism of Derrida. In contrast to Said, however, Arkoun does not read these sources as negating the value of dialogue, or of the study of other cultures. Instead, he insists, with impressive effect, on citing the strong similarities among the intellectual developments of the three monotheistic religious communities whom he refers to generally as people of the book (*Ahl al-Kitab*) hence as equally vulnerable to logocentrism.[63]

Structuralism includes a variety of diverse intellectual tendencies, and Arkoun is eclectic rather than selective, preferring to emphasize the general methodological principles upon which his own critique of Islamic reason is based rather than engage in a critique of rival structuralist methods. Structuralists have been highly critical of empiricism and positivism, even though their own methods and epistemological perspectives are oriented toward the "real" world rather than to metaphysical entities or eidetic essences. Taking neither a strictly pragmatic nor a strictly relativistic line, structuralism has emphasized the historicity of meaning, truth, and even reason in human societies, and the random variability of social organization. Its humanism, to which Arkoun subscribes, insists on human individual and social behavior as the basis of all meaning, and hence of all religious truth and morality.

> L'enjeu, on le voit, est la philosophie de la personne humaine. Pour rendre celle-ci possible dans la pensé islamique actuelle, il ne faut pas seulement réactualiser l'effort mu'tazilite pour conquérir un certain territoire propre à la raison . . . il est nécessaire de dénoncer la solidarité active entre les formes de pouvoir qui se sont imposés dans les sociétés musulmanes, et toute la théologie du serf-arbitre dévelopée pendant des siècles, dans les sociétés du Livre. Le combat pour l'émancipation de la personne humaine hors des servitudes qu'elle se fabrique, est inséparablement intellectuel et politique.[64]

This is not to argue for a relativistic theory of truth and goodness, nor to justify moral compromise as necessitated by the human condition, but rather to argue that all claims to have determined the ultimate nature of truth or reason or goodness ought to be subjected to an intellectual critique based on structuralist assumptions. Arkoun appears to be more concerned with intellectual freedom than with political freedom. He would be free to apply a multidisciplinary structuralist critique to Islamic orthodoxy as preached by the ulama, as upheld by al-Azhar and similar institutions, and enforced by Muslim governments, and he would have other scholars, Muslims and non-Muslims, free to do the same. Upon further reflection, his references to Egyptian Nasserism, to the domination of the orthodox ulama in Morocco, to the neglect of Berber culture, and above all, to the cultural significance of the Islamic revolution in Iran, indicate that he is perhaps equally concerned with political freedom.

Though his writing ranges widely over the field of Islamic intellectual history, Arkoun's special field is Islamic philosophy of the medieval period. Arkoun is particularly interested in and partial to the philosophical schools that arose after the translation of many works from the ancient Greek into Arabic, a movement which struggled against orthodox scripturalism, theological empiricism, and the jesuitical practitioners of dialectical apologetics.[65] Islamic philosophy, or *falsafa*, lost out and declined to become a secondary, even a rejected tradition in Islam, barely hinted at in the oft-repeated statement that reason and revelation both sustain the truth of scripturalist interpretations of Islamic law.

> . . . la pensé classique, comme toute construction intellectuelle achevée, a produit un *impensable* à mesure qu'elle a organisé . . . l'espace de son propre *pensable*. La théologie, par exemple, a mis au point une stratégie polémique bien plus qu'une structure heuristique pour une investigation ouverte: il en est résulté un vaste domaine encore *impensé* dans la pensée arabe moderne.[66]

The failure of the philosophical movement is, for Arkoun, the central event in the intellectual history of Islam, second only in significance to the originating "fact" of revelation itself.[67] This failure was in part due to the limitations of the various schools of philosophical reasoning, but for the most part it was due to the political need to have interpretive control over the text and its meaning. The decline of Islamic philosophy meant the triumph of Islamic scripturalism and the establishment of a *clôture logocentrique* by which possible alternative understandings of revelation became unthinkable.[68] "Islamic reason" came to be founded on this doctrinaire interpretation and Arkoun distinguishes that reason as *la raison vrai* from *la raison réel,* that is, structuralist, historical, linguistic and social reason. Among the most important examples of the consequence of such reasoning is the way in which the early political conflicts which led to the Sunni-Shiʿi division in Islam have become rigidly fixed cultural symbols, incapable of sustaining new interpretations.

But Arkoun's position is not to be equated with that of the "bourgeois liberals" who may regret that Islam rejected the Muʿtazila—the exponents of rationalism in Islam. The Muʿtazila were influenced by the philosophical concept of reason as derived from Greek culture, but their rationality operated only within the strict confines of an empiricist conception of revelation and a correspondence theory of language. They appeal to the exponents of bourgeois liberalism who have adopted the positivist and empiricist presuppositions of Western thought.

Although Arkoun displays a strongly historical sense of the development and decline of Islam, and though he consistently refers to the political aspect of intellectual controversies, his central interpretive concern is epistemological and not historical. This concern is best illustrated in an introductory sketch which he added to a collection of essays, intending to transform them into something like a systematic critique of Islamic reason.[69] This schematic analysis of the history of Islamic thought starts out with the juxtaposition of Islamic reason (*la raison vrai*) and the social imagination of Muslims, the first identified with interpretive rigidity and political power, and the second with freedom, spontaneity, change, or *différance*. The dialectic between these two is the theme of his analysis. As we expect, the *imaginaire* loses out, and its loss must be compensated for by a new, interdisciplinary, and critical analysis of Islamic reason, using the contemporary methods that will free Muslims to think all of those things which have been rendered unthinkable by the *clôture logocentrique* imposed by the orthodox clergy.

Arkoun starts with the Qur'an, distinguishing between the "writing" of the Qur'an and the orthodox "reading" of the Qur'an. In his view, the writing, far from being a rigid or violent political formulation, must be understood as transcending human language and its situational, social, and political historicity. The qur'anic writing is expression, feeling, inspiration. It goes beyond any attempt to specify the text. But the text is *read* in a logocentric way. Similarly, the Companions of the Prophet, those who knew best the teachings of Islam, are described by the tradition as unidimensional models of orthodoxy and morality, rather than as real human beings. Above all, the Sunni-Shiʿi-Kharijite conflicts are treated as doctrinal disputes rather than as power struggles. The very possibility of treating these disputes in a meaningful historical fashion has been precluded by the insistence on the qur'anic distinction between the jahiliyya society of the pre-Islamic period and the character of Islamic society.[70]

In much the same way, the hadith has been transformed from its local and customary character into a fixed and logocentric body of doctrine presumably linking the contemporary Muslim generation with all those that preceded it. In fact, the hadith continues in tension with local traditions as well as with modernity, and Arkoun hints that the contemporary (structuralist-deconstructionist) study of *the* Great Tradition may liberate the little traditions that it has obscured.

Arkoun calls the classic, orthodox, Islamic doctrine fundamentalist, referring to the literature which discussed the "sources" or "roots" (*usul*) of theology and of jurisprudence. He uses the French term *intégriste* to refer to the fundamentalist movements such as the Muslim Brotherhood or the Hizbullah. This fundamentalist/scripturalist Islam must be exploded by the new methodology of research and analysis which he proposes. This fundamentalism came not only to dominate medieval theology, but it prevented the development of philosophy, it stymied the growth of scientific rationality, it caused the neglect of the history and culture of the nonliterate Muslim peoples, it transformed Muslim poetry from an expressive discipline into a formalist, elitist, ideology, it allowed the complete overshadowing of oral literature such as that of the Berbers, it has vilified practical reason and the related wisdom of folk religion.

The modernist movement has not really come to grips with the neglect of the *imaginaire,* the devaluation of folk cultures, and the need for intellectual freedom. The *nahda,* or Awakening, produced clones of Western intellectuals, while the revolutionary nationalist movements of Nasser and the Algerian FLN produced an equally narrow exploitation of traditional symbols and attitudes in order to combat the bourgeois liberalism of the nahda. But the limitations of these ideological tendencies have left a festering problem which has become a crisis of Islamic reason. Arkoun defines this crisis as arising out of the way in which classical Islamic reason, orthodox reason, the social imagination, and what he calls *mémoire-tradition* have failed to become more closely related in recent years.

Despite the apparent revival of classical Islamic studies by Muslim writers, Arkoun rejects most of these efforts as superficially general and romantic in character. Even orthodox reason (now distinguished from the classic tradition) has been reduced to the service of existing governments, in an effort to control the growth of radical fundamentalism. Much greater efforts have been made to inspire the social imagination with an unhistorical ideology built upon the concept of revolution and using the empty symbols of socialism, nationalism, democracy, and Islam all at once. While this propagandistic effort has succeeded to some extent, it has contributed, along with extensive social and demographic change, to the near extinction of the mémoire-tradition of Muslim communities. This mémoire-tradition is the folk tradition, the cultural authenticity rooted in birthplace and early experience, in local dialect and kinship. Its loss via urbanization, mass politics, and the formalization of religion produces alienation and a loss of security—the breakdown of traditional values that is the favorite theme of liberal development theorists. In its place has come the political ideological transformation of the mémoire-tradition into a new *imaginaire social* which now incorporates Islam, and through which Muslims struggle to "master the metamorphosis of meaning."[71] The best example of this is the way in which the Shiʿite sense of the tragic in history, in the assassinations of ʿAli and Husain, has taken on a history of its own and has become transformed: "comment lire, aujourd'hui la relation Muhammed-Abu Bakr-ʿUthman-ʿAli-Muʿawiya/Husayn- . . . Khumayni?"[72]

Arkoun's critique of ʿAli ʿAbd al-Raziq and of Taha Husain is not based on the prudence of seeking a compromise between the intellectual freedom of the enlightened and the religious prejudices of the masses. Arkoun rejects the epistemological foundations of both the modernist critique and the orthodox dogma. He finds no difficulty with the idea that Muhammad and the Companions ruled over a worldly state. In fact he quotes Muhammad ʿImara approvingly as arguing that the establishment of the caliphate was an effort of a group of tribally connected political elites to maintain their newly won political power.[73] He does not argue that Islam ought not be political, but rather that it always has been and that it should be studied and understood as such, especially when it comes to the critique of Islamic reason.

Arkoun accepts Ibn Khaldun's dictum that the caliphate had become nothing more than kingship, but he would extend that perspective all the way back to the early, rightly guided caliphate as well. He is therefore critical of the Shariʿa doctrine of the caliphate as presented in the works of Sunni fuqaha. These works exemplify the narrow reading of the Qur'an which is the hallmark of Sunni logocentrism and they manifest the readiness of the ulama to sell out their independence and become a part of the established ruling authority. Arkoun, therefore, flatly rejects the ideal of the Islamic state, or the aspiration for the establishment of the rule of God on earth, either in its classical philosophical version, or in its orthodox Sunni version, or in its liberal modernist version as a form of parliamentary-constitutional-democracy.

Arkoun's goal is not the establishment of an Islamic state, but rather a democratic state in which the distinction between Islamic reason and philosophical reason will be expunged. He wishes to abolish the idea of a privileged authority based on scripturalist interpretation of the text, and it is from this point of view that he criticizes the Islamic revolution in Iran and the doctrine of Ayatullah Khomeini.

The theocratic principle which is the basis of Khomeini's personal political authority is that of *wilayat al-faqih*, usually translated as the authority of the jurist. Shiʿite political doctrine holds that the imamate, or legitimate authority in Islam ought to have passed from the Prophet via his descendants through twelve imams. Though political authority was usurped by the Sunni caliphs, the legitimacy of the imams was undiminished. The Twelfth Imam went into hiding or removed himself from this world, and will return at some unknown time. In the meantime, that is, during the occultation of the Imam, Shiʿite Muslims cannot be guided by the Imam, but must find religious and political guidance elsewhere. Presumably that guidance, whether from religious or political authorities, or both, will be inferior to the guidance of the Imam, because lesser authorities are not endowed with the *walaya* of the Imam. In fact, a considerable controversy arose among the Shiʿite ulama and among orientalist scholars regarding the extent of the authority of the ulama during the occultation and regarding the interim legitimacy of lay political authority.[74]

Arkoun makes much of the distinction between the words *walaya* and *wilaya*. The latter, though used for the administrative authority of governors, is dismissed as referring only to an administrative division or district. The term *walaya* however, has a profoundly rich and suggestive meaning in the context of the Shiʿite theory of the imamate.

> The concept of walaya . . . recapitulates all of the dynamic representations of the Shiʿite imagination: it is God's choice of the Imam and the Imam's choice of God; the inseparable complement of the prophetic mission; it is the function of the Imams as witnesses of God; it is the continuation in this world of secret, esoteric prophesy; it is the secret of the spiritual force which God has confided in man, etc. The walaya has not only been mobilized . . . for political competition; the hopes of each believer is projected in it, and his deep psychic functioning is organized thereby; in the course of celebrations and collective commemorations it takes on cosmic significance and function. In it and by it there is deployed what H. Corbin has called the *ethos* of the Shiʿite consciousness.[75]

It is clear from Arkoun's enthusiastic explication of the term, that he prefers this type of concept, representing the imaginaire Islamique, to the logocentric concepts of the jurists and the theologians. He notes that Khomeini understands how this concept has been emptied of its true meaning and reduced to mere devotion to ʿAli and the imams in the face of the rule of nonlegitimate dynasties. Khomeini insists that legitimate authority belongs only to God, and proceeds from God only via the Prophet and the walaya. But

> Here Khomeyni [sic] breaks with the classical theory which would reserve the walaya to the imams, suspending the exercise of those responsibilities during the occultation; by conferring the walaya on the clerk-jurist-theologian (faqih) and thus reinserting its exercise into history and expunging all the differences which

> divide the Sunnis and Shiʿites over the theory of the Imamate. The faqih, that is the ʿalim, . . . does not have legislative power, but (only) doctrinal authority to verify the conformity of the executive to the spirit and the letter of the divine word.[76]

Observers who have followed political developments in Iran will readily recognize that Arkoun has misjudged the meaning of walayat al-faqih as implemented in the Iranian constitution. In his zeal to identify Khomeini with his own bête noir, the scripturalist Sunni clerics, he has accused Khomeini of the cardinal sin of demystifying a rich concept and, rather than ennobling the function of the faqih, of diminishing the function of the imam by linking the walaya to the faqih. In fact, the role of the Shiʿite ulama in revolutionary Iran has not become like that of the Sunni ulama. One might argue that, prior to the revolution, it had indeed become similar to that of the Sunni ulama. Since then however, Khomeini has restored some of the mystique of the imamate by claiming to share that walaya and by asserting the possibility, even the religious obligation, of establishing an Islamic state during the continuation of the occultation.

that is clinging to state — depending upon gov't.

Khomeini's argument in his famous political tract is precisely that during the occultation, it is the ulama who hold the walaya and hence the political authority that is the Imam's.[77] This is quite an astonishing argument, and it is not a simple matter to prove such a case convincingly by the methods used by the Islamic fuqaha. It is Khomeini's claim to have achieved this proof, thereby establishing at once the validity of the doctrine and his own qualification, as the most accomplished faqih of the age, to exercise the walaya of the imams. Khomeini did not diminish the walaya. He has in fact revived it, but it is uncertain whether, in the foreseeable future, it will be bestowed upon another individual rather than the collectivity of the fuqaha via the committee of guardians of the faith.

This misjudgment of events in Iran points to some of the weaknesses in the powerful and persuasive critique which Arkoun has mounted against the Islamic revolutionaries. His refusal to acknowledge the authenticity of mass piety over against folk Islam, and the exaggerated distinction between Islamic orthodoxy and mémoire-tradition leads to a misunderstanding of much of the force of the Islamic revival in Iran, and much of the character of the revival elsewhere. Arkoun has already determined that the Islamic tradition of the ulama is inauthentic and repressive. The creative and dynamic alternative that might be invoked by a vigorous and independent intelligentsia has been seized, monopolized, and politicized by a military, bureaucratic, and technocratic elite, who have created a synthetic ideology, and captured the imaginaire social of the Muslim masses. As a consequence, la raison Islamique has become la raison d'état in Iran as in Egypt and Morocco.

Arkoun's hostility to the Iranian revolution misleads him into failing to apply his own principles of the historicity of doctrine and symbol, the balance between practical savoir faire and formal discursive, or thetic, knowledge, and the need to take account of the mémoire-tradition. The historical and anthropological fact is that the Islamic revival does not manifest itself in the same way everywhere. Nor does it seem acceptable in a frankly historicist analysis to deny the historicity or the validity of what has happened in Iran. To do so is the same as arguing that Islamic history is all a mistake that should have been otherwise. Arkoun proposes an intellectualist solution as though an epistemological critique might alter political reality. In this regard, though his epistemology is much sounder, he shares in the rational and liberal tradition of ʿAli ʿAbd al-Raziq and Taha Husain.

5

The Religious Aesthetic of Sayyid Qutb: A Non-Scriptural Fundamentalism

Modern Fundamentalism

Islamic fundamentalism, though a relatively modern movement, has its doctrinal roots in the earliest period of Muslim history. It shares with many historical Islamic movements the recurring impulse to renew the faith, to return to pristine origins, to shed the accretions of time and clime, and to recapture the vigor and simplicity of prophetic times. At the core of the ideology of this movement there is a strong component of emotional faith, but the distinctive characteristic of the most recent fundamentalist movements has been a special sort of scripturalism. Modern fundamentalism owes as much to Islamic modernism and to the scripturalist doctrine of modern orthodoxy as it does to the chiliastic Islamic impulse.

Islamic modernism and the liberal reformist movement share with the orthodox establishment a fascination with the formal structure of Islamic law. Even the scandalous views of ʿAli ʿAbd al-Raziq are built upon a scripturalist foundation. To some extent it is valid to see the increasing influence of scripturalism, which is noted by Gellner, Lewis, Geertz, and many others, as the consequence of a growing struggle between modernists and traditionalists over how to interpret the canonical texts. ʿAbduh, more than any other single ʿalim, opened the way for a new interpretation of the Qur'an based on reason. The more traditional ulama struggled fairly successfully against the threatened loss of their exclusive, professional, right to interpret scripture in accordance with the tradition.

But neither of these two alternatives succeeded in capturing the imagination of the younger generation. In effect, the new generation of high school and college students were offered a choice between Western cultural ideals and an even more rigid reaffirmation of a tarnished tradition. The appeal of some kind of a synthesis of reason and tradition, of science and faith, of intellect and the passions, was great, and nowhere was such a formula more successful than in Egypt and in pre-independence India and Pakistan. The Muslim Brotherhood, or *Ikhwan al-Muslimun,* founded in Egypt in 1928 by Hasan al-Banna, in reaction to the growing influence of Western cultural and religious influence, and the Jamaʿat-i-Islami, founded by Abu'l-ʿAla al-Mawdudi during the last phase of the struggle for Pakistan, are the two most successful and influential fundamentalist movements of modern times.

Mawdudi's application of deductive reasoning in his interpretation of the Shariʿa, and especially in his theory of the Islamic state, represents a triumph of scripturalist doctrine, both because of its logical coherence and because of its appeal to a new generation of the Muslim intelligentsia. His influence was also deeply felt in Egypt for many reasons, including the fact that his work was translated into Arabic by the Muslim Brotherhood and diffused in Egypt during the repression of the Brotherhood under the Nasser regime, while its logico-deductive form made it seem powerful and irrefutable.

Despite al-Banna's eloquence and organizational skill, his writings and speeches have not acquired an influence comparable to the charismatic appeal of his personality. Instead, the literary and ideological legacy of Sayyid Qutb has become far more important in Egypt, though it is controversial, to some extent inconsistent, and often misunderstood. There is, moreover, much evidence of the influence of Mawdudi on the work of Qutb.[1] Nevertheless, there is other evidence that Qutb, throughout his intellectual life, was deeply influenced by an emotional, rather than a legalistic, conception of the Islamic faith, and that he has contributed to the construction of a new fundamentalist orientation which has the potential to unleash great social energy in the form of a popular movement that is neither vulnerable to state control nor subservient to traditional and parochial elites.

Moderates and Extremists

This chapter will explore the most militant work of Sayyid Qutb, his *Ma'alim fi't-Tariq.* It is claimed that this book influenced the extremist fundamentalists in Egypt who have tried to seize power, have assassinated Sadat and have consistently opposed the Camp David agreements.[2] While Qutb can be read as reflecting a broad fundamentalist consensus,[3] such a reading cannot account for the influence which he is charged with having over the ideological position of the Egyptian fundamentalist extremists.[4] It is, therefore, of interest to inquire into the reasons for his particular appeal to members of the clandestine and violent movement, as opposed to the more moderate wing of the Muslim Brotherhood.

Some commentators have suggested that the differences between the moderates and the extremists among the Ikhwan is more a question of strategy than of ideology.[5] Reference to Qutb's dependence on Mawdudi, or to the emotional consequences of his long imprisonment, have the effect of minimizing his ideological distinctiveness and his philosophical originality.[6] But criticism of both the doctrines of *Hakimiyya* and of *Takfir* by Hudhaybi (the leader of the Ikhwan from 1948 to 1954) has been interpreted as a refutation of Qutb's argument in the *Ma'alim*.[7] It is no secret that a number of those identified with the Ikhwan have been engaged in a debate regarding the tactics and strategy of Islamic revolution. It has been suggested that this debate was vigorously pursued in the Nasserist prisons after the 1954 purge and repression of the Brotherhood. It is widely believed that Qutb opted for the more radical and militant alternative, while Hudhaybi, Tilmisani, and even Muhammad al-Ghazali opted for the more moderate and accommodative alternative.[8]

The more extreme position was stated explicitly in tracts circulated secretly by the extremist societies in the late 1970s.[9] While there is little doubt that Qutb's influence has found its way into these tracts, the difficult question is whether Qutb and his followers came to an explicit agreement regarding strategy and tactics of organization and revolutionary action, or whether the "Qutbists" have merely drawn their own inferences from his work. Sayed Gomaa, for example, makes much of the fact that Qutb does not refer to the Ikhwan in the *Ma'alim*, suggesting that he implied that the old organizational structure and leadership should be abandoned and replaced by micromovements comprised of jamaʿat.[10] This interpretation is vitiated by the fact that Qutb did not refer to the Ikhwan in several other works. Nevertheless, the conclusion may be correct even if the evidence, based as it is on omission, is hardly decisive. Thus Qutb might have left an explicit strategic testament to his followers, but, in the absence of any reliable report, it is probably safe to assume that much of his influence has been conveyed through the text of his *Ma'alim*.

Fanatical fundamentalism is not a necessary consequence of something inherent in Islam. Islam is only the ground upon which some special theory has been constructed. That theory, in turn, may touch upon the personality characteristics of a small number of readers or hearers. The expansion of this small group of true believers into a movement of political significance depends upon many and varied factors, possibly including some kind of exemplary individual action demonstrating a devotion that goes beyond life itself. Thus acts of terror and martyrdom are not only aimed at terrorizing or demoralizing the enemy, but at proving that the impossible is possible. From such beginnings movements which are oriented toward a charismatic-martyric ethic may be redirected toward a routinized, nomothetic, ordered, rational and prudential ethic.

The more moderate wing of the Muslim Brotherhood was led until recently by the late ʿUmar al-Tilmisani, and it still controls the name and the license of the suspended magazine *al-Daʿwa*.[11] This more moderate wing failed to win certification as a legalized political party in the elections of 1984, but it formed a semi-legal electoral alliance with the newly legalized neo-Wafd in the elections of 1984.[12] So successful was the appeal of the Brotherhood that it was able to make an even better deal with rivals of the Wafd in the elections of 1987, when it won even more seats, though still lacking legalization. The more moderate wing has gained wide respect among the Egyptian middle classes, as it has emphasized its preference for peaceful political methods, even if it has not ruled out all use of violence.

The assassination of president Sadat on October 6, 1981, resulted in the freeing of a considerable number of Brotherhood activists from prison, where they had been able to exchange ideas with other opposition groups. The period of the accelerated release of both Islamic fundamentalists and leftists from prison, or their return from exile, around January 1982, was one of political euphoria and great expectations regarding the possible collaboration of all opposition elements in the construction of a new multiparty regime. Within a year, these expectations were disappointed, and the Brotherhood has been under some pressure to become more militant.[13] These pressures were resisted in the effort to achieve legitimate participation in the 1984 elections.

The major fundamentalist magazines *al-Daʿwa* and *al-Iʿtisam* are currently banned, so that it is difficult to trace the impact of the continuing political disappointment on the ideological position of the Ikhwan.[14] Tilmisani published a couple of pieces in the licensed press, and from time to time books and tracts by those known to be close to the Ikhwan, such as Muhammad al-Ghazali, do appear in the bookshops.[15] It is apparent that tactical and ideological discussions and rethinking are taking place, but it is not easy to follow these developments from outside. Representatives of the Ikhwan, or those closely sympathetic, still refer to the articles in the old *al-Daʿwa*, to the writings of the founder, Hasan al-Banna, to the works of al-Ghazali, but not so much to the writings of Sayyid Qutb, when asked about current ideological tendencies.

It is not clear that the radical or extremist wing of the Ikhwan is organized in any unified manner. There is an inclination among observers of the Egyptian scene to lump together a number of groups and tendencies under the general heading of al-Jamaᶜat al-Islamiyya, meaning Islamic groups. Some talk as though there is only one group, that is, a single *jamaᶜa,* a usage similar to that employed to describe the Muslim community. This usage permits many quite separate organizations or groups to refer to themselves as members of the Jamaᶜa—the true Islamic community, rather than the apparent one. Such groups, whether conspiratorial combinations aimed at seizing power or mosque-based discussion circles, can equally assert membership in the Jamaᶜa, and will not repudiate one another under most circumstances. Still there seems to be little doubt that the Takfir waᶜl-Hijra group and the Jihad group were separately organized militant groups with at least a semblance of a differentiated ideology formalized in their own publications.[16]

The *Daᶜwa* group, when asked, is inclined to praise the early works of Sayyid Qutb, especially his well known *Social Justice in Islam;* but sadly regrets the excesses to which they say he was driven by the Nasser regime.[17] The excesses to which they thus refer are contained in Qutb's most famous work *al-Ma'alim Fi't-Tariq* (Signposts Along the Way) translated as *Milestones.*[18] It is this last work, written by Qutb just before his release from prison in 1965, that is said to have greatly influenced the Egyptian Islamic extremists who broke with the Ikhwan, and who have demanded a more militant Islamic confrontation with the Egyptian regime. Nevertheless, when questioned regarding the most influential contemporary Islamic thinker, many educated Egyptians name the deceased Pakistani, Mawlana Abu'l-Ala al-Mawdudi.[19]

While this response may represent a disingenuous attempt to diminish Qutb's importance, it does point up the degree to which Qutb has employed some of Mawdudi's central ideas. These notions have, in turn, been employed in the tracts printed by the Takfir and Jihad groups, so there is little doubt Qutb has served as a transmitter of the ideas of Mawdudi.[20] Still, Mawdudi's works have been available in Egypt since the early 1950s and they are still widely read and available in all bookshops. It is possible, however, that part of the reason for the current resurgence of interest in Mawdudi is due to the unavailability of the *Ma'alim,* even though most of the rest of Qutb's works, including his thirty volume tafsir (commentary) of the Qur'an, are available.

A talented native writer of Arabic, such as Qutb, has a great communicative advantage over a translated author, regardless of the eloquence of his argument and the skill of the translator. Personally, however, I prefer Mawdudi's tighter logic and leaner rhetoric to Qutb's repetitious and wordy style. Qutb does give greater expression to his emotions and uses a large and vivid vocabulary, especially in describing the horrors which Islam opposes. But aside from style and rhetoric, if we subtract Mawdudi from Qutb is there anything of importance left? Is there anything that reveals aspects of the special quality of contemporary Egyptian fundamentalism as opposed to that militant tendency presumably widely shared throughout the region since the Iranian revolution?[21]

Mawdudi and Qutb share the conviction that Islam is engaged in a *kulturkampf* with Western imperialism, and that ultimately the purpose or consequence of modernization, or development, whether as defined by capitalism or communism, is to complete the material colonization of the Muslim world by means of a moral and cultural colonization. The reassertion of Islam is a rejection of Western dominance, of Western culture, and of the identity which the West would impose upon Muslims. Hence the improvement of the material condition of Muslims is not conditioned on their becoming more westernized but rather less westernized, and there are important implications in this doctrine for the political relationships between technocrats, bureaucrats, and professionals (including the military) and cultural elites.

Hakimiyya - Sovereignty

Mawdudi's argument proceeds by logical deduction from his first, rather primitive, premise. That premise involves the principle of *hakimiyya*, or sovereignty, in the parlance of modern international law and recent political theory. The idea is that God is the ultimate and absolute sovereign of all creation. This sovereignty is interpreted in the sense of authority to command absolute and unquestioned obedience, similar to a master commanding a slave. The basis of this authority is that God created, and is consequently the owner and master, of everything in the world. Mawdudi's vision is argued as a self-evident truth:

> . . . thus did the Qur'an wish to sever the root . . . of polytheism and the illusions of individual freedom, license and disobedience: for the unquestionable result of the belief in the detachment of God . . . from the direction and organization . . . of worldly existence is either that man will conclude that his fate depends upon others . . . , hence, he will humble himself before them; or

> he will consider himself to be master of his own fate and he will live absolutely free according to his own will and whim. . . .
>
> [T]he connection between God and creation in the glorious Qur'an . . . cannot be clarified by reference to . . . concepts . . . which are linked to political authority or kingship. . . . But the meaning of the Qur'an is revealed clearly. . . . Nevertheless . . . some obnoxious and muddled critics have concluded [from these passages] that the writing of the Qur'an was accomplished during an era when the monarchical regime dominated the consciousness and the thought of man, which in fact caused its author (who, according to these evil-doers, was Muhammad, upon whom may there be blessings and peace) to portray God in the form of a king. Rather, the everlasting truth which the Qur'an expresses, and which contradicts this [view] completely, is that kingship in the heavens and the earth [alike] is kingship of a single essence only. . . . sovereignty (*hakimiyya*) is one component of that [singular] essence, and the order of this [worldly] existence is a perfectly centralized system, all of the powers of which are exercised by a single essence. Hence, as a consequence, whenever any individual or group claims for himself or for another full or partial sovereignty . . . he is doubtlessly dazzled by falsehood, untruth, and absolute slander. . . . [Consequently, humankind cannot but] believe in that essence as a single God . . . to be worshipped in the religious sense, and also as a ruler and sultan in the political and social sense.[22]

Qutb differs from Mawdudi only in emphasis, but that emphasis is important.[23] Mawdudi wishes to emphasize the unity and, consequently the coherence of creation. The key to this coherence is to be discovered via revelation, but it does not conflict with scientific findings. Rather, Mawdudi, as many other apologists, finds the ordered intelligibility of the world proof of the divine existence and creation. Hence Mawdudi's ideology is constructed along the lines of a classical syllogism starting from the first premise of an unmoved mover. But Qutb is somewhat more interested in the consequences of divine hakimiyya for human freedom. For Qutb divine sovereignty is so comprehensive that it precludes all human sovereignty and authority. Any nondivine authority is *taghut*, that is, illegitimate, irreligious, and tyrannical.[24] The purpose of Islam is to remove taghut and replace it with Islamic or divine authority. Human beings are totally bereft of any liberty vis à vis Allah and therefore, since all are equally slaves of God, none has any shred of authority over other human beings.

> In this regard Islam is unique. . . . [I]n every regime save the Islamic some men are subject to the rule of others—in some manner or other—but only in the Islamic "way" (*minhaj*) are all men

> liberated from subjection to others, in their subjection to God alone, in their acceptance of commands from God alone, and in their submission to God alone.[25]

> Verily men are slaves of Allah only. But they cannot be slaves to Allah alone except that the banner of "there is no God but Allah" be raised—No God but Allah, as understood by [every] Arab who understands the rules of his language [means] "No hakimiyya except to Allah, and no Shariʿa (sacred law) except from Allah, and no political authority (sultan) to anyone over anyone, because political authority is Allah's only."[26]

> Islam is worship (subjection?) to God alone in accepting from Him alone their ideas, beliefs, Shariʿa, laws, values and standards of fairness, and in (their) liberation from enslavement to slaves.[27]

> This Jahiliyya . . . ascribes sovereignty to humanity, and sets up some as masters over others, not in the simple primitive form that the original Jahiliyya knew, but in the form which claims the right to prescribe ideas and values, laws and regulations, regimes and institutions.[28]

> When the supreme sovereignty in society is God's alone . . . that is the only way in which humankind can achieve complete and true freedom from subjection to (other) humans . . . there is no freedom—in truth—and no human dignity—represented in each and every individual—in a society in which some are masters who lay down the law and others are slaves who obey.[29]

Qutb does not deny the importance of Islamic government and law, but he puts far less emphasis on the organization of the Islamic state than he does on opposition to the un-Islamic state. For him the spiritual transformation of what must in each instance be an individual human being is both prior to and more important than the establishment of an Islamic state.[30] He repeats again and again that Islamic citizenship or political identity (*jinsiyya*) is doctrinal (*ʿaqida*) and not territorial, national, or racial; and, of course, that belief is individual.[31] As a consequence there is an element of individualism, which, when linked to Qutb's theory of human freedom as based on divine sovereignty, tends toward an anarchy of true believers. In a community of true believers there is no need of earthly laws, regulations, and devices of enforcement.

Jahiliyya

A second concept employed by Qutb seems also to have been appropriated from Mawdudi's usage. The word, *jahiliyya,* often translated as "ignorance," is the specialized term used to refer to the cultural and intellectual state of the Arabs before the Islamic revelation.[32] Mawdudi extended the term to refer to anything un-Islamic or antagonistic to Islam, including in an anachronistic manner, contemporary influences drawing Muslims away from Islam. Since the stature of Islam is often enhanced rhetorically by elaborating on the extreme corruption and degradation of jahiliyya conditions, any contemporary phenomenon associated therewith is similarly severely condemned. In particular, there are two manifestations of contemporary jahiliyya which have been singled out for criticism by Mawdudi and Qutb, and these are Western cultural influences, and Muslim governments which are not based on the Shariʿa and which are, evidently, Western-influenced.

The paradoxical and iconoclastic element in Mawdudi's argument is that he identifies as "ignorance" a great deal of what is considered knowledge or wisdom not only in the West but by a great many westernized Muslims. Modern science and technology are not condemned as ignorance, but the notion that they can explain all of nature, or determine political or social questions, is described as ignorance. But those Muslims who are inclined to believe that Islam does somehow prevent Muslims from progressing are particularly condemned. Thus the term jahiliyya has been transferred from reference to the pre-Islamic period to reference to modern Western society and culture, emphasizing its corrupting influence, and negating the widespread ethnographic belief that it is impossible to compartmentalize cultural and ideological matters in a way that allows for selective cultural diffusion.

While all of this is acceptable to Sayyid Qutb, he adds a dimension which is, to my knowledge, not found in Mawdudi. Qutb, at various places in the *Ma'alim,* contrasts abstract or speculative theory with practical wisdom, or practical experience (but not with pragmatism which he actually condemns in the *Social Justice* volume). At several places he describes Islam as practical, realistic, concerned with life, down to earth.[33] The rhetoric which he employs in these passages seems heavily influenced by existentialism. He also describes Islam as dynamic, characterized by movement, change, development and even, at times, stages.[34] There can be little doubt that Qutb relates dynamism and change with living reality, actuality, existence, and practical matters. The best available word might be praxis, involving as it does both the idea of change and existential reality. It might be praxis, but that term suggests that the source of change is to be found in the historical, or accidental, or natural conditions of existence. Qutb wishes rather to argue that the laws of his Islamic praxis are not in the material world, but rather in the worldly orientation of the Islamic idea (*tasawwur*) or Islamic way (*minhaj*).

There would appear to be some intellectual borrowing or transposition which leads Qutb to emphasize that Islam is nonphilosophical, that it is alien to deductive reasoning and systematic intellectual structuring.[35] His usage reminds one of the neo-Marxist usage of the term theoretical praxis to counter accusations that idealistic heresies have crept into what should be a materialistic discourse. In contrast, Qutb strives to identify Islam as a praxis which nevertheless finds its origin in an idealist-religious doctrine.

Qutb insists that speculative idealism, and deductive intellectualist systems not derived from immediate religious experience, are characteristic forms of contemporary jahiliyya. Theoretical systems which are derived from worldly praxis and material existence alone are equally *jahili*. In this way Qutb rejects not only Marxism, but also Western philosophy, the medieval philosophies of Islam, and much Islamic legal reasoning, claiming that they represent the most insidious and reprehensible forms of the jahili attack on Islam. It is not, however, abstract theory itself which is jahili. Qutb condems above all that jahiliyya which pretends it is Islam.

> Today we are in the midst of a *jahiliyya* similar to or even worse than the *jahiliyya* that was "squeezed out" by Islam. Everything about us is *jahiliyya:* the ideas (*tasawwurat*) of mankind and their beliefs, their customs and traditions, the sources of their culture, their arts and literature, and their laws and regulations. [This is true] to such an extent that much of what we consider to be Islamic culture and Islamic sources, and Islamic philosophy and Islamic thought . . . is nevertheless the product of that *jahiliyya*.[36]
>
> . . . it is necessary that we tell how the Qur'an resolved the problem of the creed (ʿaqida) during the thirteen years [at Mecca before the *Hijra*]. . . . It did not expound it in a theoretical *sura* (constructed) of dialectical disputation, like those who pursue what is called *ʿilm al-tawhid* (the science of unity).[37]
>
> But the jahiliyya which is based on the sovereignty of man over man, and which deviates thereby from existential being (*al-wujud al-kawni*) . . . that jahiliyya was not represented by pure "theory." Rather, perhaps sometimes it didn't even have a theory at all! It was instead always represented by a dynamic concrescence (or congress) [*tajammu'a haraki* is the term used, meaning a form of integrative social and cultural process similar to social mobilization] manifested in a society subservient to its leadership, and to prevailing conceptions, and values, and understandings, and sentiments, and traditions, and customs. Moreover, [jahili society] is an organic (*adhawi*) society, there being among its individual members that organic mutuality, complementarity, coordination, trust and cooperation which gives that [jahili] society its dynamic quality—with or without consciously willing it—to pre-

> serve its existence and to defend its being. . . . And since the jahiliyya is not represented by abstract theory, but is represented in a dynamic concrescence, any attempt to destroy that jahiliyya and to restore mankind to God once more . . . cannot be represented by pure "theory." . . . Rather it is necessary that such a renewed attempt [to destroy the jahiliyya] be represented in a dynamic social concrescence which is even more powerful.[38]

This passage does not merely tell us that, in opposing jahiliyya, Muslims must fight fire with fire, and must develop the same social devices which are employed by jahili societies. Otherwise, it might be argued that Qutb advocated that Islamic societies must become materialistic and historical societies rather than spiritual entities in order to survive—that is, that they must become like the jahili societies. Qutb seems, rather, to be pointing not only to the sources of strength and cohesion in jahili societies, but to the sources of strength and cohesion in all societies. In other words, despite the widespread view that Qutb opposed and shunned philosophizing and theorizing, in this passage he is expressing a social-scientific conception of social systems as social processes which stand in a relationship of reciprocal support with coherent cultural systems.

Qutb's rhetorical monism in the *Ma'alim* is neither explicit nor consistent.[39] The dualism of theory and practice, of the Islamic ideal and the un-Islamic state of the world, is neither acknowledged nor perceived as a logical contradiction by Mawdudi: it is rather an historical ephemerum, which does not challenge the validity of Islam. But Qutb does not accept the idealist-epistemological position of Mawdudi. In the *Ma'alim,* Qutb's underlying problem is the contradiction between divine sovereignty and humanity's disobedience. The separation of theory and practice is precisely what Qutb attacks as jahiliyya—even perhaps worse, because it is jahiliyya posing as Islam, while the ordinary form of jahiliyya is strong precisely because it does not separate theory and practice, because it is, consciously or not, monistic, praxis-oriented, and concerned with existential survival. Islam requires that thought and action be integrally related. Islam must be lived from the inside (i.e., from belief) out (i.e., to the collectivity).

Still, jahiliyya thought fails to make certain essential distinctions of a dualistic sort which Qutb believes are essential to Islam. In the *Ma'alim* this dualism is, for the most part, expressed in statements regarding the distinction between spirit and matter and human and animal characteristics. Qutb states that the mixing, or conflation, of these contradictories is characteristic of the jahiliyya while true Islam distinguishes between them and gives each its proper place, so that spirit and matter are recognized as "separate but equal" while the human is quite clearly nonmaterial and superior to the animal.[40]

This dualism is not self-conscious. Qutb is rather concerned to maintain the separate and distinct existence of all essences. Most importantly, this concern is reflected in a virtually compulsive insistence that there can be no social circumstance or situation which is mostly Islam or partly jahili. Whatever is not Islam is jahiliyya. The only Islamic society is one which is completely devoted to the worship of God alone, that is to say it cannot be partly anything else because it is totally Islamic.[41]

Jihad

The third central concept shared by Mawdudi and Qutb is jihad, the principal purpose of which is to combat jahiliyya.[42] The central issue discussed by Mawdudi, and the one picked up by Qutb, is whether jihad is defensive only. This issue originates in the anti-Islamic polemic which characterized Islam as barbaric because it sanctions the routine use of military violence, because it acknowledges that war can be not only just but holy, and because it encourages the use of force to convert unbelievers. Modernist Muslim apologists were moved to deny these interpretations of the doctrine of jihad and they developed an alternate theory which minimized the military dimension of jihad. Moreover, they argued when Muslims did resort to arms for religious purposes it was always defensive.

Mawdudi and Qutb both rejected this interpretation, finding in it an expression of false consciousness. Muslim apologists had been tricked into adopting an idea which not only conformed to the Christian religious doctrine, but one which also suited the political preferences of non-Muslim political leaders.

Mawdudi denies that Muslims used force to convert anyone to Islam. That was not the purpose of jihad. Jihad is employed only against governments or rulers which prevent the preaching of Islam, and since the rulers of Sassanid Iran and Byzantium did not allow Muhammad's successors to preach the true faith in their lands, they were attacked and defeated. Thus the purpose of jihad is to gain freedom of religious speech.

But both Mawdudi and Qutb argue that no non-Muslim government would allow the free conversion of its population to Islam. Jihad is the struggle against jahiliyya and since all governments which are not Islamic are jahili, it follows that all non-Islamic sovereignty must be overthrown. It is, thus, Islamic political dominance which must be spread by jihad, but conversion must be left to the individual conscience.

For the most part, Muslim countries are in no position to fulfill this prescription for jihad, but theoretically it hardly allows for a system of peaceful international relations among Muslim and non-Muslim states, or even for stable treaty relations. In a more practical sense, however, this rather unforgiving definition of jihad has more impact on Muslim governments. The immediate targets are those close-at-hand Muslim political authorities who do not rule according to what Allah prescribed.[43]

Here again, Qutb's basic emphasis deviates from that of Mawdudi without disagreeing with any of his major points. Qutb argues that we learn, from the policies pursued at various times by the Prophet, that jihad is neither defensive nor merely theoretical. The Shariʿa in general, and in particular regard to jihad, is dynamic, realistic, practical, and unfolds by stages; yet this dynamic, changing and adapting Islam never deviates from its fundamental principles.[44] The basic principle upon which the relations between Islam and other societies are founded remains jihad, according to which Muslims must struggle against taghut wherever it exists.

Qutb attacks those defeatists who believe that Shariʿa law is rigidly fixed and unchanging, and who believe that jihad is defensive. Their error is based upon their interpretation of the Prophet's nonviolent policies during the early phase of Islam, and their failure to take account of later developments.[45] Thus Qutb's insistence on characterizing Islam as dynamic (haraki) links the interpretation of the Shariʿa to historical circumstances, but he also uses the notion of haraki to refer to historical circumstances and material forces themselves. He argues that the goal of Islam is to achieve a comprehensive revolution against all jahili authority. Since jahili authority is not merely theoretical or doctrinal but includes economic, social, and cultural arrangements, so these two aspects of jahiliyya must be attacked by the two aspects of Islam: *bayan* (explanation, preaching) and *haraka* (movement).[46]

It is disconcerting to find Qutb reverting now to a simple dualism of matter and spirit, but it is also helpful to grasp his understanding of haraka as material, historical, and actual. Hence, when Qutb describes Islam as a conception (tasawwur), or vision, or idea that is haraki, or dynamic, or adaptive, or active, it is clear that he is striving for a monistic formulation which unites theory and practice, or the ideal and the real Islam. Qutb does lapse into dualism at this point, and there is some hint of the reason for this lapse in the dilemma between an assertive jihad and the Islamic principle that there can be no compulsion in matters of religious belief. As is so often the case,

Qutb's religious monism does not appear to be original, but rather a rejection of an intolerable dualism which preceded it.

Islamic Revolution

The fourth area in which Mawdudi and Qutb share a common perspective concerns the method for bringing about an Islamic revolution, or, indeed, developing an Islamic community. In this regard, almost all Muslim theorists have been inspired by the history of the early Islamic group, in Mecca, each member of which was converted by the Prophet. The beginning of an Islamic movement ought to follow the original pattern of quiet, even secret proselytization; the organization of a small cooperative community which makes no serious political claims, and which pursues an organizational and propaganda strategy that avoids confrontation while quietly increasing the number of adherents, and then, eventually, asserting authority and even a readiness to use military force under favorable circumstances.[47] The foundation of the movement must be individual, religious conversion based on faith and spiritual conviction. Each individual member must be absolutely convinced and completely devoted to the cause. Nevertheless, the real character of Islam is expressed through collective Islamic life rather than through the subjective religious experience of the individual believer.

Qutb's emphases, again, differ somewhat from those of Mawdudi. It seems to me that Qutb places much more importance on the solitary believer.

> We have already stated that serving Allah is expressed in *at-Tasawwur al-I'tiqadi* . . . and it is appropriate that we say what the Islamic Tasawwur al-I'tiqadi is. . . . It is the conception (tasawwur) which originates in the human intellect as a result of man's reception of the truths of the principles of belief (ʿaqida) from its Lordly (*Rabbani*) source: and it is that by means of which man reconciles his understanding of the truth of his Lord and the truth of the (existential) being in which he lives—both in its manifest and its unseen aspects—and the truth of the life of which he is a part—both in its manifest and its unseen parts—and the truths of his own self . . . or the truth of the essence of man.[48]

In this passage, Qutb appends a label to a mental or intellectual event which is the consequence of accepting the truth of the creed. What is noteworthy here is that Qutb did not insist that the crucial mental faculty upon which Islamic belief is based is reason. Moreover, the intellectual activity which he then describes is not logical deduction, but the coordination or reconciliation of several sets of verities, one of which is divine and the rest of which are aspects of creation, both spiritual and material. Consequently, if there is a problem of the reconciliation of the spiritual and the material, of the theoretical and the practical, of the eternal and the historical, this problem can be resolved by a mental function which is activated by belief.

The relationship between this subjective understanding, originating in divine revelation, and the nature of historical Islamic societies is developed in a later passage:

> . . . Islamic society is born of movement (haraka) and in it movement is constant, and that is what determines the capacities and value of individuals within it, and consequently determines their functions and their positions within it. . . . That movement from which that society is born starts from a movement which comes from outside of the worldly framework, and from outside of the human environment. . . . Indeed it is reperesented in a creed which is conveyed from God to mankind . . . the first push which sets off the movement does not come from the souls of men nor from material being.[49]

From these passages we can see that Qutb wishes to reconcile a deep commitment to the notion that religious faith is essentially subjective and nonrational with an equally strong commitment to the belief that there is a distinctive character to Islamic community and Islamic history. While the tension between the subjective and the objective in his thought is manifest, the unifying idea seems to be the dynamic or changing nature of what one must do in order to be a Muslim under changing historical and social conditions. While the principles of Islam are always the same, the sort of Islamic action called for changes with historical circumstances. The resultant theory may be called (half seriously) an Islamic pragmatic.

> And when that single individual believes in that creed (ʿaqida), the Islamic society commences its existence (virtually) . . . indeed an individual person will not receive that creed and turn inward upon himself. . . . [W]hen the number of believers in that creed reaches three persons, then the creed itself will say to them, "You are now a society, an independent Islamic society, separate from the jahili society . . .[50]

Those areas of ideological agreement between Mawdudi and Qutb provide a doctrinal basis which is quite sufficient to justify the line taken by the extremist fundamentalists in Egypt. Starting from the similar insistence on the absolute sovereignty of God, they have argued that the Egyptian regime is not Islamic because it is not completely and exclusively based on Shariʿa law.[51] Since it is not Islamic, the Egyptian regime is jahili and taghuti. If it is jahili, it is to be combatted by means of jihad. Even though it is not Islamic, it is not a government of Christians, Jews, or even ordinary unbelievers. It is a government of Muslims who falsely claim it to be Islamic. Hence these rulers and their supporters are hypocrites, heretics, and apostates. There can be no compromise with these sinners, nor can there be any treaty as might be made with non-Muslim "scriptuaries." They are to be judged by the qur'anic verse which states that "those who do not rule in accordance with divine revelation are heretics" (*kuffar,* or elsewhere hypocrites or evildoers).[52]

Critics of the Islamic extremists among the more traditional and liberal Muslims have noted the similarity between the positions taken by the extremists and that of the Kharijite movement of early Islam.[53] In particular, the Kharijites practiced takfir, denied the legitimacy of the government of the day, engaged in jihad against Muslim regimes, separated themselves (hence their name) from the rest of the Muslims and formed their own communities, and they permitted the killing of non-Kharijite Muslims, declaring them to be not only kuffar (heretics or unbelievers) but also apostates.

But if this modern Kharijism can be based on the doctrines shared by Mawdudi and Sayyid Qutb, why is it that the Jamaʿat-i-Islami of Pakistan turned out to be such a moderate, establishment-oriented, reformist, pro-order, petit bourgeois movement? It is true that the Jamaʿat scared the wits out of the Pakistan Muslim League and the bureaucratic "steel frame" during the early 1950s; they demanded an Islamic constitution, challenged the traditional ulama, and stirred up violent demonstrations against the heterodox Qadiani (Ahmadiyya) community in Punjab province in 1953.[54] But since that time, the Jamaʿat has entered parliamentary politics, has supported the landowning classes in the Punjab, has criticized the secessionist movement in Bengal, has compromised with the traditional ulama, has formed a coalition with Zia al-Haq and has lent legitimacy to Zia's mockery of Islamic reaffirmation in Pakistan. Moreover the early work of Sayyid Qutb seems to fall in the same category. Though strongly critical of the West, Qutb's idea of social justice, equality, freedom, order, economic justice and the like conforms well enough to Western liberal notions—with the addition of apologetic discourses on usury and the position of women. We look in vain for unique ideological elements that will explain the radicalism of those presumably influenced by Sayyid Qutb.

Social Justice in Islam

Qutb's reputation as a fundamentalist-modernist theorist was made by his early and famous book, *al-ʿAdala al-Ijtimaʿiyya fi'l-Islam* translated as *Social Justice in Islam;* but many Western observers, and more liberal Muslims, found his ideas at the time to be reassuring.[55] That book is divided into two main parts with a few additional chapters interspersed. In the first major section, Qutb discusses Islamic doctrines regarding freedom, equality and social justice. His method of exposition is familiar from other apologetic works, and it presents Islam as an ideal system which fully integrates and balances all three. Freedom is derived from the hakimiyya of Allah, and is defined primarily as freedom of conscience and liberation from material instincts. Equality in Islam is derived from the equality of all believers, but most of Qutb's discussion is an apologetic regarding the unequal position of women in Islam. Mutual social responsibility balances freedom and equality, producing social justice which is expressed in concrete form by the application of Shariʿa law.

This familiar argument is followed by a description, "The methods of social justice in Islam." Islam combines appeals to faith and conscience as well as reliance upon legal and coercive institutions in achieving its goals. Hence Islam unites or integrates spiritual and material motives. This is demonstrated to be the case with regard to Islamic political and economic theory. The Islamic state is founded upon the equality of all men and all nations. It is meant to be a universal state. The Islamic economic system has all the virtues of capitalism and communism and none of their defects.

The second major section of the book is an examination of the degree to which Islamic practice conformed to this ideal. The ideal, as we have seen, reconciles belief and institutions, or thought and behavior, by means of the sacred law. In history he seeks the reconciliation of theory and practice in the sense of the ideal and the actual, real, or factual. His conclusion is that, for the most part, theory and practice in Islam did conform, except for the restricted area of politics or government.[56] The failure of Islam in this regard is due to the unfortunate, if understandable, error whereby ʿUthman was permitted to become the third caliph in ʿAli's stead. Islam was ill served at a most critical time by a leader who was too old and too burdened by family ties to do the job well.[57]

Although there are occasional references in this work to the importance of conscience and belief and to psychological matters or questions of human nature, or even the rooting of belief in real world events, there is in fact little hint of the later philosophical tendency of Qutb. He rather pursues the standard apologetic mode, with an attack on Western culture, a defensive presentation of Muslim culture, and a description of Islam as a complete, integrated, and intelligible system which surpasses all others. The values by which Islam is praised are the values of the liberal, democratic, bourgeois West. More than other apologists, Qutb argues that theory and practice have been united historically in Islam, but in singling out the political realm as an exception he seems to be arguing that all that remains to be done in order to perfect modern Islam is to establish a truly Islamic polity that will repair the damage caused by that early mistake. Had not ʿUthman been elected caliph, "the entire history of Islam would have been changed, and it would have followed an entirely different path."[58] Obviously modernization and the clash with the West are secondary issues.

Qutb writes that Islam has met many challenges in the past, but it has shown great vitality in reasserting itself after several defeats. "But the final overthrow of Islam took place only in the present age, when Europe conquered the world."[59] But Qutb was not dismayed or discouraged by this "latest" defeat:

> "I personally, quite apart from my religious faith, have an absolute belief in the possibility of a renewal of Islamic life within the Muslim world; I believe in the soundness of Islam as a worldwide, rather than a local, system for the future. I have no desire to take refuge in vain speculation, but I do believe this to be not only possible, but even easy."[60]

Despite this optimism, in the ʿ*Adala* Qutb does not demand or expect the perfect congruence of theory and practice in Islam. He accepts the classical distinction between the two, and the reformist, moderate, and anti-radical implication of that distinction.

> Nonetheless, the difficulty of such achievement and the impossibility of maintaining it do not mean that Islam is purely mental and imaginative philosophy or idealism to which men's aspirations may reach out, but short of which their achievements must always fall. For the achievement of this standard . . . is not the responsibility of all men at all times. Rather it is the prescribed objective for men to aim at today, as they will tomorrow, and as they did yesterday; the objective which they have sometimes attained, sometimes missed.[61]

No wonder the members of the Revolutionary Command Council thought he would be a congenial collaborator.

While this book contains a few ambiguous rhetorical suggestions of the philosophical turn which Qutb would later take, his attack on the American philosophy of Pragmatism stands out as being the most relevant. Qutb argues that the renewal of Islam must be the result of education, and that, too, is a standard liberal-modernist, nonradical position. But he warns against the adoption of an educational philosophy which purports to be scientific and valid regardless of cultural context. Qutb seeks an Islamic educational philosophy, and quotes a work by one Jacob Fahm condemning Pragmatism:

> According to Charles Pierce and according to Pragmatism the idea is no more than a secondary product of some act or activity; it is not itself a reality.[62]
>
> Intellectualist theory says: If God really exists, then His existence must be logically demonstrable. Pragmatism on the other hand attacks the problem from a different angle. . . . In its view the truth of the idea of God does not depend on logical necessity; it depends solely on the profit of this idea to our well-ordered life, in our daily activity and in our experiences.[63]

Analysis of the rhetoric and reasoning of Qutb's ʿ*Adala* show that his earlier orientation was scripturalist, idealist, and intellectualist. It appears that he carefully separated his earlier interests in literary aesthetics from his more mature concern with religious reform. There is, in fact, little in the ʿ*Adala* to explain either his divergences from Mawdudi or his appeal to some of the militant fundamentalist societies. If the ʿ*Adala* represents the peak achievement in the rebuttal of the arguments of ʿAli ʿAbd al-Raziq, the *Ma'alim* represents a new departure in fundamentalist literature. The *Ma'alim* is a response to a new, nonscripturalist literature of reform and reassessment of the Islamic tradition. But it is not a wholly negative response to that literature. One of the most important elements in Qutb's altered perspective is his all but admitted adoption of the pragmatic perspective which he attacked in the ʿ*Adala*. This conclusion may be controversial precisely because Qutb does not expressly admit such a philosophical reorientation, but it is even more important and controversial to consider whether Qutb's last work expresses a definitive turn against the implied liberalism of the ʿ*Adala*. Western liberalism has made a similar pilgrimage from idealism to pragmatism, however, suggesting that, in the long run, the political significance of Qutb's work may not be as violently revolutionary as it now appears. The phrase "in the long run" is an escape clause, but here it is meant to refer to the social preconditions for the emergence of a liberal bourgeois state—to be discussed in subsequent chapters.

Tasawwur: An Aesthetic Theory of the Qur'an

In the *Ma'alim* Qutb abandons the meliorative faith in the asymptotic convergence of theory and practice within the context of an historical frame of reference. He calls for activism, jihad, and martyrdom. He promises no reward in this life, and he is pessimistic about the attainment of what he called "Islamic renewal" in the ʿ*Adala* book.[64] This affirmation of militance and martyrdom is built upon a metaphysical structure which attempts to be both worldly and subjective.

The dualism of theory and practice had permitted politicians, ulama, orientalists, modernists and others to apply an apologetic sophistry in order to transform modern Islam into an imitation of Western liberal culture. Qutb's remedy for this cultural invasion and the threat of the loss of identity, is to deny this dualism, and to replace it with a monism founded upon the consciousness and the existential condition of Muslims. Qutb is more militant in the *Ma'alim,* but it is probably of greater significance that he is more pessimistic, and that he links this pessimism with subjective and nonrational symbols.

Perhaps the most important symbol used by Qutb is his insistence that Islam is a *tasawwur,* a conception, an idea, an intuition, a vision, or something depicted or imagined. The form is actually participial, so that it could be translated as a conceiving, a visioning, or an imagining. Given Qutb's statement that this conception is dynamic, the latter interpretation may be more correct. But the primary point is that Islam, and competing systems, and the world in general are all conceived of as ideas, not as things known or understood, but as things visioned or imagined.

In the *ʿAdala,* Qutb rejected pragmatism and stated that Islam sustains the intellectualist doctrine, to which it adds revelation for a complete epistemology. In the *Ma'alim* Qutb argues against intellectualism. Even though he states that the sacred law (Shariʿa) and the laws of nature (*shariʿa kawniyya*) are of a piece, the linking of the two in human behavior is not to be accomplished via some epistemological device, but by means of an ontological integration, that is, by means of bringing human behavior or motivation into coordination with the nature of all creation (including man himself). The device by which man overcomes his alienation from nature is not knowledge but belief or faith. That faith—Islam—is, as we have seen, a conceptualizing, or a sort of phenomenological understanding.

> It is necessary that these milestones arise from the first source of the creed—the *Qur'an* . . . and from the conception or image (tasawwur) which it originates in the consciousness (*nufus* = selves, souls, minds) of the elite stratum.[65]

The significance of the term tasawwur may be revealed by an examination of an early work of Qutb. The book, *al-Taswir al-Fanni fi al-Qur'an* (Artistic representation in the Qur'an)[66] is devoted in its entirety to the analysis of *taswir,* the active participial form corresponding to the passive participle tasawwur, that is, depicting and depiction, representing and representation. In the introduction to the book, Qutb writes that the original essay on which it was based was written in 1939, and the whole book was completed only in 1944.[67] Thus the work antedates his joining the Muslim Brotherhood and his trip to the United States.[68] He wrote this book during the period in which he was still influenced by the rationalist reform movement identified with Muhammad ʿAbduh, and during the time when he was writing romantic and nostalgic stories. It is also noteworthy that this was a period in which many distinguished Egyptian authors had turned to a religious-romantic genre that has drawn the attention of several of the cultural historians of Egypt.[69] Among these authors was the well-known Abbas Mahmud al-Aqqad, whose influence on Qutb has been acknowledged.[70]

It is, nevertheless, a bit surprising to find Qutb undertaking the risky task of applying a form of literary criticism to the Qur'an, and more especially in a humanistic (if not rationalistic) centered interpretation. That this was dangerous territory is well attested, not only by the fate of Taha Husain's comparison of qur'anic rhetoric to pre-Islamic poetry, but to the later attacks on Muhammad Khalaf Allah for his thesis on the art of narrative in the Qur'an.[71] In all these cases, the aesthetic analysis of the Qur'an—which would have been unthinkable in this intellectualist discursive form before the impact of Western academic culture—touches on the weighty question of the *iʿjaz,* or miraculousness of the Quran. Any analysis which might derogate from the identification of the Qur'an as the word of God and an absolute and final truth runs the risk of being declared unbelief.[72] On the other hand, an affirmation that the qur'anic rhetoric exceeds human capacities would be acceptable to the orthodox traditionals. Qutb tells us that he was fascinated by the artistic or aesthetic miraculousness of the Qur'an, and while he was criticized as denying the iʿjaz, he does not seem to have been accused of heresy for his remarkably new approach to understanding Islamic scripture.[73]

The book starts in a simple and a disarming way with a dedication to the author's mother, "Unto you, oh mother (I dedicate) the fruit of your lengthy guidance to your little child and to your grown-up young man; though beauty in chanting [the Qur'an] evaded him, perhaps beauty in interpretation will not. May God keep you with him."[74]

In the introduction, Qutb writes that he is going to reveal a personal story that he has never told to anyone before. That story relates how, as a child, he pictured the images conveyed to him in the poorly understood qur'anic verses which he heard and read. "Pictures of this sort were sketched out before my young imagination, and I was enraptured in their contemplation, and I yearned to read the Qur'an for the sake of them."[75] In passing, we note the sensuous language employed by Qutb: *iltadhdh* (rapture, pleasure) and *ishtaq* (yearning, desiring).

Later, in his formal education in Cairo, the Qur'an was presented to him in a dry, dull, and analytic manner through the medium of books on commentary. In time, Qutb came to feel that the commentators had missed the whole point of the Qur'an, and had actually misled students by their methods. As a result of returning to the direct reading of the Qur'an and the studies of the aesthetic marvels of the Qur'an he came to two conclusions: first, that artistic representation is the major expressive method of the Qur'an and the basic principle followed for all purposes except legislation, and second, that the whole of the Qur'an is marvelously integrated by a remarkable singleness of purpose and method.[76] Hence the artistic parts of the Qur'an are not to be taken as fundamentally different in nature and purpose from the rest: "For this glorious book has common characteristics and a single method for expressing all its goals, whether the intent be preaching or warning, a tale of what happened or an event yet to be, logic to convince or an exhortation to belief, a description of earthly life or of the life hereafter, a representation of something perceived or something tangible, presenting the phenomenal or the noumenal, explaining an idea in the consciousness or observed empirically."[77]

Despite the comprehensiveness of the method of taswir, or artistic representation, Qutb hesitates occasionally and limits the scope of his inquiry. "It is not the purpose of this book," he writes, to take up the matter of the message of the Qur'an from the religious point of view, but rather to restrict discussion to the area of expression alone, transcending time and place . . . in order to discover pure aesthetic beauty, originally in its independent essence, everlasting in the Qur'an itself, expressing aesthetic [value] independently of all interest and purpose."[78] We note the idealistic philosophical bent of the statement, and the echo of Kantian aesthetic theory in the phrase, "independently of interest or purpose."[79] This philosophical quest and its religious detachment is soon abandoned for a more ambitious religious argument.

In an argument reminding us of his lament that Islamic political history was distorted by the unfortunate election of ʿUthman to the caliphate, Qutb regrets that the commentators neglected the aesthetic aspect of the Qur'an and its integrated methodology. The commentators took each verse by itself, and even if they concerned themselves with aesthetic matters, they dealt with each artistic device piecemeal and never attained a general theory.[80] Tafsir, or commentary, as a discipline, has gone through two stages. The earliest was a period in which there was a fear of too much interpretation. Gradually, that was replaced by the elaboration of a cautious, plodding commentary rooted in legalistic, dialectical, grammatical, historical and mythological analysis. The great need now is to move to the third state of an integrated, wholistic interpretation based on the comprehensive ground of the qur'anic aesthetic.[81] Presumably, Qutb's *Fi Zilal al-Qur'an* was the fulfillment of this need.[82]

Qutb started with the limited notion of taswir as a method employed in certain graphic passages of the Qur'an, but he soon moved to the more general assertion that taswir is the basis of almost all qur'anic expression, and finally to the position that taswir best represents the unified purpose of the Qur'an. The various levels of emphasis may represent positions held by Qutb over the period that he was developing his doctrine of the qur'anic aesthetic, but the evidence in this book cannot resolve that question. Qutb repeatedly goes beyond describing the qur'anic aesthetic as mere device, instrumentality, or method. He insists, rather, that means and end are one in the qur'anic revelation, that the "magic" of the qur'an is to be found in its aesthetic "essence," and in both the *Khasa'is* and the *Ma'alim*, that Islam itself is a tasawwur.[83]

Instead of the art of the Qur'an being merely a device or an ancillary aspect, appealing to children, or even a marvellous proof of the divine origin of the Qur'an, Qutb insists that means and end, like theory and practice, are completely unified and without contradiction in Islam and especially in the Qur'an. Hence the artistic method is not merely an accoutrement, but it directly expresses the essence of Islam and the Qur'an. The qur'anic message is presented by means of art and it is art itself.

The significance of this conclusion, hyperbolic though it may be, is very great for understanding Qutb's thought, if not also his appeal to younger, intensely committed believers. This significance stems from two considerations. The first of these is the apparent fact that despite important changes in Qutb's position in years subsequent to his work on artistic representation in the Qur'an, he never repudiated this early work. He is reported to have regretted his early literary efforts, including those purported to have some autobiographical and personal psychological relevance.[84] But, as we have seen, he persisted in describing Islam as a tasawwur to the very end.

Qutb's Theory of the Aesthetic

The second consideration that we have to take into account in seeking the significance of Qutb's aesthetic interpretation of the Qur'an, is the nature of his aesthetic theory. Much can be concluded from negative assertions that the Qur'an is not narrative history, not a code of law, not an extended sermon, not a work of philosophy; all of which may be corollaries of the assertion that it is a work of art. Nevertheless, it makes a great deal of difference what Qutb had in mind when he used the word art.

Despite the fact that Qutb explicitly faults the traditional commentators for failing to produce a comprehensive aesthetic theory of the Qur'an, it seems to me that he does not do so either. He comes much closer to providing a comprehensive commentary on the Qur'an which is informed by his two basic principles (that the method of the Qur'an is artistic and that its art is an integrated whole) but he did not produce a theory of art itself.

It is apparent that Qutb did not question the nature of art, but seems to have adopted the post-Kantian aesthetic of liberal individualism that was the legacy of European romanticism to the cultural elite of the colonial world. The divine art, like all art, appeals essentially to the subjective and the emotional. Qutb maintains this position throughout his adult life, spanning both his literary and his religious fundamentalist periods. In a later book, apparently first published in 1962, and one which is far more analytic in intent than *al-Taswir al-Fanni*, Qutb reaffirms his earlier position, but does not elaborate a theory of art. His goal is to present an analysis of the art of the Qur'an, not of art itself. Only the first volume of the later book, *Khasaʿis al-Tasawwur al-Islami wa-Muqawwimatuhu*, has been published. In that book Qutb argues that there are six characteristic features, or patterns, in the art of the Qur'an, and these are found throughout.[85] Rather than analyzing the artistic in itself, Qutb was more concerned to show how the qur'anic aesthetic sustained six characteristic aspects of Islam. In other words, he sought to demonstrate the complete integration of the whole of revelation and of revelation and art.

As a consequence of the absence of any explicit statement of Qutb's philosophy or art, we have to rely upon his arguments attempting to prove that the Qur'an is a unified work of art. We start with his *Taswir*.

In summing up his perspective, Qutb writes:

> Taswir is the instrument of preference for the qur'anic method. Taswir expresses intellectual meanings and mental states by means of sensuous and imaginative depiction; and, by the same means, the [Qur'an] expresses the experience of events, and the perception of spectacles. It also portrays models of human characteristics and the nature of creatures of the flesh. Then it takes that picture which it has drawn, and bestows upon it a personified vitality or a self-regenerating dynamism. So it is as if the intellectual idea is a structure or a movement; and the mental state a picture or a spectacle; and the human type a live person, and human nature a vigorous corporeal form.

> As for events and perceptions, stories and ideas, it (taswir) makes them into persons, present before us, in whom there is life and movement, and should [such qur'anic representations] be further examined, they would be found to entail the equivalent of all of the methods of dramatic performance. Thus, when the presentation has barely begun, the audience imagines itself . . . transported to the original theater (the real world?) where those events have either occurred or will occur. . . . The individual listener forgets that those are merely lines which are spoken, and, as though he were struck, he imagines it to be a vision presented to his senses and an event happening. Indeed, those are persons, and not actors, going and coming on the stage, and the reaction of the audience is the outward mark of the affect on all the consciousnesses that arises from the situation accompanying the events. Those words cause the tongues to move with them, and they reveal the hidden feelings (of the audience).[86]

This passage is actually an outline of the remainder of the *Taswir* book, and is the most elaborate statement of Qutb's aesthetic. Later on, after presenting some supporting examples from the Qur'an, he writes, "As for me, I have forgotten myself, and I forgot that I was explicating the artistic aspect of this spectacle; I thought I was witnessing it in reality and not in imagination."[87] Toward the end of the book, Qutb concedes that the intellect and the conscience are among several paths for accomplishing the goals of religious conversion, but their power is much weaker than the method which appeals to the consciousness and to the senses.[88]

Thus, the primary function of art is to excite and arouse affective reactions in the consciousness by means of the diffusion of aesthetic pleasure, and thereby to arouse a latent vitality and to stimulate action.[89] Qutb's aesthetic points to the effect of art on the inner stream of consciousness, or durée, or nonreflexive experience of which Bergson and Schutz wrote.[90] Art does not merely reproduce life, it reproduces the immediate experience of life. Hence art goes beyond the mere reproduction of what is empirically observed and objectively experienced.

Against Philosophy

Thus Qutb joins many thinkers who argue that in the field of religion, as in the communicative sciences generally, it is consciousness and not knowledge upon which truth, or reality, or Being, is to be grounded. In particular, Qutb is to be associated with those who have argued or intimated that the aesthetic is the appropriate form of discourse on religious, social and historical matters. An important difference is to be found in the fact that Qutb is not referring to the role of the artist as an interpreter of the cultural consciousness of a particular era. Qutb writes rather of the role of revelation which conveys, by means of a divine art, a transcendent religious consciousness—and by transcendent I mean the conveying of a universal truth (Being) in a manner which touches without mediation on the human condition (being with a small *b*).[91] But the teaching of the Qur'an is not merely meant to affect the emotional attitudes of Muslims towards Islam, it is also meant to convince them that external social experience is to be brought into conformity with the aesthetically defined inner experience of truth. This conclusion is, in effect, the reverse of the usual existentialist argument that takes historical experience as the measure of human goals.

If Qutb seems to be taking Heidegger, Gadamer, and even Nietzsche, and standing them on their heads (knowingly or unknowingly), Western observers may be inclined to ask, "Why bother?" The purpose of the modern development of hermeneutical-existential phenomenology is to provide a philosophical ground for preserving the Western tradition, now that we no longer accept the ground of ancient philosophy or the ground of religious revelation. If everything can be founded upon the truth of Islam, then there is no need for such a substitute for the inherited intellectualist philosophies.

Qutb's system in the *Ma'alim* does not start with doubt or the search for a ground, but rather with an unequivocal acceptance of revelation. It would appear, therefore, that he had no need to elaborate an aesthetic theory to provide an alternative justification for belief. Nevertheless, the implicit question remains, and he seems to have provided the answer in the *Taswir* book. Thus, in describing the magic of the Qur'an, he shows how some early converts to Islam were won over by merely hearing a single verse of the Qur'an—much as he was charmed by the Qur'an as a child—and before becoming acquainted with the full teachings of Islam. The Qur'an is a fully integrated theological and artistic unity, but it is not necessary to know it all before one becomes a believer, nor is that process a voluntary or rational one. Belief is not based upon the intellectual understanding of the logical priority of divine creation. The event of belief precedes the lengthy process of acquiring religious knowledge. For any given individual, for the *kinunah al-insaniyya* (does it mean *dasein*?), the aesthetically grounded emotional experience must be existentially prior.

In 1962, Qutb's *Khasa'is* was published. At first glance, it appears to be a further development of the earlier *al-Taswir al-Fanni*, but in fact it represents a more restrained and Apollonian version of the qur'anic aesthetic. The main body of the book details the way in which the artistic devices of the Qur'an are employed to present the principle features of the Islamic belief system: divine authority, permanence, comprehensiveness, balance, positiveness of divine involvement in the world, immanence (practicality and actuality of Islam), and monism.[92] While the work as a whole has an analytical and expository structure, its main argument, repeated throughout, is a rejection of philosophy. The rationalistic framework notwithstanding, Qutb maintains his earlier position in all its essentials, going as far as to explicitly equate the Qur'an and al-Tasawwur al-Islami.[93]

Qutb starts out by criticizing ʿAbduh and Iqbal, because they adopted inappropriate and poorly comprehended Western philosophical frames of reference in developing their interpretations of Islam. ʿAbduh erred in equating the significance of reason and conscience, because reason varies with the individual and cannot serve as an independent basis of interpreting the Qur'an.[94] Iqbal erred in borrowing from Hegel and Comte, and thus overemphasizing the pragmatic and the experiential. Qutb states, without embarrassment, that there is no Islamic philosophy. "That doesn't diminish Islam one bit in our view. . . . It rather powerfully affirms its authenticity, its purity, and its uniqueness!"[95]

Despite Qutb's criticism, there is an obvious affinity between his idea of Islam and the philosophy of Iqbal. This similarity is most apparent in the parallel between Qutb's concept of movement or dynamism in Islam, and Iqbal's principle of movement in Islam.[96] Yet Qutb argues that Iqbal's interpretation is constrained and distorted by its philosophical dependence upon either materialistic or dualist systems. Qutb affirms that frames of reference influence the ideas they are meant to convey (form and content) but he denies that every idea is inevitably presented within some formal (language, discipline, paradigm, etc.) context.[97] Here we see more clearly one of the functions that an aesthetic perspective is to achieve for Qutb: the replacement of the need for a systematic philosophical approach, as though the artistic vision is nothing but the rapturous response of the consciousness to the affect of sensuous arousal (rather than, for example, the authentic hermeneutical determination of the form to be impressed upon random experience).[98]

Existential Praxis

The second element that we note in Qutb's later metaphysical orientation is a rejection of idealism, or essentialism, and a commitment to existential praxis. Islam is practical, worldly, and relevant to the actual circumstances of human beings. The Islamic conception and Islamic praxis are inseparable, or where separated become jahiliyya.

Where consciousness and action are fully integrated with existent circumstances, there we have Islam. The means of unifying the tasawwur and the conjuncture is the active practice of Islam.

Despite his criticism of pragmatism, Qutb describes both the Islamic tasawwur and existential reality as dynamic or moving. The metaphysical implications of this notion are far-reaching because he thereby denies the usual classical conception of a fixed and absolutely determined world which is the result of the divine creative will. The stuff of the world is not made up of things but of activities, processes, and movement. The world is constituted of intuition/representation (taswir) and action, yet this movement occurs within the apparently fixed limits of the shariʿa kawniyya or the laws of creation.

Although the shariʿa kawniyya is understood as dynamic, Qutb does fall into the contrary view that divine creation has the form of fixed laws (*nawamis*) of creation, of which man is a part, and to which man must conform by means of the knowledge gained of such laws from revelation.[99] I am inclined toward the view that Qutb was simply inconsistent and philosophically unsophisticated enough not to recognize the contradiction. The problem points once again to the question of overcoming the alienation between man and the world and the answer, in part, is to deny the reality of both the theoretically abstract world of science and theology and the objectivist and empirical world of materialism. Even the reconciliation of man and the world is described as the coordination of the movement of man with the movement of nature.[100]

It is more than likely that this apparent contradiction can be mitigated, if not resolved, by recalling that Qutb's Islamic phenomenology is based on divine revelation and creation, and not upon experience in the world. Qutb's praxis involved reconciling direct (rather than discursive) experience with the Islamic phenomenology. Hence movement (haraka) involves the dynamic reconciliation of divine phenomenology and experience in (what Husserl called) the life-world, through activity which has meaning in the Islamic sense.[101] The ambiguity that remains turns on whether Qutb conceived of the nawamis (norms) of nature as principles of movement or as a fixed and unchanging order, and I do not think the text gives us a decisive answer.

The themes of movement, dynamism, activity, and change recall the familiar criticism that Islam has become stagnant and that its rigid law prevents it from adapting to changed conditions. Qutb's exposition is meant to refute this critique, but we see that he has gone beyond the usual apologetic to locate the purportedly missing virtue in the very essence of Islam.

> Tasawwur and the ordering of (everyday) life (*nizam*) alone will not produce "Islam" in the world in an actual-dynamic way. Moreover . . . it will profit those to whom Islam is presented in this way [i.e., as tasawwur and nizam, or conception and order] only if they are actually engaged in an actual Islamic movement. The greatest benefit that can accrue to those to whom Islam is thus presented will occur if they interact with it in the measure that they actually reach [that tasawwur] in the course of action.
>
> Once again I reiterate that the doctrinal tasawwur must be immediately represented in a dynamic concrescence (coming together) and, at the same time, that dynamic concrescence must be a true representation and a faithful translation of the doctrinal tasawwur.[102]

There can be no stronger affirmation of Qutb's belief that thought and action are united in Islam, and that each grows in interaction with the other. And again, "Islam is not merely doctrine, which convinces men by means of explication (*bayan*). It is rather, a method (*minhaj*) which is represented in a dynamic organizational concrescence."[103]

Martyrdom

In the final section of the *ʿAdala,* Qutb describes the path which is to be taken in order to achieve the renewal of Islam. As we have seen, he recommended a program of Islamic education. In the *Maʿalim,* his last chapter is similarly titled, "This is the Way," but it is heavily laden with a message of pessimism and a dismaying example of martyrdom. Qutb cites the story of the martyrs of al-Akhdud from the Qur'an, *surah al-Baruj:*

> In the name of the merciful and compassionate God
> By the heaven with its zodiacal signs
> And the promised day!
> And the witness and the witnessed
> The fellows of the pit [al-Akhdud] were slain;
> And the fire with its kindling,
> When they sat over it
> And witnessed the while what they were doing with those who believed,
> And they took not vengeance on them save for their belief in God,
> The mighty, the praiseworthy,
> Whose is the kingdoms of the heavens and the earth;
> For God is witness over all![104]

After elaborating on the horrors of the burning of the martyrs of al-Akhdud, Qutb raises the question of why they were not avenged and their murderers punished, as in several other stories in the Qur'an. He argues that the purpose of this story, and the meaning of God's inaction, is to affirm that the goal of life is not material comfort or pleasure, but true belief and God's service. The people of al-Akhdud achieved a victory over worldliness and rendered true belief victorious. In this manner, they served the whole of mankind by preserving and portraying an image of the true faith. Would the saving of the lives of a few at the cost of religious truth for all have been justified?[105]

This might also explain theory ≠ practice

Qutb rejects the idea that the martyrdom of the people of al-Akhdud must be given a rational, human explanation. God's will is not known to man, and the true believer will follow his faith wherever it leads him without hope or desire for reward.

> They are hirelings of God. Wheresoever, howsoever, and whysoever he wishes them to work, they shall work and receive the known (*maʿalum*) wage! It is neither their right nor their duty to direct the call (*daʿwa*) toward any destination whatsoever, for that is the business of the proprietor and not of the hired employee.[106]
>
> [by means of faith] did true belief triumph over life. . . . Those hearts (martyrs) were freed from their enslavement to life . . . and they broke away from the shackles of the earth together with all its attraction, and they rose above their own selves through the victory of true belief (*ʿaqida*) over the life in them.[107]

There is no reference to dynamic, conceptual praxis in these passages, but neither is there any affirmation of an ordered and predictable social world. The true believer will do what he must without concern for the consequences. The overriding conception is complete subservience to God marked by the extremes of jihad and martyrdom. In the *ʿAdala,* Qutb was mostly concerned with what lies between those extremes, but in the *Ma'alim* he seems to be preparing the case for his own martyrdom. The imagery of religious martyrdom is familiar to us from both the Christian and Shiʿite Muslim traditions in which martyrdom may be considered the religious act par excellence, in which martyrdom is often portrayed in a dramatic setting, that is, as part of a progression of events, where the act of martyrdom gives meaning to a senseless world, and finally wherein identification with the martyr can be an important aspect of religious experience. There is, of course, a difference between acting out the event in a dramatic setting, and acting it out in the form of a deed of suicidal or hopeless terrorism—but there is also some obvious similarity.

While the mainstream of Sunni orthodoxy seems to have eschewed these martyrological options, it has been argued that some Sufi orientations, particularly that of al-Hallaj, did embrace martyrdom as a central religious element.[108] Consequently, it is of interest to note the way in which Qutb manages to link a strong martyrological emphasis with an equally powerful nomothetic and non-Sufi Islam. One might be inclined to say a nonmystical Islam, but I am not sure that the devices which Qutb uses to arrive at his conclusion are entirely free of mystification—particularly with regard to his notion of Islam as a dynamic tasawwur which both expresses and defines the essence of human existence.[109]

Qutb's path to his vision of martyrdom, as we have seen includes an important change from viewing Islam as reconciling philosophical opposites to a monistic system which denies the validity of dualism altogether. Secondly, while affirming the divine origin of Islam, Qutb actually takes man or human existence as the measure of the religion.[110] Thirdly, Qutb rejects speculative reason and any attempt to equate revelation and philosophical wisdom. Qutb's exposition uses a terminology which invokes the notions of praxis, existentialism and process. Hence, in contrast to other fundamentalists, he seems less concerned with legalism and the logical structure of the world. His arguments remind one of some elements of contemporary Protestant theology, especially those that are unconcerned with the question of the literal truth of revelation and more concerned with the moral phenomenology of the scriptural message.

Despite Qutb's embracing Mawdudi's theory of Hakimiyya, he turns it into a declaration of man's radical freedom. Man's absolute subjection to God's will is a matter of individual conversion and personal conviction, as is his rejection of worldly government—for no Islamic state actually exists. Man may be the measure of all things religious in the sense that Islam is an expression of the divine conception of man, but that conception is not articulated in a doctrinal formula. It is rather grasped intuitively and experienced by a living consciousness existing through time. The Islamic experience of man's Being is founded upon faith and revelation rather than upon material existence alone, but its dynamism, its capacity to change, the fact that the Islamic conception—al-Tasawwur al-Islami—is also a tasawwur haraki means that Islamic religion is conceived of as a human phenomenon and not something coterminous with God, as is the Qur'an. It is, nevertheless, important to insist that the origin of this religious experience, or enlightenment, is not historical or this-worldly experience. As a consequence, religious duties are not governed by political prudence, or natural necessity, or the laws of social process.[111]

While Qutb does sometimes, somewhat inconsistently, refer to such prudential considerations, his major emphasis is upon the (subjective) religious consciousness of the individual and the process by which that consciousness changes so as to give meaning to the life lived by the individual Muslim. In a manner of speaking, religion, or Islam, replaces the aesthetic in a rather uncertain adaptation of Heidegger's ontological phenomenology.

The ontic element in Qutb's theory, by now obvious, is given expression in the term *al-kinuna al-insaniyya* (the human existent).[112] Qutb's ontological Islam is thus linked to the "ownmost being" of the believing Muslim, in a manner that urges him to act out, to realize, to practice that faith as an expression of his being, and not with regard to practical political or social consequences of that act. When we consider once again that the absolute foundation of Islam, and of the freedom of the individual Muslim to act, is the hakimiyya of God, then the characteristic Islamic act becomes the defiance of jahili activity. Thus is the groundwork laid for acts of martyrdom which appear to be suicidal and/or hopeless acts of political terrorism.

Finally, it is relevant to note that the rejection of theory is also a rejection of the idea of the absolutely determinative character of the world. The point is not that God does not determine all, or that God does not know all, but rather that man does not and cannot know all, and Islam does not provide such knowledge.[113] Qutb does not perceive the world as does Mawdudi, nor is his debate primarily with the exponents of materialistic natural science. He does not aspire to crumple his westernized opposition by the overwhelming force of his logic. He wants to appeal to the nonrational, nostalgic consciousness, the sense of authenticity or the primordial sentiments, or simply the traditional cultural attachments of (Egyptian) Muslims. His argument is that, by practicing Islam, by doing what Islam commands, eschewing any intellectual debate or justification, and by affirmatively accepting the consequences of that practice, one becomes a true Muslim and one gains paradise. But this quite modern and quite distinctive view of Islam is beset by many contradictory themes, suggesting the ambivalence of Sayyid Qutb and the intensity of his personal struggle to give his own martyred life Islamic meaning.

Theory and Practice

The most important political aspect of the ancient dualistic distinction between theory and practice, is the idea that theoretical perfection can never be realized in practice. In religious terms, this conception had led to equating revelation with theoretical perfection, but it has also produced the standard justification of leniency in the application of religious rules regarding human behavior. The underlying question is whether religious laws define an impossibly perfect human society or whether these laws reflect a worldly adaptation of divine wisdom and will. Where we have religious doctrine or laws defining political authority and legitimacy, the case is particularly difficult, and only becomes more complicated where social control is recognized as one of the (political) functions of religion.

More specifically, the question is whether the Islamic theory of the state and/or the caliphate should be considered as abstract and speculative theory which can never be realized in full on earth, or whether revelation by definition distinguishes between the divine and the earthly, the eternal and the temporal, the ideal and the humanly real. Given the fact that all agree that extant Muslim governments and societies fall far short of the ideal, are they to be condemned as jahili, or are they to be justified as determined by prevailing historical conditions to which the Islamic ideal must, in every age, be adapted? In other words, should the Shariʿa, or revelation, be treated as theory and historical governments and societies as practice, or should human achievements be measured directly by the Islamic ideal as an ideal already adapted to take account of human limitations?

In Qutb's earlier work, developed as a comparison of Islamic theory and practice, he recognized this dualism, and, in the usual manner, strove to close the gap by intensifying religious belief and commitment. In that work, he basically agreed with Mawdudi that Muslim practice could be brought closer to, if not up to the level of, theoretical sharʿi perfection.

Hence Qutb and Mawdudi seem to agree that the contradiction between theory and practice was the characteristic problem of contemporary Islam, that the two had been reconciled in the Islamic past, and that it was possible to achieve such perfection in the future. The method of doing so was primarily objective, social, and political; that is, by means of applying the law of Islam in society, but also by means of preaching the message of Islam. That message was, however, also conceived of as a rational discourse based on logical deduction from the first premise of God's creation and sovereignty. That is to say, objective reason and objective social organization were the bases of the solution to the contradiction of theory and practice in Islam. The worldly Islamic order, it was affirmed, was thus capable of prefection, and, hence, so was the worldly order of human society.

As we have noted, this doctrine did not nourish a violent, radical, or terrorist movement. Instead it sustained a petit bourgeois, reformist, gradualist and collaborative movement, willing to form coalitions and make compromises with other groups. It represents the scripturalist tendency within the fundamentalist movement. In Sayyid Qutb's later work we find a decisively divergent tendency, although it is not bereft of many disparate and contradictory statements.

Qutb resolves the contradictions between theory and practice in Islam by declaring that Islam, as a religion revealed to mankind, is oriented to praxis. Rather than characterize Islam in terms of the absolute determination of idealized theory, he defines the Islamic understanding of the world and of religious action in terms of existence and movement.[114] Movement, change and adaptation are all more important than cognitive truth or epistemological certainty. Religious perfection is attained by performing the religious act which actually, existentially, and politically reaffirms religious truth and faith in the particular, specific, situationally defined circumstances prevailing at a given historical-social-political juncture. The world is not so much a place whose religious perfection will be realized in the form of political and social institutions. It is rather a field in which divine omnipotence and human servility are combined in a religious praxis which denies the legitimacy of political institutions based on compromise and adaptation.

The issue broached by virtue of the identification of the Qur'an with the rhetorical, dramatic and poetic arts is the same as that which Taha Husain opened with the publication of his book on pre-Islamic poetry, and it is the same issue which divided Abbas Mahmud al-ʿAqqad and Mustafa Sadiq al-Rafiʿi. That is the issue of the miraculousness, or iʿjaz of the Qur'an—or that aspect of its form or its communicative character which renders the Qur'an proof of its own divine origin. Insofar as any explanation of that special miraculous quality involves a comparison with some form of human endeavor, there remains the possibility of duplication, or of explaining away the apparently miraculous by means of the merely ingenious.

In the *Taswir* book, Qutb tells us that his quest is not the essence of Islam, but the essence of artistic beauty. While he lays out no philosophical context of this quest, it resonates with the medieval belief that revelation and pure theoretical reason can be demonstrated to be identical. Of course, the Qur'an does not present us with an aesthetic theory, rather, according to Qutb, it is itself a work of art. Its perfection is not determined by its conformity to some theoretical criterion arrived at by philosophical reasoning. Qutb assumes, but does not argue, a definition of the nature of artistic beauty. His assumption is based on his own experience and his conclusions regarding the nature of religious experience, and the connection between such experience and belief.

If a work of art can inspire religious belief, is it necessary that the originator of such art be God, Himself, or is it possible that a purely human artistic endeavor may lead to the same results? If experience demonstrates that a merely human art is capable of raising human beings to the highest level of religious consciousness, it follows that the Qur'an may not be divine, or at least, that there is no self-evident proof of its divine origin.

There is no evidence that Qutb harbored such thoughts, since he employed a form of circular reasoning whereby the method of the Qur'an is used to define art, and his definition of art is used to determine the quality of the art of the Qur'an. But, as we have seen, the foundation of this circular reasoning is not theoretical—it is in the artistic experience itself. Moreover, this circular reasoning says as much about Islam as it says about art, and one of the most important things it seems to be saying is that belief is not founded upon rational thought or cognitive process. This is not a scandalous innovation in our post-Kantian world, but it is a departure from usual Islamic self-understanding, which is simply that God revealed his will to the Prophet Muhammad at specific times and places in a completely historical, factual, and empirical sense.

If the Qur'an's account of itself is an artistic rather than a factual account, it might be argued that the truth it thus conveys is a religious and not a factual truth. Such an argument replaces the historical fact of revelation as the basis of belief with the artistic experience. This approach diminishes the significance of rationalist and objectivist doubts, and places the greatest burden of belief upon individual consciousness. But individual consciousness is a matter about which it is difficult to be absolutely certain for any continuous and lengthy period. The argument for the aesthetic ordering of the world as a way of rendering it meaningful was Nietzsche's last resort in the struggle to escape from nihilism.[115]

Qutb did not start from the edge of the abyss, but his aesthetic interpretation of the Qur'an is gratuitous unless we suppose the possibility that the cognitive apologetic has failed to convince. In most of his work, after the *Taswir,* Qutb withdrew from the brink and adapted his vision to the analytical form of the established fundamentalist discourse. Nevertheless, political prudence is the enemy of a religious consciousness that aspires to social as well as individual meaningfulness. The implicit question is, why couldn't Qutb compromise, and why did he urge his followers not to compromise? Qutb argues that the Islamic tasawwur brings forth in the true Muslim a conception of meaningful action which he calls a minhaj: a way of acting which is called for by the aesthetic appeal of the Qur'an, and which fulfills the artistic conception and completes its meaning. But if art fails or is abandoned, is there anything else?

It is apparent that there is much to be said for the common

opinion of the effect of imprisonment and political persecution on Qutb's thought. There is reason to believe that Qutb, driven back to the inner resources of his own faith, reasserted the latent aesthetic structure of his religious experience. This world was no longer viewed as a field for the "actualization" of the Islamic ideas, but rather as a setting in which the immanent meaning of religious truth might be made manifest by means of a praxis founded upon a religious consciousness inspired by the Islamic aesthetic.

> We must return to it [the Qur'an] . . . in a spirit informed by accomplishment and activity, not in a sense of academic or leisurely study. We return to it to learn what it demands of us that we become, so that we can so become. Along the way we will encounter artistic beauty in the Qur'an, and splendid stories and spectacles of resurrection . . . and the logic of intuitive consciousness . . . and the rest of those things that are sought by the advocates of study, but we shall encounter all those things without their being our primary goal. Truly, our primary goal is to know, "What does the Qur'an want us to do? What is the all encompassing tasawwur of which it wishes us to conceive? How does the Qur'an wish us to feel about Allah?"[116]

In the ʿ*Adala*, Qutb, following Mawdudi, and in the Islamic tradition, chooses theory over practice, and expresses this choice as a preference for idealism over pragmatism. In the *Ma'alim*, Qutb chooses practice over theory. Reading the Qur'an and practicing the faith produce an Islamic consciousness. But there is no guarantee that such practice can transform the world of lived experience into the ideal of the Islamic tasawwur. Qutb, isolated, imprisoned, in ill health, and dispirited, chose martyrdom over accommodative compromise. But his choice is not the only possible conclusion, nor even the most usual conclusion, drawn from the pragmatic, existentialist, ontological or historical preference for practice over theory. Qutb's *schwannegesang* opens at least a philosophical path for the cooperation of fundamentalists and contemporary political movements of both the right and the left.

6

Islam and Capitalism

revival =
1. faith/commitment ↑
or 2. material change ?

The central question in understanding the events known as the Islamic revival, is whether those events are the result of a spiritual reinvigoration of religious faith and commitment, or merely the consequence of material change. In the preceding chapter, the alternatives of reason and consciousness were addresed, and the resultant dialectic led to a new understanding of the spirit of Islamic fundamentalism and its nonscriptural, totalizing perception of Islam. In this chapter, the alternatives of the material and spiritual explanations of religious movements will be addressed by means of the analysis of a recent literature which is concerned with the "failure" of capitalism in the Muslim world. This second dialectic has produced a variety of historicist interpretations of Islam, some of which reaffirm the view that traditional Islam blocks progress, and others which assert that an historically dynamic and adaptive Islam has and will continue to contribute to the progress of capitalism in the Muslim world.

Two decades ago, when Maxime Rodinson wrote *Islam and Capitalism*, the issue was rather to explain the backwardness of the Islamic world, but the essential question is still the same.[1] Presumably, the intervening transformative events, occurring in the full view of historically conscious observers, should have allowed the issue of spirit versus matter to be decisively set at rest, and thus disposed of one of the most persisent intellectual conundrums of all time. Rodinson claimed that the truth of the materialist conception of ideology had been more than amply demonstrated by the history of his times, even if that truth were a little distorted by the excesses of his dogmatic Marxist "friends."[2] Despite his confidence in this matter, there are still many moralizing and intellectualizing idealists who are inclined to read the most recent history of Islam differently.

Rodinson, himself, is outspokenly committed to the values of political freedom and political equality, and he furthermore argues that Muslims and others are in a position (are free ?) to choose between capitalism and socialism at this historical juncture.[3] Actually Rodinson's explicitly theoretical, philosophical, and methodological statements are somewhat confused, rambling, and diffuse. But then the value of his book does not lie in the fragments of polemic against dogmatic Marxism and pan-structuralism which it contains, nor in its oversimplified populist materialism. Rodinson is an orientalist, and throughout most of this work he remains faithful to that calling, despite his apparent belief that the enlightenment evidenced by his abandonment of orthodox Marxism was an entitlement to a social-scientific pretension. The value of the book is rather to be found in its relevance to two more limited questions, one arising in the context of Marxist theory and the other in the context of Weberian theory, and both related to the general issue of development, or modernization.

The predominant theories of development, liberal and Marxist alike, hold the position that modernization, by whatever definition, is a singular phenomenon of world-historical significance, which has already occurred. Though modernization, as either or both a cultural or an economic phenomenon, first emerged in Europe, the significance of that emergence is worldwide. Hence, as far as all non-European societies are concerned, modernization or development must in some sense be westernization, and therefore alienative. The possibility of an authentic development for Third World countries depends upon the theoretical possibility of two or more entirely independent processes of development, and, at our present stage of world history, the practical possibility of reconstructing what an alternative and originally authentic process of development might look like. The complete statement of the issue for present purposes requires the further question of whether there might have been an authentic Islamic alternative development that was preempted by European imperialism and capitalism, and which might now be recovered by a revolutionary return to Islamic authenticity—as some might argue is transpiring in Iran under the leadership of Ayatullah Khomeini.

One revisionist aspect of Rodinson's neo-Marxism is his rejection of the concept and the historical reality of the Asiatic mode of production (AMP). The distinctive characteristic of the AMP is that it produces stagnation rather than conflict, contradiction, struggle, dialectic, change and revolution. If the prevailing mode of production in medieval Islam was the AMP, then no progress would ever have been attained, were it not for the intrusion of Western capitalism. This is a straightforward interpretation of Marx, although casuistical interpretations of the Althusser sort might deny it. Now, the difference it makes in the long run, in terms of the choice of socioeconomic arrangements, is not much. That is, both the Christian-capitalist West and the Muslim world are headed for, or should be headed for socialism. The question is whether it was or is necessary for the Muslim world to get there via integration within the mode of production of late capitalism. Rodinson argues that there is no alternative way, not because of the AMP, but because the Western Christian world got there first.[4] Rodinson and Samir Amin differ on why the West got there first, but both agree that capitalism has been the necessary path to socialism in terms of world history. Amin argues that it is not necessary that the Muslim world either recapitulate the experience of the West or that it become integrated with the late capitalist mode of production.[5] Amin's arguments may or may not be sound, but they have the effect of asserting that the Muslim world should and can bypass the capitalist stage, and should pursue an autarkic policy challenging the structure of the international economic order.

Rodinson's position appears to be anomalous, because he argues that Islam was not inherently antagonistic to capitalism, yet he urges the Muslims to reject the capitalist alternative for socialism. In arguing against the dogmatic Marxists, Rodinson is at pains to point out that he distinguishes between the prevalence of certain capitalistic practices which he takes as evidence of the potential historical evolution of a capitalist mode of production or a capitalist socioeconomic order, and the actual existence of a socioeconomic order whose mode of production is capitalist. The existence of capitalistic enclaves, or economic subsectors, in medieval Islam is enough to refute the Asiatic mode thesis.[6] Given the proper political, social, and economic circumstances, Rodinson is certain that a full-fledged capitalism would have emerged. It would appear that the discussion of the AMP and the assertion that Islam was, in fact, hospitable to capitalist practices and capitalist social segments at various times and places is only academic. There are, however, significant implications of Rodinson's argument both for contemporary politics and contemporary scholarship.

It is important to bear in mind that Rodinson does not treat capitalism and socialism as contradictory essences. Socialism is not only dialectically derived from capitalism, it actually incorporates many aspects of capitalism as a mode of production. Hence, to argue that medieval and even early Islam were compatible with capitalist practices is to argue that modern Islam is compatible with socialism. The key components of the capitalist mode of production and the socialist mode of production are identical as far as the organization of production is concerned. It is rather in the area of the relations of production that they differ.

From the point of view of materialist historical analysis, the theory of AMP postulates that the Muslim world had virtually no history. While the critics of Western orientalists are inclined to attribute this conclusion to the pernicious influence of those orientalists on Marx, the orientalist model is actually idealist, and is built on assumptions which are organic, biological, teleological, and functional. The orientalists tend to interpret Islamic history as the growth, development, integration, and expression of a distinctive essence; followed by decline, corruption, disintegration, and then expressive confusion, incoherence, and silence. Western imperialists are further inclined to characterize the Islamic golden age not only in terms of political success and cultural efflorescence, but also in terms of the hiatus between the spirit of early Islam and the worldly ethos permeating the high Abbasid or Ottoman times.

Obviously, the orientalists ought to be condemned for their own sins, rather than for the misdeeds of others. Rodinson's criticism of the doctrinaire Marxists is thus more to the point than the confused reasoning which would attribute every pejorative judgment on Muslims or Muslim history to the prejudices of Western Christian culture as enhanced by bourgeois idealism and Zionist manipulation. In denying the validity of the theory of the AMP, and in showing how various capitalistic segments emerged from time to time and struggled for survival, aggrandizement, and even dominance, Rodinson demonstrates the need for a careful analysis of social forces at each stage of Islamic history. In other words, he argues that the Muslim world does have a history in the sense intended by adherents of historical materialism. There were significant changes of social structure and of the organization of production at different times and places, leading up to the ongoing struggles and transformations of the present. Rodinson's method has been directly influential in Peter Gran's treatment of the historical setting of his analysis of the cultural meaning of the work of Hasan al-Attar.[7] But even among those whom we might expect to have learned from Rodinson there are lapses, as when Samir Amin writes of the continuity of a single social formation for over twelve centuries, and Gran himself, criticizing Amin, proposes six centuries for the dominant patrimonial-tributary formation of Abbasid times.

The neo-Marxists are, therefore, inclined to agree with the liberal analysts that a meaningful indigenous development process is going on in the Muslim world, but, of course, they do not agree on the essential features of that process. The neo-Marxists are struggling to define it in terms of a conflict of classes, while the exponents of the liberal theory of development are more inclined to measure the adaptation, or socialization, or the learning skills of actual ruling elites, and their ability to assert tutelary control of the cultural development of their fellow Muslims.[8]

The question of whether Islam is inherently anti-capitalist is derivative of the earlier view that Islam is inimical to progress, rationality, liberty, and democracy. These criticisms of Islam were often proffered as explanations of the backwardness of Muslim society and the military weakness of the Muslim empires. But the criticisms were not based on any scientific findings regarding the prerequisites of development. They rather reflected the self-image of Western society and those values to which the dominant classes were inclined to attribute the success of the systems they dominated. The criticisms were also linked to particular provisions of Islamic law, thus lending them a plausibility that frequently influenced Muslim intellectuals themselves.

The provisions of the Shariʿa regarding slavery, the position of women, legal reasoning, qadi justice, and the caliphate, to name merely the most popular, were taken as proof of the need to reform Islam if it were to be adapted to the needs of the modern world. In the realm of economic organization, the central symbols were the Shariʿa provisions regarding usury and gambling and their derivative judgments regarding banking, joint stock corporations, speculation and futures markets. Over against this serious critique, it was argued that Islam arose in a commercial setting in Mecca, that the language of the Qur'an actually reflects a commercial culture and commercial values, that merchants were usually closely associated with the ruling elites, that patrimonial bureaucracies were often engaged directly in commerce, and, of course, that Islam generally guarantees property rights, commercial contracts, and wage labor. Some fundamentalist Muslims are inclined to accept the literalist interpretation of the Shariʿa provisions and to argue that, if implemented by a government of pious Muslims, they will result in a more prosperous, more beneficent, and more efficient economic system than either capitalism or socialism. There are also many liberal Muslim intellectuals who are concerned to show that Islamic law and legal reasoning either were not, or need not be so rigid. Adaptations of the letter of the law were made by various regimes in the past, and these same legal mechanisms can be used in the present to bring about similar results which will be both true to the spirit of Islam and responsive to the needs of modern economic life.

Rodinson's position is fairly close to that of the liberal apologists, although his reasoning is rooted in historical materialism rather than in the principle of practical reason and the necessity of adapting the purely theoretical to the requirements of historical situations. Rodinson's method is to point out that, in fact, Muslim rulers, ulama and merchants, made adjustments and did respond to the requirements of the prevailing mode of production. The principle which governed these adaptations was not so much the preservation of a religious principle as the need to legitimate adaptive reforms. The function of the ulama might even be defined in terms of this service to the warrior elite of the Islamic patrimonial state. Rodinson argues both positive sides of the question. He argues that Islam is both rational and commercial in spirit, and that Muslims were always able to work around specific qur'anic provisions which seemed to militate against economic rationality. It is incorrect, argues Rodinson, to hold that Islamic history has been determined once and for all by either the character of the original revelation or by the social formation that prevailed at the time of its origination. Early Muslim society was not primarily a slave-holding society, nor was it primarily feudal. The function of early Islam was to integrate tribally organized bedouin with the commercial and cultural centers of Arabia. But Muslim society changed, and as it changed Islam became elaborated and complex while adapting to the superstructural requirements of the medieval state. Morever, no single socioeconomic structure became dominant or synonymous with Islam. Capitalistic enclaves existed, but so did many other modes of production, simultaneously, in a confusing arrangement of heterogeneity.

At the beginning of this book, Rodinson asks, "How far is it necessary to go in the process of drawing level in order to achieve the enviable prosperity of the industrialized countries? Must one go so far as to sacrifice values that that are especially cherished, those that constitute the particularity, the individuality, the identity of the peoples concerned?"[9] His answer, coming at the end of the work, is that it is not necessary to give up anything that is essentially Islamic, because Islam has really had nothing to do with the economic circumstances of Muslim lands. It follows that Islam cannot be responsible for the backwardness of Muslims. In other words, one may go as far as one needs to in order to catch up with the West without sacrificing anything which is essential to Islam or integral to the identity of Muslims.[10]

In his insistence upon the detachment of Islamic essences from historical circumstances, and in his refusal to validate any conclusions regarding Islam which have been drawn from historical events, Rodinson appears, paradoxically, to have agreed with a number of idealistic Muslim apologists. In point of fact, Rodinson criticizes both would-be orientalists and Muslim apologists. He does this by demonstrating that even the Islamic prohibition of usury, and of certain kinds of transactions, was no barrier to the continuation and elaboration of pre-Islamic capitalistic practices, and by similarly demonstrating that the qur'anic revelation did not bring into being an exemplary moral economic system which was fundamentally different from any other existing economic system.[11]

Rodinson insists that there is no third way. There is only a choice between capitalism and socialism. Islam, like any other ideology, is essentially epiphenomenal, even if in the short run it might have some political significance. Moreover, at the moment, the symbols of Islam are fairly firmly under the control of the conservatives. Hence, if Muslims desire to achieve greater political freedom and greater material equality in accordance with what most people now believe to be possible, then they must turn from traditional Islam and reject the chimerical notion that there is an authentic, original, Islamic third way to development. Of course, this is not to argue that Islam is a barrier to socialism any more than it is a barrier to capitalism, or even that it is essentially socialistic, capitalistic, fatalistic, or militaristic. As mere ideology, Islam may, under appropriate circumstances, serve any political design, whether that of Khomeini, or Saddam Husain, or President Sadat, or King Fahd, or Muʿammar al-Qadhafi, or General Ẓia al-Haq, or King Hassan II, or . . .

This conclusion would not have much significance if Rodinson did not also argue that Muslims may choose to become economically modern. The choice is complicated by the fact that there are actually two ways to become economically modern, via capitalism and via socialism. For Rodinson, socialism is morally preferable in terms of the rational humanitarian values which he says Marxism shares with the philosophers of the Enlightenment.

While Rodinson does not write that the choice of capitalism will necessarily lead to dependence on the Western capitalist states, he suggests that the choice of socialism is likely to produce greater cultural authenticity as well as a more just society. This argument is made in the course of his discussion of the contemporary situation, where the exposition is structured about three central questions: (1) "Is the extension of the capitalist sector in the Muslim countries external or internal in origin?"; (2) "Has the Muslim religion hindered or favored this development?"; (3) "Has contemporary capitalism taken a specific road in the Muslim countries? If so, is the cause to be found in the Muslim religion?"[12] Rodinson answers that the extension of the capitalist sector in Muslim countries is external in origin. The Muslim religion did not hinder this extension, but rather made the necessary legitimating adjustments as required by the dominant classes. There is nothing distinctive about capitalism under Islam; it is just as exploitative and just as ruthless.

Until the rise of socialism as "first presented by the experience of the Soviet Union" traditional Muslim rulers could choose only between backwardness and capitalism. But socialism gave them the choice of "the results offered by capitalism . . . along with a higher stage of society . . . and at the same time not incurring the risk of losing the power of independent decision."[13] And just in case this rather vague suggestion fails to influence those who put a higher value on Islam than on socialism, Rodinson concludes with the argument that a massive social struggle is now going on in Muslim lands; that the upsurge of the popular classes can neither be controlled nor organized by Islam or the ulama; that the most effective instrument in modern times for the mobilization of the masses for struggle is Marxism; that the exponents of Islam had better jump on the Marxist bandwagon or be left behind in history; and that they had best not delude themselves with the thought that they can produce a genuine synthesis of Islam and socialism. Rodinson concludes that, if Islam is dominated by "de facto reactionary elements . . . [t]he certain consequence will be a detachment of the masses from their traditional faith, in proportion as they emerge from their material, cultural and moral wretchedness. . . . Islam will be a barrier against the rise of the forces of change, and this barrier will not hold. It will suffer a crisis like that of Christianity in the nineteenth century, and this despite the extra strength it will draw from its role as a *national* religion" (p. 233).

For a good many observers, what has happened in Iran, especially after the break between the Mujahidin-i-Khalq and the Islamic Republican Party, is a test of the views of Rodinson. The Mujahidin believe that it is possible to devise a synthesis of Islam and Marxism. The followers of the late Ayatullah Beheshti believe that a third Islamic economic system is possible. The ancien regime of the Shah was determined to introduce modern capitalism and to make of Iran a nondependent participant in the world system. The Fidayan-i-Khalq and the Tudeh Party were apparently equally convinced of the validity of Rodinson's formula of exploiting the legitimating symbols of Islam in the struggle to establish a socialist system. The traditional clergy were successful in first allying with the Marxist revolutionary groups and then outmanoeuvering them because of their hold on the masses, even though Rodinson argued that it would be the upper classes who were bound to form alliances with the ulama. Rodinson asked, rhetorically, "Who will assemble around him in prayer and veneration, with a new theology, adherents who will be ready—

 while building socialism, of course—to denounce and attack such and such a rite or belief, and those who hold them? To believe this to be possible one needs to possess that total ignorance of the present climate of the Muslim World" (p. 231).

Of course, Rodinson wrote those lines a long while before the Iranian revolution, criticizing those orientalists who were convinced that the Muslim masses are "still living in the religious atmosphere of the Middle Ages."[14] More recently, orientalists have been criticized for failing to predict the Iranian revolution and the role of Ayatullah Khomeini. Still, it may be too early to judge Rodinson's theories in their application to Iran, because the masses have not yet emerged from their material, cultural, and moral wretchedness sufficiently to recognize the contradictions between their own interests and the structure of the regime of the clergy.

Even though *Islam and Capitalism* was first published in 1966, it is manifestly not dated, except in the sense that it does not refer to some obviously relevant recent examples of efforts to achieve development without either adopting socialism or allowing an unbridled capitalism to overwhelm traditional social and political structures. While falling considerably short of being a major intellectual achievement, the book does have a seminal quality. Although we cannot be certain of its direct influence, there exist a small number of related studies which have further amplified the issues here introduced. The most closely related are the two essays by Brian Turner, *Weber and Islam: A Critical Study* and *Marx and the End of Orientalism*.[15] Edward Said, the author of the celebrated *Orientalism* has expressed his admiration of Rodinson's work, and he, like Rodinson, has defended Islam against its critics.[16] Of greater relevance to Marxist polemics is the little book by Samir Amin called *The Arab Nation: Nationalism and Class Struggle,* in which he attempts to apply his "law of unequal development" to Arab history.[17] Amin is well known for his earlier denial of the validity of the argument that development is possible within the framework of dependency. Those who hold the contrary view are, according to Amin, constrained to "accept the Trotskyist theses according to which socialism can only come from the developed capitalist world" (p. 111). But Amin rejected those theses, asserting instead that "There are thus several evolutionary paths, as opposed to a single road mapped out in advance for the whole of human history. . . . [I]f capitalism had not appeared in Europe, humanity would doubtlessly have discovered it anyhow" (p. 91). Suggestions of this sort, based at least on the same problems which presented themselves to Rodinson on his emergence from orthodox Marxism, may give rise to a new trend in the study of Islamic history—a trend inspired by the search for an emergent indigenous capitalism which was crushed by European imperialism. Peter Gran's *Islamic Roots of Capitalism: Egypt 1760–1840* is oriented to this theme, and we may expect it to be followed by other works with a similar *parti pris*. It may be noted that, like Rodinson's, these works are critical of traditional European-oriented Marxism, which is said to be tainted with orientalism. Gran, for example, argues that the Islamic world does have a history of its own which is meaningful independently of European history, and worthy of study.

The best-known contribution of Max Weber to the explanation of the rise of modern capitalism, is his attempt to show that superstructural or ideological developments may sometimes precede changes in the mode of production. Weber did not argue that culture, or religious beliefs, or ideology can somehow be the cause of material change, but that belief systems and socioeconomic systems must necessarily bear some sort of relationship to one another if they are to last. This is but a variation of the Hegelian effort to rejoin what Kant set apart in his exposition of pure reason. It is experience, or history, that reveals the principles by which subject and object or spirit and matter are conjoined; and it is not traditional logic. Weber, of course, sought for the logic of the relationship between culture and the socioeconomic order along lines familiar from Marx's treatment of ideology. Contrary to the usual understanding of Marx, however, he did not believe that material factors are ultimately determinative. The relationship between superstructure and substructure might be described as circular, reciprocal, or even simultaneous. The implication of mutual causality further suggests an ongoing process or a continuous interaction in which adjustments are made and an equilibrium maintained. Talcott Parsons pursued this suggestion in developing the idea that social interaction tended to produce a kind of coherence of meanings and values and behaviors in any given culture—an idea which has had a profound impact on contemporary cultural anthropology. Despite the controversies which have arisen about the so-called Weber thesis, its strength lies in the very plausibility with which it describes some characteristics of Protestant Christian culture. Weber's later analyses of Hinduism and Judaism have similarly enriched the historical study of the development of those two religious and social systems. Unfortunateley, there is no similar comprehensive study of Islam; but that has not prevented any number of scholars from proposing grand generalizing interpretations which, naturally, would tell us why capitalism did not arise in the Muslim world. Obviously, Rodinson's question is a Weberian question, even though the question is a response to Marxist theory.

II

Max Weber did not write an historical sociological monograph on Islam, as he did on the religions of India, China, and Israel. As in the case of Marx, all that can be done is to piece together references from the writings we do have, and then to reconstruct what might have been a more systematic analysis. The Weberian analysis of Islam is relevant to the issue of Islam and capitalism not only because Weber shared with Marx the idea that capitalism is the characteristic form of modernity, but because the problematic of the relationship between a given religious ethic and a particular social formation is Weberian. Marx argued that a mature capitalism would be reflected in a nice balance, or coordination, between substructure and superstructure, or in Gramscian terms, between the political dominance of the bourgeois class and the ideological-cultural hegemony of that class.[18] In the long run, or eventually, substructure determines superstructure, but not necessarily in the usual sequential manner that is the foundation of naive casual theory.

Weber's position is, to all intents and purposes, similar in the sense that the link, or association, between substructure and superstructure is asserted, but no causal, or sequential, or even intellectual process of rationalization is postulated as the preferred explanation of the observed or imputed association. Interpretive social science is to find out how the social and cultural are connected.

If it were agreed that a religious ethic and a mode of production are always, ultimately, integrated, but that only the mode of production is necessarily constrained by material circumstance and extant technology, then it follows that, in the long run, the religious ethic adapts to the prevailing substructural constraints. If, however, it is argued that the mode of production is no more constrained than is the religious ethic, then it is plausible to expect some kind of reciprocal process of adjustment to bring the two into a stable, workable, and circular arrangement that "makes sense." It is also possible to hold yet a third view, that a given religious ethic is, or may become, so rigid that it is not adaptable, or that its range of adaptability is limited, and that it may be unable to "make sense" of certain substructural arrangements or certain modes of production. In the present case, the question raised by Weber is whether the Islamic ethic has, historically, developed in such a manner that it was and is antithetical to the capitalist mode of production and the other superstructural requisites of capitalism. If, as a consequence, Islam persists, and capitalism remains limited to an enclave—a partial and secondary mode of production in Muslim lands—then it is clear that either the long run has not occurred, or that the diffusion of capitalism is not "necessary," nor is superstructure always dependent on substructure in the long run.

Weber's "circular" thinking regarding the links between society and culture, reflected in the work of Parsons and Geertz, has been criticized by Schutz as inadequate to Weber's own stated task of establishing the subjective meaning of social action. Schutz distinguishes between the culturally determined meaning of social action and the subjective meaning of such action as it is in the individual consciousness.[19] Since the latter meaning in the stream of consciousness is spontaneous, prethetic, and unreflective according to Schutz, it cannot be recovered by a cultural analysis, but at best, only by sharing in the immediate experience of the subject. The meaning which is attached to a category of social action by a particular culture is an externalized, formalized, reflexive, and hence, rationalized meaning. This externalized meaning has some of the character of Heidegger's inauthenticity, and is considered by Schutz to set an absolute limit on the ability of sociology or social science to get at the reality of the meaning of social action.[20]

Hence, Weberian social science is a sociology of ideal types—of objectified models of behavior—based on superstructural or institutionalized cultural formulas. Weber, it is argued, does not seek the motive of the individual, or the cause of individual behavior, but, instead, classifies individual behavior in terms of ideal types constructed of rationally coherent associations of socioeconomic structures and ideological structures. Neither Schutz nor Weber resolves the problem of the degree to which individual, prethetic, behavior in-the-stream-of-consciousness may be unconsciously shaped by prevalent ideal-types. Turner sums up his conclusion on the matter: "Thus, Weber could be interpreted to argue that to explain actions we need to understand the subjective meanings and subjective motives of social actions, but the languages which are available for describing and explaining actions are themselves determined by social and economic conditions."[21]

From these considerations, it follows that Weberian social science poses the question of the relationship between Islam and capitalism somewhat differently than does Marxian social science. Nevertheless, the one serious effort that has been made to trace Weber's various allusions to Islam is marred by an emphasis on what is shared by Marx and Weber rather than their differences. Turner's strategic choice is based on his conclusion that Weber was inconsistent on the significance of the influence of superstructure on substructure.[22] This inference is drawn from the fact that various critics disagree in their assessment of Weber and not from Weber's work itself. In fact, it is characteristic of this study that too little space is given to the actual exposition and critique of the Weberian text.

Turner rejects those arguments which claim that Weber's theory and method assumed a circularity, or interaction of causality among material and ethical or religious factors: "his analysis of the Islamic ethic seems to stand independent of his analysis of the socio-economic structure of Islamic society. No attempt is made by Weber to connect what he regards as a warrior ethic to the patrimonial domination of the sultans and caliphs" (p. 13).

Since Turner declares invalid such widely accepted understandings of Weber's interpretive sociology, he leaves us with two disjoined theses, (1) that the patrimonial institutions of Muslim sultanism and the prebendal structure of landholding prevented the rise of capitalism in the Islamic world, and (2) that the hedonistic, anti-ascetic Islamic ethic which was the consequence of the adaptation of Islam to the needs of a warrior class prevented the rise of capitalism, but he does not argue that Weber effectively linked the two or even made a case for their circular relationship or thought in terms of some kind of overdeterminism. Turner's own argument involves crediting the critique of Muslim patrimonialism and rejecting the critique of the Islamic ethic.

Turner's analysis, despite his uncertainty regarding Weber's theoretical position, claims that this mistaken conception of the Islamic ethic is the consequence of Weber's failure to pursue his own method. Weber's understanding of Islam is based, rather, on prevalent Western conceptions, and the unwarranted assumption that this hedonistic ethic originated in the ideological requirements of a bedouin warrior class. Turner does not deny the social and political significance of the warrior class, but he argues that it was only one of several relevant groups. The bedouin military elite may have contributed to the emergence of Muslim patrimonialism, but they were not the most important group in shaping the forms of Islamic religious discourse. Turner insists that Islam comprehends several vocabularies of motives,[23] the most important of which are the Sunni (ascetic, legalistic, etc.), the Shiʿi (emotional, messianic, charismatic), the Sufi (mystical, otherworldly, resigned), and the many folk-religious idioms often expressed in the reverence for popular shaykhs or "saints." In the manner of the turath ideologists, he notes also the importance of the Kharijite movement and the Muʿtazila, and discusses the extent to which Sunni Islam managed to integrate all of these streams into the mainstream of orthodoxy.

Relying on a few Western interpretations of Islamic history and culture, Turner attempts to do what he claims Weber failed to do, and the general picture we get is one of a multifaceted Islam in which the scripturalist and formalist tendency remains dominant, and in which ascetic, affective, enthusiastic, messianic, reclusive, and mystical elements coexist, even if not always easily. As Rodinson argued, so does Turner, that capitalistic enterprise existed in some measure under the caliphate, and it may even have been associated with an ascetic ethic. Hence, Islam, though it is neither thoroughly hedonistic nor thoroughly ascetic, did not prevent a certain amount of capitalist development at either the substructural or the superstructural level.

Turner's critique of Weber concentrates on a few points. He flatly contradicts Weber's view that the Islamic ethic is a warrior ethic, the consequence of a tactical choice by the prophet Muhammad when faced by the hostility of the dominant elites in Mecca. Turner seems implicitly to accept the view that a warrior ethic is essentially a hedonistic ethic, and that it is incompatible with capitalism. On the other hand, he seems to be ambivalent regarding the relevance of an ascetic ethic to capitalism, because he argues that Weber was wrong in believing that asceticism was a necessary cultural requisite of capitalism and, at the same time, he acknowledges that there were ascetic elements in Islam.

Despite all this, Turner is inclined to accept the orientalist critique of mainstream, Sunni, Islam as a repressive, stagnant, and rigid doctrinal system that sustained the arbitrary authoritarianism of medieval patrimonialism. Since Turner attributes the failure of capitalism in the Middle East to the prevalence of patrimonialism, and since he argues that Weber never established the relationship between patrimonialism and the warrior ethic, it follows that Turner joins the orientalists who attribute the "backwardness" of Islam to scripturalism rather than to hedonism.

While Turner's characterization of Islam is pluralistic, and although he emphasizes its tendency to integrate and moderate challenging oppositional ideological tendencies, he suggests the persistence of an Islamic essence, identified by means of the juxtaposition of two types of social conduct. These two types of social conduct are summed up in two concepts which were evidently prevalent in pre-Islamic times, *hilm* (self-controlled and reasonable) and *jahl* (ignorant and wanton).[24]

Turner insists that Islamic mysticism and Christian mysticism were not the same thing. This conclusion is turned against Weber, who is blamed for not realizing this difference, and for holding the view that Islam was dominated by orgiastic Sufi beliefs. In contrast, Turner would argue that Islam nicely balanced the ascetic and the mystical, the rational and the passionate, the Sunni and the Sufi. It was the virtually totally otherworldly aspect of Christian mysticism, leading in some cases to grotesque episodes of suicide, that led to the need to control these practices, and to channel the religious passions of believers. Islamic mysticism is decisively social, communicative, and functional by contrast.

Kharijism, Shiᶜism, Muᶜtazilism, Ismaᶜilism, and Sufism are all rejected alternatives to the Sunni orthodoxy, which has become dominant in most Islamic lands. Many, if not most, Muslim scholars will agree that each of these movements left their mark on Sunni Islam, but only the traditionally orthodox hold that the cultural influence of these rejected alternatives has been sufficiently absorbed into Sunni Islam. The modernists, in their variety, are more inclined to explain some of the political and social problems of contemporary Muslims as the consequence of the failure of the cultural influences associated with these heresies to continue to influence Islamic culture. For Turner, following Weber to a considerable extent, and both relying upon the external view of orientalists, the political-cultural force which produced the orthodox Islamic ideology was the alliance of the ulama and the patrimonial rulers of the Umayyad and Abbasid dynasties. Thus: "By the end of the ninth century, Sunni Islam had become a dry and legalistic religion, offering little to the emotional needs and messianic aspirations of its exploited masses. Its official exponents, the ulama, were assimilated into the administrative staff of the centralized, patrimonial empire" (p. 87).

This baleful development of Islamic ideology was the consequence of the refusal of the orthodox to choose between the alternative ideals of the "charismatic community" as advocated by the Kharijites, and the "charismatic leader" as advocated by the Shiᶜites. For Turner, "The important historical point is that orthodox Sunnite society was able to assimilate the Kharijite emphasis on communalism in a watered-down form, but it never successfully included the Shiᶜite theory of the charismatic imamate" (p. 91). Charismatic legitimacy was rejected among the orthodox, or to some extent charisma was transferred to the Shariᶜa from the Rightly Guided Caliphs. Law, order, and obedience to civic authority became the prime values identified with the preservation of the well-being of the umma, or the Islamic community.

Some would argue that the Muᶜtazilite movement was an effort to integrate Islamic theology into this rational and orderly system. After a temporary success, the Muᶜtazilite movement was transformed from an established orthodoxy to a rejected heresy, and it might be argued that its function was better performed by the integration of the ulama into the patrimonial bureaucracy than by the attempt to instill a rational theology in the minds of a socially pluralistic clergy and laity.

Muʿtazilism lost its influence, and it is always interesting to consider the historical explanation offered by various theorists for this result, because it is sometimes taken as the reason why Muslims have fallen behind the Christians in the advancement of science and technology. At any rate, this failure produced a patrimonial establishment which was characterized by the effort to achieve order, but without at the same time striving for rationality. Hence, Muslim patrimonialism did not produce the conditions for the emergence of the equivalent of the Protestant ethic. An alternate rationalism, that of Ismaʿilism, also arose, only to be more severely defeated in a struggle that decisively defined Sunni Islam in a pragmatic, nonsystematic, disenchanted manner: "The rationalism of the Ismaʿili movement was not, however, a cold rationalism, since it was through the conception of the imamate that the movement appealed to the illiterate, exploited mass. For those who were spiritually starved by the formalism of Sunnite orthodoxy, Ismaʿilism offered the companionship of the Imams" (p. 88).

In this passage Turner reflects not a little of the orientalists' nostalgia (reflected also in the writings of Muslim modernists) for rejected Islamic alternatives that might have brought Islam and Christianity closer, and, of course, might have produced a religious ethic more compatible with modern capitalism.

This particular interpretation of Ismaʿilism, based on the ex post facto attribution of ideological "needs" to the medieval Muslim masses, seems strained, however. The implicit interpretive framework relies on a conception of ideology as a functional requisite of political community. It implies that belief in a personal and a personified God, similar to Jesus, is more functional than the abstract attachment to God's law. Yet it argues that this sort of faith need not be purely charismatic. It could include enough rationalism to sustain a capitalist order.

Turner argues that it was not because of the particularities of Islamic culture that capitalism failed to arise spontaneously among Muslims. In particular, he argues that it was not the absence of the Protestant ethic which prevented the rise of capitalism. Following Rodinson, he asserts that there were enclaves of capitalist enterprise especially among the urban merchants in the medieval period. These merchants adhered to a distinctively Muslim form of rationality. The problem of the failure of capitalism in Muslim countries must be sought in the explanation of the failure of these protocapitalist elements to achieve economic, if not political, dominance. The answer is to be found in the practices of Muslim patrimonialism, especially its "financial dilemmas," its impact on Islamic jurisprudence, and its political domination of the urban upper classes.

Thus we find Islam, though different from Christianity, nevertheless endowed with a doctrine which is, or was, adaptable to capitalistic enterprise, failing to produce modern capitalism because of the persistent domination of patrimonialism. Patrimonialism prevented the emergence of an independent urban bourgeoisie, and it also prevented the emergence of an independent feudal class. More significantly, this patrimonialism depended upon peculiar forms of military organization and fiscal processes that produced inherent contradictions whenever territorial expansion ceased. Turner sums up his position as agreeing with the views of Sami Zubaida: "It was not the attitudes and ideologies inherent in Islam which inhibited the development of a capitalist economy, but the political position of the merchant classes vis à vis the dominant military-bureaucratic classes in Islamic societies" (p. 173).

Turner's conclusion is that the political dominance of rational-pragmatic urban merchants, and a more truly feudal military organization, would have allowed Muslim countries to modernize and develop economically in competition with the West and along alternative cultural lines.

> It was under the patrimonial dynasties of mediaeval Islam, starting with the Abbasids, that a different culture with its attendant view of appropriate motivation which stressed discipline, obedience and imitation came to dominate Islam. With the formation of an alliance of necessity between the military and the ulama, the *Shariʿa* as a formalized and unchanging code of life came to embody the only legitimate language of conduct. From 1100 CE, or even 900 CE, independent judgment in legal matters had been finished with the closure of "the gate of *ijtihad*." It followed that the supreme moral stance was one of imitation (*taqlid*), unquestioning acceptance of authoritative statements of the *Shariʿa*. Under patrimonial conditions, therefore, a new vocabulary of motives was elaborated by the ulama and instilled by the madrassa, the new institute of orthodoxy, which was perfectly suited to the law and order requirements of the dominant class. Since control of the self through subjection to divine law became the highest motive, innovation (*bida*) became a criminal activity. It was under these conditions that Islam was to be characterized as a slavish, fatalistic religion, a religion of accommodation to patrimonial rule. This is not to say that alternative, critical and oppositional sets of motives did not survive. Shi'ism, the Carmathian movement, the Muʿtazilites and certain philosophical schools attempted to preserve a sense of human freedom and thereby a commitment to the idea of moral choice, but the dominant, normative vocabulary of motives was Sunnite and conservative. Furthermore, the fatalistic view of human motivation survived

> down to modern times, especially in the more remote parts of Islamic society. (Pp. 142–43)

Turner argues that capitalism is speading in the Middle East, but the ethos of Western bourgeois capitalism, or the Protestant ethic, is not spreading among capitalists so much as it is among the intelligentsia, the bureaucracy, and the military (that is, among the neopatrimonial elite). The usual historical process of ideological change is actually being subverted in the Muslim world, because a Western ethos is being substituted for Islam as a result of the call for secularization. Hence, the authentic Islam for the present era cannot readily emerge unless this campaign for secularization is defeated. Turner suggests that Muslim populations may yet reject the "mimetic" secularization proposed by some modernizing intellectuals. The Middle East may find its own path to secularism, or it may reject secularization altogether.

In a second and briefer work, Turner repents his lapse into the orientalist mode of analysis under the theoretical sociological influence of Max Weber. Unfortunately, he falls into an even more parochial or sectarian theoretical approach, which claims to follow the ideas of L. Althusser, and may be described as a Marxian epistemological teleology. The central idea in this teleology is that the Marxist system of thought is incomplete, and that a constant reference back to the original texts, especially the nonscientific texts of the early years, or of the journalistic articles, will not resolve the analytical problems facing contemporary Marxist theorists. The solution to the theoretical problems of Marxism, is to complete the theoretical legacy in accordance with the epistemological position evident in the later works. This position is described as scientific, but in the structuralist and neopositivistic manner of Althusser. Furthermore, the central feature of this process of theoretical completion is to be accomplished by means of the reconceptualization of everyday political experience in abstract terms which are logically compatible with the extant fragments of the Marxist system. In this way, Marxist theory is validated by reference to its potential logical completeness, but not with reference to any possibility of empirical testing, and not because of any claim to exclusive truth. Marxism is thus presented as an ideology, a scientific teleology, and one of several possible and competing paradigms which may be employed by diversely interested scholars for the understanding of contemporary politics and culture.

It is this rather special Marxism which is employed by Turner to refute that Marxism which is identified with the concept of the Asiatic mode of production and the view that the increased political domination of modern capitalism in the underdeveloped countries would advance world revolution, and prepare for the advent of communism. The defects of the Marxist legacy are most apparent in the weakness of its theory of pre-capitalist modes of production, and in the gaps in the theory of the relationship between substructure and superstructure. Turner knows what he wants Althusserian Marxist theory to accomplish, and that is to prove that had the Muslim world been left alone, it would have found its own path to development, modernization, and capitalism, and that it would be on its way to revolution now. Furthermore, this theory should prove that the intrusion of the West has distorted the historical progress of the Middle East through the appropriate modes of production, and has produced political forms and social formations which are inappropriate to achieving political and economic liberation from the West. A proper theory of Marxist development will show the essentially progressive character of Arab nationalism at this stage, and it will establish the essentially retrogressive character of Jewish nationalism. This theoretical advance is still in process but part of the task involves a trenchant critique of the prevailing Hegelian interpretation of Marxism, which is heavily influenced by the cultural prejudices of orientalism.

The best example of the theoretical blending of orientalism and marxism may be found in what Turner refers to as the "no revolutions" thesis.[25] According to this thesis, there is an essential cultural or ideological difference between Islam and Christianity that accounts for the absence of a revolutionary tradition in Islam. Marxism accounts for this by means of the theory of the Asiatic mode of production. Turner dismisses the idea that there can be an essential (idealistic) difference between Islam and Christianity that can account for any significant historical difference. It is rather the task of neo-Marxist theory to establish the material conditions accounting for the absence of the bourgeios revolution in oriental history, and to demonstrate the genuine revolutionary character of tribal resistance movements, fundamentalist rebellions, petit bourgeois military regimes, and contemporary nationalist movements. He writes, "A Marxist analysis of the revolutionary potential of political opposition, whether in the case of nineteenth-century tribal rebellions or in the case of contemporary resistance, has to challenge the ethnocentric assumptions and theoretical incoherence of the dominant form of Middle East studies, namely, Orientalism" (p. 79). While the task of Marxist theory is thus clearly stated, we are told that existing Marxist thought is capable of the task of destroying the idealist theory of the orientalists, but incapable of performing the more constructive task, because of the difficulty of deciding between the *determinism* of attributing revolutions to changes in the mode of production and the *vol-*

untarism of attributing revolutions to class struggles. Leaving aside the naiveté of this crude formulation, it appears that Turner and his group seem to favor the mode of production approach, and they would subordinate "voluntaristic" elements of class struggle as events taking place within the more meaningful framework.

But this only appears to be the case, for Turner concludes by expressing his firm belief that Marxism has the potential for demolishing orientalism, and that it will do so when certain theoretical difficulties have been overcome. In demolishing orientalism, neo-Marxism will also have to deal with Weberian sociology and Hegelian interpretations of Marxism. Neo-Marxism will have to establish the validity of the thesis that

> . . . once the global centers of capitalism had been established, the conditions for development of the periphery were fundamentally changed. The internalist [*sic*] theory of development fails to grasp the significance of this global relationship and consequently persists in posing futile questions about spontaneous capitalist development . . . on the periphery . . . Capitalism intensifies and preserves pre-capitalist modes of production so that there is no unilinear evolutionary path from 'traditional' society to 'modern' society. (Pp. 81–82)

If this argument is correct, then it follows that the failure of the development of modern capitalism in Muslim countries is not due to the "cluster of absences—the missing middle class, the missing city, the absence of political rights, the absence of revolutions." Insofar as this cluster of absences has been attributed to some essence represented as the "expressive totality" which is Islam, then that attribution is also incorrect, because Turner simply rejects all idealistic explanations as false. It hardly need be added that this metaphysical position precludes Turner from arguing that Islam itself might be responsible for any historical outcome whatsoever. Turner is also highly critical of his colleagues when they allow idealistic elements to slip into their own formulations. Nevertheless, he seems to be unaware of the idealistic potentialities of Althusser's emphasis upon reconceptualization as the foundation of theoretical "production." Turner is evidently more concerned with the transformation of "certain quasi-scientific problems (nationalism, the mosaic model, patrimonialism, revolutions) into proper objects of theoretical work" (p. 82). Turner's epistemological polemic leaves one with the uneasy feeling that rendering something a "proper object of theoretical work" is tantamout to justifying the relevant historical phenomenon in a moral sense. If "it" is not the fault of Islam, and if it is the fault of imperialism, what is to be done and who is to do it? If Islam is not to blame, and if it cannot provide a solution, is the Muslim world fated to continue its subordinated peripheral dependence upon the advanced capitalist centers?

III

The alliance of Third World nationalists and pro-Soviet groups which has occurred from time to time has produced a number of ideological efforts intended to explain and justify what might otherwise be seen merely as a political, and sometimes military, marriage of convenience. Even the Soviet Union, pursuing a pragmatic policy of reducing Western influence in some of the underdeveloped parts of the world, has attempted to offer reasoned and historically relevant explanations of alliances with military oligarchies, petit bourgeois regimes, and even traditional ruling classes. While some types of theory have some plausibility, in other cases the ideological explanations appear to be no more than crude rationalizations thinly veiling efforts at mutual exploitation. Dependency theory, with all its variations, has been the most successful in arguing the conflict of interest between the developing areas and the capitalist countries of the world economic core. But that negative basis has failed to provide a solid political foundation upon which to build a policy. Neither cooperation with the Soviet Union, nor autarchy, nor the attempt to build a separate Third World economic system, nor the attempt to deal collectively with the capitalist core through international agencies and within the "North-South" framework, have been validated as appropriate solutions to chronic underdevelopment. As a consequence, political ideology and economic policy have become separated. In a sense, political ideology has become severed from the test of economic realities, and has been freed to serve other purposes, such as attempts to intimidate the capitalist countries, or attempts to embarrass or cajole the Soviet government, or attempts to influence policy, or gain power at home. Marxian thought and the ideology of Third World liberation are employed in many cases in an opportunistic manner, and in others simply as a vocabulary of political activism testifying to the effectivenes of this hybrid in displacing other forms of political anad cultural discourse. Nowhere is this phenomenon of the ideological exploitation of Marxian and nationalist symbols more apparent than in the little book by Samir Amin, *The Arab Nation*.

To start with Amin's conclusion, he virtually predicts that Egypt will emerge as the leader of a group of Arab states whose national unity and international influence will be enhanced by the transformation of the mode of production and the redirection of international trade. Because of its favored situation, the consequence of the existence in Egypt alone of a large and exploited urban and rural proletariat, it will be able to serve as the core for the process of Arab national integration. Unhampered by overadaptation to the capitalist mode, Egypt will be able to develop a more advanced form of socialism. It will lead the other Arab states away from dependency by providing an alternate pole of economic attraction. The Arab nation, thus loosely integrated, will become a new and important force in international relations, and it will contribute to the breakdown of the prevailing capitalist-dominated system of the international economy.

This conclusion, justified by some interesting if unconvincing reasoning, proposes that Egypt will play a role of virtually unparalleled importance in the transformation of worldwide social and economic relations. This anticipated role will overcome the obstacles resulting from the policies of the United States and the Soviet Union alike, and lead toward a real world revolution. Amin concludes his essay with these words:

> Perhaps this sketch of a third possible outcome for the Arab world, based on its socialist transformation and unification, seems unrealistic. . . . But it is not unrealistic. All the conditions are gathered for the appearance of an invincible revolutionary upsurge in the Arab world: a large concentrated and embattled proletariat, and vast impoverished peasant masses which are exploited and close to the proletariat. The bourgeoisie has gone bankrupt and the petty bourgeoisie which has led the movement till now has demonstrated its instability and its limits. But this same petty bourgeoisie, for all its pusillanimity when it led the movement as a class, has produced thousands of revolutionaries.[26]

It is difficult to imagine Amin, or any other prominent Egyptian Marxist, contemplating so central an historical role for Egypt, had it not been for the inspiring example of Nasser's leadership. Nasser's regime is dismissed as a petit bourgeois government incapable of reaching beyond the limited notions of national independence. Nevertheless, Nasser did bring Egypt to the front rank of the nonaligned movement. He did create a very large public sector of the economy. He did institute a land reform that destroyed the political power of the largest absentee landholders. He also challenged the capitalist domination of the world economy. He defied and he cajoled the Soviets. He also intimidated the oil-rich Arab states. So promising did the Nasser regime appear as an obsacle to "imperialist" domination of the Middle East, that both the Soviet leadership and the leadership of the most important communist faction in Egypt agreed to lend it almost complete support.

 Now, after eighteen years of de-Nasserization, the proper ideological assessment of the Nasser period is still the most important theme in the discourse of Egyptian Marxists. Those Marxists who made their peace with Nasser, and later came to regret it, have generally taken the position that they are the true heirs of Nasserism, and that the first task facing them is to restore the Nasserist regime in the face of Sadat's revisionism and Mubarak's fence-sitting. Samir Amin noted the successes of the Nasser period in weakening the bourgeoisie, but he is even more emphatic about the shortcomings of the Nasserist regime. The failure of the Nasserist experiment is due to a number of contradictions, the most important of which were the conflict between petit bourgeois ideology and the land reform, the conflict between state capitalism and the dictatorship of the proletariat, and the conflict between the Soviet policy of drawing individual "countries out of the American sphere of influence without endangering the policy of peaceful coexistence by the extension of socialist revolution" (p. 56). Amin prefers a Maoist line, and one that is inspired by the Vietnamese example.

In spite of all this, the vision of Egypt's political future adumbrated by Amin appears to be similar to the Nasserist vision of an Egypt which dominates the other Arab states, virtually excludes competing foreign influences from penetrating the Arab sphere, and builds its own economic power and international influence upon its hegemonic position among the Arab states. As a consequence, it is difficult to decide whether Amin's main goal is socialist revolution or the enhancement of Egyptian state power through the exploitation of Arab nationalism. Amin seems to argue that the Nasserist goals can be reached only if the Arab nation disengages from the capitalist world and ceases to depend upon the pragmatic Soviets. The confusions of Nasserist ideology can only be overcome if the effort to achieve Nasserist goals is led by a well-organized and self-conscious proletariat.

Amin's doctrine is not only ambiguous in the matter of socialist revolution vs. nationalist aggrandizement, it also raises controversial issues regarding the justification of Egypt's leadership role within the Arab nation. Egyptian domination of Arab affairs was sharply reduced after the disastrous defeat in 1967, and even after the limited success of the 1973 war, Egypt was unable to restore its influence. The adherence of Egypt to the Camp David accords tested the extent of Egyptian influence, and Egypt's subsequent isolation among the Arab states points to an almost total loss of the Nasserist hegemony. It is safe to say that non-Egyptian Arabs are disinclined to accept the thesis that Egypt has a primary historical role to play in the destiny of the Arab nation, even though there may be general acknowledgment of the primacy of Egypt in the Arab cultural sphere. The resentment occasioned by Egyptian claims to leadership is a fact of Arab political life.

Amin's justification of the role he claims for Egypt is presumably based upon objective historical factors and not upon any idealistic interpretation of Egypt's national cultural mission. Amin departs significantly from the usual characterization of the prevailing mode of production in the medieval Islamic world. He argues that Egypt differed from both the Maghrib and the Mashriq. Most historians argue that the Islamic countries, like medieval Europe, enjoyed a feudal mode of production. Amin states that the medieval Arab world "constituted a constellation of social formations articulated around a tributary mode of production" (p. 7). The tributary mode was based on the extraction of surplus from agriculture by a town-dwelling elite. This system was generally too weak to produce surpluses capable of sustaining important advances in civilization, except in Egypt. Elsewhere, the surpluses upon which brilliant Arab civilizations were built were derived from international commerce. Even in Egypt it was generally the commercial surpluses that were channeled into agriculture that led to the improvement of the irrigation system and the increase of agricultural production. The decline of Egypt's international trade led to greater exploitation of the peasantry, but never to the sort of political and economic fragmentation that was characteristic of the other Arab areas. When long distance trade declined the towns based on it perished, "leaving the misery of a world of nomads and small isolated peasant communities to highlight its decadence. . . . Within this fragile whole, only Egypt survived: its high population density and its peasant character gave it a strong unity. One can talk of an Egyptian nation throughout history; the same can hardly be said of the Arab nation" (p. 21).

Amin's view of Egypt's uniqueness among the Arabs may be further appreciated by reading two additional statements:

> Furthermore, even during Arabisation, the Egyptian people kept a very strong feeling of their own particularity. . . .
>
> The history of Egypt during the twelve centuries between the Arab conquest and Bonaparte's expedition can only be grasped if one understands the unfolding dialectic between its permanent peasant base and the occasional integration of the country into a much larger economic whole. (P. 19)

Historians may well be somewhat uneasy with such sweeping generalizations, but they may also agree that Egypt was different from the other Arab political units, somewhat isolated, and economically distinctive. These arguments justify differentiating Egypt from the other Arab states, but they do not prove that all the Arab states have a common fate and that Egypt, by virtue of its special chacteristics, is objectively suited to lead the rest. That argument depends upon the complex issue of nationalism itself. At first glance, Amin's theses regarding Egypt's role in Arab nationalism appear to the liberal bourgeois as an expression of rank chauvinism, and to the orthodox Marxist as an expression of bourgeois idealism. Amin, however, is concerned to prove that Arab nationalism has an objective historical basis, that the Egyptian role is similarly historically determined, and that Arab nationalism is not merely a peripheral phenomenon of world capitalism, but the framework within which the "class struggle and the anti-imperialist liberation struggle unfolds" (p. 12).

Amin argues that the Arab nation is not the product of capitalist development, but the result of the "mercantile integration of the Arab world, as carried out by a class of merchant-warriors" (p. 7). This ruling class "was the cement which held things together: everywhere it had adopted the same language, the same orthodox Sunni Islamic culture" (p. 21). Because the Arab world was not feudal, and was not dependent upon agricultural surplus, it did not evolve into separate nations, as was the fate of feudal Europe. Amin does not spell out just how this integration was carried out, but we may conclude that it was the product of interregional trade itself as well as the geographical mobility of the culturally homogeneous elite. Commerce is integrative while agriculture is isolative. Egypt, of course, enjoyed both economic forms, so that it can share the wider Arab identity without giving up its own authenticity. At the level of that wider Arab identity, however, the unifying elite ideology was religious, and Islam may be understood as the religion and law of a commercial elite. Later, this ideology becomes transformed into a feeling of "struggle against a common enemy," that is, against imperialism. This argument suggests that Arab nationalism has supplanted Islam as the prevailing Arab ideology, as the consequence of the process which caused the decline of the warrior-merchant elites and the successful penetration of Western capitalism.

Amin offers his own theory of nationalism, rejecting both the bourgeois theory and the orthodox Marxist critique thereof. Nationalism, or rather, the formation of a nation, may occur at any historical period, and is not necessarily connected to the bourgeois revolution. Nations are integrated as a consequence of the prevalence of a mode of production which requires integration. The actual task of integration is performed by a dominant class which rules and which derives the most benefit from the integrative mode of production. The dominant class exploits and enhances those elements of common culture that contribute to the integration of the community, which is thus defined by a given mode of production. The best-known modes of production which have such integrative prerequisites are, of course, capitalism and socialism, but also a highly centralized agrarian-tributary mode which has been given the opaque title of the Asiatic mode. Thus, the Arab nation existed in integrated form from time to time, but the Egyptian nation antedated the Arab nation, and has had a more continuous career. On the other hand, societies which have not been characterized by class domination, such as feudal Europe, or the confessionally fragmented Levant, are not nations. Wherever the ruling elite is not a class, in the sense of having a relationship to the means of production, and in the sense of having some sort of self-consciousness and organizational unity, that community is not a nation. In other words. Amin has taken the ideal typical characteristics of the bourgeois state in Marxist thought and transformed them into elements of a general theory of development in which nationalism and development become near equivalents.

For Amin, the national integrative and developmental role played by the bourgeoisie under capitalism is to be played by the proletariat under socialism. The social framework for the establishment of socialism is national, and not international. However, there must be a relatively strong proletariat present for the integrative and developmental tasks to be successfully carried out. Amin is at pains to narrate how the earlier predominance of the combination of a tributary mode and mercantilism on a weak peasant-communal base, everywhere but in Egypt, left the Arab world without a class capable of leading them in the struggle against the intrusiveness of Western capitalism. The bourgeoisie has failed, and following those idealist nationalists, the petite bourgeoisie, exemplified by Nasserism, has failed also. Hence it is only Egypt, still a nation because of its strong peasant base, that can provide the proletariat to reintegrate the Arab nation, transform its mode of production, free it from foreign influence, and reinvigorate its culture. In this effort, Egypt's proletariat will be aided by the cultural achievements of the *Nahda* (awakening), and especially by the modernization of the Arabic language; but it will be retarded by the resurgence of religious fundamentalism—the ideological instrument, or ally, of the petite bourgeoisie.

Amin's essay is brief, so there may be some matters on which he would expand under other circumstances. Manifestly, his treatment of the role of culture in general, if not of the turath, is unsatisfactory and incomplete. For the most part culture is dealt with as coordinate with the mode of production and the character of the ruling class. Insofar as there was a unified ruling class during certain periods of Islamic history, that class of merchant-warriors adhered to Sunni Islam. The exponents of the various heretical tendencies were local elites representing communal, rather than class, interest, and they were either bedouin or rurally based chieftains. The challenge of Western capitalism and imperialism requires the modernization of Arab culture, but this has only been partially accomplished.

Aside from the modernization of language, the most outstanding contribution to the modernization of Arab culture was the controversial work of Shaykh ʿAli ʿAbd al-Raziq, who argued that there are no explicit Islamic provisions for the organization of government. Amin states that ʿAbd al-Raziq's book marked the arrival of "the modern era . . . the era of capitalism and later, of socialism. The state has to be separated from religion" (p. 39). Unfortunately, in Amin's view, the petite bourgeoisie faltered in making this necessary step, which accounts for the rise of the Muslim Brotherhood, and the incorporation of much of their ideology in Nasserism. Finally, Amin deplores the decline in the authenticity of Arab culture that is the consequence of the successful penetration of Western imperialism. The Arab world has adopted much of the bourgeois culture of the West. At one point Amin refers to the cultural consequences of imperialism as the deculturization of the Arab nation. Even the integration of the Arab world into the intellectual capitalist system through the combination of Arab oil wealth, Egyptian labor, and Western technology is rejected, not only because it will lead to dependent development, but because it will lead to the ". . . sort of development, which destroys national societies by ruining their culture" (p. 106). These suggestive references to an Arab culture which is both authentic and modern are theoretically interesting, but they are not further developed. The function of a modernized Arab culture is fairly clear: it must contribute to progress, liberation, independence, and socialism; but the substantive character of the culture is not elaborated.

There are two more hints in Amin's book regarding his position on the question of the turath and the Arab renaissance. Citing the global crisis of the world capitalist system, and looking forward to the emergence of a new international economic order, Amin foresees the new Arab role "in the form of an Arab renaissance, an affirmation of Arab power" (p. 105). This phrase may not indicate that Amin equates a cultural renaissance with political and economic power, but he is responsible for this choice of words. More significant yet, in my estimation, is Amin's statement that Arab unity, which must be unity of peasants and proletariat, "must first be a recognition of diversity" (p. 8). I take this to mean that Amin wishes at once to preserve Egyptian cultural authenticity within the framework of Arab national unity, while reassuring other Arab "subcultures" that they will not be overwhelmed. Still the lack of theoretical and terminological clarity is evident in Amin's proposed solution to the Palestine question by means of the "orientalization" of at least a portion of the Jews of Israel: "Neither Christian, Druse and Moslem Lebanon, nor Jewish and Muslim Palestine, nor the Syria of the interior and the Alid Syria, have ever been integrated into a single homogeneous nation, such as Egypt for instance. But diversity, which today presupposes mutual respect and considerable autonomy, does not preclude economic, political and even cultural unity" (p. 103).

IV

Doubtlessly the best work inspired by this neo-Marxist perspective is that of Peter Gran on the life and work of Hasan al-Attar whose career spanned the end of the eighteenth and the beginning of the nineteenth centuries. Despite a number of fairly unqualified references of religious culture to class interests, Gran seems to be more influenced by Weber than by Marx. In general, he prefers the terms culture, and even, the sociology of knowledge, to ideology. Moreover, by taking the intellectual biography of a leading scholar as his point of departure, Gran is able to discuss the social, religious, and cultural milieu of early modern Islam with an immediacy, a vividness, and an empathy not to be found in the deteached and abstruse analyses of those who would impose a universal Marxian frame of reference.

Gran's argument is found in a brief, but lucid, concluding chapter. In fact the story is so much better told at the end that one must wonder whether the book should not have undergone one more revision. On the other hand, the ambitiousness of Gran's interpretive project seems to have grown as he was writing and as he increasingly understood that the implications of his argument encompassed the economic, political, and social modernization of Egypt, Syria, and Ottoman Turkey. Obviously, the empirical evidence falls far short of what is required to sustain the conclusions reached. But what is far more important than the adequacy of the evidence presented, is the adequacy of the historical hypothesis with which the book concludes.

Although Gran's book is called *The Islamic Roots of Capitalism,* he does not argue that Islamic Egypt was on the verge of achieving an indigenous capitalism when overtaken by European imperialism. He shows, rather, that, in the last three decades of the eighteenth century, Egypt was systematically drawn into international commercial relations which opened up opportunities for capitalistic enterprise within Egypt. He argues that the merchant and warrior-merchant elites of Cairo and the Delta responded to those opportunities, bringing about some significant changes in the mode of production, and consequently in the structure of classes. The impact of these economic changes was reflected or parallelled by changes of literary style, changes in the rhetoric and subject matter of ulama discourse, and changes in the patterns of sociability and social intercourse among the educated classes. Despite the fact that the culture of merchants, ulama, and enterprising Mamluks is described in specifically Egyptian-Islamic terms, one gets the impression that the Muslim equivalent of a Weberian Calvinist class of individualistic, pietistic, fundamentalist accumulators was emerging.

This process was at least temporarily cut short as a consequence of domestic upheaval, Ottoman interference, and the French invasion. Gran sums up as follows:

> Thus between 1798 and 1815 the indigenous middle class was seriously weakened . . . the Mamluk system broke down between 1798 and 1815 . . . because the pressure of Western trade and technology was relentless and in the end too strong to be resisted. Muhammad Ali, in shifting to the use of Western advisers, was acknowledging the new realities of power and was conducting a self-conscious policy which balanced the factors favoring greater independence against those militating in favor of dependence.[27]

The period that followed, in which the bureaucratic authority of the Muhammad Ali administration dominated Egyptian life, was characterized by an alternative set of cultural patterns, styles, themes, and organizations. Gran suggests that, throughout the nineteenth century at least, Egyptian social and cultural history can be interpreted as a dialectic between phases of commercial and agrarian middle class assertiveness and bureaucratic-authoritarian domination. The commercially oriented groups were more individualistic and less scientifically minded than were the exponents of the strong state. In the course of this struggle, Egyptian social structure was transformed and modernized, and, of course, certain distinctive patterns of Islamic response to modernization took shape.

The cultural dimension of this dialectic was concentrated about two contrasting theological orientations whose counterposition had emerged as early as the tenth century. Gran notes that during the last decades of Mamluk rule, the ulama seemed to prefer the nontheoretical, discontinuous approach to questions of Islamic law and belief which depends upon the citation of discreet hadith to warrant ad hoc rulings. The post-1815 period saw the predominance of *kalam,* a form of theological disputation which depends heavily upon deductive reasoning, the syllogistic form, and dialectical argument. The position of those whom Hodgson referred to as the "Hadith folk" was greatly suspicious of abstract reasoning and of attempts to explain the meaning or intention of inspired doings and sayings of the Prophet or of revelation itself. Kalam was equally directed at the defense of Islam from heresy and from the attacks of unbelievers, but it was more concerned to respond to those infected with alien philosophic ideas. Hence, the traditionist (hadith) approach, which still predominates in Sunni Islam, conveys the image of the originality and simplicity of the naive faithful before the onset of the cultural challenge which was the result of the conquest of Byzantine and Sasanian lands. Kalam symbolized the more sophisticated cultural response, recognizing the dangers of Greek philosophy, adopting the notions of reason and logic; but carefully excluding any discussion of first principles—the place of which is taken by revelation. The Hadith folk were critical of the Kalam folk and of the philosophers, tending to lump them together. The Kalam folk were concerned lest the spread of philosophy weaken belief among the educated classes. The philosophers tended to be contemptuous of the intellectual compromises of kalam and of its adaptation to the needs of the established order; but they did not expect the masses to be able to comprehend the teachings of philosophy, nor did they think it desirable that the simple beliefs of the common people be tampered with.

Following the well-established symbolic content of these two concepts, Gran is inclined to treat the earlier period somewhat more favorably as original, creative, down-to-earth, individualistic, and permitting a degree of political competition. Perhaps most significant as an indicator of his favorable judgment is his conclusion that the cultural movement of the earlier period allowed the participation of at least some women. As we have seen, Gran does not argue that Egypt was about to invent capitalism, but he does suggest that Egypt was in the process of developing its own cultural response to the early capitalistic transformations in the mode of production.

The original cultural response of Islam was overwhelmed by the Napoleonic invasion and the establishment of the Muhammad Ali state. The social classes (or segments) identified with the late–eighteenth century cultural movement were weakened, and lost what was to be the first round in a continuing struggle. The new centralized bureaucratic state encouraged those who valued order, solidarity, technology, science, reason, and logic. According to Gran, Hasan al-Attar, after his return from a lengthy sojourn in Istanbul and Damascus in 1815, became the leading intellectual exponent of the kalam position and of an accompanying bundle of "sciences," which together constitute a neoclassical reform of Islamic culture in Egypt. This neoclassical reform movement is stated by Gran to have served the needs of the emergent state-commercial elite and mode of production.

Gran's judgment of the value of this kalam trend moves from a pejorative beginning to a more affirmative assessment, just as does his opinion of Hasan al-Attar as a personality. The negative symbolic content of kalam is associated with the repressive policies of the Muhammad Ali regime, while the younger al-Attar is described as an ambitious and obsequious job-seeker who will gladly sell his intellectual talents to the highest bidder. His apparent lack of cultural authenticity is exemplified by his fascination with the French invaders, and by the ease with which they seduce him with their physical beauty, their intellectual discourse, and their friendship. Al-Attar's lack of authenticity is further established by references to his homosexuality and, in a more ambiguous way, to his apparent misogyny. But al-Attar comes to his senses. His sojourn in Turkey and Syria leavens his learning, and after he returns to Egypt he is enabled to make significant contributions to the modernization of Egyptian-Islamic culture. His contributions range over a wide area, including theology, law, language, science, and medicine. What seems most appealing to Gran is the fact that al-Attar is able to draw upon elements already found in indigenous Islamic sources to bolster the values of science, reason, and logic. The intellectual return of al-Attar to authenticity suggests that even the adaptation to the world market and the dominance of Western capitalism might have been accomplished in an original and an Islamic manner without the wholesale adoption of an alien culture. This suggestion is strengthened further by the convincing evidence Gran presents to show that the work of al-Jabarti, a friend of al-Attar, was not the "product of an accidental genius working in a Dark Age" (p. 182). and that "most of what is regarded as European influence [on al-Tahtawi, his student] came from his association with al-Attar" (p. 185). In the end, though, the potentiality of an Islamic authentic cultural adaptation to capitalism did not come about because reason, science, logic, and modern thought all became identified with Western thought.

Gran does not examine why it was necessary or desirable for those who benefited from the rise of peripheral capitalism in the Middle East to foster the growth of Western culture and the decline of Islamic culture, although one may draw the conclusion that it had something to do with Western capitalism's preference for direct access to a comprador bourgeoisie rather than accommodating itself to the autonomous aspirations of Muhammad Ali's nascent state capitalist system. Gran does not argue along these lines; he is rather content to say, "What Europe needed was encouraged. It is not too strong to say that in science and medicine Islamic emulation of European science was suppressed, even if it emanated from the intellectual elite" (p. 167).

Obviously Gran is ambivalent about al-Attar's scientific writings. For the most part they were not published. If published they would have strengthened the cultural integration of the Muslim world, which otherwise suffered from the "regional division of labor in culture" which Gran finds characteristic of peripheral capitalism. Their publication would not have led to an alternate science or an authentic medicine, but merely to an Islamic "emulation" of Western science. Perhaps what Gran means here is that modern science would be understood to be a product of the confluence of several intellectual tributaries, including an important Islamic stream. Gran writes, for example, "Neoclassicism was a weapon which undermined the traditional authorities and pointed to a reconciliation between earlier Islamic sources and contemporary Western science" (p. 175). But it only pointed to a reconciliation. In the final analysis, neoclassicism did not permit the Islamic world to enter into the mainstream of modernity, it merely served as a device whereby the "ruling class could counteract the culture of the traditional middle class. . . . Where a strongly entrenched compradorial bourgeoisie could dispense with neoclassicism . . . it would do so—but neoclassicism would reemerge when the power of that class waned" (p. 177).

Nevertheless, Gran argues that those who regard the Muslim world as a passive element in world history after the rise of Western capitalism are misled. His counterassertion has a deductive rather than an empirical character, however: ". . . Arab and Islamic lands . . . did participate crucially in the development of the modern world through the international division of labor with its well known unequal trade relations, before during and after the colonial period. Thus, logically, Islamic culture played a part in the main phases of modern world history" (p. 188).

Small consolation, I suppose, even for those who are glad to have the patronizing approval of Western scholars—but more likely intended to reassure the author more than the reader.

If the final judgment on neoclassicism is a wistful negative, that on traditional (hadith-oriented) Islam remains hopefully affirmative. The commercial sector is the enemy of bureaucratic authoritarianism, and it prefers hadith to kalam. Our understanding of politics in the Muslim world is distorted by the fact that we take for granted the "strong state" which in reality does not exist.

> The commercial sector was and is competing and struggling with Western Europe to wrest every possible gain out of the ongoing economic flow of world capitalism. If one looks at the large masses of peasants, tribes, and workers, again one finds it is their struggle which in large measure accounts for rulers' weaknesses." (P. 188)

The traditionists are closer to the masses, and they represent an Islamic cultural orientation which is at once more authentic, more likely to lead to greater democracy, and more likely to lead to greater independence within the framework of the modern capitalist world.

The doubts raised by the stereotypical way in which hadith and kalam are used as sociopolitical symbols are enhanced by a number of difficult methodological problems. Foremost among these is the question of how it may be possible to prove the assertion that a given ideological structure served the interests of a particular class. It may be less difficult to validate the statement that large numbers of people, members of a class, adopted a certain point of view. But even that claim is not substantiated by direct empirical evidence. The difficulty is further compounded by the fact that hadith and kalam orientations have been around for a long time. There is no doubt that, on balance, the hadith orientation remains the preferred orientation among the ulama associated with the madrassas. From Dar al-Hadith in Morocco, to Zituna in Tunisia, to al-Azhar of Shaykh Shaltut in Egypt, to the teachings of the late Ayatullah Burujirdi in Shiʿi Iran, to the standard curriculum at the Newtown Mosque madrassa in Pakistan and the Lucknow madrassa in India, hadith studies constitute the mainstay of formal religious education. Whatever social meaning was attached to the opposition to Muʿtazilism and related forms of kalam in the tenth century, the hadith orientation is the standard, conservative, position today. It is not a militant position, nor is it very creative; and it certainly does not reflect the struggle of an oppressed class.

Gran argues at one point that the production of culture is the result of the struggle of a class to assert its interests, and in his development of the dialectical theme of hadith vs. kalam he is for the most part dealing with the cultural activities of the ulama. These perspectives raise the questions of whether the ulama constitute a class or whether they may be identified with the interests of some other class. Gran's effort is complicated by the fact that his approach via the intellectual biography of Hasan al-Attar depends upon either the typicality of al-Attar or his widespread influence. Neither of these is established. Rather than standing as a model for larger scale intellectual movements among the ulama, al-Attar serves better as a model of the cross pressures on the ulama and the long run subordination of their institution to the political establishment. Gran acknowledges that the neoclassicism which he identified with kalam was soon neglected for Western science, and that the ulama continued to study hadith, but he is inclined to attribute these facts to the divergence of class interests between the ulama and the modernizing political elites of Muslim lands. Thus he explains,

> Neoclassicism in this [second] phase was the product of a small number of religious and literary figures who were themselves part of, but marginal to, the ruling structure which they sought to legitimize. They were among the worst paid, and their skills were not highly respected. . . . Even in an era dominated by *kalam*, it was necessary for scholars to teach hadith and to maintain competence in it. . . . In addition, there was the question of the structural relationship of the *ulama* to the dominant class . . . the *ulama* lived from the patronage of the wealthy but their relationship to the ruling class was a marginal one. . . . It is natural that they retained, if not an actual independence, at least a range of values and concerns which were potentially in conflict with the regime. (Pp. 165–66)

These passages, it seems to me, present a more accurate picture of the situation then and now. Of course, the ulama are not simply the intellectual segment of the ruling class. During the period in question, that is from 1760 to 1860, the position of the ulama was actually challenged, and to the extent that they had served as the intellectual exponents of the ruling elites, they were fast losing that position. In some parts of the Muslim world, as in Iran, the ulama did make strong alliances with the traditional commercial elites, but even these were not ubiquitously opposed to the ruling political authorities either. But in Egypt, there is strong evidence that the formal religious institution structured around al-Azhar, has been successfully integrated with the bureaucratic apparatus of the state. The religious institution is not monolithic, and a wide range of economic interests may be represented among its members, but it is best compared to the other bureaucracies rather than to a social class. From this perspective, it is not surprising that some of the ulama became closely associated with the Mamluk merchant-warriors who were, perhaps unwittingly—in their own search for quick profits—opening Egypt to the irreversible and the uncontrollable penetration of Western capitalism. Similarly, some of the ulama were responsive to the suffering and resentment of the increasingly miserable urban lower classes.

Doubtlessly, the turmoil of the period of the Mamluk dénouement was accompanied by some interesting and even promising cultural developments. These cultural developments appear to have been hampered, or even squelched, by the emergence of a strong state committed to the opening to Western culture. It is not at all clear, however, that the revival of an Islamic neoclassicism was a centrally important part of the state-building strategy of Muhammad Ali—as Gran himself argues. But this is not to say that the revival of neoclassicism, the rhetorical style of kalam, the debate on the opening of the gate of ijtihad, and other topics discussed by Gran, did not assume a lasting cultural significance. In the same way, some of the cultural forms and issues identified with the end of the Mamluk period, for example, the concern with the battle of Badr and the small number of warriors who fought with the Prophet there, have also attained a lasting significance.

If we judge the influence of al-Attar in terms of whether he was able to offer an authentic cultural synthesis of the Islamic and the modern, drawing upon a sound understanding of the turath, then we must, with Gran, agree that his effort failed. Western science and culture were adopted in many cases, and Islamic alternatives were simply pushed aside. Al-Jabarti, al-Tahtawi, and many other transitional figures, were read only as forerunners of the Westernization movement, as critics of their own societies, and as cautious, rather than truly synthetic, in their juxtaposition of Islam and Western civilization. The cultural products of al-Attar and al-Tahtawi are, therefore, not the products of the struggle of a class, because there was no class whose interests corresponded to the synthetic/authentic position they adumbrated.

The issue is wrongly put if one emphasizes cultural production as though one were concerned with the production of commodities. It is far more important to consider the consumption of culture. The rulers of the nascent bureaucratic-authoritarian state in Egypt were not much interested in al-Attar's message, even though they found him a pliable and obedient clerk. Nor does it appear that the emergent agarian bourgeoisie was much interested in the effort to adapt Islamic culture to the needs of the modern age. It was not until after a period of direct British domination, recapitulating and intensifying the symbolic historical experience of the French occupation, and not until after the creation of an impoverished petite bourgeoisie, not until after the beginning of the decline of the position of the rich peasants, and not until the emergence of a popular, urban, nationalist movement, that there was created a mass reading public eager to consume cultural products of the sort that al-Attar had pioneered. Gran, himself, seems vaguely aware of how the cultural achievements of al-Attar came to be used, when he differentiates between a first and second period of neoclassic revival. The second period emphasized history, language, literature, and science, as evidence of "Islam's true glory now . . .[and] in the distant past" (p. 165). It is this sort of neoclassicism that would reemerge when the power of the compradorial bourgeoisie would wane, because "In fields in which indigenous scholarship was indispendible, it was transformed to fit the needs of nation building" (p. 177).

Gran does not make it clear which period he is referring to in his statement, but it might well be a reference to the cultural policies of the Nasser regime. There is no doubt that the modern Egyptian state is engaged in a conscious effort to control and direct the production of culture with a view to strengthening its own legitimacy, mobilizing human resources, and weakening its opponents. But the elements of the neoclassical revival on the one hand, and the renewed interest in the life and personality of the Prophet, are not the property of any cultural bureaucracy. From this point of view, some of Gran's theoretical conclusions are sounder than the presumed empirical findings upon which they are based—that is, they have a sounder basis in the historical facts of later periods. Thus he states,

> The best way to approach the subject of the Sufi revival of the eighteenth century is one in which the totality of culture within the life of the socioeconomic formation is seen as a complex structure, so that culture production can be seen at once as part of the processes of integration and reproduction of the formation . . . and only contingently as a part of a continuum of elite culture which has its own internal logic(s). . . . [T]he same corpus of mediaevel learning was subject to appropriation and reappropriation in different ways. (P. 100)

The cultural achievements of al-Attar, al-Tahtawi, and so many others, did not become the monopoly of the state, but were in fact "appropriated and reappropriated." These achievements were not very valuable cultural assets until there came into being in Egypt and elsewhere in the Muslim world a large number of people for whom they provided a plausible answer to their questions, and for whom these achievements were accessible in a practical sense. The Nasserist government appropriated the relevant cultural style and content for its own political purposes, but to a considerable extent it had already been reappropriated by the contemporary Islamic fundamentalist movement. This is why Samir Amin lumped the Nasserists and the Muslim Brethren together. The fact is, that the work of al-Attar has achieved a vitality in the rise of urban, petit bourgeois, militant, fundamentalist Islamic movements. It is also a fact that the ulama have, for the most part, stood aside from the growth of these movements, even though they can be shamed, or tempted by their success, to join in these movements.

This process of linking the ulama to a petit bourgeois fundamentalist movement has been carried furthest in Iran during the revolution, but in the ensuing break between the followers of Khomeini and the Mujahidin-i-Khalq, the objective divergence of interests, of institutional commitments, and of intellectual orientations, has been revealed. The orthodox ulama, in Egypt and in Iran, have not moved very much in terms of doctrine, nor have they lost their commitment to the concept of the "imperial ulama." The Islamic resurgence is a movement of laymen. It is a manifestation of an increasingly popular struggle of a growing number of bureaucrats, technicians, professionals (who have been downgraded to the technician level), teachers, skilled workers, and even kulaks, who would assert themselves politically and attempt to reshape the state in terms of their own self-image.

7

Nationalism, Liberalism, and the Islamic Heritage: The Political Thought of Tariq al-Bishri

Islamic Liberalism

There are apparently two kinds of Islamic liberalism. The first finds the idea of a liberal Islamic state possible and desirable not only because such a liberal, democratic state accords with the spirit of Islam, but especially because, in matters political, Islam has few specific requirements. The second takes the opposite view.

The view of the first group of liberals is that Islam has few or no political institutional prescriptions, and little canonical experience that can be said to be incumbent upon present-day political authorities or constituent powers. This first category of Islamic liberals does not propose the separation of religion and the state in Islam. They rather argue that the virtual silence of Islam on the question of state institutions, except for the matter of taking counsel, allows the establishment of liberal institutions if Muslims wish to do so. Moreover, they are inclined to deduce from the very fact of the silence of the Shariʿa on the matter of political institutions, that Islam is compatible only with a liberal system in which Muslims are free to choose and change their political arrangements. Nevertheless the state they propose would be an Islamic state.

The second form of Islamic liberalism would justify the establishment of liberal institutions (parliament, elections, civil rights) and even some social welfare policies, not on the basis of the absence of any contradictory Islamic legislation, but rather on the basis of quite specific Islamic legislation, which they are inclined to deduce from canonical sources and from the available anecdotal histories of the early caliphate. Of course, the result is an anomaly, since the liberal institutions would not themselves be based upon liberal political, epistemological, and moral principles (pluralism, individualism, capitalism, agnosticism, empiricism, pragmatism, utilitarianism, tolerance, etc.) but rather on explicit Islamic legislation of divine origin, such as the qur'anic provision for taking counsel, or the denial of the sovereign authority of man over man, or the sharʿi provisions for "electing" the caliph, or the hadith concerning the equality of believers.

It may well be questioned whether the political apparatus of a liberal regime can be justified in a political community in which the overwhelming majority are expected to hold similar beliefs and to obey religious authority. There is, then, a sense in which liberal political practices might be seen as a form of religious ritual—with the conclusion usually already known.

The existence of this alternative Islamic orientation, a kind of "scripturalist liberalism," more concerned with apologetics than practical politics, has led some optimistic observers to conclude that there is some tendency for modernists and fundamentalists to converge in their ideas of the Islamic state and the Islamic social order. Some say that the modernists are becoming more "Islamic" while the fundamentalists are becoming more liberal. Those who hold this view are inclined to be religious and political conservatives. Still, they point to the one principle that Islamic liberals and fundamentalists have in common, and that is the rejection of the secular state. There is even some suspicion that those who would play down the differences between the fundamentalists and the liberals harbor aspirations to exploit the potential political power of the devout masses by employing fundamentalist symbols. In their search for political allies to help in the struggle to bring reform and modernization, even a liberal parliamentary state, they try to convince themselves that the fundamentalists constitute a benign political force waiting to be guided by the more enlightened. But it may also be argued that Islamic liberalism is too lacking in explicit Islamic textual support and too weak doctrinally and organizationally to withstand the pressures of the fundamentalists. The real question is which of the Islamic tendencies would come out on top politically in the longer run.

Some observers are apprehensive that the fundamentalists would in fact establish an authoritarian religious regime, and call it liberal or democratic because it is Islamic. This possibility is all the more likely where it is argued that Western political and philosophical criteria ought not be applied to Islamic experience and institutions because those criteria are inauthentic, alien, and often instruments of exploitation. From this perspective, the differences between the modernists and the fundamentalists are exaggerated when viewed with Western spectacles because Westerners are inclined to make false and tendentious ideological distinctions based on irrelevant social categories and gross cultural misunderstandings. Some would argue that the Western model of secular liberalism is simply unsuited to the circumstances of Muslim peoples who are exploring authentic alternatives by opening their own dialogue with the fundamentalists.

In spite of the fact that the convergence of modernists and fundamentalists may only be verbal, the possibility of bringing these two groups together is a tempting political goal. The liberal modernists believe that they know how to run a modern state and how to build effective administrative institutions, but the fundamentalists or the authoritarian modernists seem to be able to mobilize and move the masses.

In light of developments in Iran, established governments and westernized intellectuals, have withdrawn in horror before the specter of the mobilization of a popular revolutionary force. Still, some westernized intellectuals in Egypt have been attracted by the idea of a coalition with fundamentalists, especially those leftist intellectuals who were thrown together with the religious opposition during Sadat's last, self-destructive, phase of attacking all his enemies at once. Egyptian Marxists are confident that Sunni Islam could never produce another Khomeini. They are also convinced that popular fundamentalism is a form of false consciousness, which obscures the objectively revolutionary impulse of the masses. That the masses, rather than the working class, or party cadres, are the focal point of attention, here suggests a vaguely leftist form of nationalism rather than an ordered doctrinal position.

The idea of an oppositional alliance between the left and the Muslim Brotherhood may already be an anachronism because the ideal target for such a coalition was Sadat, and the ideal moment was the time of his assassination. That moment came and went, and Egypt was rid of Sadat without the need of the leftist intellectuals who have once again been set back on their heels and have taken to musing about what might have been.

In the meantime, while the leaders of the officially recognized political organizations have taken to a quiet reconsideration of their position and opportunities under the new Mubarak regime, a few intellectuals and publicists have begun to play with the idea of a coalition linking one or more of the licensed parties and the Muslim Brotherhood. For the most part this is election talk aimed at legitimating additional opposition parties with a view to diminishing the virtual dictatorial majority in the parliament which was part of Sadat's legacy to Mubarak. In 1984, this strategy was successful when the (neo) Wafd was licensed, and it undertook to represent the Ikhwan, which was not licensed. The election resulted in significant representation for both opposition groups, but only limited political cooperation. Nevertheless, the prospects for such a coalition of opposition forces opened a public debate which was interesting for many reasons, including the fact that the left was very restrained in its criticism of the obviously reactionary implications of a religious-bourgeois coalition. It has become clear that the image of the Ikhwan, as well as that of the Wafd, and other pre-Nasserist groups, has been altered within the context of Egyptian political culture. If this is the case, no one has had greater influence in this regard than Mr. Tariq al-Bishri, an amateur historian, a judicial officer of the Council of State, and an unaffiliated man of the left.

Tariq Al-Bishri

Tariq al-Bishri has only recently achieved wide notoriety as a political theorist in Egypt. His work is widely respected, and it has attracted a good deal of political interest, including that of the Egyptian government. Among Egyptian rightists he was deeply suspect because of his leftist connections, sympathies, and rhetoric. But he has exasperated some of his leftist friends and admirers by his unorthodox theories of ideology, his extreme antipathy to alien doctrines and culture, and his detached, if not critical, view of the Nasser period. Yet his insistence on Egyptian authenticity, on the soundness of popular instincts, on the need to integrate Islam into the national political formula, on the symbolic importance of equal rights for Coptic Christians as full members of the Egyptian nation, and above all, on the absolute independence of the Egyptian fatherland, seem to reflect a combination of sentiments that are widely prevalent in Egypt, but not articulated in any single program by any organized movement.

The resultant combination may be eclectic, and it arouses suspicion that it is only a strategic device, such as the popular front, meant to gain allies for an increasingly frustrated and confused Egyptian Marxist movement. Nevertheless its apparent inclusion of patriotism, authenticity, Islam, equal rights, populism, constitutionalism, and multiparty parliamentarism in a single package, speaks very much to the idea of a national reconciliation based on the widespread consensus that both the Nasser and Sadat administrations offered only partial answers to the nation's needs. Al-Bishri's answer is not a reaffirmation of a real or imagined Nasserism of the mid-1960s. He seems to be interested neither in reconstructing the real Nasserist state, nor in constructing an imaginary Nasserist socialist state which is the ideological centerpiece of the strategy and tactics of the more doctrinaire younger Marxists.

But if al-Bishri's views do not please his closest ideological allies, neither are they comforting to bourgeois liberals and the Western-oriented intelligentsia. Even if his approach holds out the hope of linking the Islamic resurgence to a form of liberal government, his utter rejection of Western culture is bound to lead to the isolation of those of liberal political orientation from their Western sources of support. National consensus may lead to a diminution of political cultural and economic pluralism. It is, thus, entirely conceivable that some workable combination of a liberal Islam and a liberal bourgeois state could be established in Egypt which could be almost as anti-Western as Khomeini's Iran.

Although al-Bishri's essays are written in a theoretical style, and though he appears to be reasonably well-acquainted with Marxian theory, he does not employ a formal Marxian method. Philosophically, he is an historical materialist, emphasizing the concept of an objective material reality manifested in the praxis of the masses. The early Marx prevails over the later Marx, and Leninist elements are almost entirely absent. Though the masses must be brought to a mature understanding by means of a variety of organizational, mobilizational, and educational devices, the mass movement can only be a public movement, and ought not be sacrificed to the requirements of clandestinity and organizational integrity. Hence, al-Bishri is inclined to criticize all earlier Egyptian political organizations for failing to achieve a balance between organizational rationality and programmatic clarity, between overt and covert political activity, between doctrinal uniformity and personal affinity, between elitism and mass appeal, between sincerity and prudence, and so on. His method is historical, but Egypt is virtually his only model. He ignores European discussions of some questions which are central to his position, especially on nationalism and ideology. Nevertheless, especially in the Egyptian context, he is surprisingly persuasive.

Al-Bishri's writings comprise two large historical works and a number of essays, both historical and analytical. Some of his early essays were incorporated in his first book, *The Political Movement in Egypt 1945–1952*. The later essays that will be of most concern to us, were apologetic and polemical efforts to sustain the argument contained in the last chapters of his second book, *The Muslims and the Copts in Egypt*.[1] Al-Bishri, himself, tells us that his position changed by the time that he completed his second book, and Egypt, too, changed considerably from the late Nasser period to the early Mubarak phase.[2]

The unique and surprising element in al-Bishri's recent writings on Egyptian historical and cultural authenticity, is his inclusion of both the Wafd and the Muslim Brotherhood, the two strongest political organizations of the pre-Nasser period, as manifestations of the authentic spirit of the Egyptian people. This is surprising because al-Bishri has been identified with the left, which is usually highly critical of these prerevolutionary organizations. It also suggests that Egypt was pursuing a more authentic historical path before the coup of 1952 than it was after the Free Officers took over. And insofar as both the Wafd and the Brotherhood aspire to play a major role in contemporary Egyptian politics, al-Bishri is clearly calling for a form of ideological pluralism if not a genuine organizational and institutional pluralism.

Among the most outstanding elements of al-Bishri's new ideological position is his insistence that Islamic legal specialists find a religious formula granting equal political rights to Copts in an Egyptian nation-state which is also an Islamic state in some sense.[3] Taken together with his inclusion of Islamic orthodoxy among the essential elements of the national consensus, these positions suggest the doctrinal ground upon which an Islamic liberal polity can be constructed. But the very contradictoriness of these elements hints at the inclination to subordinate both Islam and political liberalism to Egyptian nationalism.

Al-Bishri wishes to remove religious obstacles to the realization of national unity. The Islamic movement that insists on the alienness of the Copts divides and weakens the Egyptian community. But the Copts constitute a relatively small minority in Egypt, variously estimated at 7 to 15 percent, and one might suppose that overcoming the (liberal) secular-religious (fundamentalist) split among the Muslims would be far more important for the achievement of national unity. To include the Copts at the expense of losing the fundamentalists does not appear to be a prudent strategy for maximizing national solidarity.

These intriguing positions are to be found in al-Bishri's second book, and in several articles written in the early- and mid-1980s. That book discusses the history of the prerevolutionary period from the perspective of intercommunal relations. His first book concentrated on the political movement that led up to the revolution of 1952, and it was strongly influenced by the sort of Marxspeak prevalent among intellectuals during the Nasser period. We are, therefore, interested in the first book for the light it can shed on his earlier attitude toward the Wafd and the Brotherhood, as well as for its earlier assessment of the revolution itself.

Al-Bishri's goals and values seem to conflict, and his ideological orientation changes somewhat if one compares the two books. There is a significant change in emphasis from an early commitment to the truth-value of scientific socialist theory to the later assertion that the masses are, by definition, the repository of all truth. Since such a formulation offers the theorist wide latitude in interpreting the often cacaphonous and incoherent speech of the masses, and since al-Bishri argued that apparent differences of formal ideologies actually obscured the unity of the will of the masses, it is important to determine what sort of interpretation al-Bishri was inclined to give to this speech.

The Egyptian Masses

The major actor, the hero of the political movement which al-Bishri describes, is the Egyptian masses, *al-jamahir,* or the people, *al-shaʿab.* The movement is a revolutionary movement, and its elements mark the awakening and the political maturation of the consciousness of the masses. The revolutionary process, extending for seven years, culminated in the burning of Cairo on 26 January 1952. The actual coup d'etat of the Free Officers, occurring on 23 July 1952 was more a coup de grace, following the revolution, and merely filled the political vacuum.[4] That the revolution and the establishment of the successor regime did not occur simultaneously is an anomaly which points at once to the complex character of the political movement in Egypt and to the incompleteness of that movement. The Egyptian political elite, in all its factions and orientations, is sharply criticized by al-Bishri for failing to fulfill its leadership function, given the level of political awareness achieved, and the political initiatives taken by the masses. Al-Bishri's principal conclusion in this book is that the Egyptian masses reaffirmed their political cultural heritage in the course of that political movement, and they gave to the events of 1945–52 authentic meaning, despite the ideological confusions, tactical mistakes, organizational weaknesses, and false consciousness of the elite actors. Hence, the pre-Nasserist mass movement was a true expression of Egyptian national consciousness; and an investigation of the nature of that movement will reveal the content of Egyptian authenticity.

The original cause of the political movement which began in 1945 was the growing popular understanding of the economic ramifications of the British occupation. This understanding had not been clear both because of the mixture of British motives (linking Egypt to imperial communications) and because of lack of understanding of the economics of imperialist exploitation. But after the publication of Lenin's work in imperialism as the highest stage of capitalism, the perception of the role of the British in Egypt changed.[5] By the end of the war, the masses came to understand that British domination was the source of their economic hardships and "the relationship between political domination and economic exploitation was clearly revealed" (p. 10). This awareness "permitted the national movement to achieve a new maturity . . . and the more progressive elements of the younger generation took up scientific socialist thought and used it to shape a new perception of the national movement" (pp. 10–11, 221). At first, their understanding was limited to the particular conditions of Egypt alone, but the events of World War II led them to understand imperialism as a global phenomenon.

Egyptian awareness was further sustained by the development, especially during the war years, of both an indigenous capitalism and a stronger working class.[6] The postwar period saw a rising challenge to the nascent capitalist class in Egypt, so the capitalists sought a new political formula that might preserve and strengthen their wartime gains. As a consequence, postwar politics was increasingly based on class interest, a situation which "contributed to making the masses aware of the various class interests which were hidden behind the diverse policies proposed for dealing with the national question. This [awareness] was one of the factors that advanced the popular consciousness in its understanding of the attitude of big capital toward the national movement" (p. 12).

Al-Bishri then goes on to quote from the Egyptian and foreign press of the time to show that postwar changes provoked an economic crisis affecting both capital and labor in Egypt: ". . . the working class was knocking on the door, trying to achieve a coalition with the petite bourgeoisie, the intellectuals and the peasants in the struggle for political and economic independence" (p. 13). Al-Bishri contends that economic hardship played the most important role in arousing and maintaining the political consciousness of the masses in the face of the government's manifold efforts to control, or modify, or direct the popular movement.

This key argument is made in the introduction to the book on the postwar political movement, and the validity of its empirical and theoretical components is not thereafter questioned. It constitutes the largely implicit framework for the historical narrative which follows.[7]

> The effort required to overturn the regime was not beyond the capacity of the masses, but it required of them their utmost strength, and most extensive action, . . . mobilization and association, since it was understood that the goal was to change the institutions of domination as a whole and not merely the government or some institutions. And that raises an essential question, what next? [What should be] the basis of the desired regime? . . .

> it is insufficient to understand what is to be rejected, it is rather necessary to understand what the alternative possibilities are as well.
>
> If the [political understanding] of the masses depended on the extent of their power and maturity, those, in turn depended upon . . . the power of the organizations which bound the masses together, gave their movement revolutionary direction, and explained their goals, and by the way [these organizations tried] to reach out to the masses, and the extent to which these organizations could agree on specific goals. (P. 31)

The Egyptian Capitalists

In contrast to this new political awareness of the masses, even the most enlightened exponents of capitalist development gave priority to economic development above the solution of the national question.[8] For the capitalists, the national question was primarily that of Egypt's sterling balances. They were more concerned with the availability of foreign capital than with the evacuation, with financial markets than the Canal Zone, with the expansion of irrigation than with the union of Egypt and the Sudan, with the efficient organization of the instruments of the state rather than with civil rights, with social coexistence rather than class struggle, and with reducing the cost of production rather than raising the standard of living.[9]

In point of fact, British policy hampered the growth of Egyptian capitalism, pushing the conservative politicians to attempt to pass various measures to reduce the influence and control of foreign capital. But al-Bishri argues that these were half-way measures which merely reaffirm the comprador character of Egyptian capitalism. "The bill was a modest effort on the part of capital to partially Egyptianize the economy, an effort which conforms completely with the methods of Egyptian capitalism whereby it sets fragmented goals of limited scope and tries to take advantage of small gains in order to get by" (p. 192). Because of its modest goals and timidity, Egyptian capitalism failed in its attempts to limit foreign capital and to restrict the political influence of the larger landowners.[10] In sum, Egyptian capital, at the end of World War II, faced almost insurmountable obstacles that prevented it from offering solutions to either the domestic or the foreign problems facing Egypt at the time. In particular, Egyptian capital did not play the progressive role expected of "national capital." Al-Bishri accuses larger capital in particular of "a willingness to move from relations of dependency to a relationship of the junior partner (of imperialism)" (p. 202).

The popular movement "called not only for independence, but

it also attacked reaction, exploitation, and the concentration of wealth. So there was no other choice for capital other than to accept a situation which tied them to the large landowners and foreign interests and in which the apparatus of the state served them all as a protective dam against the masses" (p. 206). Al-Bishri reaffirms his argument that the masses were the hero of the revolution of 1952, which was at once a class conflict and a struggle for independence:

> Thus capital determined its policy—internal and external—with skill and talent, and it thought thereby to guide its ship with success. But the basic problem was that the ship was too small and too weak to withstand the mountainous waves that swelled all around it . . . the popular movement and the movement of the working class caused the dreams of the awakening to spread. (P. 207)

It may well be that the "awakening" has been only a dream, but al-Bishri does not seem to be conscious of the implications of this odd expression.

The Wafd

Al-Bishri's ambivalence toward the Wafd party is reflected in his description of it as a social and ideological hybrid. Despite the differences in social outlook and strategic sense between the more progressive wing of the capitalist class and the more reactionary wing of the landowning class, al-Bishri lays much blame on the Wafd for the political failures of the period.[11] The Wafd was too interested in returning to power, too much committed to social order, and too frightened of the mass movement.[12] The Wafd played a noble role in Egyptian history in leading the 1919 revolution, but its leadership was dominated by large landowners, capitalists, political opportunists and admirers of Western culture. Though the Wafd sought to limit the power of the king, in 1942 it was willing to be installed in office by the force of British tanks. It could be pushed to the unilateral abrogation of the bilateral treaty with Britain of 1936, but it could also invoke martial law against the rioting mob after the British attacked and destroyed an Egyptian police post in the Canal zone in 1952.

With the signing of the treaty of 1936 the Wafd began its retreat from the national goals and, at the same time, reactionary elements began to infiltrate the Party ranks. Nevertheless, the Wafd remained popular and was often in the parliamentary opposition. Because it still mobilized mass sentiment, the king considered the Wafd to be dangerous in spite of itself. "If the position of the Wafd among the masses prevented many of them from joining the more progressive and revolutionary tendencies in the society, it nevertheless created a broad political 'rally' of the masses which objectively benefited those (radical) tendencies in their effort to attract groups rather than isolated individuals, and it also created the democratic context which is necessary for the growth of new ideas and new streams (of thought)" (pp. 38, 361). Hence one of the greatest virtues of the Wafd was that the reactionaries opposed it.[13] The Wafd became a prisoner of its own "radicalism," and its very popularity prevented it from manipulating its supporters. In fact the opposite was the case.[14]

Al-Bishri describes the political forces supporting the king as "the institutions of the state, the security apparatus, indirectly . . . the occupation forces, and some of the large landowners and capitalists" (p. 361). Hence, the leaders of the Wafd could not be differentiated from many of the supporters of the king as far as social class and economic interest were concerned. The Wafd, he argues, was originally the product of objective social and historical conditions which forced upon it a policy of "nonviolent constitutional" action, and thereafter the Wafd remained a prisoner of those historical origins.[15]

The great virtue and the great defect of the Wafd was its commitment to nonviolent, constitutional politics–the Wafd leaders worked the system, they did not overthrow it. Still the Wafd retained its wide popularity among the masses and even for a group of young, radical intellectuals, it was the vehicle of choice for their efforts to change the system.[16]

In the mid-30s the Wafd began to appeal to the expanding group of educated youth who became active in street demonstrations at the time.[17] Their success in attracting this progressive and ideologically "mature" element led eventually to the development of a radical group within the Wafd. This younger group served as a link between the conservative wing of the Wafd, including both the traditional leadership and the newly infiltrated landowners, and those sections of the masses that were more politically conscious, including, especially, the youth of the 1940s and the postwar period.[18] Nevertheless, this radical tendency in the party was never able to dominate party policy or to reach the workers and the peasants.[19] Its most important function was that of maintaining the historical connection between the revolution of 1919 and the postwar movement. It also made an important ideological contribution to the consciousness of the mass base of the Wafd by increasing their "scientific understanding of social problems" (p. 41).

One of the most important of the political campaigns of the

"Wafdist Vanguard" (the organized section of the progressive Wafdist youth) was its defense of parliamentary life against the Ikhwan slogan, "No Party Politics and No Parties!"

> Dr. Mandur wrote that the party system was a national and a constitutional necessity, and that the call for a simple nationalism without party politics was a device . . . to destroy the Wafd; and it was incumbent on every young person to support the constitution . . . in the belief that the country's problem would not be solved so long as the will of the nation was not realized first via self-government. . . . This [was a] statement . . . of the most important political beliefs adopted by the Wafdist Vanguard . . . maintaining the constitutional and parliamentary system, and the party system as a point of departure for achieving political reform . . . and social justice, and [asserting] that the victory of the oppressed classes . . . would come through a just and constitutionally legitimate regime. [There was] some effort to blend the traditional Wafdist thought and the new social ideas. (P. 158)

The following month Dr. Mandur wrote more explicitly and more critically that "the correct solution . . . was to adopt the principle of the socialist character of the state" (p. 221).

The resulting division of labor between the parliamentary leadership and the younger radical wing sometimes "led to blind outbursts which lost sight of clear goals and practical plans . . . and that led the enthusiastic tendencies to get bogged down . . . and led some parts of the masses to hive off to those organizations that raised glittering slogans and called for total change, wherein the masses found strict organizational ties and a practical and focused movement, but [also] one which led them to goals which were opposed to their national goals and their social demands" (pp. 42, 530).

Thus al-Bishri finds the Wafd's dual nature responsible, in part, for the rise of the Muslim Brotherhood. Ultimately, however, the Wafd did lose its popularity, or rather the masses lost faith in the Wafd, whose commitment to nonviolent and nonrevolutionary methods appeared to be inappropriate after the burning of Cairo. The Wafd's willingness to institute martial law and other repressive legislation in a dubious effort to preserve public order and private property, after the burning of Cairo, appeared to play into the king's hands.[20] But al-Bishri also lays a good deal of blame on the other leaders of the popular movement for their failure to support the Wafd immediately after the abrogation of the 1936 treaty. Instead, the leaders of the communist groups, the Socialist and the Watani parties all issued statements of their differences with the Wafd, leading to great confusion among the masses.[21]

There is little doubt though, that al-Bishri regretted the political demise of the Wafd. He quotes from an article written by Mustafa Amin: "When the public discovers the deceit of one of its own men, it is not that man only who loses his position, but the people lose faith in all those like him" (p. 363). Al-Bishri explains further that

> . . . this means that the demise of the Wafd's leadership, the traditional leadership of the nation (umma) had the effect of leaving an obvious political vacuum . . . it had the effect of spreading a sense of being orphaned . . . and under such conditions, freedom becomes a burden. . . . The right to choose, to choose a goal, or a party, or a ruler, is the basis of the practice of democracy, but . . . the individual must be able to have confidence in the foundation and structure which will render his choice sound . . . but when doubt becomes the ruler of the situation . . . then destruction alone becomes the absolute good. (Pp. 363–64)

confidence in leaders declined

The Muslim Brotherhood

There was little ambivalence in al-Bishri's attitude toward the Muslim Brotherhood or the Jamaʿa al-Ikhwan al-Muslimun.[22] Al-Banna's Jamaʿa was founded in 1928, and by the mid 1930s had grown to become second only to the Wafd in popularity and power, and even greater in actual membership. The Jamaʿa appealed not only to the religious sentiments of the lower middle classes, but also to the economic interests of the religious establishment.[23] As al-Bishri sees it, the Jamaʿa was able to take advantage of the moral disgust that accompanied the dismaying increase in corruption, vice, and the breakdown of tradition.[24] Disappointment with the failure of other parties, especially the Wafd, led many Egyptians to seek alternative paths, and a surprisingly large number were drawn to the Jamaʿa in spite of, or even because of, its vague doctrine, its autocratic leadership, its tight organizational discipline, its opportunistic political line, and its religious obscurantism.[25] Al-Bishri describes the movement as a protofascist organization which could be manipulated by its megalomanic leader in any direction, and he argues that its success was the result of political despair and the resort to desperate and irrational solutions.[26]

The bases of Ikhwan politics were the two important principles that arose out of the caliphate controversy. The first was the inseparability of religion and politics in Islam, and the second was the obligatory character of the caliphate as the central institution of Islamic government.[27] The Ikhwan denied that they were a political party and, as we have seen, strongly condemned party politics. Above all, the Ikhwan claimed to be a religious, and not a political movement, but al-Bishri is at great pains to insist that they were hypocritical on

① unity of politics/religion
② obligatory character of caliphate

 this point.[28] According to al-Bishri, al-Banna was insufficiently forceful on the "national" questions of evacuation and independence, subordinating those issues to pan-Islamic and pan-Arab policies aimed at reestablishing the lost caliphate.

> It appears that the quest for the Islamic caliphate was prior to any other national goal. . . . A demand like the demand for the caliphate, given the doctrinal obscurity regarding its relationship with the meaning of Egyptian nationalism, and the meaning of freedom, and . . . the priority of each of these, such a demand was not in itself hostile to imperialism. . . . It is well known that the Turkish caliphate was the main gate through which imperialism and foreign concessions streamed into . . . the Middle East. . . . King Fuad tried to [assert the religious legitimacy of his throne] after the abolition of the caliphate by Turkey in 1924 . . . [whereupon] the democratic forces in Egypt joined the battle against [Fuad's attempt to claim the caliphate] and they contributed to the failure of the project, and after that King Faruk tried to do the same thing. (P. 55)

Al-Bishri is particularly critical of al-Banna himself, accusing him of political opportunism, of inconsistency, of riding roughshod over his opposition, and of allowing parallels to be drawn between himself and the Prophet or, alternately, the caliph.[29] He cites several sources, Western and Egyptian, that illustrate al-Banna's dictatorial style and his reactionary politics. In particular he emphasizes al-Banna's denunciation to the palace of some members of the pro-Wafdist opposition within the Jamaʿa.[30]

Al-Bishri emphasizes al-Banna's inconsistency on the question of the Jamaʿa's political role. The Jamaʿa always sought the "high ground" in declaring themselves to be nonpolitical in the sense of nonpartisan. But, at the same time, the Jamaʿa insisted on the unity of religion and politics. Thus al-Banna wrote in the first issue of *al-Nazir,* ". . . Islam is worship, leadership, religion, state, spirituality, practice, prayer, jihad, obedience, judgment, the Book, and the sword" (p. 52).

The concomitant of the Jamaʿa's claim to be all things to all men, that is, "a fundamentalist calling [*daʿwa salafiyya*] . . . a sufi tarika . . . a political organization . . . an athletic club . . . a cultural and scientific association . . . an economic enterprise . . . a social concept" (p. 53), was a lack of clarity regarding the ideology of the organization. Al-Bishri returns to this matter frequently, using the word *ghumudh,* meaning vague or obscure, to describe Jamaʿa doctrine, and frequently taking al-Banna to task in this regard: "In his treatise *To What do We Summon the People,* the guide [al-Banna] referred to the problems of the times, saying that universalism and nationalism and socialism and capitalism and bolshevism and war and the distribution of wealth and the link between the proprietor and the consumer are all comprehended in Islam, but he did not clarify his theory nor the position of the Jamaᶜa regarding these issues, begging off with the statement that space did not allow details" (p. 59).

The obscurity of the Jamaᶜa doctrine and al-Banna's global characterization of the movement, and of its conception of Islam, allowed the Ikhwan to take advantage of the discontent and the political despair of the masses.[31] But the Ikhwan misled the people on both the national question and the social question by directing their attention to two false issues, that of replacing positive legislation with the Shariᶜa and that of preventing the further intrusion of Western culture and social mores. Al-Bishri, who is a judge, it will be remembered, writes regarding positive legislation:

> A detailed study of the matter shows that the problem is not in that the legal system is positive, it is rather in the social relationships between the exploited and the exploiting classes and in the statutes which support those relations, just as it is in the problem of foreign control over the economy . . . the peasant debtors suffer from usury not because it is *haram* [forbidden by the Qurᶜan] but because it is a form of economic exploitation. Hence, positive legislation can free us from this exploitation. (P. 67)

Al-Bishri argues that the call for Shariᶜa legislation by itself would change nothing.

He is also contemptuous of the identification of imperialism with the work of missionaries, with the externalities of life-style, and with the affluence of the minorities. Al-Bishri accuses the Ikhwan of having an exaggerated hatred for all foreign cultural elements that were brought into [*al-wafid*] Egypt, identifying Western culture with the goings on in the night clubs and places of entertainment.[32] He was particularly critical of the fact that the Jamaᶜa obliterated class distinctions and prevented the development of class consciousness by blaming exploitation on the minorities and by insisting that religion alone divided social groups (especially Muslims and Copts).[33]

Finally, al-Bishri describes the Jamaᶜa under al-Banna in the 1940s as a bomb about to explode, and no one knew who its victims were likely to be.[34] Thus the strengths of the Ikhwan were in its doctrinal obscurity and its dictatorial leadership. But these were also its weaknesses, for, when al-Banna was assassinated, the succession problem could not be resolved. Al-Bishri concludes with the surprising thought that ultimately the large size of the Jamaᶜa was not a source of strength, suggesting that some smaller organizations and parties were more active and successful "such as the communist organizations and Misr al-Fatat" (p. 74).

Even under al-Hudhaybi, al-Banna's successor, whom al-Bishri believes to have been the king's choice to lead the Jamaʿa, the Ikhwan retained its appeal to an important segment of the masses and the youth. Hence the Jamaʿa might have played an important and a progressive role in the Egyptian revolution, but it did not.[35] Al-Bishri further states that, in order for the Ikhwan to have played such a role, they should have given up their policy of avoiding cooperation or coalitions with other groups.[36]

The Communists

As for the communists, despite al-Bishri's Marxist orientation, he did not believe that they played a great role in the revolution. Al-Bishri traces the development of the movement, identifies the various groups, and describes their rivalries and their tactics. The main contribution of the communists was ideological, and they had a significant influence on the ideas of the younger, educated, urban segments. Apart from this role of enlightenment and critique, the communists were too few, too riven by doctrinal disputes, and too concerned with secrecy and organizational discipline to do very much.[37] Of course, they had good reason to be wary, but the result was that they failed to influence the workers or the peasants, and they failed to set up mass line groups. Above all, they could not decide whether to form a national front or to maintain the purity and integrity of their cadre structures.

The Haditu group (The Democratic Movement for the Liberation of the Fatherland) was typically favored by al-Bishri over the more doctrinaire, French-influenced Egyptian Communist Party (ECP) because it was more willing, in theory at least, to join with other organized groups in a national progressive front.[38] The most important part of the Haditu program, for al-Bishri, was the decision to back an alliance with "national capital" which was declared to be an ally of the working class in its struggle against imperialism.[39]

The Egyptian Communist Party, by contrast, was criticized for being too theoretical, too antagonistic toward other Marxist factions, and too concerned with individual conversions. Above all, the ECP condemned the Wafd, and opposed any sort of cooperation with it, but, at the same time, it held the view that the country was not ready for a popular revolution. The ECP position upheld the two-stage theory of revolution, whereby a national democratic revolution precedes the socialist revolution, but they believed that the first revolution is accomplished by an alliance of the proletariat, the peasants, and the lower middle class. The Wafd, representing national capital, were thus necessarily excluded. As a consequence the ECP held back from a full commitment to revolution in the early 1950s.

All Communist groups condemned both the Ikhwan and the Misr al-Fatat (later to become the Socialist Party of Egypt) as fascists.[40] This position was modified as a consequence of the common sojourn of various members of these groups in jail in the late 1940s. As a consequence of this opportunity to talk in a more open and non-competitive manner, an opportunity repeated several times in recent Egyptian history, the antagonistic views of many were altered. The members of the Democratic Movement later took the position that it was impossible for a "true fascism" to occur in a colonial country, thus justifying cooperation with Misr al-Fatat.[41] And the ECP formed an even closer alliance with Ahmad Husain, leader of the Misr al-Fatat in the early 1950s despite the unwillingness of the ECP to cooperate with either the Wafd or the Ikhwan.

Al-Bishri believed that capitalist development was not a viable alternative for Egypt in 1945. It was not a question of the ultimate morality of capitalism, or of the ultimate historical inevitability of socialism. It was rather a question of the weakness and the dependence of Egyptian capital. At the same time, al-Bishri wished to see an alliance between national capital, as represented by the Wafd, and the other popular forces. He believed that it was possible for Egypt to pursue a noncapitalist path to development by means of a broad, comprehensive coalition of national patriotic forces.[42] The Wafd had to be a part of this coalition because of its popularity, its political tradition, its economic base, and its organization. But the Wafd could not lead the revolution, despite its radical wing, because it was committed in logic and in ideology to both constitutional methods and the preservation of the existing regime. Al-Bishri believed that a regime change was necessary, but he also wanted to preserve the political values, practices, and heritage for which the Wafd stood. In other words, he sought a kind of republican regime that would be able to make the transition to a form of democratic socialism. He felt that the Wafd, or something like it, might be able to play a positive role in such a new regime, but not as its sole leader.

Al-Bishri did not believe that any of the communist groups was able to perform the revolutionary-cum-integrative function that was necessary. Nor could the Ikhwan do so, though it enjoyed wide popularity and a strong organization, because of its reactionary orientation and its vague political program. In fact, the question was how to overcome the long-standing opposition of the Ikhwan to any form of coalition or long term political cooperation as well as their opposition to party politics. Al-Bishri did not believe that it was possible or desirable to win over individuals, and to recruit them away from existing parties and movements. He rather believed that disorganization was the great enemy, and that virtually any form of popular organization was superior to atomistic mass politics—the sort of phenomenon which actually did bring on the revolution.

Hence al-Bishri did not believe that Egypt was ready to leap into socialism, but rather had to undergo a transition in which both indigenous capitalism and competitive parliamentary politics would be preserved. He does not even suggest that the Marxist parties would have an important role to play in the new regime. The sense we get of the sort of regime he had in mind is not very different from the situation under Nasser, except that Nasser followed the line of the Ikhwan in suppressing all the prerevolutionary parties, and charged the apparatus of the state and the *partie unique* with the task of achieving the transition.

There is more than a tacit criticism here, because al-Bishri minimizes the significance of the role of the Free Officers in bringing about the revolution, and describes them ideologically as reflecting the range of activist groups found in the society at large. Their solidarity, based as it was on personal affinity, should have been writ large among the social movements of the whole Egyptian community, but, unfortunately, the defects of leadership, organization, and tactics prevented this. But was anything lost by this substitution of a microcoalition for a macrocoalition? National independence was gained. The British army evacuated Egyptian territory. The Canal was nationalized. The Tripartite aggression of 1956 was contained. Foreign monopolies were nationalized. Egyptian hegemony among the Arab states was established.

Misr Al-Fatat

Yet al-Bishri seems to argue against the view that the developmental transition from early dependent capitalism and autocratic government can best be accomplished by a form of bureaucratic authoritarianism and a policy of political mobilization directed by the apparatus of the state. The implied criticism of the Nasser regime is linked to al-Bishri's portrayal of the masses as the hero of the revolution, and expresses his regret that the revolution was not completed by some form of organized mass movement. This romantic view of the masses dominates al-Bishri's conceptions of nationalism, of independence, of socialism and of liberal democratic politics, and perhaps it is this romanticism which led him to the astonishing notion that the best possible vehicle for organizing and leading the popular coalition which never happened was the Socialist Party of Ahmad Husain.

That al-Bishri is aware of the anomaly of his choice for the leadership of the revolution and the transitional regime is evident because he reports the discussion among his Marxist friends regarding the objective possibility of a fascist movement arising in a colonial country. Tacitly admitting that Ahmad Husain's Misr al-Fatat had all the marks of a fascist party, al-Bishri seems to agree with the view of the moderate Marxists that under the conditions prevailing in Egypt in 1951–52, the Socialist Party could play an objectively progressive role.

What al-Bishri admired about the Socialist Party was its willingness to form a broad coalition including both the Marxists and the Ikhwan. He faults the Socialist Party, however, for its consistent hostility to the Wafd, while forgiving it its frequent dalliances with the court. What al-Bishri does not consider, despite his assumption that the Wafd was a prisoner of its own radicalism, is that the objective function of the Socialist Party in that revolutionary situation might have been to provide for a developmental transition to a capitalist-dominated state rather than a socialist one. As it turned out, of course, the authoritarianism of the apparatus of the Nasserist state was an environment within which the Marxists were able to exert considerable influence, but for the last decade the military-bureaucratic elite have suppressed the Marxist "ideocrats" and have brought the capitalists into the governing coalition, along with the rural notability.

The question of whether the Socialist Party could really be a fascist party was connected with another Marxist doctrinal issue, and that was whether the coalition of popular forces should be constructed as a single mass movement or as a federation of existing parties and organizations. Al-Bishri criticizes those who preferred the unified mass movement for their lack of realism and their preference for doctrinal purity above taking advantage of the historical moment.[43] Consequently he appears to have preferred the preservation of a multiparty system within the context of a national alliance. This accords with his later call for readmitting the Wafd and the Ikhwan into the national consensus, and it suggests that he did not support the Nasserist one-party system which excluded both.

Yet one cannot suppress a feeling of uneasiness about al-Bishri's willingness to put the best possible construction on every one of Ahmad Husain's maneuvers.[44] He admits that the party was a personal vehicle of its somewhat charismatic leader, and that his personalist leadership allowed it to make a 180-degree ideological reversal after the defeat of European fascism in World War II.[45] He praises the efforts of the Socialist party to bridge the gap between the Marxists and the Ikhwan, as though recognizing the volatile possibilities of such a union—now apparent to all who have studied the Islamic revolution in Iran. He admits that the party was wider than it was deep, but argues that it played an outstanding role in arousing the masses, which, as he also argues, it was in no position to lead, because it had neither an effective organization nor a well–worked out political program.[46] He blames the Socialist Party for carrying on a senseless feud with the Wafd and for emphasizing corruption rather than exploitation and the need for a change of regime.[47] He is even inclined to blame the Ikhwan for refusing to accept the members of Misr al-Fatat as members of the Jamaʿa, when Ahmad Husain offered to disband his own group.

At no point does al-Bishri attempt to reconcile the inconsistent elements in the politics of Ahmad Husain: his sudden religiosity, his connections with the reactionary politicians and the court, his state socialist program, his overriding hositility to the Wafd, his abstention(?) from participation in the burning of Cairo, the lack of any consistent social doctrine, and so on. Al-Bishri seems to be telling us that Ahmad Husain's Socialist Party walked like a duck, talked like a duck, but was not really a duck, because there can be no such thing as an objectively fascist movement in a colonial country. Anti-imperialism is a sufficient condition, transforming what might otherwise be considered fascist into a progressive, patriotic movement. He does not consider the extent to which the political tactics and the ideological animadversions of Ahmad Husain might have had the affect of preventing the unification of the popular movement and clarifying its political goals, that the Socialist Party and its noncapitalist path was the Trojan Horse of Egyptian reaction.

But for al-Bishri's stinting critique of Ahmad Husain's attitude toward the Wafd, one might draw the conclusion that he was not much committed to parliamentary democracy. And even taking that into account, there lingers the sense that, for al-Bishri, the highest values are national unity, cultural authenticity, and national independence. While he is not unconcerned with the question of regime transitions under the conditions of peripheral capitalism, he implicitly identifies the noncapitalist path of the Nasserist state with the ideological position of the Socialist party, and he implicitly criticizes the Nasserist state for its failure to create a real popular front. And with regard to his position on the current situation in Egypt, his relatively uncritical attitude toward the Socialist Party casts doubt upon his motives in urging the political rehabilitation of the Wafd and the Ikhwan. Is he truly committed to some kind of Islamic Liberalism, or is this a renewal of an old Marxist strategy of exploiting fascism in order to hasten the ultimate capitalist contradiction? Is it a more modest tactic aimed at providing a wider constitutional scope within which the Marxist can more easily maneuver, or is it simply a nativist response to the continuing intrusion of Western culture, Western capital, and Western political influence?

The Burning of Cairo

Al-Bishri sees the burning of Cairo on 26 January 1952 as the culminating event in a revolution. The old regime was overthrown in January, but the new regime did not take over until some time later. There is no doubt here that al-Bishri attributes the revolution to the people, and not to the Free Officers who carried out their coup in July. Nor was the revolution accomplished by the Wafd, which abrogated the Anglo-Egyptian treaty of 1936 and thus precipitated the armed conflict in the Canal Zone. None of the parties or popular organizations was ready, willing, or able to carry out a revolution. The Wafd was committed to constitutionally legal action only, and was induced to dig its own political grave by King Faruk after 26 January when it declared martial law and suspended civil liberties. Ahmad Husain and the Socialist Party had actually tried to claim that they were not involved in the rioting, and that Ahmad Husain himself had stayed home and telephoned Ali Mahir (to set up an alibi?) to urge the dismissal of the Wafd government. The various communist factions were confused, unprepared, and divided among themselves. The army was split, and the police, for the most part, joined the rioters. The Muslim Brotherhood, now led by the conservative al-Hudhaybi, was accused of inciting to violence in a manner calculated to aid the king, or of otherwise remaining aloof from the popular protest.

Following Lacouture's account fairly closely, al-Bishri argues that it all began with the protest march of the police from the Abbasiyyah barracks and security block to Giza where student protests were underway.[48] The protests were nonviolent, if vigorous, and culminated before noon in a kind of discussion between high government officials and the crowd. The first arson was of a "casino" or café, on Opera Square, where a police officer was sitting having a "drink" with a "dancer". This event is explained as being the result of the spontaneous anger (and scandalization) of the crowd, which included other policemen. It was only thereafter, it is claimed, that unknown conspirators, believed to be connected either to British intelligence or the royal court, began the systematic burning of the movie houses and other places of amusement.

While al-Bishri claims that all order broke down and that, to all intents and purposes, Egypt was without a government on 26 January, he nevertheless portrays the event as originally nonviolent, spontaneous, and led by popular but disorganized groups (police, students). The protest was not controlled, or directed, or exploited by any of the popular oppositional movements. They are, in fact, criticized for failing to take advantage of the opportunity to organize, rationalize, and lead the revolution. The protest was exploited instead by the king to bring about the dismissal of the Wafd government, to engineer the loss of its remaining popularity, and to end the conflict with the British. But the maneuvering of the court gave only the illusion that royal power had been restored, in the absence of any organized force to carry out the popular will. Thus the revolution was popular, spontaneous, disorganized, and essentially nonviolent; expressed no particular ideology other than a diffuse anticolonial nationalism; it was the result of episodic, mass, popular participation; it did not immediately change the governmental institutions; and, in fact, its occurrence was not even immediately realized.

Those familiar with recent Egyptian history will recognize similarities between this image and the way in which some Nasserists describe the events of 9–10 July 1967, when Nasser was "induced" to withdraw his resignation by the spontaneous, nonviolent, effusive demonstration of the Cairene masses. Al-Bishri does not refer to that event, but he does link 26 January 1952 with a series of prior "revolutions" going back to Muhammed Ali's time, the ʿArabi movement of 1879, and the revolution of 1919. The revolutionary experience of Egypt is described as a consistent, though not invariable, component of the Egyptian political culture and the Egyptian national heritage, or turath. In a quite remarkable passage, al-Bishri proudly describes this political cultural pattern:

> . . . despite the exposure of the regime to division, and despite the appearance of the seed of a new regime within the society, the general political orientation of the popular movement continued . . . to work from within the regime, pressuring it, and directing it toward the revolutionary path by means of partial changes. . . . It does not seem that the revolutionary movement seriously considered the demand for the total destruction of the regime as a direct and overt goal. . . . In none of these occasions of great change [1805, 1879, 1919, etc.] do we notice that the revolutionary movement resorted to arms against the ruler or the local ruling groups, even if such was known to have occurred in

the face of foreign occupation. . . . There is no suggestion that [the need to] change the regime or the social system required of the revolutionaries some rapid, destructive and decisive operation, or the resort to arms.

It was not only the revolutionary movement that was averse to total destruction or armed force, but the forces of the existing system were more inclined to yield rather than to use such methods. So we see [that they preferred] to preserve stability and to confront the state not by destructive methods but by means of a siege, and to bring about change by means of infiltration, not by direct attack for fear of anarchy. . . . Nor does it seem that [this strategy] was dictated by any revolutionary weakness or some spirit of social or political conservatism, for the political and social demands which were raised by the popular movement in each of those periods were revolutionary, given the historical circumstances. . . .

And [these movements] succeeded—in accordance with the historical conditions—in changing the political regime . . . thus establishing that they were no more backward in . . . development and civilization than other similar movements, and they might even be placed ahead of some. . . .

[In Egypt] the methods of demonstration and strike are frequently sufficient to decide issues which in some other countries cannot be resolved by the shedding of blood. . . .

This is not meant to distinguish the merits of the diverse revolutionary methods, but . . . it means that whether or not a movement is revolutionary is not to be determined by the [political] method employed but by what sort of demands are made and by what, in practice, is successful in achieving those goals. Nor is this observation an effort to attribute a theoretical character to these methods, nor an attempt to lay down some [unchanging] "certainties" in Egyptian history; rather all that we would argue is that these methods bear the impress of the turath (heritage) of Egyptian political praxis. There is no doubt that this is one of the constituent elements of the political culture (*fikr* = thought) which prevails among the Egyptian people . . . and as it is with a turath, it can change, but only slowly, with difficulty as the objective conditions which dictated its existence change. . . .

[My] purpose is to describe the general intellectual and political framework that structured rational thought at the time, not only among the political organizations, but among the broad "front" of the people which was compelled to move to impose a particular change, not only in accordance with their economic and political interests, but also in accordance with their intellectual and historical composition at a particular moment; and should the political organizations reject those [intellectual and historical] elements [of the prevailing political culture] . . . they

> will be unable to realize their goals except . . . by changing the [political culture] of the masses. (Pp. 544–47)

There can be little doubt that this passage sums up much of al-Bishri's political message, just as it lays the logical groundwork for the nationalist vision which he develops in the book on Muslim-Coptic relations and in his subsequent essays. Again, it is important to note that no credit is given to any organized party, to any movement, nor to the Free Officers. This is not a pro-Nasser or pro-Marxist interpretation. There is here some evocation of the constitutional methods of the Wafd, which al-Bishri describes as based upon arousing mass popular participation via demonstrations and the like, but only in connection with periodic parliamentary electoral campaigns. Thus, the Egyptian urban masses, from time to time, even episodically, when deeply discontented (*sukhut*) may be mobilized (*hashada*) whereupon they express their protest more as a form of siege than as a violent frontal attack, leaving it to the political authorities to work out in practice what the relatively inarticulate masses wish to have changed. This process does not quite conform to the usual conception of the dictatorship of the proletariat. It certainly suggests a unification of popular groups in the face of a division among organized parties and their leaders. These protests lead to social as well as political change, and it appears that al-Bishri believes that these changes conform to historically determined objective conditions. As a consequence, Egypt has progressed about as well, or even somewhat better, than might have been expected. There is a hint that an ideologically adaptive, integrative party, based on mass-line organizations might be more efficient, but al-Bishri does not, in this book explicitly call for anything of the sort. He does seem to warn the existing regime that it must pay attention to the popular will, even though it is not efficiently expressed via the legitimated political structures, lest popular demonstrations (such as the food price riots of January 1977) catch the government by surprise.

If the burning of Cairo in 1952 was an expression of the popular demand for change, consistent in method with Egyptian national character, did it represent anything more than an expected, but not anticipated, adjustment of political arrangements to the substructural (social and economic) arrangements which had been undergoing continuous and gradual change since 1919? Were 1919 and 1952 simply two similar episodic events, coordinating superstructure and substructure as moments in a pragmatic process, or should they be seen as representing stages in the historical development of Egyptian society? The answer to these questions, despite al-Bishri's use of neo-Hegelian and post-Marxian terminology, is not entirely clear. For al-

Bishri, the revolution of 1919 limited the domination of Egypt by "feudal" latifundists, and allowed the nascent capitalist class represented, for the most part, by the Wafd, to share power.

From the point of view of al-Bishri's leftist friends, the question which arose in 1952, and which may still be first on the agenda in contemporary Egypt, is whether the demise of the Wafd signified the end of the capitalist phase of Egyptian development. Some Egyptian communists hold the view that, for most of Nasser's administration, Egypt was correctly pursuing the noncapitalist developmental path, continuing to restrict the power of the landowners, associating national capital with the regime, and developing a strong public sector based on nationalized companies. The pressure on national capital was increased after 1961, and the Marxists sought to develop a revolutionary cadre party within the legitimate, regime-dominated, political structure from the mid-1960s. Sadat's *infitah,* or economic and political liberalization program, is often judged as capitalist reaction, but the capitalist sector has grown stronger and more outspoken if not really self-confident under Mubarak (and as a consequence of vigorous American support). The public display of wealth, the mixed results of the peace treaty with Israel, the ambivalence of the populace toward Sadat's assassins and toward Islamic fundamentalism in general, all suggest that there is a growing public discontent which is leading to some sort of gradual mobilization which will result in the laying of a siege to force the government to alter its policies.

There is, however, nothing in al-Bishri to suggest that he holds doctrinaire Marxist views. He does not argue that Egypt is now ready for a socialist revolution, or that the revolution of 1952 should have led to the establishment of a socialist system. He rather argues that Egyptian political organization, political ideology, and political institutions should conform to the heritage of Egyptian political culture, or express Egyptian authenticity. The result will be a gradual, possibly episodic, adaptation of the Egyptian social and political structures to the objective historical requirements of the time. He does not yearn for integration and participation in a universal culture, as does Abdullah Laroui. He is opposed to the intrusion of alien cultures via American capitalism or European Marxism. He favors the integration of Islam as adumbrated by the Ikhwan, mass political participation as achieved by the Wafd, national identity as expressed by Ahmad Husain and Misr al-Fatat, and the socialism of the popular front as expressed by Haditu. But he seems to have an unrealistic vision of the ability (and desirability) of Egypt to isolate itself, or at least its domestic political process, from both the great powers and its regional neighbors, and he does not say whether he prefers a pluralist or a corporatist solution to the problem of political organization. While he appears to be inclined toward a corporatist political formula, his vision of the meaning of the burning of Cairo is unequivocal on the residual autonomy of the Egyptian urban masses and their ultimate determination of their political arrangements by means of an authentic form of political democracy. But it is at least as likely that he would charge the apparatus of the modern Egyptian state, of which he is a part, with the burden of achieving the national unity he seeks by means of adopting al-Bishri's new definition of Egyptian national authenticity.

Since the Nasserist regime was but one of many similar arrangements where the apparatus of the state, led and dominated by the military, seized power from quasi-traditional authorities in an early, peripheral, capitalist setting, al-Bishri's view of the matter has some general theoretical relevance. The neopatrimonial, or Bonapartist, or bureaucratic-authoritarian, or praetorian state remains a question mark in development theory, because there is such disagreement regarding whether its function is to establish the order that is a prerequisite of development, to complete the process of state-formation begun under the traditional regime, to protect and further the interests of the national bourgeoisie, to protect and further the interests of international capital and its compradors, to subordinate capitalist development to the interests of the state and those social segments whose high status is determined by the traditional culture, or, last but not least, to pave the way for an eventual socialist revolution.

Al-Bishri does not tell us where he stands in this matter, but one might not be blamed for supposing that he may be telling us that the transition to socialism (stage II) from the pursuit of the noncapitalist path (stage I), might have been more successful under some sort of national front leadership. Alternatively, he might be telling us that the mobilizational techniques of the Nasser regime exacted too high a price in terms of the repression of Egyptian cultural authenticity without really advancing toward socialism. Since, as a matter of fact, Egypt turned toward the capitalist road, under Sadat's infitah, one might even be inclined to draw the conclusion that the function of the Nasser regime was to rescue Egyptian capitalism from both the imperialists and the traditionalists. It is true that few of Egypt's capitalists look with nostalgia upon the Nasser period, so they might be inclined to believe that the same historical materialist function might have been better performed by a national front including the Wafd, the Ikhwan, the Marxists and Ahmad Husain's Socialist party. If all of this speculative structure makes any sense, then I suppose it makes equally good sense to ask whether there is, in 1988, any possibility of putting Humpty Dumpty back together again.

Reprise

In the introduction to al-Bishri's most important work, *The Muslims and the Copts in Egypt*, he tells us that he began that work in the aftermath of Egypt's defeat in the 1967 war. He was motivated by a concern for national unity and the question of when and how Egypt would be able to regain the political and moral strength to recover its territory.[49] It is interesting, but otherwise unexplained, that his concern with national unity should have turned him to the question of the Coptic minority rather than class differences, given his Marxist proclivities. Still, his interest in the Copts, as symbolic of the weakest element in the common identity of the Egyptian national community, is both rare and courageous. Even if he cannot be considered sympathetic to the self-understanding of the Copts, as a persecuted minority and as the "true exponents" of Egyptian authenticity, his advocacy of complete civic equality for the Copts is unusual. There is no doubt that he means to challenge the Muslim religious extremists on the grounds of their contribution to national unity.

If his previous book could plausibly be read as a Marxist history, or at least as a crucial episode taken within a Marxist theoretical context, this work is presented as a history of institutions: the Coptic church, al-Azhar, the monarchy, parliament, and the important political parties. Al-Bishri tells us that he began this book as a series of disconnected institutional studies some of which he published in the journal *al-Katib*.[50] As he worked on these studies in his spare time, he began to change his views regarding Egyptian history and politics. He does not tell us how his views have changed, but he says that his ideological reorientation led him to rewrite most of his material. Rather than treating his institutional studies as background for a more dynamic analysis, he has retained the institutional focus, while setting his analysis in the context of important conjunctural events. The result, he argues, is an appreciation of the nature and role of those institutions in the context of the existential reality of the *Lebenswelt* (the life-world or, in Arabic, actuality = *al-waqʿa*).

There is no doubt that al-Bishri places a great deal of emphasis upon the understanding which is to be gained from the continuous "interaction" of conceptual notions with the actuality of events in the life-world. This is the theme of his critique of political movements in Egypt and the explanation of their failure at critical junctures. There is an element of pragmatism in this approach, which, when added to the emphasis on institutions and on the postulate of national unity as the highest value, emerges as the most consistent intellectual theme in this work. The central historical theme is the emergence of Egyptian national consciousness through the period from the Napoleonic invasion to the revolution of 1952. The national unity expressed in the popular movement of 1952, seems somehow to have diminished, and al-Bishri's purpose is to urge the restoration of that national unity and its preservation via institutionalization. His narrative is never very far from the composition of the Egyptian political community, and the elimination of conflict among its constituent elements. His view of Egyptian political history is dominated by the theme of religion and politics and the way in which various political groups used religious institutions and symbols, rendering them divisive rather than unifying forces in Egyptian life.

The structure of social forces and class conflict are lightly touched upon in this study, which is primarily concerned with superstructural themes, or what Gramscian scholars might call the struggle for hegemony. The institutional struggle concentrates on the preservation of the constitution of 1923, on limiting the powers of the king, on maintaining equal rights for the Copts and, thus, perhaps for all citizens who might be uncomfortable under an Islamic fundamentalist hegemony. But al-Bishri does not come out simply as a westernized liberal urging upon us the political ethic of pluralist pragmatism. The pluralist theme is confounded by the apparent rejection of Western culture, and by the great value placed on Egyptian authenticity and the Egyptian tradition. National unity conflicts with pluralism.

Al-Bishri's ambivalence, or ambiguity, on this contradiction, is demonstrated by his assessment of the various political organizations and their respective ideological positions, and one of the most important issues discussed by al-Bishri was the caliphate. He takes up the issue as it broke upon Egypt after the abolition of the caliphate by the government of Kemal Ataturk in 1924, just as the first Egyptian parliament under the constitution of 1923 was sitting.

Al-Bishri's analysis generally follows that of Muhammad ʿImara.[51] The king sought to use the caliphate issue to weaken the bourgeois parties and parliament, and to regain autocratic powers. In particular the king wished to attack the Wafd and to force his current parliamentary allies, the Liberal Constitutionalists, to be more amenable to the leadership he wished to impose upon them. Al-Bishri argues that ʿAli ʿAbd al-Raziq was genuinely intellectually motivated, rather than politically inspired to write his famous book, because it would have been sufficient to argue that the Egyptian king was disqualified for the caliphate because of the British occupation, even if one believed that the caliphate was obligatory. Al-Bishri further accepts al-ʿImara's criticism that ʿAbd al-Raziq failed to test his theoretical abstractions against the political and social reality of the Prophet's time. Al-Bishri concludes that ʿAbd al-Raziq's understanding of the distinction between the Prophet's religious mission and his political role was insufficiently pragmatic. ʿAbd al-Raziq's views on the separation of religion and politics in Islam are therefore rejected, but his right to express those ideas without civic or ecclesiastical penalty under the 1923 constitution is staunchly defended by al-Bishri as it was by al-ʿImara.[52]

For al-Bishri, in this book as in the previous one, the model he holds in the highest esteem is the 1919 revolution, led by the Wafd, and keynoted by slogans like "Religion is for God, but the fatherland is for all," celebrating the political cooperation of Muslims and Copts. Henceforth the Wafd symbolized political equality for the Copts, and Copts were equal members at all levels of party organization according to al-Bishri. In this manner, the Wafd practiced the constitutional and legalistic principles which it preached in its conflict with the king. Consequently, with the rise of the issues of the caliphate and the Islamic character of the state, the Wafd was vulnerable to attack on the grounds that it was too favorable to the Coptic minority. It is on these grounds that al-Bishri explains the relative quiescence of the Wafd during the controversy over ʿAli ʿAbd al-Raziq's book. The liberal constitutionalists, of whom ʿAbd al-Raziq was a member or supporter, were allowed to twist slowly in the wind. After all, they had joined the government of Ziwar Pasha and helped to push the Wafd out of office.

In his introduction, al-Bishri tells us that perhaps his most important discovery was that 1928 was a critical year for the transformation of Egyptian politics, even though no outstanding events took place in that year.[53] The importance of that year is immediately evident as the year in which the Muslim Brotherhood was founded. Al-Bishri explains the founding of the Brotherhood and other militant Islamic organizations as a consequence of the caliphate controversy and, even more importantly, as a consequence of the decision of a number of Christian missionary societies to step up their efforts to convert Muslims. Al-Bishri places particular importance on the Edinburgh conference of 1910.[54] Thus monarchical despotism and imperialist cultural "hegemonism" combine to explain the proliferation of Islamic groups starting in 1928. It was this defensive movement, beginning in the critical year, that subverted the consensus of 1919 and put the Wafd in a weak position. Implicitly, the Egyptian problem is thus defined as the need to restore the unity and the tolerance of 1919, while accommodating the popular religious identity.

This apparently straightforward liberal, nationalist solution is brought into question by al-Bishri's ambivalent treatment of the

 Young Egypt (Misr al-Fatat) movement of Ahmad Husain.[55] Al-Bishri describes the movement as a virtual caricature of Mazzini's Young Italy. He also acknowledges its affinity for Mussolini's Fascist movement. He again points to the arbitrary ideological changes which were made by Ahmad Husain. He refers to Ahmad Husain's support for the king on several occasions, but he does not expatiate on the question of whether Husain was merely an agent of the royal court. He tells us that Misr al-Fatat consistently competed with both the Ikhwan and the Wafd, seeking to win over some of their popular support. But for the most part, al-Bishri narrates the stages by which Misr al-Fatat, later the National Religious Party, and later still the Egyptian Socialist Party, moved from being a nationalist organization that subordinated religion to the national culture, to a religious organization that subordinated the class question to the establishment of an Islamic state.

Al-Bishri eschews the obvious explanation of the Misr al-Fatat phenomenon as "peripheral" fascism, nor does he argue that Ahmad Husain was for hire by the highest bidder, or that he was a political spoiler who was willing to blackmail any and all parties—including the king. He does show that Ahmad Husain worked to increase the political tension, especially by advocating demonstrations and direct action.[56] Al-Bishri does not dissuade us from the widely held belief that Ahmad Husain was anti-Copt. He also points out that Misr al-Fatat was organizationally weak, and could maintain its following only by means of mass communication and demagogic speeches.[57] Thus Ahmad Husain moved toward Islamic militancy and a kind of Islamic socialism in dialectical response to the mass support he received or sought.[58] Yet, throughout his discussion of Misr al-Fatat, al-Bishri retains a wistful sense of regret mixed with a certain admiration. Ahmad Husain's nationalism, his Islamic militance, and his petit bourgeois socialism are all apparently admirable in themselves and insofar as they correspond to the consciousness of the Egyptian masses.

Admittedly, Misr al-Fatat started out as a fanatically nationalist movement, subordinating religion to nationalsim—with the giveaway being Ahmad Husain's praise of Ataturk.[59] But toward the end, al-Bishri deduces that the organization had become a religious movement, rivaling the Muslim Brotherhood.[60] In this manner, Misr al-Fatat responded not only to the resonances of the masses, but also to an emergent historical reality. Misr al-Fatat was more a weather vane than a product of fascist opportunism or an instrument of reaction. Misr al-Fatat, like the Jamaʿa of Hasan al-Banna, was an unknowing instrument of Egyptian authenticity. The Wafd may have had the right idea about the place of the Copts in the Egyptian political community, but the nature of that community, by virtue of historical and cultural necessity, had to be religious and Islamic.

Still the community was an Egyptian community, and broader conceptions based on either Islamic or Arab definitions were diversions from the true path of Egypt's political destiny. This perception of both "comprehensive Arab nationalism" and of the caliphate issue or of pan-Islamism as diversions, indicates that al-Bishri prefers that both the religious and the cultural questions find Egyptian solutions. He clearly prefers solutions which affirm Egypt's Arabism and its Islam; and he expects the Copts to go along with these solutions in return for absolute political equality. It is essential, al-Bishri argues, to remember that the Copts are a part of the total equation. It is, however, not at all clear whether he considers the Copts a burden on national unity requiring a costly solution, or whether he invokes the Coptic question in order to compel a solution which is not shared with other Arab or Islamic countries.

Thus the Ottoman caliphate, the Palestine question, the Sudanese question, all enhanced the growing sense of Islamic political identity among participant Egyptians, but they all seemed to point to trans-Egyptian solutions. Insofar as they increased the political relevance of Islam, they reinforced the affect of the imperialist occupation, the missionary campaign, the despotic machinations of the king, and the idealist conception of the "social problem." But the failure to take account of the Copts as an essential component of the Egyptian political community led to the adoption of inappropriate solutions. The historical failure of the Misr al-Fatat was that Ahmad Husain abandoned his original conception of Egyptian nationalism. The more appropriate solution required a reconciliation of the Islamic character of the Egyptian nation with equal Coptic membership of that nation. Al-Bishri is consistent in his admiration of Ahmad Husain's integral nationalism.

Al-Bishri points out that al-Banna was favorably disposed toward nationalism, toward Arabism, and toward patriotism, but within the framework of a fundamental commitment to Islam.[61] Islam was the absolute, and nationalist considerations were matters of prudence and of the practical accommodation to historical circumstances. In concrete terms this comes down to the distinction between the clear and unequivocal, absolute commands of Islam, and those that require interpretation. Nationalism and certain proposals for an egalitarian solution of the "social problem" were matters of judgment requiring an interpretive construction of the canonical sources of Islamic law. For such issues, requiring interpretation, there was a further question of whether to insist on cultural authenticity or to accept alien solutions and approaches. On the question of the Copts, the Ikhwan rejected the position of the Wafd as enunciated in 1919.[62] Politics and religion could not be separated, and the Copts were to have the honored status of protected peoples with whom the victorious Muslims had made treaties.

In general, al-Banna argued against alien solutions.[63] As a Salafi, or fundamentalist, he urged the return to the original Islamic sources in the search for new solutions. Al-Banna believed in ijtihad and in the importance of interpreting the holy text in the light of existing circumstances.[64] There were, moreover, among the Ikhwan, many who were willing to take account of new circumstances. But there were also many who rigidly opposed ijtihad.[65] Unfortunately, al-Banna was more flexible in theory than in practice, although there were some indications that he was able to compromise—as when he argued for the Islamic character of the state on the *constitutionalist* grounds that the majority of the citizens are Muslims.[66]

Al-Bishri implies that the Ikhwan might have been brought around to an appropriate constitutional compromise on the Coptic question under some undefined circumstances, but before 1952 they had just not come far enough. Among the reasons for this failure to live up to their own ideology was the cultural defensiveness into which the Egyptian Muslims were cast by the powerful and disturbing intrusion of Western culture.[67]

> The struggle between tradition and innovation (modernism) was the crucial battle in Egypt in the nineteenth and twentieth centuries. And the legislative system was one of the fields of that extended conflict. The issue for the Egyptians was not that of choosing between an imported system and an inherited system; nor is it a simple matter like pointing to one or another of two items displayed before one in some store, which one picks up on the spot and takes home. Rather, the difficult task is to reconstruct everything that is available to the Egyptians, whether imported or indigenous, . . . to render it into a more useful and effective form in order to secure liberation, prosperity, and justice. . . . This conflict still goes on today, and certainly was not settled during the time of the first General Guide of the Muslim Brotherhood. It rather continues to go on in alternating cycles [of westernization and reaffirmation of the tradition] and this indeterminacy is a good thing, maintaining qualitatively and sequentially differing systems side by side, while the harmonization [of the two] depends upon the efforts of those with insight into their circumstances (*al-waqᶜa*), [so that] the noble will be distinguished from the base . . . in bringing about the beneficial and in warding

> off evil, in the manner of the ancient Imams of the Islamic Shariʿa. (P. 505)
>
> The interpretation of the text . . . is not merely an explanation of the meaning of its words, and sentences, and expressions, rather the essence of the act of interpretation is linking that text, in spite of its discursive limitations, to an undefined reality; that is, linking the text with reality (*al-waqʿa*), and applying the text dynamically in the context of a lived reality. (P. 509)
>
> The Ikhwan movement . . . took the view that the modern, alien, patterns were (destroying) [the system of the Islamic Shariʿa] . . . [hence] they generally took a cautious stand in explicating (their) doctrine of innovative reform in the face of existing, but unacceptable, conditions lest it be conducive to the justification of those conditions. The immediate reality of their preaching in the course of pursuing what they took to be the (inescapable) conditions of their life circumstances, dictated [their belief] in the imperative of pointing out the contradiction between their doctrine and those conditions, that they concentrate on those aspects of reality that they rejected rather than those that they could work with . . . [hence] the Ikhwan seemed [to represent] a doctrine which negated reality [and thus] failed to respond to its problems. (P. 509)

Al-Bishri has argued that the Ikhwan ought not be categorized among the groups having interests because they do not represent class interests, but rather merely represent an ideological position which may be appropriated by others. Thus he argues at one point that they did not really compete with the Wafd because they had no clear political program, and they lacked a consciousness of themselves as a group ready to seize power. While these are dubious judgments, both with regard to the class base of the Ikhwan and their political program, they seem either to have influenced other leftists or to be shared by them. The structural and doctrinal weaknesses of the Ikhwan, the Sunnism of Egypt, and the lack of fanaticism among Egyptian believers, are among the ideas put forward by some leftists to sustain the view that Egypt will not be another Iran—that a revolution planned, designed and executed by a sophisticated leftist movement with intellectual support, will not be commandeered by a fanatical religious minority of obscurantists. As a consequence, the Egyptian left seems willing, even anxious, to sup with the saints, in spite of the fate of the Iranian left. There are, in fact, many past and present, younger and older Marxists who believe that the revolutionary potential of Islam ought to be exploited. There is, however, a significant difference between those who think that an extremist outburst may be the signal for the seizure of power by a well-prepared leftist cadre, and those who are convinced of the possibility of building a strategy on continuous cooperation with the Ikhwan and other "moderate" religious elements.

Nasser's Legacy

If al-Bishri was silent on the nature of the Nasser regime after 1952 in his first book, he was explicitly critical in this one. Al-Bishri writes that the postrevolutionary regime, which as we have seen was not really a product of the popular mass movement, failed to deal with the problem of defining the Egyptian political community; so that the problem still persists and awaits a solution. Nasser was not antireligious, but simply unconcerned with the issue of the religious element in Egyptian national identity. This remained the case despite the bloody suppression of the Ikhwan in late 1954 and again in 1965. Al-Bishri explains that the new regime and its policies were essentially oriented to alien and imported institutions and methods. Especially important was the fact that the army was not only Western in orientation, but that few Copts held positions of influence within it. Secondly, the Nasser regime relied on the administrative apparatus rather than a popular party. The administration was similarly overwhelmingly Muslim, and the inclination of the regime to select "trusted people" for critical jobs kept it Muslim in all vital areas. Thirdly, the Copts were more prominent in the private sector, so the nationalization of enterprises and the creation of an important public sector hurt the Copts, and created a new Muslim managerial elite which largely ignored the plight of the Copts. Fourthly, the Muslim conservative opposition to the regime adopted an Islamic posture; but it was unpopular, and given the suppression of the Ikhwan, fewer people were attracted to the Islamic movements. To further limit the political significance of religion, the Nasser regime supported only a limited and not very popular segment of the religious elite. Fifthly, the Nasserist state was autocratic and despotic, and in the absence of democratic structures, political cooperation broke down and was replaced by a fierce competitiveness and selfishness.

The upshot of this unhappy situation was that not a single Copt was elected to parliament in the elections of 1968, 1971, 1976 and 1979. Finally, under Sadat, the government encouraged the religious groups against the leftist opposition, and when communal disturbances occurred in Alexandria and al-Khanakah, the government took action against the opposition rather than against the perpetrators of the violence. Ultimately, the government found itself both encouraging and suppressing the religious opposition, and thus hastened its own demise.[68]

Insofar as the resolution of the question of the religious character of the Egyptian political community is a prerequisite for the achievement of national unity, liberation, and economic development, then it is clear that the Nasser regime and its successors failed. In the course of elaborating this criticism, al-Bishri attacks the whole Nasserist system of domination via the state apparatus, of cooptation of "trusted" elements, and of the suppression of democracy. But perhaps the greatest defect of the present regime is that it is alienated from the spirit of the people. It has failed to understand how the political consciousness of the Egyptian people has been formed in the context of its historical evolution over the last two centuries, and in particular since 1919.

But it is not only the Nasserist elite that has been misled about the meaning of events in Egypt. The whole, westernized national movement has been mistaken about the meaning of the religious movement in Egypt. The democratic nationalist movement (the Marxists?) believed that the religious tendency was artificially contrived in order to combat the progressives. Those who sought national independence were only concerned to get the British out so they could establish a constitutional democracy, while the religious-political trend was concerned with "building an Islamic society and building the Muslim individual on the basis of the renaissance of a civilization that was all but extirpated by alien thought" (p. 681). The misunderstanding and misjudgment between the two was profound, for the religious militants considered the alien cultural influence of the West the most powerful weapon of imperialism, while the liberal nationalists and democrats were using Western ideas against the West.

The error of the westernized was the consequence of their rigid inclination to classify political movements by their ideology. Hence a religious ideology represents feudal interests; liberalism represents capitalism; socialism and Marxism in particular represent the interests of the proletariat. The resulting attitude toward the religious movement appeared to be confirmed because the religious parties were slow to develop social programs and practical political strategies. But, al-Bishri argues, this perspective is mistaken with regard to the religious militants in Egypt on two grounds: "first, that it fails to take account of the historical constituents of popular ideology, and second, that it fails to take account of the function of a particular ideology within a given socio-political context" (p. 681).

The westernized have been inclined to see Islam as the cause of the decline of the Muslims, but, al-Bishri argues, that is not the case. It is rather the defeat and the cultural decline of the Muslims that has led to the intrusion of alien culture into all of the local schools, "whether reactionary, conservative or progressive" (p. 682). As a consequence of this destructive influence, a cultural ambivalence permeates all, and Egyptian society has become divided into two separate cultural camps. There is an urgent need to close this gap and to unite the national forces, but great effort will be required and it will take a great deal of time.

"There are, then, two separate spheres, one is the political-economic and the other is the intellectual-ideological. The meaning of their separate but simultaneous existence is that no one system of thought is the exclusive expression of a coherent set of political-economic interests" (pp. 682–83). Thus, al-Bishri argues forcefully for the disjunction of ideology and interest, and he suggests that Anwar Abd al-Malik, the Egyptian expatriate scholar at the Centre National de Recherche Scientifique (CNRS) in Paris, agrees with him. The coincidence of ideology and interest is fortuitous, and one cannot deduce the interests, and hence the political strategy, from the ideology which may be espoused by any collection of human beings. To prove his point, al-Bishri cites the fact that neither liberals nor religionists agree among themselves.

> . . . when assessing the political orientation of any group or tendency, one must not stop with the general intellectual framework, rather [the true political orientation] can be determined only by observing the way in which those political positions and intellectual specificities function together in the social context, . . . any general intellectual framework is of no use by itself in the rigorous deduction of fixed socio-political positions. In the assessment of positions regarding imperialism and foreign influence and national liberation, the main point is whether they contribute to progress and reawakening. (P. 683)

Al-Bishri's main point may not be the main point for a devoutly religious Muslim fundamentalist, or for a staunchly liberal bourgeois nationalist. Though his theoretical arguments are not likely to convince either the Muslim faithful or the doctrinaire Marxists (and certainly not the hard-pressed Copts), one suspects that the pragmatic element in his thought might have a certain appeal to the growing middle class. Al-Bishri would, of course, deny that his intellectual orientation has any more of a determined relevance to a given class position than do the alternative positions he criticizes.

The Political Community

Al-Bishri devotes his theoretical conclusion to the discussion of two major issues: the nature of the political community, and the nature of citizenship. Al-Bishri wishes to establish the compatibility of Islam and Arab nationalism. His target audiences include the Muslim militants, the secular nationalists, and the Christian minority; but he is really trying to persuade the Muslim militants more than the others. Al-Bishri eschews any general discussion of the nature of the political community or its purpose. He does not dwell on the transcendant goals of Islam, and he ignores the transcendant claims of some nationalists. Al-Bishri ignores the issue of whether Islam serves Arab nationalism or Arab nationalism serves Islam. Their compatibility is not external or instrumental, but internal in the sense that they are one and the same to a certain extent. Similarly, al-Bishri ignores the possible differences between Arab nationalism and Egyptian nationalism. They are also the same thing to a certain extent, and the greater prominence of one over against the other is a matter of circumstances.

The relationship between Islam and Arab nationalism is not, therefore, one of instrumentality. Arab nationalism does not exist in order to realize the otherworldly aims of Islam. Their compatibility is in part due to their partial identity, and in part due to their sharing certain common aims. The most important of these aims are independence of foreign political domination and the related one of communal and political integration.

The rhetorical device which is most consistently employed by al-Bishri is the citation of presumed authorities that are clearly identified as religious fundamentalists, Arab nationalists, or Christian Arabs. The four fundamentalists quoted by al-Bishri are Abu'l-Ala al-Mawdudi, Yusuf Qaradawi, Muhammad al-Ghazali, and of course, Hasan al-Banna. Al-Mawdudi, in his opposition to Indian nationalism, is used as the straw man for his extreme attack on nationalism as alien, Western, prejudiced, and socially disintegrative. All the rest are quoted as in some way recognizing the important relationship of Arab culture and Islam, the naturalness of love of country, and commitment to native language and culture. Al-Ghazali is quoted as arguing that, despite the limitations of nationalism, Islam and Arab nationalism are compatible, and that Arabism without Islam would be nothing.[69]

For al-Bishri the crucial question is whether nationalism unites or divides. In the nineteenth century, separate Muslim nation states were thought to divide the Muslims, but in the twentieth century they may be taken as stepping stones toward a greater unity, or a league of Muslim states, the core of which will be the Arab states.[70] As long as these states join together against the imperialists, as in the case of the nonaligned movement, it cannot be argued that they divide Islam or that Islam divides the nonaligned movement. Al-Bishri concludes from both al-Banna and Qaradawi, that Islam does not negate the multiplication of Muslim states, and he takes it for granted that such separate states are based on a form of nationalism.[71]

Al-Bishri is not arguing for an Islamic definition of the political community. He is arguing that Islam is accommodative to historical circumstances and is compatible with those political forms that are dictated by the overriding values of independence, cultural authenticity, and political integration. It is a formula which may permit an Islamic liberalism, but its principal feature is a definition of Islam which sharply limits the specificity of its social and political prescriptions; hence the compatibility of Islam and nationalism (if not also liberal government) is based on what Islam does *not* say rather than what it does.

In practice, and at the current historical stage, argues al-Bishri, both nationalism and religion are directed against the imperialist attack on the peoples of the Third World. Hence, al-Qaradawi is wrong when he states that nationalism divides those peoples, and misunderstands the meaning of the slogans "Africa for the Africans" and "Asia for the Asians" (p. 690). In the particular case of Egypt, it is incorrect to argue that the Ottoman caliphate represented either Islam or the solidarity of the Muslim peoples. It was instead a thinly veiled Turkish nationalist form of imperialist domination over the Arabs. Moreover, the Turks were unable to protect the Arabs against European imperialism. Hence, the Egyptian struggle for national independence against the Ottomans was not anti-Islamic.

Since there can be no external juxtaposition of Islam and Arab nationalism, only an understanding of particular historical circumstances, what is most important is to determine the function of each under the circumstances. When the Ottoman caliphate and Ottoman Islam were no longer able to withstand the onslaught of imperialism, Egyptian nationalism, narrow though it was, was able to make some headway, culminating in the partial success of the 1919 revolution. Later, during and after World War II, Western imperialism supported Arab nationalism, and that permitted the Arab nationalists to turn against the imperialists.[72] Under yet other circumstances, when the imperialists sought to use Islam against the Arab nationalists, religion was turned against the imperialists. The point is, writes al-Bishri, that these two categories are real and not artificial. Both refer to a living, struggling, existent being. They are not identical, but the issue here is not their essence, he writes, it is their historical function under specific circumstances with particular regard to their ability to stand up to imperialism. "In its concrete form, the issue here is which of the several aspects (of the community), has more of the type of consciousness most appropriate to . . . the movement of struggle, which will not long tarry in rising from that base [either religion or some form of nationalism] to challenge imperialism" (pp. 692–93).

This argument is spoken by al-Bishri in his own voice. Thereafter, he returns to the rhetorical mode of citing authorities. Against both Khalid Muhammad Khalid (a liberal ʿalim) and Muhammad al-Ghazali (a fundamentalist) he quotes Shaykh ʿAbd al-Mutaʿal al-Saʿidi as arguing that every Muslim has two kinds of citizenship and two loyalties, to Islam and to his country, and that these do not conflict (assuming, of course, that he is the citizen of a Muslim majority country). Saʿidi adds that the caliphate is not identical with Islamic government, which may, in fact, take many forms. "It is incorrect to limit the form of Islamic government to that one form. The republican system of government is identical with the system of the caliphate" (p. 695).

The Indigenous and the Introduced

Al-Bishri's exposition is based on three dichotomies, one separating interests and ideologies, one separating national interests from the interests of alien imperialists, and a third dichotomy distinguishing two types of ideology, belief system, or discursive formations, that which is introduced or diffused from alien sources and that which is indigenous. The terms which al-Bishri uses to designate these two (always unmixed) types are *al-wafid* for the introduced and *al-mawruth* for the indigenous. Combinations or new discoveries, borrowings, appropriations, adaptations, collaborations, and any other conceivable alternative to these two absolutely unhistorical and unrealistic categories of cultural expression are disregarded.

Despite the simplicity of al-Bishri's system of dichotomies, and the apparently obvious meaning of the term al-wafid, the term turath is not so simple and one-sided in its meaning in the contemporary ideological context of the Arab countries. The term turath provides a way of attaching oneself to the religious heritage of Islam without declaring oneself a true believer; it is a ground on which secularists and religionists may meet, but not without many opportunities for misunderstanding and disagreement. In this sense the liberal declares that everything that a religionist may deem essential in Islam may be included in a modern liberal state as *turath* or culture, or ideology, or symbol, thus satisfying the religionist without imposing upon the non-Muslim, the secularist, or the atheist.

The second dimension of the term relates to the debate on authenticity and westernization, or cultural autonomy and alienation. The maintenance of a strong cultural identity (*hawiyya*, or *dhatiyya*) or authenticity (*ʿasala*) is thought to be either desirable or necessary for national independence, dignity, and mental health. While the religious revival may seem to some to be an exaggerated, irrational, and atavistic response to this issue, the revival, rebuilding, and restatement—in a word, the renaissance—of the turath, is thought to be a suitable answer to this problem.

These two meanings or applications of the term are not mutually exclusive, but they tend toward rather different definitions of the turath, with the first being defined by what religious authoritarians believe is absolutely essential, and the second being defined by the character of external cultural and political pressures. At times these two may clash, as over issues of usury, the rights of women, minority political rights, and the nature of Islamic political institutions. The underlying issue is, of course, to what extent the turath is Islam, simply and absolutely, as opposed to some distillation of the historical and cultural experience of the Muslim or Muslim-Arab people.

At a seminar on "Western Political Thought and Arab Political Thought," al-Bishri argued that Western political forms were introduced into Egypt and were adopted largely without attention to or understanding of their political-theoretical aspects.[73] Of particular importance for al-Bishri is the "fact" that Egyptian nationalism developed in a nontheoretical, nonintellectual context of mass rejection of foreign intervention. Nevertheless, there emerged in Egypt a kind of cultural ambivalence in which the wafid and the mawruth, in the form of institutions and political ideals, existed side by side and created confusion. Al-Bishri insists again on the importance of intrafactional and intragroup conflict, but also now states that adherents of the cultural alternatives of the wafid and the mawruth were also often in conflict.

In the context of the seminar, in which most of the participants were prominent leftists, it is clear that al-Bishri means to minimize the significance of Marxist analysis in explaining what this confusion of interests and ideological forms meant. For al-Bishri the explanation was not to be referred to class differences among Egyptians. He rather states that adherents of both the wafid and the mawruth wanted to achieve the same goals, but they were often moved to greater attacks on one another than on their common enemies: "That compels me to repeat what I have been saying, and that is that the single (common?) interest has two different forms of expression in accordance with the origin of the thought . . . of each of the two [*wafid* and *mawruth*]" (p.443).

The solution to this problem of the ambivalence of Egyptian political culture is, however, not to go back to the wafid, but to find a way of uniting both. What al-Bishri has in mind is best expressed by his interpretation of some of the salient events of Egyptian history:

> If we look at Egyptian history we find that the . . . Watani party which struggled against the English, had some Islamic connections. . . . Thereafter, we find that the Wafd party dispensed with those associations and became a party without any connection to Islam, in its political sense, in the aftermath of the 1919 revolution. Consequently, when the 1919 revolution was transformed into the regime of 1924, it was not more than four years before another organization was founded—the Muslim Brethren—to give expression to one of those parts of the divided society . . . the Watani party was a more inclusive structure, which, to some extent, prevented the split which [later] occurred. Because the Wafd party became polarized about alien (*wafid*) understandings, there was, as a consequence, a (counter) polarization on the part of the Islamic tendency, and that is what is needful of a remedy today. (P. 428)

Al-Bishri has implicitly distinguished between the objective historical reality of the "popular interests" (*al-masalih al-sha*ʿ*abiyya*) and the schizoid subjectivism of the two prevalent forms of cultural expression of those interests.[74] As rhetorical forms, the wafid and the mawruth justifications of popular interests are functionally equivalent, and if they can be brought together they will unite the divided nation. The Watani party had the right idea. The ideal organization and ideological orientation for today would bring together the Wafd and the Ikhwan. In this union al-Bishri professes to see only the expression of national, popular interests.

Another of al-Bishri's formulations of his theory of *al-wafid w*ʿ*al-mawruth* is presented in a paper prepared for a symposium on "The Problematic (Character) of the Social Sciences in the Arab World."[75] The very purpose of the symposium was to raise the question of whether or not social science, especially as practiced in America, is not itself an expression of Western culture, and therefore distorts rather than explains in its application to other societies.

Al-Bishri does not inquire into the nature of this social science in any systematic fashion. He rather lumps it together with the whole of that cultural complex which he calls wafid, and which he believes is an expression of the triumphant culture of a unified entity which he calls the West. The military, political, and economic triumphs of the West have permitted it to penetrate into the Islamic-Arab world, and now that world is culturally split into precisely two tendencies. Al-Bishri argues that Egyptian Muslim Arabs are culturally divided, with some standing well inside of Western culture while others are still in the midst of traditional Islam. It is the westernized that use the term tradition or heritage, rather than Islam, because for them it is a culture of the past which is no longer with us. If any part of that culture is to be "selected," it must be brought back, preserved, and reapplied. Moreover, the stance of the westernized is that they are detached, external to, or separated from Islamic civilization, and therefore are in a position to perform an operation such as a selection among alternatives without involving their own selves in any serious way.

Al-Bishri now introduces the concept of identity, asserting that the mawruth, which is properly speaking Islam, is the identity, the dhatiyya or hawiyya of the Egyptian Muslim Arab. Al-Bishri does not pause to critique the concept, or to wonder about its political content or its philosophical origin, or even about how it works in political or psychological discourse. He plunges in with the simple-minded and misleading question "Who are we?"

It seems obvious that we must desperately have an answer to such a question. Our very survival in society depends upon being somebody, especially when we are small children. So the question is a terrifying and an intimidating one; but it is false and misleading when it is applied to a whole society, which is defined historically to include many generations long dead and not yet living. National, communal, social, group, and familial, as well as individual, forms of identity have their uses and abuses, and ought to be approached with caution if not with scholarly neutrality—but this is a problem of social science that the Middle East shares with the West.

Once the concept of identity is introduced, it is easy for al-Bishri to argue that the idea of a free choice between *al-wafid wa'l-mawruth* is nonsense, because to choose the wafid is to deny one's identity—and one does not have a choice of identity. It sounds much as though one is choosing to be another person, but insofar as the issue is one of culture, belief, or life style, Western liberalism argues precisely that one can and may change that aspect of one's identity. Thus the false consciousness by which al-Bishri earlier characterized the clash of cultures is now put aside, and in its place a new structure is used which argues that the Egyptian Muslim Arab has forgotten that "we belong to one of the sides in this relationship (of struggle)."[76] In setting al-wafid and al-mawruth up as alternatives, Muslims are struggling against themselves. "Hence, the question regarding who are we is urgent, and so is the framework which we fabricate or create, for what we choose. If (material) interest is the framework, then in the end it all goes back to identity, and no alternatives to it will do" (p. 393).

Some critics might argue that al-Bishri has it backwards, in the sense that interest defines identity, but, of course, interest is in turn defined by the situation in which one finds oneself—and that is often determined by previous generations, especially in countries with a rigid social order. Still there is a big difference between arguing that the criterion of choice within a given cultural heritage is interest, as opposed to arguing that the condition of survival is to cleave to an identity which one has inherited.

> And as we have said, in general and in principle, the question of identity and membership does not entail a matter of choosing. For in choosing there is a kind of liberty, and in liberty there is a kind of incompatibility with belonging. . . . Identity and self, these are the framework of choice, and they are the first premise. For if not, the soldier could not sacrifice his life for it. (P. 395)

Islam is no longer something in which a person believes, to which he may come by conviction, and through which he may change his identity. It is rather something "internalized," a part of the self which cannot be altered. This is a difficult position for a universal religion to maintain, and it does not. In this passage, instead of making Islam the core of the identity which he is explicating, al-Bishri writes "we are Egyptians." Obviously the focus of his identity shifts about somewhat, but some of the not-so-liberal implications of this type of theory of nationalism are nevertheless clear in the assertion that such a national identity is homogeneous and beyond choice.

Al-Bishri's dualistic bent is further exposed in a parallel, but mirror image, characterization of the West. Modern Western civilization is an expression of *the* (only one) Western identity. It is not characterized by ambivalence, by conflict between tradition and modernity, or by tension between the religious and the secular. Moreover the three great cultural achievements of the West, religious reform, democracy, and socialism, were achieved under conditions of "freedom from the threat of foreign invasion and assurance against a foreign threat. Nor [was there] a danger of loss of identity, or the disintegration of the society's power of perseverance against an avid enemy" (p. 398). This hardly appears to be a reasonable historical characterization of Europe in the course of developing these cultural achievements—but we may forgive the embarrassing inadequacy of this statement, reading it rather as a reverse characterization of the situation of Egypt and other Muslim countries.

The Copts and Islamic Authenticity

Having established, to his own satisfaction, that Islam and/or the turath may function as the ideology of a progressive, revolutionary movement that will unite the Egyptian nation and reaffirm its national identity, al-Bishri turns to what seems to be the specific question which occasioned the writing of his second book.[77] The specific question is, what is the place of the Copts in an overwhelmingly Muslim, Egyptian, political community?

Al-Bishri begins by establishing the compatibility, even the objective functional identity of Islam and nationalism insofar as both are objectively progressive, opposed to imperialist influence, and conduce to the liberation of the political community in Egypt.[78] Neither nationalism nor Islam are credited with unique and independent meaning. Each acquires meaning with regard to the situation defined in terms of imperialism, subjection, and alien influence. The conception of nationalism is perhaps more directly connected in logic to this framework of meaning, but not via any theoretical analysis. Nationalism and Islam derive their progressive character and their meaning from their functional value, insofar as they were actually opposed to imperialism, and any intrinsic meaning which they may claim as statements of universals is evidently beside the point.

Al-Bishri argues that Mawdudi's views are inapplicable to Egypt because Egypt's historical circumstances are different, and his position is unexceptionable. A Pakistani nationalism directed against Indian unity might well be comparable to a Coptic nationalism focusing on some regions in Upper Egypt, and would arouse (or has already aroused) intense Muslim-Egyptian majoritarian religio-national antagonism. It is just this sort of religio-national separatism which further invokes plausible and meaningful arguments meant to prove by means of history, culture, language, and everything except religion, that Hindu and Muslim Indians are one nation, and that Muslim and Coptic Egyptians are one nation—and of course they may be, if they will it, and if they are willing to accommodate one another, and if no outside force interferes and if. . . .

But one of the most important questions that has to be settled is, which nationalism are we talking about? That is, are we talking about an Egyptian nationalism or an Arab nationalism? Al-Bishri usually talks about Arab nationalism, despite his concentration on the Egyptian experience and emphasis upon the notion of identity. This nationalism, which Muslim and Copt share, is defined, to a considerable extent, by the turath, an Arab-Islamic turath, which must be willingly shared by the Copts for his argument to make sense. Some might argue that the majority of Copts, but at least some Copts, believe that a form of Egyptian nationalism, drawing on the turath of pre-Islamic Egypt, is a more appropriate and a more reassuring formula. Nevertheless al-Bishri appears to be asking the Copts, in the name of national unity and the common interests of all

Egyptians, to accept a broader Islamic-Arab formula in which Coptic concerns will naturally suffer more of a shrinkage.

But al-Bishri is not primarily interested in winning the Copts over to Arab nationalism.[79] He is rather concerned to establish the compatibility, if not the identity, of Islam and Arab-Egyptian nationalism. Islamic political doctrine, in al-Bishri's exposition, includes two elements, the first of which is that the Muslims constitute a political community—that is, a human community which legitimately rules itself and has its own government—and the second of which is the requirement that the laws of the Shariʿa be implemented.

This approach allows al-Bishri to put aside any notion that the Islamic theory of government insists upon particular institutional forms or a fixed set of offices, some or all of which must be held by Muslims only. The community is a political unit, but its government is not specified except in the most general references to the shura, to those in authority, and to the *ahl al-hal wal-ʿaqd*.[80]

The implementation of the Shariʿa presents some problems, however, because al-Bishri finds that most modern (fundamentalist?) commentators agree that non-Muslims may not serve as head of state, commander-in-chief of the armed forces, nor as qadis. In order to weaken this widely held view, al-Bishri quotes fundamentalist as well as nonfundamentalist apologists on Islamic tolerance and the spirit of egalitarianism which permeates Islam. He hopes to see this tolerance legislated into guarantees for the minorities within the framework of Shariʿa legislation. He suggests that the restriction of certain offices to Muslims depends upon the assumption that certain forms of government, especially the historical caliphate, are actually established and maintained. But under modern forms of democracy, where all officials enjoy only delegated authority, and all are required to carry out impersonal roles as defined by law, he suggests that all officials, including the highest, are in effect only functionaries representing the democratically determined will of the majority—which, in Egypt, is overwhelmingly Muslim. Moreover, under such demographic conditions there is really no question of a non-Muslim ever becoming head of the state.

Al-Bishri concludes that the issue is only a formal, or a theoretical one, but not a practical issue. In practice, in an Egyptian Arab national state the Shariʿa will not be infringed upon, even if the constitution grants complete equality to Copts, as it is now believed to do. The task which is now required to be accomplished is to find some way to restate the Shariʿa requirements so that they take cognizance of Egyptian realities; but this is a task which al-Bishri requires of the fundamentalist theorists he so copiously quotes.

To urge them on to this important task, al-Bishri makes two

 major arguments about the nature of Islam and its view of politics. The first argument is that Islamic political thinking is flexible and adaptive to changed conditions, and the second is that Islam cautiously avoids disruption of political order. The first argument is then directed at the so-called fact that nowadays states are based on nationalism and not on belief, and therefore Islam has to adapt to this historical circumstance.[81] But, of course, this is exactly what the fundamentalists reject. They believe that Islam requires not only that the political community be defined by the existence of Muslims, but that the political order itself be based on Islam. They also believe that Islam constitutes a complete system of thought and a way of life, and ought not be fragmented and applied in bits and pieces.

In elaborating the second argument, al-Bishri quotes one of his favorite sources as saying that "The *ahkam* [the religious commandments] change with changing conditions, and the principles of Islam render such change a certainty. Among those principles is the duty of avoiding a *fitna* [a rebellion] in accordance with the rule of the Shariʿa that states 'If two harmful things combine against you, take on the easier [challenge].' " (p.712.)

Turning to religious authority as he has done throughout in order to convince his Muslim readers, al-Bishri quotes Shaykh ʿAbd al-Wahhab Khallaf to the effect that the position of the *dhimmis* [non-Muslim subjects] is not only a question of the Shariʿa but is also a political matter, from which Khallaf draws the conclusion that "we must respect the rights that our Christian brothers have (actually or properly) acquired" (p. 713). There is no doubt that there is something of a warning implied in this exposition—or at least the suggestion—that to take away the rights which the Copts have under the present constitution (and that constitution states that the Shariʿa is the major source of legislation in Egypt) would threaten national unity and political order.

Conclusion

Several observers have hinted that a scholarly analysis of al-Bishri's work is beside the point, that his argument should rather be seen as a strategic effort to manipulate the formation of a new national consensus and develop structures that will maintain that consensus, that his antitheoretism is meant to minimize intellectualist confusion, that the mixture of identitive referents is meant to legitimate alternative formulations, and that the legitimation of fundamentalism is meant to lead to a reinterpretation of Islamic political requirements. It is likely true that some of the intellectual weaknesses of al-Bishri's work are due to the subordination of scholarly pedantry to political purpose, but the ultimate political purpose is also left obscure. This obscurity is the result of the formula which states that, in the pursuit of national independence via national unity, democracy, socialism and religious reform can be attained, but these desiderata may not "look" like they do in the West.

Al-Bishri reasons from historical counterfactuals, and the resultant inadequacy of his comparison of European and non-European conditions, raises questions regarding his enterprise. History is nonhistorical in his treatment, it is rather the reification of a number of ideas; and this reification of ideas is particularly troubling when it is applied as a form of apotheosis of events, institutions, and personalities in contemporary Egyptian history. Instead of logical analysis, al-Bishri transforms events or reality (*al-waqᶜa*) into principles, and instead of reconciling logical contradictions, he argues that integrative organizational forms will overcome the contradictions born of the external, empirical counterposition of these principles. Thus, al-Bishri denies that the Wafd, the Ikhwan, and Nasser's Socialist Union represented real social forces, rather than superficially divergent verbal formulations of the same idea. Although he writes of reality, al-Bishri's exposition is that of an idealistic dialectic.

In the light of al-Bishri's rejection of al-wafid, it is difficult to avoid the temptation of pointing out that the absolute inalterability of identity is itself a product of the confluence of a number of Western ideas, all of which represent the troubled reaction of Western intellectuals to the very crises of modernization which al-Bishri argues did *not* occur in the West.

As we have seen, al-Bishri is not primarily concerned to resolve social-scientific problems or to satisfy the qualms of Western, liberal, professors. A little obscurity may serve his purposes better than such quibbling, especially if it allows antagonists to resolve differences and to get together. The device of allowing others to speak for him through the use of selective quotations works well in this manner, leaving the author somewhat detached and his own views unknown.

Still, there are times when it seems clear that al-Bishri has taken a position of his own, or adopted a certain interpretation, and in at least two cases, it seems to me he has missed or distorted the important point made by his source. The first of these is in his critique of Mawdudi's rejection of nationalism, which is in part attributed to the special condition of Muslims in India, where nationalism meant Hindu-dominated Indian nationalism. That was indeed the situation, but as W. C. Smith pointed out long ago, Mawdudi was opposed to the Muslim League's Pakistan project, and his attack was directed against precisely the kind of *Islamic Nationalism* which al-Bishri has in mind—that is, the pragmatic use of Islam as an expression of the national interests of a certain class or social segment.[82] I think that the fundamentalists understand this point very well, though it may not prevent them from joining political forces with others for a brief ride.

The second misunderstanding occurs where al-Bishri argues against the standard modernist interpretation of the destruction of the Janissaries. He first quoted Dr. Muhammad ʿAbd al-Latif al-Bahrawi as saying that, while the destruction of the Janissaries freed the Sultan from their tyranny, it also "freed the Europeans from any fear of the Ottoman empire, which now appeared before them as virtually naked."[83] Al-Bishri goes on to quote the memoirs of ʿAbd al-Hamid II, as though in the same vein: "The big mistake actually snowballed from the days of my grandfather [Mahmud II] to the present time. We had gotten rid of the Janissaries, but we did not get rid of the reasons for the corruption of the Janissaries" (p. 400).

It seems to me that the lament of Abdul Hamid II is not that the Janissaries were destroyed, but that a reform which concentrates on formal structures does not go deeply enough. Al-Bishri seems to want to have socialism without socialists, religious reform without reformers, and democracy without democrats. Al-Bishri would establish a system which has all the integrative benefits of liberalism, but which would avoid the pluralist costs thereof. Would not such an approach to the construction of a liberal regime also merit the lament of Abd al-Hamid II?

Al-Bishri began with the use of revolutionary terminology and the need for radical change of existing circumstances. His later statements suggest that he has moved from the Marxian notion of the objectively revolutionary character of mass Islam to the idea of the functional substitutability of Islam for Western revolutionary ideologies, to the view that indigenous and introduced elements might be suitably combined under the right circumstances, to the conclusion that Egypt might best learn from its own *mixed* experience of adapting Western forms, and thus evolve toward full national liberation rather than necessarily undergo a revolution. It appears that al-Bishri's radicalism has waned as his conception of the indigenous alternative has become broader and more sophisticated. Not only has al-Bishri become more religiously committed himself (according to reports) but his judgments of the Wafd and the Nasserist experiment have become more tolerant. In a way it is possible to see both an intellectual evolution and the logic of the ideological process at work in the gradual shifts in his thinking. The full development of his ideas is still some way off, and we have yet to see how he will integrate the state apparatus and the neo-Wafd or the bourgeoisie in his total picture. Al-Bishri may be able to produce the right formula to sustain a broader movement, or he may encourage others to produce similar syntheses—essentially combinations of familiar Egyptian political ingredients—while working his way back from independent Marxism to liberal, nationalist, Islam.

In recent years, Tariq al-Bishri has grown more popular, and he has become more religiously observant. His most important disciple and colleague, Adil Husain—son of Ahmad Husain, the late leader of the Misr al-Fatat—has also emerged as an influential oppositional political personality, openly carrying forward the ideological and political heritage of his famous father. This is a surprising revival of a long dead and ignored political tendency, usually identified with the moral and political corruption of prewar Egypt, or, ironically with the inauthenticity of European fascism. But this strange ideological hybrid has been strengthened by the support of Ibrahim Shukri, a crafty political broker, who was not only Ahmad Husain's deputy, but was later appointed by Sadat as leader of the Labor party, one of the four licensed political parties. To hold such a license under the Egyptian system is like holding a television station franchise in the U.S. Ibrahim Shukri has used this asset to woo the Ikhwan while rebuilding the support of the middle classes. In 1987, Shukri successfully outbid the Wafd for the right to list Ikhwan candidates, and he was handsomely rewarded with a greatly increased representation of his own in the new parliament.

In pursuing this policy, Shukri has reversed Ahmad Husain's policy of competing with the Ikhwan, but he has finally succeeded in Husain's aspiration of defeating the Wafd—even though it was only the ghost of the Wafd that Shukri outmaneuvered. Above all, Shukri and his Labor party have extended a serious challenge to both the neo-Wafd and the ruling National Democratic (Watani) party, by positioning itself to represent the interests of the Egyptian bourgeoisie.

At the same time, it should be noted that the Mubarak government has given its tacit support to the informal entry of the Ikhwan into legitimate politics. The Mubarak government is betting that the increased influence and legitimacy of the Ikhwan will provide an outlet for Islamic political aspirations, and thus reduce the dangerous political potential of the Jamaʿat. Mubarak and his advisers hope that de facto participation by the Ikhwan in parliamentary politics, reinforced by the challenge from more extreme groups, will convince the Ikhwan of the virtues of political liberalism.

This may also be the hope of Tariq al-Bishri, Adil Husain, and Ibrahim Shukri, but liberalism is not very well established in Egypt, nor is the Egyptian bourgeoisie or the liberal intelligentsia strong enough to counterbalance the influence of the petite bourgeoisie and the sansculottes. Mubarak may be committed to an attenuated liberalism as the best alternative to either Nasserism or Sadatism, but the prescription offered by Tariq al-Bishri may produce a modified Nasserism—bureaucratic authoritarianism plus Islam.

8

The Hermeneutic of Authenticity

From the time of the Napoleonic invasion, from the time of the massacre of the Janissaries, from the time of the Sepoy mutiny, at least, the West has been trying to tell Islam what must be the price of progress in the coin of the tradition which is to be surrendered. And from those times, despite the increasing numbers of responsive Muslims, there remains a substantial number that steadfastly argue that it is possible to progress without paying such a heavy cultural price.

There are two important issues here, and not one. The first is whether Islam poses a substantial obstacle to modernization and development, and the second is whether Islam proposes a radically different and possibly much better social order than that which is adumbrated in the Western theory of development. The first issue assumes that Islam may be the barrier to development, while the second assumes that the West may be the barrier to development in the Islamic world. The first question identifies Islam and tradition, generically, while the second denies that westernization is the only form of modernization. Each of these perspectives provides us with an alternative evaluation of an Islamic renaissance as either a reaffirmation of tradition or the very condition of the possibility of an authentic modernization.

Islamic Authenticity

The crossing of the Suez canal in 1973, the overthrow of the Shah in 1979, the battle of Karameh in 1968, have all been treated as "meaning events" in the jargon of phenomenological existentialism. From this perspective there can be no question of the truth of something which has occurred and which has influenced, as it must, the self-conception and the value orientation of human beings. Such a "meaning event" or an "understanding event" or such a "disclosure of being" provides for its own validation simply because it is in history and has had an impact.[1] In this sense Islam may be taken as ontically true or historically valid by believers and nonbelievers alike, but we are still faced with the Heideggerian problematic of distinguishing the authentic from the inauthentic in the Islamic experience. Following Gadamer, the authentic historical meaning of Islam for our time can be discovered by means of the phenomenological hermeneutic.[2]

The task of the phenomenological hermeneutic is to distinguish between inauthentic or unacceptable historical manifestations of Islam and authentic manifestations, between the inauthenticity of the "decline" and the authenticity of the period of the salaf. The renaissance of Islam is, consequently, the reassertion of the historical truth of the earliest period of Islam as the true being of Islam and the authentic being of the Muslims of today. The Muslims of today are to reaffirm that authenticity by choosing to live their lives in accordance with their "own most being."

The authentic Islamic turath will then be disclosed by the things Muslims do—that is, by the way they reenact their heritage in modern times. But what they do is likely to be the result of material circumstances as well as the result of the role of intellectuals who are interpreting the turath for them. Which is the historically authentic? The meaning event of the Palestinian revolution, or the meaning event of the Iranian revolution? Are they really two distinguishable meaning events? The question is transformed from that of the historically true in a simple factual sense to one of the juxtaposition of the contemporaneously authentic vs. the merely "fallen" in the Islamic experience.

Heidegger wrote in his *Introduction to Metaphysics,* "Only as a questioning, historical, being does man come to himself; only as such is he a self. Man's selfhood means this: he must transform the being that discloses itself to him into history and bring himself to stand in it."[3]

But this questioning still requires an answer, and the answer depends upon how the past is understood, how understanding is interpreted, how it is taken from the merely passive and rendered active, and thus related to the present. The past is obviously not to be reenacted like some ritual, and it is not to be adjusted to someone else's preferred values. Above all, the past is to be taken as real, ontically true, as an aspect of the being of Muslims by virtue of an understanding event that is evidently to be an act founded upon a living experience of the Islamic tradition. That tradition cannot be seen as having been abrogated by the decline. Indeed, the decline is inauthenticity. Authenticity is the life-choice which the preferred elements of the tradition demand under present circumstances in order that they be reaffirmed as real, and appropriated as aspects of the being of the Muslim *Dasein.* That is the theory, but after all is said much remains to be done. The tradition must still be defined in terms of the present, and a course of action must be determined. It is necessary to formulate a project.

The central problem is, therefore, a hermeneutical problem—one of how to interpret the tradition, or the turath, whether by means of the philological methods of objectivist research on ancient Greece, Rome, and Israel, or by some other method by which the hiatus between subject and object is overcome and an understanding event can occur that will produce the ontic truth of the being of the modern Muslim. In all of this there is no doubt an important religious subtheme, in that the Heideggerian problematic is rooted in the Hegelian truth of the historicality of religion as at least a moment in the dialectical composition of Absolute Spirit. To simplify greatly, the issue is how to establish the truth of religion on other than an objectivist rational basis in the post-Kantian world.

Hegel's answer, which is not unrelated to the ancient Semitic view, historizes religion but then detemporalizes history. Heidegger, like Nietzche, and others, rejects the Hegelian eschatology and also the atemporality of the Hegelian dialectic. The existentialist process of self-understanding is a temporalized dialectic. One of the consequences of this scheme is that the relevance of religious teaching remains, even if particular parts of revelation are no longer literally accepted. But since the validation of religious experience is the end, there is some awkwardness about employing the traditional methods of theological reasoning as the means to that end. The understanding event which will render religious experience ontically valid is unlikely to be mediated by formal theological discourse. It is more likely to be mediated by an experience which discloses authentic being—an experience which *Dasein* prepares for by resisting the temptation of "fallenness," of everydayness, of the *lebenswelt,* of the natural attitude, or of self-objectification.

For the religious hermeneuticist, the most important goal is the event of faith rather than the event of knowledge. He is more concerned with the effect of the word—the logos—on the inquirer (*Dasein*), than with his understanding in any epistemological sense. The most important thing is that the logos become a part of his being, that his changed state represent an expression of his potential for true being, or his consciousness of his authentic self. Hence every act of interpretation leading to understanding leads to a changed state of mind, a new approach to the world, a new course of action, a new attitude toward death, but not necessarily to an articulation of a truth in the scientific sense.

H.-G. Gadamer, the German hermeneutic philosopher writes: "But according to the Christian teaching there is a 'final' failure. The Christian meaning of proclamation, the promise of resurrection that sets us free from death, consists precisely in putting an end to the constantly repeated failure of self-understanding, its eventual collapse in death and finiteness, in faith in Christ. Certainly this does not mean that one steps outside one's historicalness, but rather that faith is the eschatological event."[4]

Of course the secular version is historical and noneschatological, but rather political in the sense that resoluteness replaces faith for Heidegger, and commitment to a collective authenticity replaces incorporation in the body of Christ. The worldly rise of Islam is to be distinguished from the deepened faith of Muslims—or is it?

Is the historicality of Islam related to its eternal truth in a manner inverse to that of Christianity? Heidegger could only be a Christian even though his teaching has widely influenced non-Christians. Only a Christian could write of being-toward-death as the ontic verity of *Dasein*. What is the Islamic equivalent?

Gadamer suggests the manner in which historical consciousness grasps and resolves the issue of the emendation of history, that is the simultaneous desire to retain and yet to expunge from history what is inauthentic.

> [Historical consciousness] By claiming to transcend its own conditionedness completely in its knowing of the other . . . is involved in a false dialectical appearance, since it is actually seeking to master, as it were, the past . . . the dialectical illusion, which historical consciousness creates and which corresponds to the dialectical illusion of experience perfected and replaced by knowledge, is the unattainable ideal of the historical enlightenment.[5]

But the past cannot be mastered and replaced by knowledge; instead, "historical consciousness . . . must, in fact, take account of its own historicality." Gadamer argues that each of us stands within a tradition, and that, if we try to transcend that tradition, to deny our prejudices, we, in fact, lose control of our prejudices. Instead, real historical consciousness ought to be open to what the tradition has to say to it. But what the tradition has to say depends upon what we ask of it. Knowledge depends upon questioning, and the answer for Gadamer is essentially dialectical. Gadamer writes approvingly, "Aristotle says that dialectic is the power to investigate contraries independent of the object." And of even greater relevance to the condition of Islam he writes, "logically the negativity of experience implies a question."[6]

This question is to be posed to the heritage, the tradition, or the turath, in the form of a hermeneutical dialogue or a conversation within the text, of which the dialectic of Hegel is for Gadamer the outstanding example. Gadamer's goal is something he calls actual-historical-consciousness. This goal takes the place of what the Enlightenment called knowledge, and it is achieved by means of a hermeneutic which is for Gadamer the antithesis of method. In its place there is rather a dialectic in which the tradition is interrogated, and its various moments speak to the inquirer in a manner that is meaningful to his actual historical condition. These moments are not dissolved in synthesis, nor do they become clarified as what actually was the case at some time in the past, nor do they articulate unequivocally the essence of the tradition. The answer they give is simply the actual meaning of the tradition for a given inquirer.

For Gadamer, the essential task is to bridge the gap between the author and the interpreter, to allow the author to speak to the reader, while the reader is almost passive, allowing an experience to occur, not operating on the text. That which for Gadamer allows the "unity of horizons" is language, and the aesthetic form par excellence which uses language is poetry. Hence it is openness to poetic experience which allows a contemporary reader to be open to the speech of his heritage, and to reexperience it in a way that he will realize its truth for his situation, and be enabled to appropriate it and carry it on in a way which gives his being-toward-death authenticity.

The experience of poetry may be the central conceit in the hermeneutical approach, but all understanding, like all being, is essentially historical. The notion of history in this existential orientation conveys more than mere temporality, it really stands for positionality, perspective, intentionality, or that which sets apart the authenticity of one group from another. Hence, historicality is not simply temporality, mortality, or relativity. Historicality is an essential part of the being of *Dasein* and as such is essential to truth. Historicality justifies as many truths as there may be authentic ways of relating to a heritage.

The hermeneuticist view of history is deeply imbued with Hegelian idealism. It is not the materialist history of Marxist thought, with its emphasis upon the interrelationship of social forces and the mode of production. Were it otherwise, it would not be possible to speak meaningfully of carrying on a dialogue with history. History does not really reply to our efforts to put a meaningful construction upon it. History, in the sense of political outcomes, may, however, defy our efforts at interpretation insofar as those efforts imply some program of future action. Either we believe that we are more or less free to resolve to pursue the results of a dialogue with history, or we believe that there is no sense talking to history, because history is deaf, and because we ourselves are within history. This is not to argue that historical discourse is idealistic or else simply nonsense. It is not impossible for man to understand his own history, even if that history, including himself, is materially determined.

But the hermeneuticist argues that we can choose. Heidegger poses a choice between authenticity and inauthenticity. Gadamer allows us to choose objective historical truth or to live in the alienation of ignorance. Neither really argues that we can change the world. We can only change our attitude toward the world, and the way we live in the world. For the existentialists, and not only the existentialists, the world, especially the modern world, is not an easy place in which to live. But it follows from their doctrines that it may be harder for some than it is for others, depending upon the content of their authenticity. Because the choice of authenticity does not change the world, it may in fact make it more difficult to live in the world than might otherwise be the case. Hence, it might be argued that, for good or ill, modernity is closer to Western authenticity than it is to Islamic authenticity. This is, in fact, the meaning of the argument that modernization and westernization are the same thing. The existentialist view that modern man is alienated in inauthenticity is one kind of rejection of the identification of modernity and westernism. Another rejection is the argument that modernity or development may take more than a single cultural form and that the historical fact of Western domination is the cause of the alienation of the non-Western peoples. Their reluctance to choose inauthenticity has been an obstacle. The obstacle may be removed by a proper understanding of their history.

The search for meaning in Islamic history is the goal of the turath literature. That literature is rich, varied, and growing, despite the scripturalist gains in Iran and Pakistan. But the political and ideological implications of the turath genre are far from clear. In fact, there may be no single political meaning imbedded in this literature. It is relatively easy to find divergent interpretations of the turath, employing, respectively, idealist and materialist methods of interpretation. It is also noteworthy that the idealist trend is mostly concerned to liberate Islamic thought from the rigid limits of traditional legalism, while the materialist trend seeks freedom from the rigid limits of orthodox Marxism.

These two parallel but ideologically distinct tendencies are well illustrated in the work of Zaki Naguib Mahmud and Abdallah Laroui, as will be shown in the remainder of this chapter. The two approaches express alternative methods of interpreting the turath, but they are not without their own convergent inclinations. Mahmud's idealism, as we shall see, is tempered by the influence of neo-Kantian dualism and pragmatism. As a consequence, the Islamic ideal is never permitted to negate the turath as historical praxis in its entirety. In a similar fashion, the intellectual critique of humanist Marxism by structuralist Marxism, that is, of ontological existentialism by epistemological existentialism, inspired a number of "Third World Marxists" to produce similarly hybrid ideological forms. According to these mixed forms, historical praxis produces authentic idealist conceptions much in the way in which structuralist theory is supposed to be produced (i.e., by theoretical praxis). The paradoxical result is that Mahmud's idealism becomes an apotheosis of Islamic praxis, while Laroui's materialism becomes the ground upon which an idealist synthesis of the universal and the particular may be constructed.

Zaki Naguib Mahmud

Zaki Nagib Mahmud has acquired notoriety as a courageous and outspoken defender of liberalism and reform in modern Egypt. He is an octogenarian, a retired professor of philosophy, a prolific author, and a frequent contributor to the weekend press. In recent years he has debated the redoubtable Shaykh Sha'arawi, an extremely popular television preacher and the leading exponent of traditional and populist Islam in Egypt. Mahmud's theme is the reform or renewal of the Islamic Arab turath, a matter which he approaches from a philosophical standpoint, championing the idea of reason. He has tried to explain what reason is, how it works, how it manifests itself in the turath, how it has been misunderstood by Muslims, and how it has been subordinated to unreason.

Over the years, Mahmud has gained stature and experience as an exponent of Islamic liberalism and modernism, and he has refined his arguments and his rhetoric. Still, he has not wholly overcome the reputation of being extremely secularly-minded—a consequence, no doubt, of his frequent references to European philosophical literature, and his analytical style of writing. By the same token, part of his influence must be attributed to his excellent command of the literary language and his skill in expounding on abstract themes.

300 In view of the considerable range of Mahmud's intellectual talents and the many works which he has written, the present exposition must necessarily represent but a fragment of his thought. It will be based on only a single work, his *Renovation of Arab Thought*, an early, somewhat eclectic, but ambitious contribution to the debate on the turath.[7] That is to say, early in terms of the time when Mahmud's interests turned to public affairs, but certainly not early in terms of his intellectual maturity. In fact, Mahmud admits that he was no expert on the Islamic tradition, even though he was long fascinated by the problem of whether it was possible to synthesize Arab culture and the culture of modern Western civilization. His academic retirement allowed him the leisure to read some of the great works of the Islamic tradition, and to ponder, philosophically, their relationship to the Western systems of thought with which he was well acquainted. Mahmud does not hesitate over the question of whether his reading of the texts of the turath might be considered an "outside" reading that must fail of the depth of the reading of one long steeped in the Islamic tradition. Rather, Mahmud more than once criticizes those who are so attached to their own conception of the tradition that they are like someone who crouches frightened in a dark corner, for fear of exposure before the eyes of those who go about freely in the world.

In a most interesting passage, Mahmud writes that it appears to many, superficially, that educated Arabs are at home in both Western and Arab cultures, but, actually, they live in two separate worlds, as in two rooms, staying now in one and then in the other.[8] His own views on the question shifted; at first he thought that culture could not be divided into compartments, and he even developed some sympathy for those who advocated a withdrawal into a purely Arab culture after the Arabs had been defeated by "modern" enemies.[9] His conclusion, though, was that the question had been badly put. Like squaring the circle, the blending of two distinct cultures is impossible, so the answer lies in the pragmatic application of whatever will be of practical utility, regardless of whether it is modern or traditional.[10] Mahmud further insists that the pragmatic principle of utility can be applied in the spheres of the social and humanistic disciplines just as it can in the applied sciences.[11]

Zaki Nagib Mahmud set out to examine the turath to discover, as he puts it, what may be useful today and what is simply of antiquarian interest. His premise is not that there is something wrong with modernity, but rather that there is something wrong with contemporary Arab and Islamic thought. But even then he does not dwell on the question. It is self-evident that one must take a position regarding the Islamic heritage. His procedure is supposed to be rational and scientific: a systematic investigation of the cultural heritage of Islam from the advanced perspective of modern science, philosophy and social studies. His judgments are unhestitating, and his method that of unrelenting repetition. His is not really a dialogue with Islamic history, but rather an interrogation or an examination. The Islamic heritage does not speak to him so much as he listens to what it says literally in its own time.

Mahmud's conception of the turath is analytical and intellectual rather than historical and hermeneutical. The single period which receives attention in an historical sense is that of the Abbasid overthrow of the Umayyad caliphate, and the subsequent establishment of the Abbasid political and cultural regime. It is during this period that the fateful turn was taken against philosophical reason and in favor of theological dialectics. Like Arkoun, another philosopher, Mahmud finds the rejection of the Greek cultural alternative to have been greatly damaging to Islam. But unlike Arkoun, Mahmud does not use his philosophical framework as a structure within which to explicate the authentic meaning of the historical and aesthetic constituents of the turath. Mahmud believes that it is better to separate pragmatic reason and the turath in order to protect what is most essential to each. He does not even make a strong pragmatic argument for the need to preserve the turath. The turath represents the nonrational side of human nature, but not the rational necessity of political society, for example.

Mahmud found much to decry in the series of strategic moves whereby the Abbasid conspirators succeeded in seizing power. They encouraged anti-Arab (*Shuʿubi*) sentiments, and the diffusion of gnostic and mysterious religious beliefs. Having been helped to power by the enigmatic Abu Muslim, the Abbasids betrayed and disposed of him, and tried to contain the spread of deleterious irrational ideologies by reaffirming a Sunni orthodoxy, and also by encouraging the spread of a rationalist philosophical ideology (by means of translations from the ancient Greek). The paradoxical result was that the very same political forces that were responsible for bringing Greek rational philosophy into Islam were also responsible for bringing irrational, mystical, and gnostic distortions of philosophical theology into Islam. The political opposition to the Abbasids exploited the doctrines of the *Zanadiqa*, the *Batiniyya* and all the rest, ultimately enfeebling the Abbasid caliphate by means of its very own revolutionary instrument. And the consequence of all this for Islam has been the deep rooting of three intellectual obstacles to modernization: the beliefs that (1) the ruler has unlimited legitimate authority; (2) that the past should prevail over the present, and; (3) that miracles can supercede natural law.[12] These obstacles must be removed before progress can be made, and the way to remove them seems to be to lock them in a closet marked "nonrational elements of the turath." All three are rooted in the misconceptions regarding reason and truth which prevailed under the Abbasids, and especially during the period of the intellectual and ideological ascendancy of the Muʿtazila. The neo-Platonic idea of reason was based on the assumption of a fixed and eternal order of creation defining the framework within which deductive logic might be used to determine what is true. Mahmud's conception of reason is pragmatic, reflecting the views of Kant and Dewey.

The early Abbasid period has attracted much attention already, so Mahmud's interest is not idiosyncratic, but reflects his ideological position. One loosely argued cultural conclusion often drawn from those events, which Mahmud does not share, is that had the Muʿtazila been allowed to flourish, Islam would have developed a rationalist-deductive strain of thought which might have prevented the intellectual stagnation of later times, and might have allowed for the indigenous development of what is called modern science. Mahmud does not deny the possibility that, if left alone, the Muʿtazila might have contributed something of lasting intellectual value; he is rather concerned to show that the teachings of the Muʿtazila cannot be used for the standard apologetic purpose of claiming that all that the West has achieved is already known to the Islamic turath.

Mahmud ruthlessly relativizes the Muʿtazila, drawing on the two best-known medieval heresiologies, that of Abd al-Qahir al-Baghdadi and that of al-Shahrestani, showing how they were regarded by the orthodox.[13] Aside from placing them alongside the *Zanadiqa,* the *Batiniyya,* and the various Sufis, Mahmud points out that the issues on which all of these and the orthodox (especially the *Ashaʿira*) differed, were impractical matters of no account to modern nonreligious needs. Mahmud manages to praise the Muʿtazila spirit while yet placing them at the rationalist extreme opposite the mystical extreme, leaving the middle position for the orthodox *Ashaʿira.*

Mahmud sides with the Ashʿarites and with Sunni orthodoxy against these two forms of extremism, but he is careful to point out that he does not find the Ashʿarite position intellectually worthy.[14] The nonrational extremists, such as the various Zindiqs, represented the political and economic demands of the non-Arabs, or the *Shuʿubiyya.* The Muʿtazila reflected the interests of rational administration, and their extremism was expressed through the inquisition, which they supported. The Sunni orthodox represented the interests of the Abbasid establishment. It is noteworthy that Mahmud equates the interests of the community (Sunni orthodoxy) with the maintenance of order and with the elite (the Abbasid establishment). Mahmud's conception of reason may be "radical" in contemporary Egypt, but his politics are not.

Mahmud further elaborates his views on the religious intolerance of the turath by citing the works of the best-known medieval heresiologists. He ridicules the concern with metaphysical detail, and the imaginative invention of ways in which the prophetic inspiration was supposed to have been transmitted to pretenders. The heretical and the orthodox alike are criticized for their concern with matters which not only could not be known, but need not be known. All of these theological controversies, often politically or culturally motivated, are parts of the turath, but they are to be discarded. The effort to impose irrational belief by murderous force is not a cherished part of the turath. Religious belief is, or ought to be, an area of freedom of choice. Freedom should similarly characterize artistic expression and the whole range of subjectivity and the formation of the self.

Mahmud's conclusion from all of this is quite negative. He believes that virtually none of this is useful for the contemporary Muslim or Arab when it comes to relations between man and man rather than between man and God. For him, these matters of belief, despite their political significance historically, are not of practical interest. The Arabs and Muslims must choose between living in the past and living in the present where problems are solved. Objective conditions have changed so that the modern world is different from the traditional. What was culturally possible in the past is no longer practical. The culture of the past belongs in a museum. Its main purpose in any case was as a form of amusement to while away the leisure hours.[15]

Unlike the historically oriented theorists of the turath, who are seized of the great ideological consequences of the controversies surrounding the Kharijites, the Shiʿites, the Muʿtazila, and the gnostic extremists, Mahmud is inclined to view the turath as the juxtaposition of a number of philosophically relevant intellectual standpoints. Even when he discussed the merits and the defects of Muʿtazila rationalism and the benign and malevolent aspects of Sufism, he does so in analytical rather than in historical terms. The turath is not constituted by the historical and social consequences of the emergence of these movements so much as it is by the intellectually confusing and distorting presence of these tendencies.

Mahmud is most sympathetic to that philosophical culture which is recognized as one of the great contributions of the Islamic turath, but which was, nevertheless, a secondary intellectual tendency. But the cultural figures he cites are not only philosophers. Mahmud is enamored of classical Arabic literature and, especially poetry. He cites al-Farabi and al-Ghazali, but also Abu al-ʿAla al-

 Maʿarri; ibn Miskawaihi and al-Razi, but also al-Jahiz. His own rhetoric evidences a wide reading in the tradition and substantial literary skill. His turath is a literary one and a philosophical one, and not primarily concerned with Shariʿa, fiqh, kalam, and devotional practices.

It is not surprising that he praises the role played by al-Ghazali, and implicitly adopts his strategy of seeking a compromise that would allow the coexistence in Islamic culture of philosophical rationalism and religious faith. He sees these two as expressions of reason and unreason, but both reason and unreason can have their good and bad sides, and both have their place. In fact, the dualism of religion and science, of the Islamic and the Western, is the central argument for Mahmud.

Mahmud confronts these traditional intellectual and ideological orientations as a rationalist, but his ambivalence emerges and becomes stronger as he proceeds with his examination of the turath. It is apparent not only in his frank dualism, but also in his vacillation over the significance of aesthetics and feeling which he identifies with culture. In the end we shall find that even his dualism is strained to the breaking point as he seems willing to abandon his neo-Kantian pragmatism for what he calls an existentialism of belief (or a religious existentialism).[16] Mahmud is not consistent in his argument. He begins forcefully, all but rejecting the turath, only to end up in praise of poetry and nonutilitarian ethics. He condemns the confusion by which some Muslims have equated the divine law with the "laws" of a divinely ordered nature, but later calls on Muslims to subordinate their will to God's will. He starts with the critical stand of the falasifa, but in the end he sides with al-Ghazali and al-Ashʿari against the falasifa and against the Muʿtazila.

One has the sense that Mahmud started out bravely, to free the modern Arab of the fetters of the past, believing that the obstacle to modernization was and is the turath, and that much of that tradition had to be ruthlessly discarded if the Arabs were to be able to confront their problems and overcome them in the modern world. But his critical attack on the Islamic-Arab turath was almost wholly negative. His point of departure did not reserve the premise that the self, or the Islamic-Arab identity or some form of authenticity had to be maintained even while modernizing. His insistence on the importance of separating form and content allowed him to abstract the concepts of rationality, freedom, responsibility, and social "engagement," from the turath, while rejecting the historical and situational "content" which is the substance of the traditional Arab-Islamic culture.

In proposing an "Arab philosophy" toward the end of this book,

Mahmud focuses on the universal contribution of Arab thought before he has identified its particular characteristics. It is, therefore, almost as an afterthought that he returns to the question of the Arab identity and the special place which Islam has. Prior to this surprising reversal, he treated identity as a subjective matter, to be understood in his dualistic paradigm as linked to the nonrational, to the intuitive, to belief, to the emotional, to the arts, to expressiveness, to the nonutilitarian, and hence to a sphere of unconstrained freedom of choice. It is almost as though Mahmud couldn't care less about such matters. Yet, throughout the volume he keeps returning to the theme of the arts, Aristotelian and Arab-Islamic aesthetics, and especially to poetry (not philosophy) as the prime expression of Arab authenticity.

Mahmud locates all the elements of authenticity in those mental regions in which neither pure nor practical reason function. He is certain that once his dualistic perspective is accepted by Arab Muslims as authentically their own, then there need be no fear that modernization or westernization will undermine their identity. The great error of the traditionalists and the fundamentalists is that they believe that faith and reason are governed by the same logic. Some Muslim scientists actually argued that sending a man to the moon, or transplanting human organs, were un-Islamic as well as against nature.[17] Hence, no matter how, or even whether, Muslims choose to preserve their turath, that choice ought not impinge on any adaptive political, economic, or social changes they may be constrained to adopt in order to modernize.

Manifestly, the world below is a realm of change and of ephemerality, while the heavenly world is a world of permanence and eternity. Yet, for Mahmud it is not religion, but nature, or the world of everyday reality, that is fixed and determinative, unyielding and demanding. Everyman, Arab and American and Englishman and Frenchman, must accommodate himself to the realities of nature, and to the structure of the world as it is at the moment. Survival, progress, prosperity, all depend upon obeying the commands of nature. Reason begins with experience, writes Mahmud, echoing Kant.[18] Reason gives rise to will, to a project, and then to practical action, the success of which depends upon a sound understanding of the natural world. Given a goal determined by human will in a particular situation, there is, in fact, no choice, according to Mahmud. In matters of faith, however, there is room for disagreement, and there is wide latitude for choice among alternatives, because there can be no validation of religious claims.

Though at any given time nature poses absolute constraints, the world here below is constantly changing. As a consequence, human communities must constantly change also if they are to survive and prosper. The turath is best analyzed as composed of form and content, or principle (theory) and practice. Practice represents an adaptation of the general principle to the requirements of some historical time. Because of ignorance, superstition, prejudice, wickedness and the like, the time-bound practice rather than the ideal form, or abstract principle, has been invested with an unwarranted religious sanctification. As a consequence, the turath has been misunderstood because it has been taken too literally. The most valuable aspects of the turath have been forgotten or ignored, while the least valuable aspects have been rigidly preserved. Muslim Arabs who believe they are preserving the turath are therefore unable to adapt to the pragmatic requirements of the time because they are constrained to make the wrong choices.

Change and choice are linked to the question of human freedom. There is no doubt that Mahmud is, in political matters, a Lockean liberal, and he is absolutely uncompromising in concluding that the Arab-Islamic turath is devoid of examples of political freedom upon which modern Arabs may draw.[19] In the absence of indigenous cultural examples of political freedom and equality, the Arabs must perforce borrow from the West.[20] Thus the model of electoral democracy has been borrowed, but it has not been well applied in the face of the prevailing despotism and imperialism, and it cannot be well applied given the extremes of wealth and poverty in the Arab countries. Moreover, the contemporary borrowing of alien or *wafid* cultural elements merely repeats the practice of the turath, for the origin of Islamic rationalism was Greek, while many of the mystical and gnostic influences in Islam were borrowed from India and Iran. In fact, the former were encouraged in order to combat the latter, but once rationalism began to gain the upper hand, the intelligentsia of the Islamic establishment split among themselves, with the conservatives claiming that a rationalism which is not subordinated to religious belief was itself as dangerous a heresy as the irrational beliefs of the *Batiniyya* or the *Zanadiqa*. This deplorable division forced al-Ghazali to call for a balance and a harmony between reason and faith, rather than insist on the clear separation of the spheres of application of the two.

Mahmud is centrally concerned with political freedom, to which he refers the freedom to change as well as the freedom from tyanny. Mahmud also makes the briefest of references to economic freedom and to the liberation of women, but he does not elaborate. Individual political freedom is opposed to Sultanism, and collective freedom is opposed to imperialism. But the freedom to change must be contrasted with the constraint of nature, the absolute limits of means-end rationality, and the religious definition of ends. The situation is further complicated by the fact that, for Mahmud, the sphere of choice is essentially nonrational: religion, art, and identity; while the sphere of constraint is rational and experiential.

Though the second, and larger, section of the book is influenced by a more or less consistent theme, it ranges over such topics as a critique of language in Arab culture, a proposal for an Arab philosophy, a celebration of the importance of reason in Arab culture, and, finally, an argument which establishes the primacy of "human" values over rational values in Arab Islam. The most surprising elements in this part of the book are the insistence that the turath is culturally and philosophically dualistic, and the remarkably severe attack on expressive styles in contemporary Arabic usage.

As we have seen, Mahmud's own ambivalence regarding the value of the turath is expressed by means of his dualist analysis, but, in the second part of the book, Mahmud is less concerned with separating the good from the bad in the turath than he is in separating the turath from instrumental rationality. But even in this he is inconsistent, concluding eventually that reason and technology must serve consciousness and religious identity.

Despite these inconsistencies, the major theme of this more affirmative section remains the initial theme of freedom. Mahmud returns from time to time to the matter of political freedom and the absence thereof in contemporary Egypt, but he is primarily concerned with the freedom to reinterpret the turath, and to define one's cultural identity for one's self. He is, consequently, at pains to insist on the irrelevance of the apologetic argument which finds the concept freedom in the turath, and draws the conclusion that the historical notion of freedom in Arab culture is the same as the contemporary liberal political understanding thereof.[21]

Mahmud denies apologist argument about freedom in Turath

The freedom of self-definition is to be attained by means of philosophical enlightenment, so Mahmud's argument proceeds at two levels. At one level Mahmud is, by turns, critical and laudatory of the Islamic-Arab turath, at the second level, Mahmud presents his own metaphysical dualism, distinguishing between fact and logical postulate, between object and subject, between world and self, between technology and art, between action and thought, between science and ethics, between things and words, between reality and imagination, between constraint and freedom, and between modernity and authenticity.

For Mahmud, fact is constraining, but one is otherwise free to adopt or discard beliefs, religious ideas, values, or even metaphysical postulates. Above all, freedom is related to the realm of art and expression. But if the two are confused, if one comes to believe that faith or religion determines factual reality, the result can be disastrous. It is also important to understand that the world of factual reality is always changing, hence it is not so important to focus on the beginning and end, the salient themes in medieval religious philosophy, as on the process itself. The world appears fixed and unchangeable only to those who draw the wrong conclusions from the conception of divine creation and omnipotence. Hence that world of factual reality which is constraining, which grants no freedom, is also a world of constant change to which man must adapt or be lost.[22] Furthermore, the Marxists who claim that changing material conditions will bring about a concomitant cultural and ideological change are wrong. In fact, intellectual change is not automatic or inevitable; it is voluntary.[23] Technical and scientific change start with epistemological change. The realms of freedom and of constraint are conjoined by a philosophy based upon the recognition of the difference between the two, and, consequently, the manner of their interdependence. Learning how to push the buttons on a machine is not becoming truly modern.

In Mahmud's exposition, modernity and tradition are made to correspond to the duality of practice and theory, and to the logical duality of synthetic and analytic statements. These two logical forms are then linked to characteristic forms of speech: speech referring to existing things in the world, and speech which is both general and abstract. Speech is related to language, language to thought, and thought to experience. Traditional Arabic speech, reflecting the fact that the language of culture is not the language of everyday affairs, is theoretical, analytical, general, abstract, subjective, fanciful, complex, artificial, and nonpurposive.

This attack on the Arabic language of culture is particularly severe, and significant because Mahmud asserts that the Arabic language is the *essence* of the turath.[24] He emphasizes the fact, long noted by orientalists and Muslims alike, that the Arabic language is the language of revelation, that qur'anic rhetoric is thought to be miraculous, that the language is considered to be so unique that expression is an end in itself.[25]

Arabs and Muslims must realize, according to Mahmud, that they are in a period of transition—transition from tradition to modernity. They must either leave tradition and the turath behind or continue to live in the past. To make this transition successfully, the Arabs must change their language from one of consummatory enjoyment to one of practicality and usefulness. Tradition is merely expressive; modernity is productive.

Arab Culture as a Regional Culture

Mahmud recognizes the existence of what he calls regional culture, wherein the cultural identity of a particular community is expressed in their dominant philosophy. Without specific reference to his own philosophical inclinations, Mahmud illustrates this idea by describing French thought as Cartesian, British thought as empiricist, and American thought as pragmatist, almost as if these were matters of style rather than of substance.[26] In a similar sense, there is an Arab philosophical style, which he characterizes as dualist, based on the distinction between self and other and especially between man and the complete otherness of God. Mahmud asserts that the relationship of the Arab to the world is governed by language rather than experience. In fact Arab intellectuals prefer verbal signs, or the world of words, to the actual world, or the world of things.[27] The Arab looks upon the world in a detached, instrumental, way, but he is emotionally involved with language, relishing the "taste" of its expressions as though they were food or drink.[28] The Arab would rather read a poetic description of a beautiful garden than see the garden itself.

From this reference to taste, Mahmud moves on to contrast Islamic art with that of ancient Greece, India, or Egypt. Islamic art is geometrical (*handasi*), as we see in the complex design of the arabesque or the structure of the *qasida*. This design expresses the Islamic view of the world as a complex and infinite ordering of an integrated whole which continuously returns and repeats itself. As a consequence, the world is conceived of as governed by lawlike arrangements which fix its component parts in eternal relationships. Change is accidental, a momentary aberration.[29]

Mahmud insists that the core problem is linguistic, in the sense that the reservation of language for the expression of the beautiful prevents its practical use in adapting to mundane change. On the other hand, the geometric and architectural aspects of Arabic thought lend themselves well to the task of resolving the ubiquitous modern contradiction between man and the world, between "regional" cultural authenticity and the civilization of modern science, technology, and industry.

Mahmud's ambivalence toward Arab-Islamic culture emerges more clearly now, and it becomes clearer yet when he goes on to argue that the Arabs have made some progress in modernization, primarily in the field of literature—but not in the field of philosophy. Even in literature, the greatest achievements of the Arab tradition are not to be found in genres built around individual experience, such as plays and novels. And as for philosophy, well, Arab philosophers are for the most part teachers of the history of Western philosophy, and they do so in a manner detached from the realities of Arab life. This brings Mahmud to his tentative proposal of a modern Arab philosophy, a "regional" philosophy, reflecting Arab authenticity while providing for a synthesis with modernity.

In proposing an Arab philosophy for the modern age, Mahmud claims to draw upon the essential principles of Arab culture as revealed in the turath. While he takes intellectual responsibility for his own proposal, it is nevertheless proposed as an interpretation of something which already exists.

Arab thought, writes Mahmud, is based on the duality of matter and spirit; but spirit is the more important of the two.[30] Hence, Arab thought rejects the views of the materialists, the idealists, and the pantheists, along with those dualists who make no distinction between matter and spirit. Nor does Arab thought assume the Platonic dismissal of individuals as lacking true being. Mahmud would rather divide the universe of agents into absolute (God) and contingent individuals, and then further divide contingent individuals into those governed by freedom of the will (human beings) and others. Hence man, though a contingent being, is morally free, and not completely subject to scientific prediction. Concomitantly, Arab ethics are founded upon the concepts of duty and absolute value rather than upon interest and utility. This ontic structure is further reflected in the Arab conception of beauty, which is based upon the pursuit of rational, geometric forms in all the arts—a perspective which sees the world as an eternal, infinite, complex, order.[31] Arab culture, as expressed in its art, begins with the observed and the experienced, but leads on to that which is only understood intellectually. It goes from nature to metaphysics, and this movement from the seen to the unseen, from the sensed to the intellectual is, in Mahmud's opinion, the essence of the Arab spirit.[32]

No other culture, writes Mahmud, makes so sharp a distinction between the here and now, and the infinite.[33] And this distinction calls forth the well-worn methodological controversy between idealists and empiricists, to which Mahmud replies in Kantian candor, "Why not pursue two intellectual methods, depending upon the matter in question?" The controversy is itself the result of an error that arises from the attempt to impose the methods of pure reason on the problems of practical reason.[34] But this separation of the spheres of matter and spirit fails to sustain the argument for the superiority of spirit.

This proposed Arab philosophy will bring great benefits to the Arabs because it will allow them access to the rewards of Western technological and scientific progress, without the loss of their absolute values, and without cutting them off from a kind of knowledge which permits of adaptation to changing conditions. Mahmud explicitly denies that he intends any sort of relativism by his insistence on the principles of human freedom and moral responsibility, because those principles are absolute despite changing historical circumstances. Mahmud concludes with a dubious observation, "Whether or not I have erred in this proposal, I am convinced that the present contradiction between science and human values is not a necessary one."[35]

Mahmud now turns to the matter of art and its relationships to nature. Here he drops the notion of the arabesque and the essentially intellectual character of Arab aesthetics. He rather sets nature against art, referring to the former as the realm of necessity and to the latter as the realm of freedom. In order to achieve a renaissance of Arab culture the Arabs must adopt a second dualism in addition to that of matter and spirit, and that is the duality of science and freedom, the dualism of objective necessity and the freedom to express one's identity as one wishes.[36] To realize this duality, the Arabs must cease to concentrate upon external form alone, while ignoring content. The Arabs, writes Mahmud, take appearance for reality, and this leads them to tolerate tyranny and immorality when they have only the appearance of legitimacy and piety.[37]

In the very next section Mahmud argues that rationality is the essence of Arab thought, even in its poetry and art. Sufism and similar irrational excesses are aberrations, and not characteristic of the Arab spirit.[38] Beginning with Aristotle's aesthetics, he explains that the idea that art copies nature is not to be taken literally, but functionally. Hence, the upholding of traditional values is not to be achieved by a slavish copying of the practices of the past, but by means of a creative adaptation. A good example of this, he states, is the way in which John Dewey did for his generation what Aristotle did for his own![39] Presumably, Mahmud will perform a similar function for the Arab regional culture in his own day.

There are, writes Mahmud, three types of cognition: rational, sensual, and speculative.[40] The rational, which the Greeks defined, and which the Arabs adopted more readily than other ancient peoples, has been defined in pragmatic terms. The sensual is nontheoretical empiricism. The conjectural is, however, identified with mysticism and the irrational rather than with philosophical contemplation in the classic sense. Thus, speculative consciousness is characteristic of the thought of women and children, who act whimsically, without thought of the consequences, but such a consciousness can become widespread among a people (literally "the men" = *al-nas*) during times of weakness and defeat, as has been the case with the Arabs during the last three hundred years.[41]

But having thus, obliquely, attacked contemporary Arab culture as irrational, defeatist, effeminate, and childish, and having identified it with the philosophy of Bergson rather than Dewey, he swings back again to the praise of Arab culture.[42] Arab culture is expressed in poetry above all, hence the Arabs excel in speculative and imaginative consciousness, but they balance reason and speculation without subordinating one to the other. The Arabic language is, in fact, well-suited to the expression of both reason and consciousness, while Arabic poetry differs from other poetry in that it is more intellectual, more rational, and has objective, worldly aims.[43] It is difficult to make complete sense out of these inconsistencies, but the answer may lie in Mahmud's attempt to differentiate between the turath as abstract culture and the turath as the majority of Muslims understand and practice it.

In the concluding section, Mahmud takes up the notion of Islamic humanism and, in typical fashion, sets his discussions within the framework of the philosophical dichotomy between man and nature. The unifying conception that Mahmud employs in his last two essays, is that of Islamic moral responsibility expressed in both the obligation of obedience to the Shariᶜa, and the obligation to serve the collective interests of the Islamic community. This conception is explicated by Islamicizing the principle that reason is always practical.[44]

Though Mahmud has already criticized the anachronistic conflation of concepts that sound similar when taken out of context, he is ready to do so himself if the contemporary meaning is imposed upon the traditional usage. So Mahmud cites the medieval *falasifa* who "always" linked reason, not only with wisdom and justice, but with purposive action. Mahmud compares the views of Bentham and Mill with those of Abu Bakr Muhammad ibn Zakariyya al-Razi, who is cited as saying that the reason why the intellect should dominate the passions is because it is more conducive to useful benefits (*al-manafiᶜa*).[45]

Mahmud contrasts the Western and Arab approaches to the relationship of man and nature in a manner that raises many questions about his purpose and his method. The idea of a communally based philosophy is not explicitly contrasted with the idea of universal reason, but we already know that Mahmud would resolve such problems by means of an appropriate or a convenient dualism. Hence, when Mahmud contrasts the Western and the Arab views of "man and nature," he states that the Western view is dominated by concern with the relationship between the knower and the known, but the

Arab is concerned with the morality of human, purposive, action in the world. The Western philosophical problematic is epistemological, while the Arab problematic is ethical. Naturally, Mahmud is going to work toward some sort of synthesis of the two as a remedy for the Arab predicament.

Mahmud now defines the role of the philosopher[46] as that of working out the systematic order and unity of all of the disparate elements in divine revelation, thereby expressing the unity of Islam, which, of course, reflects the unity of God, which in turn is manifested in the integrative Islamic conception that requires man to subordinate his will to God's. Islamic ethics govern the social action of man, and this action must complement true belief and a good conscience. The West may be concerned with a passive knowing, but the Arab is commanded to act and to serve his community. Mahmud returns again and again to this distinction, finally drawing the conclusion that the resolution of this contradiction does not lie in some Islamic dualism, but rather in the complementary relationship of the West and the Arab East.

In the final pages of his book, Mahmud seems to abandon his concern with a universal humanistic rationality altogether. Arab culture, he writes, is mainly characterized by poetry and the arts, and the main feature of Arab aesthetics is its identification with nature![47] But which nature? The nature of constraint, or the nature of imagination and conjecture? Mahmud tells us that western culture would turn man into mere nature, but the Arab would turn nature into a living thing with which they would interact. The only Western philosophy which has any affinity for Arab thought is that of Bergson, or a form of religious existentialism that "insists that man must be active, free, and responsible for his acts, and that no human being should disregard any other in any way in pursuing his responsible actions."[48] Mahmud then proceeds to complete the statement of this pragmatic reinterpretation of Arab-Islamic culture by referring to the epistemological views of the sage who is most admired by contemporary fundamentalists. Ibn Taiymiyya held the view that man cannot know God's "quiddity" or essence. The only way to know God is via His will, as expressed by the prophets. Man must obey God's will, and through such obedience is there created a community, an umma. Such an *umma* is characterized not only by geography, culture, history, or language, but, according to Ibn Taiymiyya, by means of their cooperation in common action in which each transcends himself and opens himself to the others.[49] Indeed, man may not know the quiddity of the things of this world, or "things in themselves," but he can create valid truths by means of will and common action.

Mahmud, for all his references to the Aristotelian tradition, and for all his commitment to Western industrial modernity, calls upon the Arabs to make themselves in the modern age by an act of will which is founded on the truth of a liberated artistic conception of the turath rather than on the alienating truth of universal reason.

Tarif Khalidi's Analysis of Turath Literature

Professor Tarif Khalidi, an historian at American University, Beirut, has attempted a survey of various contemporary approaches to the interpretation of the turath, which for him is the Islamic element in Arab national culture and history.[50] Although he does not deny the accusation that he is a traditionalist and an orthodox Muslim himself, his own position is stated in terms that are academic, intellectual, and political. He writes, for example:

> Insofar as Arab-Islamic thought is concerned, the glorious Qur'an is the absolute. And it behooves us to revise its commentaries in each age in the light of innovations in the literary, linguistic, psychological, philosophical, historical, and sociological theories—for we should understand the Qur'an from within the context of science, rather than understanding science from the context of the glorious Qur'an.[51]

Khalidi's inquiry was inspired by the problem of whether the failure to redefine the turath is the root cause of the lack of development. To further this inquiry Khalidi has surveyed some twenty books dealing with the turath, and he gives us a very brief statement of the summary conclusions of his survey. He tells us that there is a profusion of diverse assessments of the turath, of what is to be preserved and what is still useful. So many different points of view have been presented that the intelligent public is confused. Khalidi laments the passing of a time when the size of the reading public, the number of publicists, and the range of intellectual approaches was so much more restricted that it might be said that the whole intelligentsia of the Arab world was engaged in a single debate.

Having thus established his problematic, Khalidi turns our attention to the issue of classifying the diverse approaches to the turath, with the presumed purpose being the simplification and clarification of the choices, so that the Arab public may decide upon the path it should follow. The merely academic discussion of the turath is a luxury which can no longer be afforded, and one which will no longer be tolerated.

The proposed classification system is itself a rhetorical structure, which should convince the reader of the correctness of the author's preference. Khalidi proposes three classification schemes. The first reflects the three political problems which emerged clearly after the disastrous war of 1967, and gave rise to three ideological groups: the traditionalists, the nationalists, and the Marxists. The events of 1967 gave none of these an advantage over the others, so comprehensive was the disaster.

Second, Khalidi noted with some measure of approval Abdallah Laroui's classification of Arab theorists into three groups: the traditionalists, the eclectics, and the historicalists. The first two groups are roughly identifiable with the interests of the feudalists and the bourgeoisie. The historicalists are not explicitly identified with the interests of the proletariat, but the classification scheme is obviously Marxist in orientation.

Khalidi's own classification scheme employs only two categories, the historicalists and the nonhistoricalists, and it is noteworthy that he does not discuss the traditionalists or specify in what way his notion of history differs from the position of the Marxists. His explicit criticism is directed rather at the nonhistoricalists (very similar to Laroui's eclectics) who reject the specifics of the Islamic heritage, while preferring the general method of Islamic thought, or who selectively discover in the Islamic heritage only evidence of such essences as rationality, progress, freedom, authenticity, and the proletarian spirit.

The circumstantial evidence leads to the conclusion that Khalidi would seek some synthesis of the Marxian position and the traditional orthodoxy, which he identified with the turath. Khalidi explictly states that he not only prefers the historical approach, but that he accepts the Hegelian-Marxist approach to history as essentially a dialectical process. Thus Islamic, or Arab, history is to be studied to overcome and surpass that history. The historical turath is to serve as thesis over against the antithesis of Western culture, and the synthesis will be of universal character.

The conclusion is more Hegelian than Marxian, but Khalidi commits no great distortion of the position of those with whom he identifies. In fact, he gets to the point much more directly than does Abdallah Laroui, with whom he most agrees. But Khalidi stops abruptly short of drawing any practical conclusions from his analysis. He argues that the historicalist position (which is not an historicist position) requires that Arab scholars first undertake the meticulous study of a great many modestly defined problems, especially social and economic problems, that have not yet been dealt with. Only through such work can a modern-day Ibn Khaldun be produced. In more general terms, Khalidi argues that the historical approach identified with the model of Ibn Khaldun's work eschews idealist synthesis, and takes due account of the objective differences among Arab states, and among the variety of historical conditions that have prevailed during different periods.

The selection of Ibn Khaldun as the example to be followed directs attention to the intellectual heritage of the Islamic-Arab people rather than to a particular period of development and expansion. Ibn Khaldun's political thought provided for the legitimation of regimes which fell short of the Islamic ideal. His historical analyses tended to bring the understanding of politics out of the theological clouds and down to earth. He inspired no revolution, but may have helped some rulers to accommodate themselves to the harsh realities of the times.

Muslim historiographical thought was influenced to some extent by the perspective of the Old Testament, but the classic historians are far from the view that history is the narrative of *gesta dei per Musulmanos*. Khalidi argues that the origins of Muslim historiography are to be found in the desire to explain the connections between the Muslims and their predecessors, and the relationship between Islam and the world.[52] A second source of historiographical effort was in the desire to clarify the obscure and confused ideological situation prevailing during Islam's earliest period. The third contribution is the result of the more fixed and differentiated ideological position that emerged in the fourth Islamic century, which gave us the beginnings of Shiʿite and Muʿtazilite history. The Shiʿites, in their search for factual historical proofs of their doctrine of the imamate contributed to the development of empirical method. The Muʿtazila, because of their rationalistic theology, contributed to the development of reasoned explanation. Khalidi believes that the turath presents to Muslims examples of a tradition of critical historical writing which transcends the merely ideological and the sectarian concerns of the heresiologists. The reinvigoration of this tradition will contribute toward an Arab-Islamic renaissance. It will permit a dialogue with history as called for by the ontological-hermeneuticists, and a dialectical confrontation with Western historiography.

Khalidi's concluding strictures against the ideological temptations to generalize, to construct a univocal conception of the Arab-Islamic turath, and to propose a singular political solution to the institutional problems of contemporary Arab states, may be contrasted with the position of Abdallah Laroui. Laroui does not envision a renaissance as the result of the slow accumulation of scholarship culminating in the emergence of a second Ibn Khaldun. He rather emphasizes the importance of certain processes of restratification, or restructuring, which have led to the emergence of a new "national state" in some countries. The affect of these processes is to be experienced in all of the Arab states, and the cultural renaissance which is to respond dialectically to the presently dominant Western culture, can arise only as the result of the liberation of intellectual activity from domination by the apparatus of the state.

The difference between the two seems at first to be substantial, but it may be argued that the kind of intellectual renaissance which Khalidi would like to see can only occur in the kind of state which Laroui would like to see. It is also instructive to note that both Khalidi and Laroui define an Arab-Islamic cultural renaissance in terms of a synthesis with Western culture rather than in terms of a purging of Western cultural influences.

Abdallah Laroui

Abdallah Laroui, historian, professor at the University of Rabat, and one of the best-known Moroccan intellectuals, has been deeply influenced by European intellectual trends. Laroui is a cultural and philosophical hybrid, capable of interpreting Europe to the Muslim world and Muslim culture to Europe. His reading of the Western literature on Islam, and on political development, the two components of "contemporary orientalism," is both subtle and penetrating. His critique of orientalism, in all probability, influenced Edward Said's work.[53] Though he is vaguely *marxisant,* and shows the growing, if limited, influence of Althusserian scholasticism, Laroui is an eclectic—a superb dialectician, whose rhetoric includes both phenomenological and pragmatic tropes.

In one of his essays, Laroui argues that Islamic historiography is dominated by the idea of a period in which Allah was close to the Muslims.[54] That closeness no longer obtains. The task of Muslims is to restore that period—to close the gap between themselves and Allah. They have been trying hard for some time, and, it may be argued, they have begun to succeed in recent years. Whatever success may have been realized is not so much the result of the advance of historical research as of either renewed piety or of windfall material gains. However this may be, Laroui does not think that the renewal of the Muslim historiographic tradition is as important in the short run as is the need for a confrontation with Western prejudices.

There is a point of view which holds that a meaningful dialogue with history is culturally impossible or unlikely for Muslims because of the defects of their historical consciousness as evidenced in Muslim historiography. Indeed, Khalidi's work is largely an effort to refute this argument. Nevertheless, despite the admittedly remarkable achievements of traditional historians, the Western assessment remains that Muslim history writing is insufficiently critical, insufficiently objective, insufficiently comparative, and insufficiently synthetic. The views of Gibb, von Grunebaum, Zurayk, and many others may be cited in support of this perspective.[55] Of course, the hermeneuticists are not very satisfied with Western historiography either, insofar as it is positivistic, social scientific, empathetic, or "antiquarian" in the Nietzcheian sense.

But if a dialogue with the texts of the turath is unlikely to occur, a reasonable equivalent may be found in a dialogue with the critical and unsympathetic Western histories of Islam. Abdallah Laroui, in an admirably ambivalent treatment of the work of Gustave von Grunebaum, calls for precisely such a dialectical confrontation with the clearly unsympathetic work of that late and great scholar.[56]

Laroui genuinely admires von Grunebaum's intellect, but he is, if anything, even more impressed by his culture, and his remarkable career. Von Grunebaum's antipathy for Islam is duly noted, and some illustrative evidence is footnoted, but Laroui eschews the outrage of the unmasker of imperialist scribbling. After an extremely perceptive and intelligent exposition of the academic influences on von Grunebaum, he makes two telling but gentle points against von Grunebaum's scholarly monuments. He shows that von Grunebaum's Islam is an a priori singularity, and that it is unhistorical. But he does not wish to see the writing of a dozen tiresome treatises that will prove that Islam was not always, and in every way, inferior to Greek culture and its Western heirs. The only way to refute von Grunebaum is to show him (by actual deeds) to be incorrect in the historical present.[57] This will not only prove that von Grunebaum did not properly interpret the essence of Islamic culture, but it will also divert the energies of Muslims from the fruitless task of justifying the past.

Laroui rejects von Grunebaum's characterization of the essence of Islam as decadence, even though he appears to be willing to accept the hermeneutical consequences of that Gustavian suggestion. There is some evidence that Laroui is in general agreement with von Grunebaum's argument that the vitality of European culture is related to its curiosity about other cultures, and the critical self-knowledge which is the result of studying the other. In a truly brilliant little essay, reflecting wide critical reading in American development literature—but an essay which is curiously appended to a long rambling and obscure critique of the Arab intelligentsia—Laroui writes:

> One could maintain that an hermeneutic tending to relativize Western culture is an indirect result of the infringement of extra-European cultures on the consciousness of Europe. But as yet,

> apart from circumstantial writing, we can accredit to no great name of the extra-European world any radical critique of the fundamental European ideology: rationalism applied to nature, man, and history.[58]

Europe, he argues, is in the throes of a profound philosophical and ideological reevaluation of itself which "will have been the result of a non-European reflection of Europe, but it will be a self-enrichment, not an about-face of perspective."[59]

Laroui calls upon the Muslim intellectual to struggle against the pernicious influence of fundamentalist traditionalism by embracing what he calls the historicist Marx. But he is almost apologetic, and he is certainly obfuscatory, about his definition of historicism, and about the remainder of Marx which lies beyond historicism. Laroui concludes by vindicating particularism as a necessary and preliminary stage before the Third World can adopt the rationally scientific universalism of the Marx of Althusser. Laroui appears to regret the fact that he is unable to accept the then trendy, but highly abstruse, Marxism of the French philosopher, but he does not fail to identify him with the Cartesian, Kantian, mainstream of rational bourgeois thought.[60] We are, consequently, led to the conclusion that Laroui's exhortations of Muslim intellectuals to historicism and to Marxism are not two, but a single summons to the early humanist Marx—the Marx concerned with the particularisms of the German condition. Only when they have similarly demystified the ideology of retardation can they go on to the universal scientific rationality which Althusser finds in *Das Kapital*.

The title of Laroui's major philosophical work invokes comparison with Marx's *The German Ideology,* and the relevant references in Laroui's later essays might lead one to expect an unmasking of Islamic or even nationalist idealism based upon a trenchant critique of class structure in Muslim countries.[61] Nothing of the sort. Laroui's problem is modernization, and he believes that there is only one possible form of modernity, and that is exemplified by the modern liberal state and by the rational scientism of the late Marx. The difficulty for Muslims, or rather Arabs, is that modernity, even if it is a universal human destiny, is existentially Western. It represents alterity and not authenticity. His problem is, how do we get "there" from "here" without giving up our identity.

Laroui proceeds by means of what he calls a dialectical method. He successively rejects an authenticity which is equated with rigid tradition or with a romantic glorification of history, and an alterity which is rather loosely defined as an unsympathetic positivism. These two alternatives are found wanting both with regard to the search for authenticity (identity) and the search for continuity (history). The third moment is the search for universality, and here positive social science is rejected as alien, as is rigorous or positivistic Marxism. Neither accord with the need for authenticity, although both accord with the desired goal of modernity. The trouble is that they cannot serve as an interim ideology. A loose or vulgarized set of Marxian ideas, which he calls objective Marxism, is acceptable insofar as it may be adapted to the pre-modern condition of Muslim societies, and insofar as it is critical of the West. But the real solution is identical to the method that Laroui himself has employed, in contradistinction to logical analysis, and that is dialectic. The structure of the dialectic, is, of course, the juxtaposition in tension of authenticity and alterity, or us and them; it is "the ideological utilization of the dialectic which has the mission of facilitating the definitive passage from the traditional me to the non-me."[62]

The turath is the guide to self-understanding for most of those who are concerned with Arab or Muslim identity or authenticity. There is, however, an important difference in the range of connotation between the notions of identity and authenticity. Identity has an important psychological referrent, which is often expressed in a discourse of tautologous subjectivity. Erikson and other members of the psychocultural school have linked identity to socially defined roles, gender, rites of passage, and the cultural self-definition of the community. A group of European *marxisants* who have been influenced by psychoanalytic theory, including such luminaries as Sartre, Merleau-Ponty, and Habermas, have emphasized the emancipatory significance of freeing the ego from various kinds of identity which are imposed upon it by culture, or prejudice, or ideology, or power. Foucault dwelt upon the same issue, but from the other point of view, that is, the way in which discourse imposes an identity which impedes emancipation.

It is at this point that identity and authenticity converge in the debate over whether an historically determined authenticity is emancipatory or enslaving. The Heideggerian position substitutes authenticity and inauthenticity (or alterity) for the freedom or bondage of Hegel's dialectic of the master and slave. Authenticity thus stands for the freedom to be what one, in some sense, already *is*, while identity may also be referred to the freedom to be what one wants to be. Authenticity is to accept, or even embrace, a fate, and it is linked to a self-knowledge which is derived from an "archaeological" investigation of cultural and historical origins. Identity may also mean the negation of one's past, overcoming the particularities of kinship, culture, community, and even personal experience. For many, this kind of freedom is unnatural, frightening, grotesque, socially destructive, and politically suicidal. For others, its meaning is expressed in the hopeful slogan, "today is the first day of the rest of my life."

It is not surprising that *marxisant* theorists should be critical of the concept authenticity, given their commitment to revolutionary change, historical transformation, and the substructural determination of ideology and culture. There is probably no more thorough, intemperate, long-winded, and scathing castigation of Heideggerian authenticity than that of Theodor Adorno, who pronounces it a sinister mystification serving as a bulwark of the ideological hegemony of the dominant classes.[63] Authenticity refers to that which does not change; and even if one argues that it always entails adaptation to the contemporary situation, it must pose a dilemma for those in the Third World whose consciousness has already been affected by European culture, and who are strongly committed to both national independence and economic development.

In his analysis of the issue of Arab authenticity, Laroui tries to shift the focus of attention from Heideggerian authenticity to the emancipation of the Arab identity. His Marxism is sustained in the form of historicism rather than in a concern with class struggle, or the social determination of ideology. His pragmatism is obscured by the discursive forms he employs, but his understanding of the dialectical method, the dynamic definition of authenticity, and the historical process, allow him to loosen the connection between authenticity and the tradition. At the same time, he conceives of the future as conforming to some preordained pattern to which the evolution of Arab identity must be adapted. He seems to believe that it is essentially possible to understand the present, that is, to acquire valid social knowledge, by means of a form of critical and dialectical analysis that eschews the pitfalls of various forms of "positivistic" dogmatism, including religious dogmatism, Marxist dogmatism, behaviorism, empiricism, and a number of uses and abuses of history.

He also believes that one can define the future "ideologically," by which he means intellectually or morally, in a manner that is essentially undetermined by social and historical conditions. The future must be among the logical possibilities of the present, but the concept of the future liberates one from the "positivities" of the present. That concept is transformed into an emancipatory principle in Laroui's reification of the grammatical category of the future perfect—a linguistic form which evidences man's ability to conceive of things being different in the future from what they are now.[64] But even if the future can be grasped as an idea, it cannot be approached by the direct methods of the positivist and objectivist planners and technocrats. The future, which is already an historical potentiality, can only be approached dialectically.

The vision of the future realization of Arab authenticity revealed by Laroui, has both pessimistic and optimistic moments. The bad news is that, for Laroui, it is no longer possible to realize a pure Arab authenticity. The Arab identity has been so tied to that of Europe that it is no longer possible to engage in a cultural monologue. There can be no Arab self-understanding which is not also an understanding of the European other, and it is gradually becoming clear to the European intelligentsia that the same is true for them. Hence, the good news is that Arab authenticity can and will be realized in a transcendant universalism to which they will contribute at the two levels of defining the goal and participating in its substantive realization.

This appears to be a liberal and idealist doctrine that accords with the general character of bourgeois ideology and, hence, falls well within the range of the superstructural prerequisites of the liberal bourgeois state. In the context of Moroccan politics, its implications are clear. But it stands in theoretical contradiction to the many Marxian allusions by which Laroui suggests the substrate of his conception of an historical eschatology. The realization of Arab authenticity-within-universalism will, of course, be conditioned by the socioeconomic situation, even if the concept is not determined by those not-yet-extant conditions. Hence the goal of authenticity is linked to—perhaps even conflated with—the Marxian utopia. The bourgeois state can only be a transitional arrangement, to be surpassed in the course of the historical dialectic.

Laroui's ambivalence toward the bourgeois state and bourgeois culture results from the double function he wishes it to perform. On the one hand, the bourgeois state is the necessary vehicle for participation in the world historical process, but on the other, it must serve as the setting for the rejection of Western culture, and the realization of Arab authenticity. Laroui differentiates among the colonial state, the liberal state, and the national state. The national state struggles against imperialist exploitation without fully overcoming it, while the liberal state accepts its exploitation with fatalistic defeatism.[65] The national state is only imperfectly understood in terms of its class structure, or even in terms of "its intermediary position between the liberal capitalist state and the planned socialist state."

> . . . it is a state in the process of embourgeoisement, with all of the social and cultural characteristics which that implies, but under the direction of a social fraction other than the bourgeoi-

> sie. . . .[I]t is at the cultural level that the preceding definition seems most adequate. The national state imposes a bourgeois culture, rationalist, and universalizing, on a society which has not given birth to it by means of an endogenous development. The embourgeoisement is general, rapid and more immediate there, compared to that of the liberal state [where it is] slow and fragmentary.[66]

The national state is also inauthentic in that it represents Western experience and history. Nevertheless, it will perform the function of integrating the world-historical experience of the bourgeois state into the consciousness of Muslims. Western culture and politics are at once alien *and* bourgeois. The bourgeois experience is an essential component of world historical experience, and it has already conditioned the present predicament of the Arabs. As such, it is an essential historical prerequisite of the eventual realization of socialism (or some Hegelian alternative). Socialism, in its complete form, will produce a universal order and a universal culture. But if the Arab-Muslim people have not participated in the historical experience of the bourgeois era, they will be but passive beneficiaries of the transition to universalism. It is even possible that the exclusion of the Arabs, Muslims, and other Third World peoples from the historical process will distort the process itself.

In the light of Laroui's cultural analysis, this formulation of the sociopolitical character of the national state is somewhat misleading. The description of the national state invokes the Marxist problematic of the transition to socialism and the necessity of passing through a capitalist stage. There the question is whether this sort of transitional state is actually preparing the way for a more complete bourgeois domination, as in the paradigm case of the government of Louis Bonaparte, or whether it is possible to find a noncapitalist path to development. The cultural emphasis, when combined with Laroui's description of the function of the national state as *embourgeoisement,* suggests that he is going to explain how the national state and its petit bourgeois apparatus employs certain ideological structures in order to further the interests of a nondominant bourgeoisie. Laroui appears to be arguing that the national state serves as a functional equivalent for the bourgeois state.

In fact, Laroui does not argue that the national state performs a necessary historical function. Nor does he argue that it is a benign, humane, authentic, and liberal form of government. It is rather a setting in which the alien *techné* of the West, the *non-moi,* stands in contradiction with the Arab self. More precisely, it is the arena in which the aspiration for a modern, centralized, industrial economy, confronts the aspiration for an authentic self-understanding. The national state poses the challenge, but since it struggles to realize its independence of the West, it comprehends the potentiality of self-transcendance.

It is important, however, to remember that this transcendance is not defined in socioeconomic terms, but in cultural terms. In fact, Laroui questions the validity of the Western discourse on class structure in its application to societies which did not produce that discourse originally.[67] Marxism applies to Europe, but not to the Arab world. Hence, Laroui argues that there is a danger that the process of embourgeoisement will determine the culture of the Arab countries, but it is not a foregone conclusion. Embourgeoisement does not necessarily lead to the dominance of bourgeois culture and ideology; it leads to industrialization, to bureaucratization, to technocracy, and to rationalization. The economic policy goals of the national state are never in doubt. What is in doubt, however, is the question of Arab authenticity.

The various forms of positivism, that is, intellectual methods which employ fixed and immutable definitions of their objects, all pose dangers in the form of limitations to the possible future development of Arab authenticity. It is the task of the Arab intelligentsia to combat those ideological forms of false consciousness which sustain, not the domination of the bourgeoisie, but the technocratic and positivistic mentality of the dominant elites of the national state.

It is, of course, possible to read this argument in terms of a potential conflict between the emergent bourgeoisie and a hegemonic, Bonapartist, bureaucracy (read: apparatus of the state). For the time being, it is obvious that the bourgeoisie is unable to stand alone even in Egypt, let alone Morocco or Iran, but the Egyptian *infitah* is an indication that the national state is, indeed, an arena of conflict, and one in which the bourgeoisie has greatly benefited from the reassertion of Islamic-Arab identity.

Laroui opines that the conflict between Hasan II, the Moroccan king, and the bourgeoisie as represented by the Istiqlal and other parties, was politically gratuitous in that they both represent the same social forces.[68] It is possible though, that, as in Iran, the monarchy masks the extent to which the apparatus of the state has already gained dominance, and has limited the influence of the bourgeoisie.

The doctrine of the relative autonomy of the state suggests that the bourgeoisie always depends upon the apparatus of the state, and that the apparatus of the state must define its own function in nonclass terms if the capitalist state is to work, but Poulantzas also makes the point that there is a constant shifting of the balance within the "power bloc," and a continuous adaptation of the hegemonic pattern.[69] Following this form of theoretical discourse, the political function of the emphasis upon cultural expression during the transition to universalism, that is, during the dialectical process of discovering one's authenticity, becomes more intelligible.

The question of Arab authenticity is approached by Laroui as a question of method: the intellectual method by which the Arabs are to understand themselves. Having employed a vaguely construed Marxism to refute the ideological failings of the ʿalim, the liberal, and the technophile, Laroui admits that he might now be expected to elaborate on his earlier allusions.[70] Instead, Laroui argues that Marxism serves rather as a means of understanding the other, in this case, the West. Objective Marxism, as opposed to formal or positivistic Marxism, is ubiquitous among educated Muslims as a stereotypical understanding of the external relationships of Muslim society, but it does not reflect the lived realities of Muslims themselves.[71] Objective Marxism is merely an abstraction, a system for dealing with the world, but not an acceptable method for self-understanding. The limitation of objective Marxism is virtually the same as the limitations of positivism and empiricism. None of these allow for change, for development, for the ideological validity of the future perfect (i.e, the idea that the logical consequences of presently obtaining conditions have, already, the character of historical fact—of what will have been the case in the future).

In fact, no existing state form or substructural condition, can provide the material basis to guide Muslims to an authentic understanding of their being. The only foundation for such an understanding must be ideological, and is only possible insofar as ideology is given primacy over society.[72] The concept must precede its realization in the sense of the future perfect. This is the case for the Arabs because it must logically be the case if a true authenticity is to be realized, otherwise the solution offered would be inadequate to its intellectual objective, as Laroui might say.

Throughout his critique of the contemporary Arab ideology Laroui has rejected various interpretations of Arab authenticity because the methods employed were inadequate. In general, the inadequacy stemmed from the fact that the methods adopted could lead to only a fixed, non-dynamic, understanding. "It seems," writes Laroui, "that the preceding developments all lead to one and the same conclusion: discard all objective knowledge [*toutes connaissances objectives*] of Arab society."[73] This is now the attitude of the Arabs who anticipate a better future, and who reject the present which they hope will become their past. They do not want to be analyzed now. And Laroui asks, "Are we going to give the same answer?"

No. He does not. Laroui's answer is that there is only one method which may be employed: "The dialectic, and only the dialectic, can explain and surpass the persistent opposition between technocracy and the call for authenticity. The national state, by adopting it [the dialectic], can put an end to the duality of doing and understanding, it can continue to do and begin to understand itself."[74]

Moreover, the dialectic is not alien to the Islamic turath, it is rather to be found in the mystical tradition. This consequence of the ideological vicissitudes of medieval Islam renders the dialectic culturally accessible, and hence potentially authentic, but it also poses a problem in that the mystical involves a flight from reality. There is a danger that the adoption of the dialectical method of analysis will lead to the same result as in the past, especially since the contemporary problem is the same as the medieval problem: "The progressive unification of the me (tradition) and the non-me (occident)."[75]

Laroui offers no solution to this problem, except to suggest that the marginal position of Morocco, not yet a national state but capable of integrating the experience of other Arab states, may put it in a position to realize, in the dialectic, a fully adequate logic of Arab consciousness.

The dialectical method, which is preferred to any objective characterization of Arab authenticity, and the redefinition of the problem facing the national state (it is now the reconciliation of the me and the non-me and not the reconciliation of development and authenticity) point to Laroui's conclusion: "To recognize the universal is to become reconciled with oneself."[76] The West however, has hesitated to pursue the logic of its own thought, and has preferred a plurality of alterities to a single, universal, authenticity.

Laroui's concluding chapters, devoted to the question of how Arab authenticity is to be expressed, are a three-part essay on contemporary Arab literature. In the first part, Laroui establishes the distinction between art and folklore, defining folklore as at once narrowly parochial and inauthentic. Folklore has been fostered in the national state to serve the cultural inclinations of the bourgeois and petit bourgeois classes, representing a romanticized, distorted, and nostalgic view of traditional peasant and tribal customs. The more exotic and atypical, the more appeal one finds in folklore. Creative artistic work, by contrast, must include universal elements. Folklore is a manifestation of the backwardness of Arab society, while artistic expression is an attempt to compensate for that inferiority.[77]

This discussion sets the stage for Laroui's critique of Arabic belletristic literature; but it also provides him with yet another means of attacking the national state. The national state, whose function, we have seen, is to accelerate the embourgeoisement of Arab society, is responsible for promoting folklore at the expense of artistic creativity. It does so for political reasons because it vaguely senses the persistent bourgeois significance of the prevalent literary forms. But since the alternative folkloric form is itself a product of embourgeoisement, the petit bourgeois state and the petit bourgeois elites have contradicted themselves.

Laroui goes on to criticize the contemporary "expressive" (i.e., not folkloric) literature in the second part of this concluding section, but here, too, it is apparent that his central theme is the conflict between the bourgeois and the petit bourgeois impulses. This preoccupation is obscured by his orientation toward a vaguely conceived universalism of the future, and the frequent reference to the self-other problematic of authenticity. Nevertheless, the sort of authenticity which is folkloric, parochial, and autistic, is identified with the petit bourgeois mentality, petit bourgeois politics, and petit bourgeois art. The bourgeois cultural impulses are indirectly approved because, contrary to the petit bourgeois, they do not entail a rejection of the dialogue with the West.

In discussing what is wrong with contemporary Arab literature, Laroui analyzes two forms of criticism, the academic and the social or ideological. Academic criticism is dismissed as essentially formal. The works of Arab authors are compared to those of Western authors and the Arabs are found lacking in their mastery of the received artistic forms. These shortcomings are attributed to the single cause of the underdevelopment of Arab society. The inappropriateness of the forms themselves is almost never suggested. This criticism is rejected as uninteresting because it only restates the problem, and offers no solution. It does not tell us how literary expression can help, both to overcome underdevelopment and to attain self-understanding.

Laroui's discussion of ideological criticism is complex. He has divided modern Arab literature into three phases: a neoclassic phase, a sentimental and "romanesque" phase, and a realist phase. The first is personified, again, by Muhammad ʿAbduh and the naive optimism and empiricism of the cleric.[78] The second is identified artistically with Taha Husain and politically with Lutfi al-Sayyid, the liberals. The third is identified with the work and the petit bourgeois mentality of Najib Mahfuz. Mahfuz is, in turn, linked to the third of Laroui's inauthentic *hommes-fetiches:* "It is, in effect, Salama Musa which he describes under the name Adli Karim; the manager of the review, courageous and solitary, the 'guru' of the progressive youth."[79]

These three categories are in turn related to three types of criticism: bourgeois, petit bourgeois, and Marxist positivist, each of which contributed to the passing from one phase to the next to the present. Bourgeois criticism called for subjectivism, for freedom from classical rules. The *liberté anarchique* that was practiced as a result of this critique was justly identified as European and bourgeois, but Laroui urges us not to forget the positive role that the bourgeois writers played despite their historical "devaluation."[80] Petit bourgeois criticism of bourgeois literature found fault in its narcissism, its lack of concern for the rest of society, and its use of a language which is unintelligible to the masses. The petit bourgeois critics and writers called for realism, for the elaboration of the social and historical context, and for the use of spoken language. The Marxist (positivist) critique of petit bourgeois literature praised its realism, but found fault with its pessimism and its naturalism. Progressive literature should seek to portray the image of a popular hero, and to project hope.

Each of these three critical tendencies corresponds to a literary phase, and each is personified in one of the three ideological orientations united in the national state; the derivative type of inauthenticity which each represents corresponds to the inauthenticity of ʿAbduh, Lutfi al-Sayyid, and Salama Musa, or Shawqi, Taha Husain, and Mahfuz.

The neatness of this triadic arrangement is disturbed by Laroui's difficulty in deciding how to treat Najib Mahfuz. Mahfuz is first pigeonholed in the petit bourgeois realism box. But then Laroui tells us that the bourgeois phase produced no genuine bourgeois *roman*. It remained for the petite bourgeoisie to produce a novel that portrayed exemplars of a social class detached from context, that is, a proper bourgeois novel: "Quand le roman objectif s'épanouira en langue arabe, il le fera donc sous le signe de la petite-bourgeoisie et c'est là un trait de la plus haute importance, a garder toujours en mémoire si on veut juger sainement la valeur du 'réalisme' qui sera proclamé comme un dogme intouchable."[81]

Laroui concludes this exposition with the pronouncement that all of these forms of ideological critique depend upon the formal categories of academic criticism, and they are all inauthentic. Authenticity is not to be found in the application of a pretended universal form to a new case. The only way to an authentic expression is by means of calling the literary forms themselves into question, something which neither abstract analysis nor petit bourgeois realism, nor progressive realism has done. The petit bourgeois national state, which would produce writers like it would produce metallurgists, has recoiled from facing this problem.[82]

In the third part of Laroui's critique, the consistency of his analytic scheme is also marred. Here, he proceeds with an analysis of the three principal literary forms, *théâtre, roman,* and *nouvelle,* as though they correspond to the bourgeois, petit bourgeois realist and progressive realist schools, or as though they correspond to the orientations of the cleric, the liberal politician, and the technophile. To manage this, he takes the plays of both Shawqi, the neoclassicist, and Tawfiq al-Hakim, the bourgeois narcissist, as jointly exemplary of the first category, and he suggests that the drama itself represents a single class orientation.

More interesting, Laroui declares that tragedy, which is evidently what he means by theater, is inauthentic in Islam. This conclusion is derived from the historical and doctrinal resolutions of the early Islamic religious crises, which have contributed to the unwavering Islamic commitment to the principle that God has not and will not abandon the world.

> Or, dans le théâtre arabe, Dieu peut il être mis en question[?] . . . Non, Dieu ne peut être mis en doute, il doit rester le garant de passé, pour qu'il puisse garantir aussie le futur. . . . D'ou peut naître alor la tragédie?[83]

Tragedy itself is described as a royal form, challenging the legitimacy of kings and pretenders. But Shawqi and al-Hakim reflect the legitimating orientation of the legists, the scribes and the mystics,

> . . . trois tendances constantes de la pensée islamique; ce sont aussi et surtout trois solutions, fallacieuses mais étonnement efficaces, de noyer le tragique[84]

The *roman,* which is the bourgeois form par excellence, is equally alien, because the Arab bourgeoisie was born in an instant, taking over the places of the Ottomans or the Europeans. This social transformation has nothing of the *romanesque* in it. The role which is more familiar in Arab society is that of the petit bourgeois, preserving traditional mores. Laroui argues that, as a consequence, the Arab *roman* has peripheral content which is expressed in a form alien even to that content. "And this what gave rise to the greatest Arab *romancier,* N. Mahfuz, himself."[85]

Laroui does not, therefore, criticize the inauthenticity of the borrowed bourgeois form of the *roman.* He rather criticizes the work of Najib Mahfuz for his failure to understand the bourgeoisie, for his nostalgia, for his constant repetition of the same themes, and for his symbolic, rather than realistic, treatment of time. In other words, Mahfuz is criticized as being incapable of using the bourgeois form.

The third literary form is the *nouvelle,* which Laroui defines as the conclusion of an unwritten *roman,* the description of a situation and its immediate impact on an isolated human being without pretending to explain how the world works. The *nouvelle* deals with fragmentary, marginal, or interstitial topics and roles. It is the expressive form of the inductive.[86] This dark, pessimistic, directionless, essentially symbolic form has been borrowed from the French and American realist schools, and it is in this form which Mahfuz and his followers have excelled. The false image portrayed by this borrowed form has come to shape the Arab self-image—the image of a society dominated from afar by a foreign capitalism—an image which could only be acknowledged during a period which paved the way for the national state. "The more that the latter [the national state] liberates society in the course of reconstructing it, the more is there the risk that this [literary] form will perpetuate the image of a fixed and completed past, which will impede the grasping of a new reality."[87]

The meaning of this passage is by no means transparent. It isn't clear in context which past must not be miscontrued as historically complete and just what difference it will make regarding the understanding of the present. Laroui answers these questions indirectly in asserting that the perpetuation of false literary forms, especially the petit bourgeois *nouvelle,* is the act of the national state which needs the sort of ideology that promotes change in the socioeconomic sphere while retarding change in the formal, superstructural areas. Moreover, the solution which, as we have seen, lies in adopting the dialectic, can only be attained during the prolonged transitional waiting period represented by the liberal state. If it is not thus attained, if the liberal bourgeois experience is too short, or somehow incomplete, then one will bear the limitations of these inadequate forms, like a curse, for a long time.

Laroui asks: "Toutefois, pendant cette période d'attente où le libéralisme n'en finit pas de s'épuiser, comme celle que vit présentement le Maroc, faut il voir dans cette critique des formes une justification indirecte du formalisme?"[88]

His answer is, more or less, yes. Laroui's dialectic has brought him to the point of arguing against the exponents of a parochial authenticity, and against those who would break off the dialogue with the West. The historical interpretation that he would deny, and which he fears will become fixed in the Arab consciousness, is the one which condemns the bourgeois experience. And most astonishing of all, if least important in a substantive sense, after lambasting the inauthentic formalism of Arab literature he ends with a justification of formalism. Laroui argues that the Arabs should borrow freely from the West because Western thought allows the contemporary Arab ideology to advance beyond experience and actual practice, so even though the Arabs are "objectively" backward vis à vis the West, they are "really" in advance ideologically.[89]

The aporetic element in Laroui's exposition is manifest in the structure of the book itself, when examined in the light of his commitment to the dialectical method. The book is divided into four parts: authenticity, continuity, universalism, and expression. These correspond to thesis, antithesis, and synthesis, for the first three, but the fourth section appears to direct itself to a secondary, or peripheral problem. But we have also noted that Laroui's dialectical method consistently leads him to the conclusion that many things turn out, on close examination, to be just the opposite of what they claim to be. This is Laroui's judgement of the national state, of Marxism, and even of authenticity, itself. The national state, the vehicle of petit bourgeois reform, is actually engaged in the embourgeoisement of Arab society; Marxism is acceptable as a "system" in understanding the "other," but not as a "method" (process) for understanding (and changing) oneself; and the true authenticity can only come via the universal. It is not unreasonable, as a consequence, to contemplate the possibility that what appears to be Laroui's aesthetic afterthought conveys, in fact, his central conclusion, representing his major purpose in this book.

The theme of this last section is that contemporary Arab literature is both artistically poor and inauthentic, not because of the borrowed content of that literature, but rather because of the inauthenticity of the modern literary forms: the tragic drama, the romantic novel, and what he calls *la nouvelle*. These forms have been sustained, along with their virtually necessarily inauthentic content, by the petit bourgeois leadership, intellectual and political, of the national state. While Laroui uses a rhetoric continuously condemning the national state for the bourgeois function that belies its populist and nativist posture, in this section he maintains that the national state places political obstacles in the way of the (authentic) expressive realization of universal values and in the way of an unhampered experimentation with new literary forms.

Since these authentic, but universal, forms have not yet been found, Laroui cannot tell us what they will be. He can only tell us that they may be discovered only if the Arab intellectual and artist is allowed to express himself with complete freedom. In the end, therefore, Laroui demands cultural and political freedom for the Arab intelligentsia, because it is the independent intelligentsia—and not the petit bourgeois apparatus of the state—that will direct the Arabs toward the path of authentic self-understanding *and* universalism. There is little doubt that Laroui's message, when disencumbered from its dialectical trappings, is a strong plea for bourgeois liberalism in the classic forms of academic and artistic freedom, justified by reference to the idea of development as an open-ended process—a universal pragmatics of communication and production.

Whatever Laroui may be saying about Islamic-Arab authenticity, his argument is also a contribution to the debate on the political roles of the petite bourgeoisie, the intellectuals, and the apparatus of the state. Some theorists lump all three groups together as fractions which support or sustain the hegemony of the bourgeois class in a social formation defined by the predominance of the capitalist mode of production. Others recognize, at least implicitly, the possibility of the temporary dominance of a petit bourgeois fraction within a ruling "power bloc," but they do not agree on the significance of such a situation. Some assert that the dominance of a petit bourgeois fraction, say a bureaucratic authoritarian elite, is a consequence of an equilibrium between the feudal and bourgeois forces, while others argue that such dominance is a form of Bonapartism and, therefore, merely a transitional device leading to the full assumption of power by the bourgeoisie, after it has been strengthened by its association with the state. And others, yet, believe that the petite bourgeoisie, especially in its bureaucratic and intellectual fractions, can play a "progressive" role in the transition from the bourgeois state to socialism or social democracy.

The Marxian cast of this debate has not precluded the intellectual appropriation of the issue by functionalists, pragmatists, critical theorists, rational choice theorists, and structuralists, each in accordance with their own paradigmatic apparatus. Laroui who appears to be a left-Hegelian, with appropriate pragmatic-historicist inclinations, argues that the national state, or petit bourgeois Egyptian state, represents not a transition to bourgeois domination, but a premature overthrow of the bourgeois state in Egypt. It was premature because the process of embourgeoisement, and of the development of an authentically modern culture had not yet been achieved when the bourgeois state of pre-1952 Egypt was overthrown.

Since Laroui conflates embourgeoisement, economic development, and modernization, he can conclude that the national state produces substructural development and superstructural retardation and inauthenticity. The consequence is a contradiction similar to that found in modern Western societies in which alienation prevails. The major defect of the petit bourgeois state, against which Laroui rails, is the bureaucratization of intellectual and cultural expression.

Written in the early '60s, and hence before the publication of Mahfuz's works that are critical of the Nasser regime, Laroui's book singles out the literary oeuvre of Najib Mahfuz for castigation because its portrayal of the hopeless misery of the petite bourgeoisie served as the ideological justification of the narrow-minded Jacobinism, authoritarianism, and bureaucratism of the Nasser regime. Laroui's conclusion is unmistakable. He believed, at the time, that the prospects for Morocco, still a bourgeois or liberal state under Hasan II, were better than those of Egypt, despite its revolution.

Objectively, it can be argued that Laroui, the petit bourgeois intellectual, has supported the hegemonic bourgeoisie of Morocco, the same bourgeoisie which had made a deal with the monarchy, allowing the king to maintain formal domination. The resulting power bloc included the monarchy, the landed grandees, the bourgeoisie, the landed gentry, the clergy, the military, and the intellectuals. Within that bloc, however, there was a great deal of competition over hegemony, in the sense of precedence within the coalition.

The competition over ideological hegemony has been very subdued, with virtually no serious attempts to cross the boundaries between cultural enclaves. Laroui deplores the slow progress being made in Morocco, and he criticizes the king for gratuitously insisting upon ruling rather than reigning as a bourgeois monarch. Nevertheless, he is against any premature overthrow of the regime, and especially against any attempt to establish a national state in Morocco.

Within the context of the power bloc in Morocco, this particular intellectual allied himself (objectively) with the coalition between the monarchy and the liberal bourgeois parliamentary factions, against the petit bourgeois elements in the apparatus of the state, in the military, and even among the clergy. It is patent that the intellectuals are almost as bureaucratized as the civil service in the national state, or the bureaucratic authoritarian state, nevertheless, it is frequently the case that they do not define their interests in the same way as does the bureaucrat. If the various petit bourgeois fractions often ally themselves with the bourgeoisie, they seem to do so differentially and in competition with one another. The disunity among the petit bourgeois fractions offers the bourgeoisie the possibility of forming tactical alliances which may allow it to gain hegemony of the power bloc without resorting to force, or even formal (party) organization. Laroui's thesis makes more sense in this theoretical context than it does as abstract cultural theory, especially since Laroui subscribes to this theoretical context, himself, in the form of what he calls "objective Marxism."

The central component of this ideological discourse is the theory of the bourgeois state, and the core of this theory, say, as formulated by Nicos Poulantzas, is the paradox of the bourgeois revolution. Poulantzas argues that the bourgeoisie is incapable of leading its own revolution; it must ride to power on the vehicle of temporary alliances with kings, feudal aristocracies, landowners, bureaucracies, army officers, priests, and various segments of the petite bourgeoisie. The bourgeoisie thus gains control of the state, while the

bourgeoisie can not run its own revolution —

legal formal character of the state masks its class character. The relative autonomy of the state is thus the very device which permits bourgeois domination through a coalitional power bloc, without the necessity of the bourgeoisie organizing itself in class-based parties. The state itself is the organization of the bourgeoisie insofar as it is integrated and pursues a coherent public policy based on a rationally ordered system of legislation.

Manifestly, the ideological hegemony of a bourgeois doctrine of political liberalism is absolutely essential to such an arrangement. It is also manifest that the power structure of the bourgeois state is far from rigid, and it is always possible to challenge the dominance of the bourgeoisie. The constant adjustment among the forces of the coalition, the constant tactical concern about whether to admit or exclude new elements or existing members of the power bloc, the continuous need to agree on the extent of the concessions to be made to those who are not part of the power bloc, and, above all, the ongoing requirements of adjustment to incremental changes in the socioeconomic and cultural contexts, complete a picture of a political system that is similar, indeed, to that of the pragmatic, pluralist theory identified with the key liberal concepts of function, equilibrium, and process.

There is, from within the context of this sort of theory, some question as to whether the national state, or the petit bourgeois state, or the bureaucratic authoritarian state is merely a Bonapartist stage leading to bourgeois domination, or whether it represents, at least, a temporary retreat of the bourgeoisie from dominance. As Poulantzas never tires of repeating, the precise arrangement among the fractions of the power bloc depends on the "conjuncture," which, in turn, is defined as the sum of the political activities of the individual agents of production. It is this pragmatic perspective, and his refusal to identify petit bourgeois regimes with a theoretically defined stage in a universal revolutionary process, that has permitted a convergence between the marxisant and the pluralist analyses of Third World regimes. And it is this discursive nexus that permits an intelligible discussion of the political tactics and strategy that are employed among the factions allied in the power bloc. This is the major content of the literature on the bureaucratic authoritarian regime in Latin America. That literature focuses primarily on the problems of cooperation and competition between the bourgeoisie and the apparatus of the state. Laroui calls our attention to the way in which intellectuals may play a role in this process, and he clarifies the ideological tactics that can lead to a diminution of the hegemonic power of the apparatus of the state. Given the facile tendency of so many "theorists" to identify the notion of the relative autonomy of the state with a bureaucractic monopoly of power, it is instructive to have this example of the relative autonomy of the ideological process.

It is possible that Laroui is more interested in diminishing the influence of the apparatus of the state than was the Moroccan bourgeoisie. In addition, the liberal intellectuals are not the only possible allies of the bourgeoisie in their ideological struggle for hegemony. Both the ulama and the fundamentalist organizations are potential members of a bourgeois coalition aimed at controlling the state apparatus, but the outcome of such a coalition in Iran must be somewhat dismaying, at this stage at least.

It is probably a rare case, but possibly a very fortunate one, in which both the bourgeoisie and the petit bourgeois apparatus of the state are vying for the support of the liberal intellectuals. Such a conjuncture may offer a limited opportunity for the creation of a liberal regime, since liberal regimes are, it seems, dependent upon very special conditions. Would anyone be so bold as to read such a situation into a political context dominated by the idea of an Islamic resurgence? As Laroui writes, "Conclusion trop optimiste? Pourquoi pas. . . . Conclusion équivoque aussi."[90]

9

Conclusion: The Prospects for Liberal Government in the Middle East

Abdallah Laroui makes a powerful argument for the importance, if not the necessity, of the bourgeois state by means of his biting attack on the petit bourgeois state. Since Laroui was influenced by Althusser, it is not surprising to find in his work certain interesting parallels with the structuralist arguments of Nicos Poulantzas. For both, as for anyone acquainted with the contemporary history of the Middle East, the crucial question is that of the nature or function of the Bonapartist state, that is, the Ataturkist, the Nasserist, or the Pahlavi state.

Poulantzas criticizes the French Revolution as an incomplete bourgeois revolution. Because it is incomplete, it blocks the historical dialectical process, but it is also the cause of the inadequate realization of bourgeois democracy in France. The root cause of the lack of completion of the French Revolution was the bourgeois fear of the proletariat and the subproletariat. In order to prevent a serious political challenge from the working class, the bourgeoisie allied itself with the petite bourgeoisie and supported both a strong centralized bureaucracy and an autocratic, militaristic ruler. By means of this institutional structure, the bourgeoisie fails to dominate the "historical bloc," and it fails to achieve ideological hegemony. Its interests are protected by, if subordinated to, the interest of the state elite, while the hegemonic ideology expresses Jacobinist, Poujadist (or fundamentalist Islamic) tendencies. In the context of the Islamic Middle East, a fundamentalist resurgence has petit bourgeois and Bonapartist implications.

Laroui seems to think that a traditional monarch can do a better job of completing the "bourgeois revolution" and constructing a bourgeois state than can a Bonapartist ruler such as Nasser or Ataturk. But like other exponents of the neoliberal paradigm, who seek the establishment and consolidation of bourgeois states, he does not argue that the bourgeoisie can do the job alone. Others argue that there is no such thing as a bourgeois revolution because the bourgeoisie is incapable of seizing power by itself.

But if the bourgeoisie cannot produce a bourgeois state without political allies, and if reliance upon the apparatus of the state produces a petit bourgeois state which is authoritarian, chauvinist, and culturally reactionary, what alternative is there? Poulantzas, following Gramsci, suggests that the bourgeoisie must ally with the other segments of civil society against the state, that the bourgeoisie, in the enlightened pursuit of self-interest, must take the leadership of the "historical bloc," and achieve political hegemony by forming a cross-class parliamentary coalition. The only way in which this sort of an alliance of the forces of civil society can be forged against the power of the Bonapartist state, is through the achievement of cultural hegemony or the establishment of a new political consensus. And, of course, the role of the intellectuals will be crucial in any such process.

Abdullah Laroui's Marxian perspective leads him to identify state-led development with a petit bourgeois state. Yet this petit bourgeois state is relatively autonomous, in the sense that it is not directed by petit bourgeois segments of civil society. The petit bourgeois state is, nevertheless, still influenced by petit bourgeois culture, because culture is thought to be relatively autonomous of both politics and economics. Besides, for many Marxian thinkers, the intelligentsia as well as the bureaucracy are petit bourgeois in the main and, hence, incapable of producing a viable bourgeois state without bourgeois direction.

One does not have to agree with Laroui to appreciate the value of his effort. His, alone among the works studied, proposes a synthesis of the cultural and the socioeconomic in an integrated and mutually determinative system. He is critical of those conceptions of authenticity that legitimate the petit bourgeois state, or rather the authoritarian role of a state bureaucracy drawn in large part from the petit bourgeois class. He argues that it is the culture of this class, rather than anything inherently Islamic or Arab, which leads to the rejection of the dialogue with the West. He recognizes that formulas such as those proposed by more orthodox Marxists, by nationalists who reject *al-wafid*, and even by those who would compartmentalize religion and save it from any political or cultural critique, are products of a class, or an historical consciousness, rather than manifestations of the true Islam. His conception of Islam and Arabism is founded upon a developmental or evolutionary conception that rejects cultural defensiveness as itself a barrier to development. He believes that the establishment of a bourgeois state is a prerequisite to the achievement of an Islamic-Arab cultural authenticity, which can then enter into a conversation with the West on the basis of cultural equality. Hence, Laroui's response to the challenge of orientalism is not to call for the "dispersal of man," but to seek a universal cultural formulation in the way of Gadamer or Rorty. And, perhaps most important of all, Laroui has pointed to the role that Arab intellectuals can play in encouraging the development of liberalism by offering to ally themselves with bourgeois interests against the authority of the apparatus of the petit bourgeois state.

It is doubtful that Laroui believed that Egyptian intellectuals alone could change the course upon which that country had been set. He strongly suggests that there is a contradiction between the goals and the methods of the "national state" that will cause some sort of a breakdown, which may produce a reorientation. Nevertheless, he implies, if only by his own writing, that Arab intellectuals are capable of transcending their own class consciousness. For Laroui the interest of the Muslim intellectuals is in freedom of expression and they must seek to produce the political circumstances in which free expression is possible.

Egypt

For some observers, the Nasser regime was the prototype of the autonomous state, suspended twixt heaven and earth, without support from either God or man. Tariq al-Bishri's argument is, however, more subtle and realistic. He ticks off the various classes, groups, and ideological tendencies, and then tells us that the July Revolution simply filled a political vacuum left by the events of January 1952. If that which the Free Officers seized in July of 1952 was power, then they continued well into the remaining years of the decade in their effort to consolidate that power and to work out a domestic and a foreign policy. In the course of this effort, the Free Officers had to resolve factional and ideological conflicts among themselves. Those conflicts resulted, in part, from the usual kinds of personal rivalries, but far more importantly, they reflected a number of conflicts which derived from the divisions within "civil society."

When Nasser's faction gained control, it proceeded to weaken or destroy representative organizations and associations, while establishing corporatist structures of the party, or the state, or the public sector to mobilize the support as well as the interest of all of these groups. If one looks only at the destruction of the party system, at the repression of strikes, at the proscription of the Ikhwan, and at the land reform, one may come to the facile conclusion that neither workers, nor peasants, nor students, nor civil servants, nor rural notables, nor petit bourgeois shopkeepers actually supported the regime. The absence of voluntary associations or their "incorporation," does not mean that the Nasserist elite had no support, it only means that it allowed no organized, overt opposition, and that it had no legitimate competition.

Most observers are inclined to agree that the Nasser regime was generally supported by most of the groups mentioned, even though there is some disagreement about whether the most important thing about the regime was its military base or its petit bourgeois character, or its tacit alliance with the rural notability, or its willingness to work with what it called the "national bourgeoisie." At any rate, it hardly seems possible to make sense out of the political history of Egypt since 1952 unless we recognize that Nasser himself, and Sadat as well, conceived of Egyptian society as constituted of diverse social classes, interests, and ideological tendencies, and pursued a domestic political strategy based upon the assumption that the regime required the support of the very alliance of social forces which it claimed to represent.

Tariq al-Bishri argues that the Wafd and the Ikhwan, each in its own way, represented an integral part of Egyptian cultural authenticity. In making this argument he wishes to minimize the class character of each movement, for the Wafd is usually identified with the landed classes, and especially the emergent Egyptian bourgeoisie, while the Ikhwan are usually identified with the petite bourgeoisie. Al-Bishri's goal may well be to find a common ground upon which both classes may cooperate. He may be arguing, as does Abdullah Laroui, for a bourgeois state in which the petite bourgeoisie will take a secondary but honored role. Islam, along with other nationalist cultural symbols, will serve to integrate, or to unify the nation, and thus permit democracy despite class differences.

Hence, al-Bishri, like Laroui, does not deny class differences. He seeks a way to overcome these differences without the absolute equality of a classless, socialist, society. Rather than condemn the ideology of fundamentalist Islam as false consciousness, he credits fundamentalism as an authentic expression of Egyptian consciousness, and argues that, by embracing Islam, the Egyptian polity can overcome not only an ideological division, but a class division as well. Implicitly, al-Bishri criticizes the Nasser regime for failing to pursue such a policy, and for exacerbating the cleavage between the state elite and the religiously oriented members of the lower middle classes.

At the outset of the July Revolution there was a good deal of cooperation, and even some ideological affinity, between the Ikhwan and the Free Officers. In fact, there was a much closer affinity between the Nasser regime and the lower middle class/petite bourgeoisie than there was with either the workers, or the peasants, or the lumpenproletariat. The falling out between the Ikhwan and Nasser was not a mere misunderstanding. It was the result of an open struggle for power; and when Nasser won, he had to decide how to deal with the Ikhwan organization, with Islamic fundamentalism and voluntary Islamic organizations, and with those classes and groups that had been most responsive to the appeal of the Ikhwan.

There were many superficial aspects of Nasser's Islamic policy which, in retrospect, appear to have been of little effect, but the central feature of Nasser's policy was highly successful, if unspectacular. Nasser simply continued and intensified the policies of earlier rulers of Egypt who patronized, bureaucratized, expanded and elaborated the Azhar academy of Islamic learning and its complex array of adjunct institutions. More than any other institution or organization in Egypt, al-Azhar is the official clerical and religious establishment. Increasingly over the last century and more, it has become a part of the state bureaucracy. It is the official spokesman for Islamic orthodoxy, and as such it is a target of those who oppose the government's religious policy, as well as an instrument to be used against any who would usurp the role of the orthodox clergy.

Even though the judicial and general educational role of al-Azhar and the clergy was diminished under Nasser, the institutional strength, the material wealth, the political prestige, and the size itself of al-Azhar greatly increased. Al-Azhar, as the symbol of the Islamic character of both the state and the nation was not directly attacked, and has retained a vague kind of general legitimacy, despite attacks on the religiosity of the regime itself. Even when Sadat was assassinated as a renegade, most fundamentalist extremists admitted that the state and the society remained Islamic, and they rejected the views of a minority faction that called for religious flight from the society of unbelief.

In contrast to the continued consolidation and expansion of al-Azhar, the Ikhwan organization was suppressed, and many of its leaders were either killed, imprisoned, or fled into exile. Although the movement retained some of its earlier vitality, it was gravely weakened by both external repression and internal dissension. Many younger adherents came to believe that the strategy of the older generation, especially that which sought legitimation by the state and reintegration into the political system, was defeatist. In any case, while in political and organizational limbo, the Ikhwan could neither hold the allegiance nor nourish the religious commitment of a new generation of fundamentalists. Many new, local, and often small and secret organizations were founded after 1965, some of which challenged the vestige of the Ikhwan, and others of which simply did their own religious thing. Some were highly politicized and militant while others sought the comfort of fraternal association and the consolation of mutual cooperation. Most of those who joined such groups were, again, members of the petite bourgeoisie, students, and others on the periphery of the modern, bourgeois, or technocratic center of Egyptian society.

The growth of such groups and, especially, of the religious tendency among university students, is not the consequence of the diffusion of the spirit of the times so much as the political consequence of the 1967 defeat, the increased influence and wealth of the conservative, petroleum exporting countries, and the conscious policies of Sadat to at once encourage the patronage of Saudi Arabia and strengthen domestic antileftist ideological forces.

But even though fundamentalist groups and religiously oriented students have caused much difficulty to the Egyptian state, the fact remains that the religious opposition (with its powerful and resourceful foreign support) is fragmented, while the official religious establishment remains powerful, united, active, and under the control of the state. The Egyptian government retains what the Turkish state has dissipated, and what the Iranian Imperial state was never able to get hold of. The Egyptian state or polity is still empowered to seek Islamic solutions to political problems.

It seems to me that there can be little doubt that it is the division between al-Azhar and the profusion of fundamentalist groups that has allowed a number of intellectuals to take up the question of Islam, and to ponder the issue of Islamic liberalism. In Egypt more than in any other Muslim country, the class basis and the policy implications of the religious question are well understood. Despite the urging of Tariq al-Bishri and many others, Mubarak refused to legitimate the Ikhwan as a political party, or rather as *the* Islamic party. On the other hand, the fact that both the neo-Wafd and the leftist Tagammuʿa Party sought an electoral alliance with the Ikhwan indicates that they understand the class appeal of the fundamentalist groups. Al-Bishri argues that the Wafd and the Ikhwan, in terms of their appeal to the masses, really represented identical social and cultural forces. The Egyptian Marxists are inclined to accept that formulation, even if they are careful about restating it in terms of the false-consciousness doctrine. The result is that the state upholds scripturalist Islam as its main line of defense against fundamentalist extremism, while the leftist opposition embraces fundamentalism and jacobinism in a Faustian bargain aimed at breaking the state's political control. Between the two there may be a common interest in the expression of an Islamic liberalism which would provide for the coexistence of both groups, but the space between, as measured by the enlightenment of the bourgeoisie and the courage of the intelligentsia, is so narrow that it is difficult to be optimistic.

Throughout the period from 1955 to 1968, the Nasser regime did not meet with open protest or a severe clandestine threat. Opposition existed, but it was mostly passive or directed from abroad, and it was to a large extent unorganized. Nevertheless, the regime was constantly at odds with the intellectuals, it was continuously in conflict with the fundamentalists, it systematically alienated the remaining large land owners, and the industrial bourgeoisie. Perhaps even more important was the fact that it could not continue to improve the condition of either its major constituency, the petit bourgeois bureaucrats, or its secondary constituency, organized labor. Only its support among the rural middle class was relatively undiminished by the time of the outbreak of the 1967 war.

The Nasser regime faced a severe crisis in the mid-1960s. That crisis was brought on by the failure of the economic development program, by political fallout from the renewed suppression of the Ikhwan in 1965, by the continuing consequences of the secession of Syria from the United Arab Republic, and by the increasingly brazen assertiveness of the Marxist factions within the ruling elite. Factional strife grew, and the leftist challengers sought to increase their power by the creation of new organizations to mobilize activist elements among peasants, workers, students, soldiers and civil servants.

Most analysts date the turn away from doctrinaire socialism in Egypt from the student demonstrations of 1968, but some find evidence of the shift as early as 1965. The turn began before Nasser's death. Sadat's pursuit of the same policy was not merely, or even mainly, a continuation of the Nasserist line. It was rather a strategic device to protect his own position against the challenge of the powerful leftist faction within the apparatus of the state. Sadat began by appealing to the rural gentry again, then to the bourgeoisie, then to the intellectual elite, then to the Islamic fundamentalists. He actually began to open the political system as well, but then he realized that he could not control all of these diverse groups. In backing away from truly liberalizing political reforms, Sadat again began the process of alienating wider and wider social segments, and by late 1981 he had all but isolated himself from the left, from the intellectuals, from the

fundamentalists, from the students, and from the petite bourgeoisie.
Only the urban and rural bourgeoisie remained supportive to the tragic end.

It was due to Sadat's ill-conceived strategy, rather than to any competitive political process, that the Egyptian bourgeoisie now finds itself isolated and in desperate need of domestic allies. It is not inconceivable that the Egyptian bourgeoisie will form some cooperative relationship with either or both the fundamentalists and the intellectual and professional classes. At the moment, however, even among those who are most vocally supportive of political liberalization, both the fundamentalists and the intellectuals condemn Sadat's infitah and those who have benefited from it. The rhetoric of political liberalism in Egypt does not include capitalism, while the rhetoric of Islamic reform does not preclude socialism.

Egyptian capitalism currently benefits from the ambivalent support of the Egyptian state and from the more enthusiastic support of a variety of foreign firms and foreign powers. As a consequence, we find the semblance of a bourgeois state in Egypt, yet the bourgeoisie does not hold hegemonic power, it has no coherent political strategy, no effective organization, and seems incapable of forming efficacious coalitions with other groups. Under the circumstances, though tempted to work out an independent political and ideological position, the Egyptian bourgeoisie cannot risk biting the hand that feeds it.

Given the unfinished character of the Egyptian bourgeois state prior to 1952, it is easy enough to understand the ease with which the Nasserist economic policies could be put in place. The Nasserist economy did not replace, much less crush, a previously existing capitalist economy. It attempted to expand the Egyptian economy via state action. The result may be seen as actually facilitating the later expansion of capitalist enterprise. In this sense, the Nasser regime has been seen as the ally (unwitting, perhaps) of the Egyptian bourgeoisie.

Gradually, but deliberately, Anwar al-Sadat dismantled the single-party system of political domination and mobilization built up by Nasser. At first he restructured the secretariat, then he broke up the secret elite apparatus, then he encouraged the formation of ideological factions, then he transformed the factions into embryonic parties (platforms) within the party, then he limited the function of the official Arab Socialist Union, turning its participatory responsibilities over to the platforms, and finally he licensed the platforms as parties alongside a centrist residual party made up of the bulk of the representatives in parliament.

The original single party, though it was called the Arab Socialist

 Union, represented all classes and groups. It was supposed to be a mirror of all of the patriotic social forces of Egypt, including "national capital." Its successor, now known as the National Democratic Party, or the Watani party for short, still presents itself as a patriotic "rally" rather than a class-based party, and, to the extent that it is the regime's instrument, it does exercise a kind of corporatist responsibility. It is, nevertheless, dominated by the ruling coalition of bureaucrats, notables, and capitalists, which, along with the military, continues to dominate Egyptian political life.

The new parties hoped to capitalize on the reaction of so many Egyptians to the political repression of the Nasser years, but their lack of clear ideological position or social identity, and their often irresponsible rhetoric, when combined with the caution of the Ministry of the Interior, has led to the disappointment of such expectations. For a brief moment, under Sadat, when the pre-1952 Wafd party was revived to an enthusiastic public response, there was a genuine belief that all of the old parties would return, and that the Egyptian masses would once again become the targets of competitive party maneuvering. Sadat overreacted, and refused to license either the Wafd or the still illegal Muslim Brotherhood, although he pursued policies favoring both capitalist entrepreneurship and religious fundamentalism. It was apparent that the regime feared the opposition of these social forces if they were allowed to detach themselves from government control.

Mubarak, after some persuasion, decided to license the Wafd for the elections of 1984, but not the Ikhwan. The election law of that year also set a minimum requirement of 8 percent of the popular vote nationwide as a prerequisite for winning any seats in parliament, thus encouraging the smaller parties to ally. The Wafd allied with the Ikhwan, promising to seat Ikhwan candidates running under its banner, and hoping at once to win religious support, to strike a blow for political liberalism and against the restrictive policies of the government, and to present itself as a party of national unity in a direct challenge to the claims of the Watani party, and as an indirect dismissal of the licensed parties as regime lackeys.

The Wafd-Ikhwan effort tested Mubarak's commitment to liberal parliamentary practices, and he, eventually, made certain concessions. Beyond this limited opening of the system, the opposition coalition didn't achieve much. The Wafd won 57 seats out of the 448 contested and 9 were allocated to the Ikhwan. The parliamentary opposition remained weak and fragmented. Some three years later, the 1983 electoral law was struck down, not because of the 8 percent rule, but because it effectively prevented independents from winning since they could not win 8 percent of the national vote by themselves.

The new law set aside some seats for independents, and new elections were held in 1987.

The new law was a small step toward a more liberal electoral system, but the quota was maintained, and the Ikhwan were still not licensed. As a consequence, the Ikhwan remained available for an electoral alliance, and all the opposition parties sought to share its wide religious appeal. The Wafd was the logical candidate to renew the 1984 alliance, but it had failed to build a cooperative political relationship with the Ikhwan since the previous election. The Wafd lost out in the competitive bidding, and the Egyptian Labor party, led by Ibrahim Shukri, a former leader of the defunct Egyptian Socialist party, formed an electoral alliance with the Ikhwan and the Liberal party (another of the splinter parties licensed by Sadat). The coalition won 56 seats, with the Ikhwan taking 35 and the Labor party 18. The Wafd won 35 seats on its own.

The Wafd has turned out to be a weaker force than anticipated, but its success is no measure of the strength of the Egyptian bourgeoisie, which is well represented in the ruling Watani party and elsewhere. The Ikhwan were shown to enjoy wide popularity, but they were unable or not permitted to convert their popularity into votes. Ibrahim Shukri's Labor party has emerged to a kind of prominence as a result of the electoral alliance and its new presence in parliament. The Labor party has also gained important attention recently by its increasing support of Islamic religious and political initiatives.

But the Labor party is not just another political splinter of the bourgeois class. It is not antibourgeois, but its tactics, drawn from the experience of the Misr al-Fatat party as it was under Ahmad Husain, are aimed primarily at mobilizing the urban masses. If the Wafd offered the idea of a bourgeois-fundamentalist coalition, Ibrahim Shukri offers the alternative of a petit bourgeois–fundamentalist coalition. Mubarak will have to ponder which of these two makes him more uneasy.

The Ikhwan are ambivalent about direct participation in parliamentary elections, and they did oppose all party politics in the pre-1952 period. Nevertheless, they seem to be moving toward full entry into the system. When and if they do, the current employment of surrogates and the attendant competitive bidding will end, though it is likely that the Ikhwan will seek coalition partners. The growing legitimation of the Ikhwan, alongside of the state religious establishment, will continue to limit the ability of individual intellectuals to speak for Islam. But the exigencies of political competition within the system, and the rivalry with the jamaʿat outside the system, are likely to influence the Ikhwan's conception of its role, and thereby determine, in part, whether Islam will sustain or weaken the increasingly liberal tendency in Egyptian politics.

Turkey

The history of Turkish development has been, for the most part, a history of bureaucratic centralization, challenged seriously only in the last two or three decades. The diminution of the role of the apparatus of the state, often identified as the bearer of an ideology known as Ataturkism, is usually dated from the elections of 1945. At that time a competitive multiparty electoral system was inaugurated, but the two major parties represented the two major ideological and economic orientations among the ruling elite. These two tendencies, the statist and the bourgeois, emerged and matured during the period of apparently unchallenged autonomy and/or hegemony of the apparatus of the state during the 20s and the 30s. It may be that the growth of the Turkish bourgeoisie within the structure of the bureaucratic-authoritarian regime itself was made possible only because that regime ruled through parliament and via the instrument of a single party. It may also be argued that the emergence of a Turkish bourgeoisie which could then ally itself with the other propertied classes, such as the merchants and landowners, was in fact the consequence of the etatist policies of the autonomous state itself. Even so, the Turkish case illustrates that the apparatus of the state is not isolated from either social process or the class system. It is itself a part of "civil society," and therefore vulnerable to the impact of the unintended consequences of its own policies, as well as the conflicts which arise out of the fact that the state elite is not a single, integrated, and homogenous unit characterized by a common interest.

Most students of Turkish politics identify the Republican People's Party (RPP) with the apparatus of the state and the ideology of Ataturkism. The emergence of a multiparty system after 1945 is, nevertheless, traced to longstanding divisions within the RPP, especially with regard to choices between state capitalism and private capitalism. The electoral successes of the Demokrat Party (DP) and then of the Justice Party (JP), and more recently of the Ozal coalition, are indications of the continuing consolidation of private capitalism, and of the political influence of the Turkish bourgeoisie. During the same period, the RPP became transformed, especially in the mid-1970s, from a "state party" to a left-of-center party representing the interests of low-ranking civil servants, the intelligentsia, and the more moderate segments of the working class, the residents of the *gecekondus*, and even the poorer peasants of Eastern Turkey. The transformation of the RPP coincides with the occurrence of profound changes in the structure and ideology of the state elite. The most important of these changes has been the growth and differentiation of the bureaucracy itself. The Turkish state could no longer function as the "political organization" of the petit bourgeois class of civil servants, university graduates, professionals, and intellectuals. Hence, as the RPP was gradually taken over by more radical elements, those who were concerned to maintain the sovereign integrity of state power were increasingly drawn to cooperate with those bourgeois interests (domestic and foreign) which sought to control and limit distributive demands.

While the large public sector, the legacy of the autarchic development strategy of the thirties, has been maintained, it is no longer considered an alternative to bourgeois capitalist development. The relations between state enterprise and private enterprise in Turkey have passed beyond the troubled and ideologically confused situation prevailing in Egypt. The identification of bureaucratic and organized labor interests with the public sector will prevent any serious effort to dismantle that sector, but public enterprise is not now seen as a viable alternative to private capitalist development. This is not to argue that the emergence of a "bourgeois state" in Turkey is either complete or irreversible, but merely to describe where we are at now.

With the differentiation of the state apparatus in Turkey and the strengthening of both the rule of law and the parliamentary system, it can be argued that the relative autonomy of the Turkish state has been significantly diminished. If state capitalism produced a viable and influential bourgeois class, that class is no longer the passive instrument of the state. From an alternative perspective, however, it may be argued that the actual autonomy of the Turkish state is masked by the façade of bourgeois parliamentarianism, while the ultimate power continues to rest with the military. The question of political liberalism in Turkey is less a matter of the rise of the bourgeoisie than it is a question of the meaning to be attributed to the military interventions of 1960, 1971, and 1980. In this regard Egypt differs significantly from Turkey, because the Egyptian parliamentary system has not, since 1952, been allowed the scope to get itself into as much trouble as has the Turkish parliament since 1945.

The standard meaning attributed to these three military intrusions into Turkish parliamentary politics is that they reflect, at once, the commitment of the Turkish military (a segment of the Ataturkist elite) to the preservation of democracy, and the precariousness of that democracy as practiced by either self-interested bourgeois parties or antibourgeois extremists of the right and the left. This questionable interpretation is based on the assumptions that Ataturkism involves a deep commitment to democratization, and that the state elite has opted for a policy of direct and indirect support of the bourgeois class and its allies in order to achieve democratic development. This interpretation does not deny that one of the goals of the state elite is to maintain the autonomy and sovereign authority of the state. It merely argues that this goal is instrumental to the higher purpose of democratic development.

The fate of the present coalition between the state elite and the bourgeoisie will depend, in part, on the economic success of the Ozal government, and it is already apparent that it will be limited. Besides we know that the military preferred a more authoritarian government to that of Ozal and his allies. The inclination of the state elite remains more conservative and more cautious about power sharing than their bourgeois allies. Nevertheless, the legacy of this last military intervention seems to be the realization that change from the top can only go so far until it must accommodate itself to the prevailing social structural and ideological forces in Turkey.

The partial emergence of a bourgeois state in Turkey has influenced more than the role of the state and the identification of relevant political interests. It has also affected the political and ideological position of Islam. The historical role of Islam has been first and foremost as state religion and secondarily as social protest or spiritual withdrawal. The Ataturkist state denied itself the support of an official religious establishment, partly because the state was unable to control it, and partly because the state elite believed it would constitute an obstacle to development. Turkey did not, however, separate religion and politics as one might expect in a liberal state. The Turkish state maintained control over Islamic institutions and decreed the restriction of their scope as a matter of national policy. This policy resulted in the near elimination of all those state institutions which defined Islamic law, education, theology, and social ethics. At the same time, state policy did not diminish popular belief or practice, especially in the rural areas and the gecekondu districts where rural migrants settled. Nor did state policy effectively suppress movements of religious opposition and social protest.

With the opening of the political system to competitive party politics after 1945, the religious issue was transformed into a topic of legitimate political discourse. It is still imprudent to advocate a complete reversal of the Ataturkist religious reforms, but one can advocate reforms of the reforms. In fact, the electoral victories of the Demokrat and Justice parties have been attributed to the religious appeal of these parties, to their promises to change government policy, and to the considerable official support which Islam now enjoys.

The key to the electoral success of the bourgeois parties has been their ability to convince rural voters to support them. Since the

DP and the JP both advocated the interests of the larger agriculturalists, their support poses no interpretive problem. The support of the poorer peasants is explained as due to the cultural influence of the rural notables and the identification of these parties with religion. Both the RPP and the state elite responded to these successes by first diminishing their opposition to the political legitimation of Islam and then actually encouraging the expansion of Islamic educational facilities. Belatedly the state elite began to realize that an established religion might help to enhance authority and social control and limit the intensity of interest or class politics. The RPP, also belatedly, realized that it could not win the support of landless labor in the rural areas or of the migrants in the gecekondus so long as it attacked all religion as obscurantist. The state, the bourgeoisie, and the groups which coalesced in the RPP all had a common interest in challenging the increasingly strident and extremist leaders of Islamic fundamentalist movements and Islamic movements of social protest.

By the mid-'70s the transformed RPP and the JP were openly competing for the support of the religious masses, the JP by direct religious appeals and the RPP by recasting its demands for social justice and equality into religious terms. For a brief period, during which petroleum and agricultural prices rose, it looked as if a stabilized parliamentary system might become consolidated in Turkey. But then the inability of the two major parties to work out a compromise representing the moderate sector allowed extremist groups to move the political arena from parliament to the streets and campuses. Political violence grew, but the established parties could not agree on sharing responsibility for repressive security measures against either the left or the religious-nationalist right. The state elite lost confidence in the parliamentary regime, and intervened to reestablish public order to the paradoxically combined relief and dismay of the Turkish public.

We still do not know whether the Turkish system is "working," nor do we know what role religion will play in the long run in Turkish politics. For the moment, and despite the Iranian revolution, religious extremism does not appear to be the central issue. Despite the weakness of the major parties in the pre-1981 period, it appears that they are responsible for the fact that the classic political cleavages between the bourgeois and the nonbourgeois, between the urban and rural, the industrial and the agricultural, are no longer translated into pro-Islamic and anti-Islamic. Surveys of the Turkish electorate show that rural "traditionals" and urban migrants affected by modernization are inclined toward stronger religious commitments. Increasingly, lower-ranking civil servants fall into the second category, while the intellectuals split up in even more complex ways. There is no longer an official ideology that denies the legitimacy of religious thought. But neither has Islam become an instrument of the Turkish state. Nor can the Turkish bourgeoisie any longer freely manipulate the symbols of Islam in order to induce the Turkish peasantry to vote against its own interests.

Iran

The Islamic revolution in Iran was not a bourgeois revolution, though in the long run, the new regime may become increasingly responsive to the interests, and even the influence of the Iranian bourgeoisie. The gradual integration of Iran into the world economic system, and the concomitant growth of the Iranian bourgeoisie lagged behind the parallel developments in Egypt and Turkey. Iran had its own pseudo-Bonaparte in Reza Shah, modeled after Ataturk, as was Nasser to some extent. But despite that fact, the Reza Shah regime had little in common with bureaucratic-authoritarianism as we know it from the Latin American model. It was not based on an alliance with a subordinated bourgeois class: it did not develop and patronize its own labor movement; it did not act as the implicit representative of petit bourgeois interests; even though Reza built a new army, increased petroleum revenue, built important infrastructural facilities, centralized administrative authority, and was inclined to encourage import substitution industrialization. Nevertheless, the Reza Shah regime was not a bourgeois regime, and it did not lead to the emergence of an assertive bourgeois class.

It was rather the largely traditional commercial bourgeoisie which gradually grew and consolidated its position from the last quarter of the nineteenth century, through the constitutional movement, and up to the forced abdication of Reza Shah in 1941. The period from 1941 to 1953, beginning with the wartime occupation of Iran by Britain and the Soviet Union, and ending with the overthrow of Mosaddeq, is sometimes known as a democratic interlude. It was a period of intense political competition and almost continuous foreign intervention. During this period, the Tudeh party was founded, and a self-conscious labor movement was organized. It is from this period that we can date the emergence of a national bourgeoisie that can be differentiated from the traditional merchants of the bazaar. It was during this period that the clergy again became politically active in opposition to the monarchy, but it was also during this period that the owners of the largest agricultural estates attempted to assert their political power.

Reza Shah, the Iranian Bonaparte or the Iranian Ataturk, did not succeed in transforming the Iranian polity, and he did not bequeath a stable regime to his successors. He did, however, rationalize the structure of the political contest, and he did establish the rudiments of an army and a state which could serve as prizes for any who might seize control thereof. Reza Shah established the apparatus of a modern state, all but crushed the clergy, and ruled in an extremely tense association with the great latifundists, the Qajar nobility, and the mercantile bourgeoisie. The Tudeh Party, with support from the Soviet Union, and the National Front, with support from the United States, each tried to gain control of postwar Iran, as though it were a mature capitalist society in which the proletariat and the bourgeoisie were arrayed against one another in splendid isolation. In fact, neither group really represented a class, neither class had developed a sophisticated consciousness, and neither group could pose a challenge without external support. There was consequently, something artificial about the political conflicts of the Mosaddeq period and its immediate aftermath.

The same artificial and largely ideological dualism appears in the political crisis of the early 1960s. That was the period in which American pressure on Iran led to, first, a strengthening of the National Front, and then to land reform, the beginning of the White Revolution and the suppression of the clerical opposition movement led by Ayatullah Khomeini. Sharing power with the National Front, for all of the facile identification of that group as both liberal and bourgeois, would have done little to create a liberal regime in Iran because of the questionable social support of the Front. The Shah, in any case, was more inclined to keep tight control of the state apparatus, while making extensive concessions to liberal preferences in other spheres. The White Revolution was the answer to both American pressures and the demands of the liberals. Its most important component was the land reform which weakened the landed classes and encouraged the rapid growth of the indigenous bourgeoisie. At the same time, this new bourgeoisie was directed toward cooperation with foreign capital and industrial enterprise, while the state embarked on a development program that increasingly overshadowed the efforts of the private sector.

For at least one doctrinaire Marxist revolutionary, the land reform was the equivalent of a bourgeois revolution, but Bizhan Jazani then argues that the development policies of the White Revolution induced the *national* bourgeoisie to become a *comprador* bourgeoisie, acquiescing in the domination of imperialism and its oppressive autocratic ally.[1] Jazani further points out that the clergy was divided in its attachments to both the landed ("feudal") elite and the (merchant) bourgeoisie. The clergy was, however, constrained to oppose the land reform, not only because of the dependence of the clergy on landed endowments, but because of the traditional Islamic position on private property, and because behind the White Revolution lay the threat of a renewed Pahlavi effort to bureaucratize and control the clergy itself as a part of the state apparatus. Jazani argues, convincingly, that the peasantry accepted the land reform enthusiastically, as did the liberal intelligentsia and the petite bourgeoisie. As a consequence, the clergy, led by Khomeini, sought to fight the reforms on other grounds, such as opposing equal rights for women and the extension of extraterritorial privileges to American forces. The clerical opposition was based primarily on the threat to Islam and Iranian culture.

The 1960–64 crisis period led to a series of reforms that strengthened Iranian capitalism, while alienating the clergy and excluding the liberal nationalists from political participation. As things turned out, the liberals and the clergy made no common cause and found no common ground. Their failure to form a political alliance, despite the limited precedents of the constitutional movement and the Mosaddeq period, foreshadowed the break which was to occur shortly after the Islamic Revolution. The mass rising of 5 June 1963 was the model for the mass involvement in the revolutionary activities of 1978 and 1979, but they demonstrated the influence of the clergy over the petite bourgeoisie and the urban lumpen strata rather than any emergent alliance with the urban bourgeoisie. Faced with a threat to the autonomy of their own institution, guided in part by Khomeini's personal ambition to leadership of the clerical establishment, influenced by the willingness of a few liberals to join in support of Khomeini's campaign, a large segment of the clergy put itself in opposition to the emergent bourgeoisie, maintaining its traditional reliance on the landed proprietors and the bazaar. The postrevolutionary position of the clergy has been defined in large part by the positions taken in the early 1960s.

If the period of the White Revolution (1964–1978) was one of the growth of capitalism and the further integration of Iran into the world market and system of international finance, it was not a period of the growth of an autonomous and influential national bourgeoisie. During this period Muhammad Reza Shah completed the construction of a powerful, centralized, and technocratic state apparatus, and a powerful modern military machine. These, together with enormously increased petroleum resources and generous international political support, created the illusion that the Shah needed virtually no domestic support at all, but could take on and challenge all sections of society at once. This illusion of autonomy, that the state was not part of Iranian civil society, and the political style of autocracy, undermined the confidence of even the closest supporters of the regime. No one was indispensible, no one was safe from suspicion, no one was immune from political sacrifice.

Certainly, there was continued preferment of the interests of the comprador bourgeoisie over the national bourgeoisie, of industry over commercial interests, of foreign trade over domestic trade, of joint-stock agribusiness with foreign involvement over indigenous agrarian capitalism. The growth of the apparatus of the state and the expansion of the education system contributed to the expansion of the petite bourgeoisie without improving their material circumstances. Agricultural policy actually encouraged the expansion of holdings and accelerated the migration of landless peasants to the cities, swelling the ranks of the urban dispossessed.

As the regime gained self-confidence, it alienated its social support, and created an atmosphere of suspicion and anxiety, which was exploited and enhanced by the tactics of new urban guerilla movements. The regime was enticed into increasingly violent repressive responses, while denying the need to share authority with either the bourgeoisie or the liberal intelligentsia. In time, despite the material wealth which Iran gained in the 1970s, and despite its importance to U.S. policy in the Middle East, the foreign and domestic beneficiaries of the Shah's regime began to worry about the degree to which it was alienating opposition elements.

In the end, though, it seems to me that the Iranian state collapsed from within. When the Shah sought to respond to economic difficulties and to political pressures at home and abroad, he sent out a number of mixed signals, making it difficult to discern whether he intended to increase repression or to liberalize the system. Given the arbitrariness of the Shah's autocracy and the precariousness of political power and position within the system, some simply drew aside to wait it out, while others began to maneuver desperately in an effort to survive despite the Shah's uncertainty.

When increasingly challenged in the late 1970s, the regime responded equivocally, thus encouraging the opposition to express itself in new ways. As the battle for control of policy within the regime proceeded, it is apparent that some felt that it was to their tactical advantage to exaggerate the threat. But the "natural" allies of the regime were neither mobilized nor intimidated by the assertiveness of the opposition, or the weakness of the regime. The orthodox left was not leading the attack on the regime, it was following the initiatives of the educated middle class, the clergy, the bazaar, and various student organizations, whose ideologies included a mixture of rationalism, Islam, and socialism. There was, in fact, little fear that the left would gain control of the revolutionary movement and direct the activity of the urban masses. There was even less fear of the role that the lower middle class might play. The educated classes did not believe that the clergy could or would lead the movement. Under the circumstances, the combination of mass demonstrations and work stoppages in some of the major state institutions seemed both rational and an effective means of bringing down the regime.

The class character of the Islamic revolution was not manifest, and still is not manifest. The provisional government established after the collapse of the Bakhtiar effort was composed of members of the educated middle class, technocrats, intellectuals, and professionals. The pattern reflected Khomeini's earliest orientation based upon the excellent rapport he had established with a number of exiled intellectuals. It was as though the alliance that should have been forged in 1963, was now realized in 1979, and that the future of the revolution would be determined by the obvious confluence of class interests, despite the ideological distance that separated the extremes of the revolutionary movement. The emergence of the bourgeois class, heralded by the initiation of the White Revolution but blocked by the arbitrariness of the Shah's autocracy, would now be completed. The Iranian bourgeoisie would join with its natural allies among the clergy and the educated middle class to restore state authority, while opening the system to wider participation. American support would, if anything, become even stronger, though some of the multinationals might be discomfited, as might some of Iran's Arab neighbors and OPEC colleagues.

The revolution did not turn out as expected because the local revolutionary committees and the bands of revolutionary guards, both in Tehran and in the provinces, refused to disband and to acquiesce in the restoration of the authority of the government and the central bureaucracy. Various revolutionary groups of workers, peasants, students, and government employees took over buildings, administrative functions, and even security or judicial functions. The Bazargan government struggled to establish order, prefering to postpone the redefinition of the regime. But wherever local groups had seized power, or property, or authority, they were reluctant to give it up. Moreover, a sizable component of Khomeini's clerical support came from those associated with the petite bourgeoisie who were suspicious of the educated classes, distrustful of the liberal intellectuals, and eager to increase their own power and prestige. Many clerics, who were themselves leaders of local revolutionary committees, were disturbed by attacks from the left and concerned about the ineffectiveness of the liberals. Nor did the liberals always hide their contempt for the journeymen clergy. Consequently, many were induced to encourage the continued recalcitrance of the revolutionary committees with which they were charged.

The "radical" clergy, redefining Khomeini's concept of *vilayat e-faqih* to represent the collective political precedence of the clergy, asserted their own direct leadership. In alliance with groups of students, revolutionary guards, and then organized groups of street fighters, the leaders of the Islamic Republic Party (IRP) crushed the left, undermined the liberals, and intimidated the bourgeoisie. Responding to various demands for economic improvement and the diffusion of authority, the revolutionary government approved policies of the nationalization of industry and banking, the distribution of land, and even total regulation of commerce. Gradually, however, the IRP gained control of the situation in the streets, and began to reestablish the authority of the government they now dominated. More recently, the conservative views of Khomeini and the members of the Guardians Council have come to prevail. The commercial bourgeoisie is again favored by government tax and trade policy. Agricultural land has been restored to its Iranian owners in many cases, though the operations of the mixed foreign and domestic agribusiness enterprises have been taken over by the government. Industry is still largely government controlled, although there is some inclination to restore private enterprise to the extent possible.

In its early phase, the Iranian revolution manifested strong anticapitalist and antibourgeois tendencies. Gradually, as domestic opponents of clerical power were defeated, and as the war with Iraq became the major focus of ideological and political concern, the Islamic Republic has relented in its pressure on the propertied classes. At the same time, the government has consolidated its power, and it has gained much more control of both the committees and of the revolutionary guards. Increasingly, the role of law, that is Islamic law, is emphasized, and the idea of the adaptive reinterpretation of Islam is neglected. Ideas such as the universal imamate of all Muslims, or the contingent nature of the right of private property, or the right of laymen to interpret Islamic law or the Qur'an, have been identified with the defeated liberals, who are regarded as having succumbed to the influence of Western culture.

The revolutionary Iranian state is still evolving, but its general lines are now discernible. In place of a bureaucratic authoritarian regime dominated by an alliance of the military and the administrative elites, we have a similar regime dominated by a clerical faction. Instead of a one-party system based on an ideology of national unity and interclass harmony, we have a similar party based on Islamic solidarity and the authority of the mujtahids. The expansion of the public sector and the continuing emphasis on prosecuting the war with Iraq have produced a pattern of state authority and autonomy which is familiar from the experience of Egypt and of Turkey. The

 Iranian state is similar in many ways to Laroui's national state. It is also based on an implicit alliance between the apparatus of the state and the petite bourgeoisie. The traditional merchant and landed allies of the clergy are admitted to the periphery of the coalition, while the educated classes are admitted only to the extent of their involvement in the state administration, one of the state enterprises, or the military. There is a quite different cast of characters in charge in Iran, but there are important similarities with the situation of Turkey in the 1920s and Egypt in the 1950s. The question is, what difference does it make that the Iranian revolution and successor petit bourgeois state is led by the clergy?

Neither the regime of Ataturk, nor that of Nasser, nor that of Khomeini was or is liberal or bourgeois. None of the three revolutions associated with these heroic figures was a bourgeois revolution. But, as we have seen, neither the Turkish national state nor the Egyptian national state, as defined by Laroui, was able to sustain and reproduce itself for more than a generation. In each case, petit bourgeois regimes linked to relatively autonomous state apparati and relying on rural traditional authority, gradually turned toward cooperation with the urban bourgeoisie and the nontechnocratic or liberal intelligentsia. Both regimes took an early anticlerical or antireligious stand, but gradually relented. Can we expect that Iran will follow a similar path on the question of the urban bourgeoisie and the liberal intelligentsia, and a reversed path on the Islamic question? And if such an evolution is possible, what are the prospects for political liberalism in Iran?

The revolutionary regime in Iran has rejected the very foundation of Islamic liberalism, and has embraced the orientalist caricature of Islamic scripturalism. This was not an inevitable development, though not a surprising one, either, given Khomeini's political doctrines and the nature of Shiʿite orthodoxy. Moreover, the exigencies of the revolutionary conflict and of the subsequent and not unexpected war, place a high premium on the maintenance of centralized control and unquestioned authority. But neither can we ignore the social basis which produced the revolutionary divisions, and the social forces which determined the winners and the losers in the postrevolutionary struggle for power. For the moment, the spirit of Shiʿite martyrology, cultural xenophobia, and petit bourgeois pessimism dominates over Iranian nationalism and the ideology of development and modernization. Not only is there no need for the clergy to share power; so long as the war persists, it may even be politically unwise or dangerous to do so. In the longer run, however, the claims that have been made in the name of Khomeini's ability to translate the will of God into current policy will have to be made good or rescinded. So long as the infallible interpretations of God's will leads to war, self-sacrifice and martyrdom, to a rejection of this world, the pretensions of the regime may indeed be unassailable. But when one turns to the possibilities of life, of material well being, and of hope for the future, a different form of discourse is required.

Islamic Fundamentalism

Islamic fundamentalism has been identified as the cause of the revolution in Iran, of domestic terrorism in Turkey, and of the assassination of President Sadat. In our concern with this newly invigorated Islamic tendency, and in our anxiety about where it may next erupt, we have all but forgotten that this brand of fundamentalism is still very much a minority orientation. There is relatively little chance that fundamentalist Islam will overwhelm and replace the traditional Islam of the mullahs, the schools, and the neighborhood mosques. But there is a significant possibility that fundamentalist Islam will successfully challenge the liberal Islam which has until recently attracted the Western-educated, the modernizing bureaucratic elite, the academic elite, the lawyers and the urban bourgeoisie.

Fundamentalist Islam and liberal Islam appear to have ready sociological, cultural, and political referrents, and they lend themselves to ideological analysis as two of the significant aspects of the contemporary political process in Muslim countries. Still, both fundamentalist Islam and liberal Islam draw on the same religious sources, they often employ the same types of reasoning, they usually concentrate on the same authoritative pronouncements, and in some cases the differences between the two may be difficult to discern. The absence of a clear doctrinal break, and the fact that fundamentalists and liberals joined forces in the Iranian revolution, have led some observers to argue that, in recent times, the two have tended to fuse, ideologically and politically.

On the face of it, this observation seems to contradict established social scientific expectations that, over time, differences in social position will be manifested in practical politics, and that relevant interests will be justified by ideological differentiation. Hence, if it is true that Islamic fundamentalism and liberalism are in the process of fusion, this development should be paralleled in terms of social restructuring, political organization and strategy, and in ideological communication. It is also possible that the appearance of ideological and political fusion is the consequence of the recent intimidation of the liberals, resulting from the dual affect of political repression from above and the threat of violent lawlessness from below. It is even more likely that the apparent convergence of Islamic liberalism and

 Islamic fundamentalism is but the ideological dimension of efforts to forge an alliance among the bourgeoisie, the petite bourgeoisie and the professional intelligentsia. Just as the competition among these classes and groups is frequently masked, so are the ideological issues covered by the obscurity of doctrinal or exegetical disputes. At this time, nearly every group has an interest in minimizing the extent of its ideological differences with the others, but with the unfolding of events in the future it is likely that the new Islamic synthesis will be found to favor either some form of authoritarian regime or a liberal regime in which the bourgeoisie will play a leading role.

The Muslim bourgeoisie does not have powerful instruments at its disposal, despite its links with the military and the bureaucracy. The intellectual and liberal segments of the bourgeoisie are largely unable to exercise leverage through political parties or parliaments. Moreover, those social segments, bourgeois, petit bourgeois, bureaucratic bourgeois, and so forth, that support a strong state, may well not find fundamentalist doctrine to be worrisome. Hence it is only a section of the modernized strata which is committed to liberalism, and only part of that section emphasizes the compatibility of Islam and political liberalism. Yet this section of a section bears the intellectual responsibility for facing the challenge of fundamentalism and of bureaucratic authoritarianism in Muslim countries.

But liberalism is not merely an idea. It is also an expression of the practical interests of a number of groups, such as intellectuals, journalists, free professionals, private entrepreneurs, religious minorities, ethnic minorities and even segments of the rural gentry. These may be influential groups, but they are hardly powerful enough to attain political hegemony without allies. In Iran, the liberals formed an alliance with both the left and the religious establishment, and their role was absolutely indispensable in moderating American opposition to the revolution and in inducing the Shah to abdicate without further struggle. But the liberal leadership was of little further use when it came to consolidating revolutionary power and rebuilding state authority. When brushed aside by the militant clergy, all but a handful of the liberals went quietly into political retirement or exile. Liberalism will not be established by force, and even those few who were willing to martyr themselves for it, like Ghotbzadeh and Bani Sadr, or even Mosaddeq and Kasravi, are thought of as eccentric or quixotic personalities.

The situation is not hopeless, but neither is the time quite right. It is enormously difficult to develop liberalism outside of a sustaining bourgeois culture in which a high value is placed upon liberal education, individual dignity, the rule of law, freedom of the press, freedom of artistic expression and criticism, not to mention life itself, health, privacy, leisure, quiet, and even space. It is impossible to isolate the middle classes from the impoverished, traditional and ignorant mass upon whom they depend for vital and daily services. The culture of Middle Eastern societies is profoundly affected by the constant need to communicate with the illiterate and the poorest classes. There are no cultural enclaves or social settings which are truly insulated from this interdependence. Hence the lowest classes, while not dominating Middle Eastern society, weigh upon it so heavily as to make it impossible to escape their massive, glacial, and pitiable presence. For the most part passive, this underclass has nevertheless shown that it can be moved by religious appeals which promise change, and that it will be moved by sudden price changes which threaten its marginal existence. In the face of such a dismaying reality, it seems foolish indeed to attempt to rally the sansculottes to the barricades on behalf of a concept which is as complicated as Islamic liberalism.

Until the circumstances render the concept self-evidently meaningful to mass and elite alike, the prospects for Islamic liberalism will remain dim. But in the interim it may be possible to reassess those prospects in terms of the continued rise of the Muslim bourgeoisie, the continued elaboration of the doctrine of Islamic liberalism, and the continuing attrition of state autonomy.

The attrition of state autonomy is not the same thing as the decline of the power of the state, even though it serves the interests of some to conflate the two ideas. There are good reasons to fear the decline of state power and authority, if only to take Lebanon as an example. But there are also circumstances in which liberalism may strengthen, rather than weaken, the state, as indeed, is the central argument of the neoliberal development paradigm and its post-Marxian theory of the capitalist state. In Egypt and Turkey, Syria and Iraq, Tunisia and Algeria, Islamic militance challenges the autonomy and the authority of the state and, therefore, may, in the long run, advance the cause of political liberalism, if only pragmatically. An alternative possibility is, however, suggested by Iran where the clergy have become the state elite par excellence, and where Islamic legitimacy may solve the problem of the capacity of that authoritarian state to reproduce itself.

Notes

1

1. J. Habermas, "What is Universal Pragmatics," in *Communication and the Evolution of Society* (Boston: Beacon Press, 1979), 1–68, 208–9.

2. Hans-Georg Gadamer, *Truth and Method* (New York: Seabury, 1975). This work is discussed at greater length in chapters three and eight.

3. Richard Rorty, *Philosophy and the Mirror of Nature* (Princeton: Princeton University Press, 1979).

4. Michel Foucault, *The Archaeology of Knowledge and the Discourse on Language*, trans. A. M. Sheridan (New York: Harper Torchbooks, 1972). Foucault's ideas are discussed at greater length in chapter three.

2

1. Aidan Southall, "Stateless Society," in *International Encyclopedia of the Social Sciences*, D. Sills, ed. vol. 15, 155 ff (New York: Macmillan, 1968). See also E. E. Evans-Pritchard and Meyer Fortes, eds., *African Political Systems* (London: Oxford University Press, 1940).

2. David Easton, "Political Anthropology," in *Biennial Review of Anthropology 1959*, Bernard J. Siegel, ed. (Stanford: Stanford University Press, 1959), 210–62.

3. J. P. Nettl, "The State as a Conceptual Variable," *World Politics* 20:4 (July 1968): 559–92.

4. Samuel P. Huntington, "Political Development and Political Decay." *World Politics* 17:3 (April 1965): 386–430. J. P. Nettl. *Political Mobilization* (New York: Basic Books, 1967).

5. C. J. Friedrich, *Constitutional Government and Democracy: Theory and Practice in Europe and America*. Rev. ed. (Boston: Ginn, 1950).

6. E.g., C. Wright Mills, *Sociology and Pragmatism* (New York: Paine-Whitman 1964), 173 et passim; and Jurgen Habermas, *Knowledge and Human Interests*, tr. Jeremy J. Shapiro (Boston: Beacon Press, 1971), 91–112.

7. Arthur F. Bentley, *The Process of Government: A Study of Social Pressures* (Chicago: The University of Chicago Press, 1908).

8. Talcott Parsons, *The Structure of Social Action* (New York: Free Press, 1949); H. Lasswell and A. Kaplan, *Power and Society, A Framework for Political Inquiry* (New Haven: Yale University Press, 1950): "Part One: The subject matter of political science is constituted by the conduct of persons with various perspectives of action and organized into groups of varying complexity" (facing p.xxiv); David Easton, "An Approach to the Analysis of Political Systems," *World Politics* 9:3 (April 1957): 383–400; Karl Deutsch, *The Nerves of Government: Models of Political Communication and Control* (London: Free Press of Glencoe, 1963); David B. Truman, *The Governmental Process: Political Interests and Public Opinion* (New York: Knopf, 1971).

9. J. David Greenstone, "Group Theories," in *Handbook of Political Science*, vol. 2, Fred I. Greenstein and Nelson W. Polsby, eds. (Reading: Addison-Wesley Publishing Company, 1975), 243–318; Paul F. Kress, *Social Science and the Idea of Process* (Urbana: University of Illinois Press, 1970).

10. Stanley Rothman, "Systematic Political Theory: Observations on the Group Approach," *American Political Science Review* 54:1 (March 1960): 15–33, esp. 23–25.

11. C. Wright Mills, *Sociology and Pragmatism*, 426 ff; John Dewey, *Freedom and Culture* (New York: Capricorn Books, 1963). *See also* David Apter, *Choice and the Politics of Allocation: A Development Theory* (New Haven: Yale University Press, 1971). Much of the "feedback" literature (e.g., Easton, Deutsch) is based on this idea.

12. Greenstone, "Group Theories," 260–62.

13. Ben Page, *Who Gets What from Government* (Berkeley: University of California Press, 1983).

14. Amartya Sen, "Social Choice and Justice: A Review Article," *Journal of Economic Literature* 23 (December 1985): 1764–76.

15. Jon Elster, *Making Sense of Marx* (Cambridge: Cambridge University Press, 1985), esp. Section 1.2, p.8f.

16. Mancur Olson, *The Rise and Decline of Nations: Economic Growth, Stagflation and Social Rigidities* (New Haven: Yale University Press, 1982); Michael Hudson, *Arab Politics: The Search for Legitimacy* (New Haven: Yale University Press, 1977), 280 ff.

17. Mancur Olson, *The Logic of Collective Action* (Cambridge, Mass.: Harvard University Press, 1971), 121–25.

18. *SSRC Annual Report 1953–54* (New York: SSRC, 1954), 40 and 47.

19. Gabriel A. Almond and James S. Coleman, *The Politics of the Developing Areas* (Princeton: Princeton University Press, 1960), chap. 1

20. Parsons, *The Structure of Social Action*, p. 751; and, T. Parsons and E. Shils, *Toward a General Theory of Action* (Glencoe: Free Press, 1950).

21. J. Habermas, *Legitimation Crisis* (Boston: Beacon Press, 1975), 7, 89, 117ff.

22. G. McT. Kahin, G. J. Pauker, and L. W. Pye, "Comparative Politics of Non-Western Countries," *American Political Science Review* 49:4 (December 1955): 1022–41.

23. Daniel Lerner, *The Passing of Traditional Society: Modernizing the Middle East* (New York: Free Press, 1958); K. Deutsch, *Nationalism and Social Communication* (New York: Wiley & Technology Press, 1953).

24. Daniel Lerner. *The Passing of Traditional Society*, 43f.

25. Karl Deutsch, "Toward an Inventory of Basic Trends and Patterns in Comparative and International Relations," *American Political Science Review* 54:1 (March 1960): 34–57; and K. Deutsch, "Social Mobilization and Political Development," *American Political Science Review* 55:3 (September 1961): 493–514. *See* S. Eisenstadt, "Modernization and Conditions of Sustained Growth," *World Politics* 16:4 (July 1964): 576–594; and J. S. Coleman, in *Crises and Sequences*, 73 (See note 35, below).

26. John Taylor, *From Modernization to Modes of Production: A Critique of the*

Sociologies of Development and Underdevelopment (Atlantic Highlands: Humanities Press, 1979).

27. Ibid., 36.

28. Ibid., 32.

29. T. S. Kuhn, *The Structure of Scientific Revolutions* (Chicago: University of Chicago Press, 1962).

30. Taylor, *From Modernization to Modes of Production*, 36.

31. Ibid., 29.

32. Samuel P. Huntington, *Political Order in Changing Societies* (New Haven: Yale University Press, 1968), 21, 25, 98, 341; Samuel P. Huntington and Joan M. Nelson, *No Easy Choice: Political Participation in Developing Countries* (Cambridge, Mass: Harvard University Press, 1976). *See also* L. Binder, "Political Participation and Political Development," *American Journal of Sociology* (Autumn 1977).

33. Edward Shils, *Political Development in the New States* (London: Mouton, 1965); Reinhard Bendix, *Nation Building and Citizenship* (New York: Wiley and Sons, 1964); Lloyd Rudolph and Suzanne Rudolph, *The Modernity of Tradition: Political Development in India* (Chicago: The University of Chicago Press, 1967); Robert A. Nisbet, *Social Change and History* (New York: Oxford University Press, 1969).

34. J. P. Nettl, *Political Mobilization*; Aristide Zolberg, *Creating Political Order* (Chicago: Rand McNally 1966); Joseph G. LaPalombara and Myron Weiner, *Political Parties and Political Development* (Princeton: Princeton University Press, 1966); M. Janowitz, *Military Institutions and Coercion in the Developing Nations* (Chicago: University of Chicago Press, 1977); and Joseph G. La Palombara, *Bureaucracy and Political Development* (Princeton: Princeton University Press, 1963).

35. L. Binder et al., *Crises and Sequences in Political Development* (Princeton: Princeton University Press, 1971); Mark Kesselman, "Order or Movement? The Literature of Political Development as Ideology" *World Politics* 26:1 (October 1973): 139–54.

36. Charles Tilly, ed., *The Formation of National States in Western Europe* (Princeton: Princeton University Press, 1975).

37. Gabriel A. Almond and G. Bingham Powell, *Comparative Politics: A Developmental Approach* (Boston: Little, Brown and Co., 1966); G. A. Almond and Scott C. Flanagan, et al., *Crises, Choice and Change: Historical Studies of Political Development* (Boston: Little, Brown and Co., 1973); S. Huntington and J. Nelson, *No Easy Choice.*

38. Greenstone, "Group Theories."

39. *Proposal to the SSRC for a Research Planning Committee on States and Social Structures*, submitted by P. Evans, A. Hirschman, P. Katzenstein, I. Katznelson, S. Krasner, D. Rueschemeyer, T. Skocpol, and C. Tilly, dated April 1983. Covering letter reporting approval of proposal signed by M. Gephart, dated August 1983.

40. Theda Scocpol, "Bringing the State back In," SSRC *Items* 36:1/2 (June 1982): 1–8.

41. Ibid., 4.

42. Ibid., 7.

43. The literature on these subjects is immense, but the following may provide a basis for further inquiry: Shlomo Avineri, ed., *Marx on Colonialism and Modernization* (New York: Doubleday, 1969); Karl A. Wittfogel, *Oriental Despotism* (New York: Vintage Books, 1981); Anne M. Bailey and Joseph R. Llobera. *The Asiatic Mode of Production* (Boston: Routledge & Kegan Paul, 1981); Maxime Rodinson, *Islam and Capitalism* (Paris: Éditions du Seuil, 1966), 61.

44. André Gunder Frank, *Capitalism and Underdevelopment in Latin America* (New York: Monthly Review Press, 1967). *See also* Samir Amin, *Accumulation on a World Scale: A Critique of the Theory of Underdevelopment*, trans. Brian Pearce (New York: Monthly Review Press, 1974); Raul Prebisch, "The Economic Development of Latin America and Its Principle Problems" (New York: United Nations, 1950).

45. Samir Amin, *Accumulation;* Arghiri Emmanuel, *Unequal Exchange: A Study of the Imperialism of Trade* (New York: Monthly Review Press, 1972).

46. John Taylor, *From Modernization to Modes of Production;* Barry Hindess and Paul Hirst, *Precapitalist Modes of Production* (Boston: Routledge & Kegan Paul, 1975); B. Hindess and P. Hirst, *Mode of Production and Social Formation: an Auto-critique of Precapitalist Modes of Production* (London: MacMillan, 1977).

47. Shimon Shamir, "The Marxists in Egypt" in *The USSR and the Middle East*, M. Confino and S. Shamir, eds. (Jerusalem: Israel Universities Press, 1973), 293 ff.

48. Mahmoud Husain (pseud.), *Class Conflict in Egypt: 1945–1970* (New York: Monthly Review Press, 1973). *See also* Samir Amin, *The Arab Nation*, trans. Michael Pallis (London: Zed Press, 1978).

49. Ralph Miliband, *The State in Capitalist Society* (New York: Basic Books, 1969); Ernst Mandel, *Late Capitalism*, trans. Joris de Bres (London: New Left Books, 1975); Jurgen Habermas, *Legitimation Crisis*, trans. Thomas McCarthy (Boston: Beacon Press, 1973).

50. Geoffrey Kay, *Development and Underdevelopment* (London: Macmillan, 1975).

51. For example, Samir Amin, *The Arab Nation*, 111 ff.; Adil Hussein, *al-Iqtisad al-Misriyya, min al-Istiqlal ila al-Taba ʿiyya*, 2 vols. (Beirut: 1982); Abdallah Laroui, *L'Ideologie arabe contemporaine* (Paris: F. Maspero, 1967), 139 ff.

52. Bill Warren, *Imperialism: Pioneer of Capitalism* (London: New Shelf Books, 1981).

53. F. H. Cardoso and Enzo Falletto, *Dependency and Development in Latin America* trans. Marjory Mattingly Urquidi (Berkeley: University of California Press, 1979); Guillermo O'Donnell, *Modernization and Bureaucratic Authoritarianism* (Berkeley: Institute of International Studies, University of California, 1973); Theda Skocpol, *States and Social Revolutions* (Cambridge: Cambridge University Press, 1979); Immanuel Wallerstein, *The Origins of the Modern World System* (New York: Academic Press, 1974).

54. Ted Benton, *The Rise and Fall of Structural Marxism: Althusser and his Influence* (London: Macmillan, 1984), xi. 2–3, 14–23.

55. Steven B. Smith, *Reading Althusser: An Essay in Structural Marxism* (Ithaca: Cornell University Press, 1984), 30–70; Benton, *Rise and Fall*, 58.

56. Smith, *Reading Althusser,* 45, 210; Maurice Merleau-Ponty, *The Phenomenology of Perception,* trans. Colin Smith (New York: Humanities Press, 1962); Jurgen Habermas, *Knowledge and Human Interests,* trans. Jeremy Shapiro (Boston: Beacon Press, 1971).

57. Frantz Fanon, *The Wretched of the Earth* (New York: Grove, 1968).

58. Benton, *Rise and Fall,* 12; Smith *Reading Althusser,* 68 et passim.

59. Benton, *Rise and Fall,* 67, 100; Smith, *Reading Althusser,* 132.

60. Nicos Poulantzas, *Political Power and Social Classes,* trans. T. O'Hagan (London: NLB, 1975); John Taylor, *From Modernization to Modes of Production.*

61. Benton, *Rise and Fall,* 89, 203 f., 228–9; Smith, *Reading Althusser,* 106–7, 213 f.

62. Benton, *Rise and Fall,* 40; Smith, *Reading Althusser,* 87–8.

63. Benton, *Rise and Fall,* 50–1, 205.

64. Poulantzas, *Political Power and Social Classes,* 178, 193, et passim.

65. Ibid., 259–262.

66. Ibid., 29–47, footnote 17, 110 et passim.

67. Ibid., 101–14, 130 f.

68. Ibid., 247, 286, 296 ff.

69. Ibid., 81, 247 et passim.

70. Taylor, *From Modernization to Modes of Production,* 71 ff.

71. Ibid., 266, 274, 275.

72. Ibid., 240.

73. Ibid., 276, footnote 12.

74. Peter Evans, *Dependent Development: The Alliance of Multinational, State and Local Capital in Brazil* (Princeton: Princeton University Press, 1979).

75. R. Packenham, "Plus Ça Change . . . The English Edition of Cardoso and Falleto's, *Dependencia y Desarollo en America Latina,*" *Latin American Research Papers* 17(1):142–46.

76. O'Donnell, *Modernization and Bureaucratic Authoritarianism;* David Collier, ed., *The New Authoritarianism in Latin America* (Princeton: Princeton University Press, 1979).

77. Guillermo O'Donnell, "Tensions in the Bureaucratic-Authoritarian State and the Question of Democracy," in Collier, ed., *The New Authoritarianism,* 285f.

78. Collier, ed., *The New Authoritarianism,* 386–87.

79. Ibid., 395.

80. Ibid., 369.

81. Ibid., 387.

82. *Review,* A Journal of Fernand Braudel center for the Study of Economics, Historical Systems and Civilizations (by Research Foundation of the State University of New York), publishes articles which conform to a perspective described by the editors as one "which recognizes the primacy of analyses of economics over long historical time and large space, the holism of the social-historical process, and the transitory (heuristic) nature of theories," *Review* 3:2 (Fall 1979). Issue 1 was printed Summer 1977 (quarterly).

83. Immanuel Wallerstein, *The Modern World System: I* (New York: Academic Press, 1974), 348.

84. J. A. Goldstone, "The Comparative and Historical Study of Revolu-

 tions," *Annual Review of Sociology,* vol. 8, eds., Ralph H. Turner and James F. Short, Jr. (Palo Alto, 1982), 187–207.

85. Ibid., 194. *See* Barrington Moore, *Social Origins of Dictatorship and Democracy* (Boston: Beacon Press, 1966).

86. Goldstone, "The Comparative and Historical Study of Revolutions," 193–94.

87. Crane Brinton, *The Anatomy of Revolution* (New York: Vintage Books, 1965); Goldstone, "The Comparative and Historical Study of Revolutions," 189–92.

88. Moore, *Social Origins,* 468 ff.

89. Theda Skocpol, "A Critical Review of Barrington Moore's *Social Origins of Dictatorship and Democracy,*" *Politics and Society* 4:1 (Fall 1973): 1–34.

90. Skocpol, *States and Social Revolutions,* 116 and 154.

91. Ibid., 285–86.

92. Hans Rosenberg, *Bureaucracy, Aristocracy and Autocracy: The Prussian Experience 1660–1815* (Cambridge, Mass: Harvard University Press, 1958).

93. Ervand Abrahamian, *Iran Between Two Revolutions* (Princeton: Princeton University Press, 1982), 441; Theda Skocpol, "Rentier State and Shi'a Islam in the Iranian Revolution," *Theory and Society* 11 (1982): 265–83.

94. François Furet, *Penser la Révolution Française* (Paris: Gallimard, 1978).

95. Ibid., 133ff.

96. Ibid., 191.

97. Ibid., 129.

98. Skocpol, *States and Social Revolutions,* pp. 13, 34–5, 174f.

99. Ibid., 112–7.

100. Furet, *Penser la Révolution Française,* 123, 125.

101. G.O'Donnell and P. C. Schmitter, *Transitions From Authoritarian Rule: Tentative Conclusions about Uncertain Democracies* (Baltimore: Johns Hopkins, 1986).

102. Laurence Whitehead, "International Aspects of Democratization," in *Transitions from Authoritarian Rule: Comparative Perspectives,* G. O'Donnell, P. C. Schmitter, and L. Whitehead, eds. (Baltimore: Johns Hopkins, 1986), 3–46.

103. Adam Przeworski, "Some Problems in the Study of Transitions to Democracy," in G. O'Donnell, P. C. Schmitter, and L. Whitehead, eds., *Transitions from Authoritarian Rule,* pp. 47–62.

104. Binder, et al., *Crises and Sequences;* J. Habermas, *Legitimation Crisis;* O'Donnell, *Modernization and Bureaucratic Authoritarianism;* Collier, *The New Authoritarianism.*

105. Perry Anderson, *Lineages of the Absolutist State* (London: Verso, 1979), 18ff. et passim.

106. Ibid., 490, 495.

107. Theda Skocpol, "Rentier State and Shi'a Islam in the Iranian Revolution," *Theory and Society* 11 (Amsterdam 1982): 265–83.

108. Ibid., 267.

109. Ibid., 275.

110. Ibid., 269.

111. Ibid., 276.

112. Ibid., 276–77.

113. Ibid., 280.

114. Furet, *Penser la Révolution Française,* 130.

115. Ibid., 127.

116. Adil Hussein, *al-Iqtisad al-Misriyya,* Jalal Ahmad Amin, *Mihna al-Iqtisad w ʿal-Thaqafa fi Misr* (Cairo: al-Markaz al-ʿArabi lil-Bahth wal-Nashr, 1982).

117. Marnia Lazreg, *The Emergence of Classes in Algeria: A Study of Colonialism and Socio-Political Change* (Boulder, Colo.: Westview Press, 1976); Robert Bianchi, *Interest Groups and Political Development in Turkey* (Princeton: Princeton University Press, 1984).

118. William Zartman, "Political Science," in Leonard Binder, ed., *The Study of the Middle East* (New York: John Wiley and Sons, 1976): 265–325.

119. John Waterbury, *The Egypt of Nasser and Sadat* (Princeton: Princeton University Press, 1983).

120. Manfred Halpern, *The Politics of Social Change in the Middle East and North Africa* (Princeton: Princeton University Press, 1963).

121. M. Janowitz, *Military Institutions and Coercion;* Lucian Pye, *Politics, Personality, and Nation Building* (New Haven: Yale University Press, 1962); D. Apter, *The Politics of Modernization* (Chicago: University of Chicago Press, 1965), 164–66 et passim; M. Halpern, "Middle Eastern Armies and the New Middle Class," in J. J. Johnson, ed., *The Role of the Military in Underdeveloped Countries* (Princeton: Princeton University Press, 1962).

122. John Waterbury, *The Egypt of Nasser and Sadat,* 233–34. In private communication, Waterbury has acknowledged that he exaggerated both the capacity and the autonomy of the Egyptian state and was too ready to dismiss "societal" forces as of little account. I have cited a couple of hyperbolic summary statements which seemed to carry a great deal of interpretive significance, even though the evidence which contradicts the image of the all-powerful state abounds on the pages of the book itself. Careful readers will readily discern the disjunction between the narrative meat of the book and the interpretive *garniture.* As in his study of the Moroccan political elite, Waterbury manifests a penchant for personifying social forces and ideas. The result is confusing because he invokes the theory but neither employs it nor criticizes it. Consequently, in the case of Egypt as of Morocco, we get a social science without society, or political actors whose stature is so distorted by the stage lights that the scene behind them is obscured by the shadow of erudite hero worship.

123. Ibid., 203–4., 332.

124. Edward Said, *Orientalism* (New York: Vintage Books, 1979). *See,* for example, pp. 38–39, 119–20, 312–13.

125. Richard Dekmejian, *Egypt Under Nasser: A Study in Political Dynamics* (Albany: State University of New York Press, 1971); R. H. Dekmejian, "Marx, Weber and the Egyptian Revolution," *Middle East Journal* 30:2 (Spring 1976): 158–72.

126. Daniel Lerner, *The Passing of Traditional Society;* Manfred Halpern, *The Politics of Social Change in the Middle East and North Africa.*

127. Daniel Lerner, *The Passing of Traditional Society,* 45: "Whether from

 East or West, modernization poses the same basic challenge—the infusion of 'a rationalist and positivist spirit' against which, scholars seem agreed, 'Islam is absolutely defenseless.'"

128. M. Halpern, *The Politics of Social Change*, 52, 221–23.

129. Bernard Lewis, *The Emergence of Modern Turkey* (London: Oxford University Press, 1961); Manfred Halpern, "Middle Eastern Armies and the New Middle Class"; Keith Wheelock, *Nasser's New Egypt* (New York: Praeger, 1960); Nadav Safran, *Egypt in Search of Political Community* (Cambridge, Mass.: Harvard University Press, 1964); Joseph M. Upton, *The History of Modern Iran* (Cambridge: The Center for Middle Eastern Studies at Harvard University, Harvard University Press, 1960); Richard W. Cottam, *Nationalism in Iran* (Pittsburgh, Penn.: University of Pittsburgh Press, 1964); Donald Newton Wilbur, *Iran, Past and Present* (Princeton: Princeton University Press, 1976); Dankwart A. Rustow, "The Near East and North Africa," *Politics of the Developing Areas*, G. Almond and J. Coleman, *The Politics of the Developing Areas;* Clement Henry Moore, *Tunisia Since Independence* (Berkeley: University of California Press, 1965).

130. P. J. Vatikiotis, *The Egyptian Army in Politics* (Bloomington: Indiana University Press, 1961); R. Dekmejian, *Egypt Under Nasser;* Raymond Baker, *Egypt's Uncertain Revolution Under Nasser and Sadat* (Cambridge: Harvard University Press, 1978); Amos Perlmutter, "The Praetorian State and the Praetorian Army," *Comparative Politics* 1:3 (April 1969): 382–404. From p. 385: "Praetorianism occurs when the civilian government comes to a standstill in its pursuit of nationalist and modernist goals (modernization, urbanization, order, unification, and so forth). Thus, praetorianism is generally associated with the disintegration of an old order and the rise of a decapitated new one." And, from pp. 383–84: "In view of the general trend toward modernization, it may be said that various types of praetorianism probably represent certain stages of development."

131. John Waterbury, *Commander of the Faithful: The Moroccan Political Elite* (New York: Columbia University Press, 1970).

132. Bernard Lewis, "Communism and Islam," in *The Middle East in Transition* W. Laqueur, ed. (New York: Praeger, 1958), 311 ff.

133. P. J. Vatikiotis, "Dilemmas of Political Leadership in the Arab Middle East—The Case of the United Arab Republic," *American Political Science Review* 55 (March 1961): 103, 111; Sylvia Haim, *Arab Nationalism* (Berkeley: University of California Press, 1962).

134. Bernard Lewis, "The Return of Islam," *Commentary* 61:1 (January 1976): 39–49.

135. Ernest Gellner, "A Pendulum Swing Theory of Islam," *The Philosophical Forum* 2:2 (Winter 1970–71): 234–44; Ernest Gellner, "The Moslem Reformation," *The New Republic* 187:20 (November 22, 1982): 25–30.

136. B. Lewis, "The Return of Islam," 44–48.

137. Ibid., 48–49.

138. E. Gellner, "The Moslem Reformation," 27.

139. Idem.

140. Ibid., 30.

141. Ibrahim Abu-Lughod, ed., *Arab Studies Quarterly: The Islamic Alter-*

native 4:1–2 (Spring 1982); Hassan Hanafi, "The Relevance of the Islamic Alternative in Egypt," in Abu-Lughod, ed., *Arab Studies Quarterly,* 4:1–2, 54–58, 65, 71.

142. Edward Said, *Orientalism,* 301: "the Orient is at bottom something either to be feared (the Yellow Peril, the Mongol hordes, the brown dominions) or something to be controlled (by pacification, research, and development, outright occupation whenever possible)." And p. 40: "But . . . everywhere to stress the fact that the Oriental lived in a different but thoroughly organized world of his own, a world with its own national, cultural, and epistemological boundaries and principles of internal coherence"; p. 121: "The modern Orientalist was . . . a hero rescuing the Orient from . . . obscurity, alienation, and strangeness"; p. 296: "He (von Grunebaum) has no difficulty presuming that Islam is a unitary phenomenon, unlike any other religion or civilization, and thereafter he shows it to be antihuman, incapable of development, self-knowledge, or objectivity, as well as uncreative, unscientific, and authoritarian"; p. 303: "[in the *Cambridge History of Islam*] Islam is understood to mean an unrelieved chronology of battles, reigns, and deaths, rises and heydays, comings and passings, written for the most part in a ghastly monotone." *See also* Marwan Buheiry, "Colonial Scholarship and Muslim Revivalism in 1900," *Arab Studies Quarterly: The Islamic Alternative* 4:1–2, 1–16, esp. 4–5.

143. See discussion in Maxime Rodinson, *Islam and Capitalism,* 58–68.

144. Bryan S. Turner, *Weber and Islam* (London: Routledge & Kegan Paul, 1974), and *Marx and the End of Orientalism*(Boston: Allen and Unwin, 1978).

145. Hassan Hanafi, "The Relevance of the Islamic Alternative in Egypt," 54–74; *see also* Hassan Hanafi, ed., *Al-Yasar al-Islami* (The Islamic left) 1:1 (January 1981).

146. Dr. Ali Mukhtar, organizer and rapporteur, "Symposium of Western Political Thought and Arab Political Thought," (Nadwa hawl al-fikr al-siyasi al-gharbi wal-fikr al-siyasi al-ʿarabi), *Al-Fikr al-ʿArabi* 3:23 (October-November 1981), 420–43, with the participation of Dr. Fu ʿad Morsi, Tariq al-Bishri, Dr. Ibrahim Sa ʿd al-Din, Lutfi al-Kholi, Dr. Ibrahim Saqr, Dr. Qasim ʿAbdu Wasim, and Muhammad Sayyid Ahmad. *Also* Hassan Hanafi, *Al-Turath wa al-Tajdid* (Beirut: Dar al-Tanwir, 1981).

147. Sa ʿd al-Din Ibrahim, *al-Ahram al-Iqtisadi* (April 1983).

3

1. For example, Wittgenstein's *Philosophical Investigations* (Oxford, 1953) for linguistic analysis; and Raymond Geuss's *The Idea of a Critical Theory* (Cambridge, 1981) for critical theory; Rorty's *Philosophy and the Mirror of Nature* (Princeton, 1979) for pragmatism: "edifying philosophers have to decry the very notion of having a view, while avoiding having a view about having views. This is an awkward, but not impossible position. Wittgenstein and Heidegger manage it fairly well" (p. 37).

2. Michel Foucault, *The Order of Things: An Archaeology of the Human Sciences* (New York: Vintage, 1973), pp. 313f.; H. L. Dreyfus and P. Rabinow, *Michel Foucault: Beyond Structuralism and Hermeneutics* (Chicago: University of

 Chicago Press, 1982), 26–32. *See also* Jacques Derrida, *Writing and Difference* (Chicago: 1978), 114: "This is why the modern philosophies which no longer seek to distinguish between thought and language, nor to place them in a hierarchy, are essentially philosophies of original finitude."

3. Edmund Husserl, *The Cartesian Meditations* (The Hague: Martinus Nijhoff, 1960), 72: "since every eidetic universality has the value of an unbreakable law, eidetic phenomenology explores the all-embracing laws that prescribe for every factual statement about something transcendental the possible sense (as opposed to the absurdity or inconsistency) of that statement."

4. Hardly a last effort in fact. We note the parallel effort of Leo Strauss in political philosophy, esp. in the title of a recent and posthumous collection of some of his essays, *Studies in Platonic Political Philosophy* (Chicago: University of Chicago Press, 1983).

5. Martin Heidegger, *Being and Time* (New York, 1962), 67: "The essence of Dasein lies in its existence" (author's italics).

6. Ibid., 436.

7. Werner Marx, *Heidegger and the Tradition* (Evanston: Northwestern University Press, 1971), 262: "The present treatise was guided by the fundamental conception that for Heidegger the sense of Being and of the essence of man is 'creative.'" Marx then cites his own pages 106ff., 139ff., 155f., 218f., 227f., and 237.

8. Vincent B. Leitch, *Deconstructive Criticism: An Advanced Introduction* (New York: Columbia University Press, 1983), 60–86 et passim.

9. Hans-Georg Gadamer, *Truth and Method* (New York, 1975), 433: "we have endeavored to liberate the mode of being of art and history, and the experience that corresponds to them, from the ontological prejudice that is contained in the ideal of scientific objectivity; and, in view of the experience of art and history, we were led to a universal hermeneutics that was concerned with the general relationship of man to the world." For Gadamer, the idea of a universal hermeneutics makes the world understandable; but he also argues that the finitude of *Dasein* is the very condition of intelligibility: "there is no possible consciousness, however infinite, in which the 'object' that is handed down would appear in the light of eternity. . . . The paradox . . . proves all interpretation to be, in fact, speculative" (p. 430).

10. Jean-Paul Sartre, *Critique de la Raison Dialectique, précédé de Question de Méthode*. Tome I: "*Théorie des Ensembles Pratiques* (Paris: Gallimard, 1960). *See also* Wilfrid Desan, *The Marxism of Jean-Paul Sartre* (New York: Anchor 1965), 235ff.

11. Michel Foucault, *The Archaeology of Knowledge and the Discourse of Language* (New York, 1972); Edward Said, *Orientalism* (New York, 1979), 3, 23; Derrida, *Writing and Difference*, p. 31f. "Cogito and the History of Madness," et passim.

12. Christopher Norris, *Deconstruction: Theory and Practice* (London: Methuen, 1982), 34.

13. Ibid., 39.

14. Ibid., 41.

15. Foucault, *The Archaeology of Knowledge*, 38, 114–7. "Behind the com-

pleted system, what is discovered by the analysis of formations is not the bubbling source of life itself, life in an as yet uncaptured state; it is an immense density of systematicities, a tight group of multiple relations" (p. 76). Yet, Foucault seems to take a position that is very close to that of Wittgenstein in some passages: "[discursive practice] is a body of anonymous, historical rules, always determined in the time and space that have defined a given period, and for a given social, economic, geographical, or linguistic area, the conditions of operation of the enunciative function." (p. 117). But, "Enunciative homogeneities (and heterogeneities) intersect with linguistic continuities (and changes), with logical identities (and differences) without any of them proceeding at the same pace or necessarily affecting one another" (p. 146).

16. Ibid., 186–87.

17. Ibid., 120.

18. Said, *Orientalism*, 11, 12.

19. Ibid., 6, 22, 25.

20. See Christopher Norris, *Deconstruction: Theory and Practice;* Jonathan Culler, *On Deconstruction: Theory and Criticism after Structuralism* (Ithaca, 1982); Leitch, *Deconstructive Criticism;* also, G. L. Bruns and M. Verdicchio reviewing Culler in *Diacritics* 14, no. 1 (Spring, 1984): 12–35.

21. Norris, *Deconstruction*, 88.

22. Said, *Orientalism*, 23 and 226ff., but the section entitled "Latent and Manifest Orientalism," beginning on p. 201, takes a quite different direction minimizing the significance of "the various stated views about Oriental society. . . . Whatever change occurs in knowledge of the Orient is found almost exclusively in manifest Orientalism; the unanimity, stability, and durability of latent Orientalism are more or less constant" (p. 206). "For de Man, however, the point is to recognize the fundamental urging of a rhetoric which nevertheless persists in the text when deconstruction has employed all the means at its disposal. . . . It is to this end of saving the text that de Man so carefully stakes out the limits of deconstruction and the gap that persists between the reductive grammar of tropes and the rhetoric of textual performance. . . . Derrida himself . . . gives little sign of accepting any such 'performative' check to the free play of deconstruction" (Norris, Deconstruction, p. 108). *See also* Culler, *On Deconstruction*, 180ff. Quoting Derrida, on p. 91, "The *Verbarium* shows how a sign, having become arbitrary, can remotivate itself. And into what labyrinth, what multiplicity of heterogeneous places, one must enter in order to track down the cryptic motivation ("Fors," pp. 70–71/114)." *See also* Leitch, *Deconstructive Criticism*, p. 102ff. "The random flights of signifiers across the textual surface, the disseminations of meaning, offer truth under one condition: that the chaotic processes of textuality be willfully regulated, controlled or stopped. Truth comes forth in the reifications, the personal pleasures, of reading. Truth is not an entity or property of the text. No text utters its truth; the truth lies elsewhere—in a reading. Constitutionally, reading is misreading. Deconstruction works to regulate controlled dissemination and celebrate misreading" (Leitch, p. 122). *See also* Foucault, *The Archaeology of Knowledge*, p. 68: "Lastly, this authority is characterized by the *possible positions of desire in relation to discourse.*"

23. Derrida, *Writing and Difference*, 76, 78, 108, 152–3

24. Muhammad ʿImara, *al-Islam wa 'l-Thawrah* (Beirut, 1980), 28.

25. E.g. H. A. R. Gibb, *Modern Trends in Islam* (Chicago: University of Chicago, 1947), 129. *See also* E. Said, *Orientalism*, 263.

26. J. Habermas, *Knowledge and Human Interests* (Boston: Beacon Press, 1972), 196ff.

27. Patricia Crone and Michael Cook, *Hagarism: The Making of the Islamic World* (Cambridge: Cambridge University Press, 1977), 134 and elsewhere, referring to "rabbinic Islam."

28. Fazlur Rahman, *Islam and Modernity: Transformation of an Intellectual Tradition* (Chicago: University of Chicago Press 1982), 17–22; Sayyid Qutb, *al-Taswir al-Fanni fi al-Qur'an* (Cairo, 1963), 26–32.

29. Said, *Orientalism*, 326. *See* Clifford Geertz, *Islam Observed: Religious Development in Morocco and Indonesia* (New Haven: Yale University Press, 1968).

30. Geertz, *Islam Observed*, 39.

31. Ibid., 97.

32. Ibid., 104 et passim.

33. Ibid., 29.

34. Ibid., 42–43.

35. Ibid., 53 et passim.

36. Ibid., 48.

37. Ibid., 105.

38. Ibid., 93, 131: where Geertz refers explicitly to one of Schutz's essays; but compare the discussion on p. 108 ("Worship and analysis are simply impossible to carry out together . . .") with Alfred Schutz, *The Phenomenology of the Social World* (Evanston: Northwestern University Press, 1967), 70.

39. Schutz, *Phenomenology*, 70.

40. Geertz, *Islam Observed*, 108.

41. Crone and Cook, *Hagarism*, 90–91.

42. Ibid., 132.

43. Marshall G. S. Hodgson, *The Venture of Islam: Conscience and History in a World Civilization*, vol. 1, *The Classical Age of Islam* (Chicago: University of Chicago Press, 1974).

44. Ibid., 71.

45. Edward W. Said, *Orientalism*, 326.

46. Foucault, *The Order of Things*, p. 365

47. Ibid., 340, 367.

48. Ibid., 373.

49. Habermas, *Knowledge and Human Interests* (Boston: Beacon Press, 1972), 212.

50. Foucault, *The Order of Things*, 377.

51. Ibid.

52. Michel Foucault, *The Archaeology of Knowledge*, tr. A. M. Sheridan Smith (New York: Harper Torchbooks, 1972).

53. Said, *Orientalism*, e.g., pp. 24, 201, 327.

54. Ibid., 202, 261.

55. Ibid., 326.

56. Michel Foucault, *The History of Sexuality,* vol. 1, *An Introduction,* tr. Robert Hurley (New York: Vintage Books, 1980).

57. Said, *Orientalism,* 301.

58. Ibid., 25.

59. Ibid., 24, 215, 299.

60. Alexandre Kojève, *Introduction to the Reading of Hegel,* ed. Allan Bloom, trans. J. H. Nichols, Jr. (New York: Basic Books, 1969), 212f., n.15.

61. Steven B. Smith, *Reading Althusser: An Essay on Structural Marxism* (Ithaca, N.Y.: Cornell University Press, 1984), 202.

62. Ibid., 56–58; Kojève, *Introduction,* 157–62.

63. Claude Lévi-Strauss, *Structural Anthropology,* trans. C. Jacobson and B. G. Schoepf (New York: Basic Books, 1963), 24.

64. Ted Benton, *The Rise and Fall of Structural Marxism: Althusser and His Influence* (London: Macmillan, 1984), 58–61, quoting *The German Ideology,* p. 122.

65. Michel Foucault, "The Subject and Power," afterword to Dreyfus and Rabinow, *Michel Foucault,* 216.

66. Jacques Derrida, *Writing and Difference,* tr., with an introduction and additional notes by Alan Bass (Chicago: University of Chicago Press 1978), 79.

67. Ibid., 105.

68. Ibid., 153.

69. Ibid., 130.

4

1. Albert Hourani, *Arabic Thought in the Liberal Age* (London: Oxford University Press, 1962), 190.

2. Ibid., 184–92.

3. Muhammad ʿImara, *al-Islam wa-usul al-hukm li-ʿAli ʿAbd al-Raziq* (Beirut, 1972), 92.

4. Ibid., 93.

5. Muhsin Mahdi, *Ibn Khaldun's Philosophy of History* (London: Allen and Unwin, 1957), 247–48.

6. Ibid., 238.

7. Ibid., 239, n. 1.

8. Ibn Khaldun, *The Muqaddimah,* tr. by Franz Rosenthal. vol.3, 2d ed. (Princeton: Princeton University Press, 1967), 428.

9. Ibid., 414–15.

10. Ibid., 427.

11. Ibid., 399.

12. Ibid., 416–17.

13. ʿImara, *al-Islam,* 116–17.

14. Ibid., 119.

15. Ibid., 120.

16. Ibid., p. 117.

17. F. Dieterici, ed., *Alfarabi's Abhandlung der Musterstaat,* [*Ara ahl al-madina al-fadila*] (Leiden, E. J. Brill 1964), 59.

18. Mahdi, *Ibn Khaldun's Philosophy of History,* 284, n. 3.

19. ʿImara, *al-Islam,* 121.

20. Abu Mansur ʿAbd al-Qahir Ibn Tahir al-Tamimi al-Baghdadi, *Usul al-din,* (Istanbul: Government Press, 1928), 281–82.

21. ʿImara, *al-Islam,* 123.

22. Ibid., 123.

23. Ibid., 125.

24. Ibid., 130.

25. Ibid., 135.

26. Ibid., 130.

27. Ibid., 146.

28. Ibid., 149.

29. Ibid., 155.

30. Ibid., 165.

31. Ibid., 170–71.

32. Ibid., 174–75.

33. Ibid., 62.

34. Ibid., 65.

35. Ibid., 66.

36. Ibid., 71–72.

37. Ibid., 34.

38. Ibid., 32.

39. Ibid.

40. Ibid., 34–35.

41. Ibid., 46.

42. Ibid., 49.

43. Ibid., 50.

44. *See* L. Binder, "Definitions of the Political Community in Islam," in *Governing Peoples and Territories,* D. J. Elazar, ed. (Philadelphia: Institute for the Study of Human Issues 1982), 33–46, for an alternative approach.

45. Muhammad Zìa al-Rayyis, *al-Islam w 'al-khilafa fi al-ʿasr al-hadith: Naqd kitab al-Islam wa-Usul al-Hukm,* (Cairo: Maktabat Dar al-Turath, 1972 [?]).

46. Thomas W. Arnold, *The Caliphate* (Oxford: Clarendon Press, 1924).

47. D. S. Margoliouth, *Mohammedanism* (London: Williams and Norgate, Home University Library of Modern Knowledge, n.d. [1911?]).

48. al-Rayyis, *al-Islam w 'al-Khilafa fi al-ʿasr hadith,* 230.

49. Ibid., 234.

50. Khalid Muhammad Khalid, *al-Dawla fi 'l-Islam* (Cairo: Dar al-Thabit, 1981), 104.

51. Emmanuel Sivan, *Radical Islam: Medieval Theology and Modern Politics* (New Haven: Yale University Press, 1985), 132.

52. Khalid, *al-Dawla fi 'l-Islam,* 71

53. Ibid., 36.

54. Ibid., 23.

55. Ibid., 28, 60.

56. Ibid., 70; Sivan, *Radical Islam,* 103; Gilles Kepel, *Le prophete et pharaon: les mouvements islamistes dan l'Egypte contemporaine* (Paris: La Decouverte, 1984), 184.

57. Khalid, *al-Dawla fi 'l-Islam,* 57

58. Ibid., 13–16.

59. Mohammed Arkoun, *Pour une critique de la raison islamique* (Paris: Maisonneuve et LaRose, 1984), 28.

60. Ibid., 10.

61. Mohammed Arkoun, *La pensée arabe,* 2d ed. (Paris: PUF, 1979). Chapter 1, "Le fait coranique," pp. 5f.

62. Mohammed Arkoun, *Essais sur la pensée islamique,* 3d. ed. (Paris: Maisonneuve et LaRose, 1984), 191.

63. Arkoun, *Pour une critique,* 162f.

64. Ibid., 38.

65. Arkoun, *La pensée arabe*, 48.

66. Ibid., 51–52.

67. Arkoun, *Pour une critique*, 18–21.

68. Arkoun, *Essais*, p. 189 and the accompanying note referring to the use of the term by Derrida in his *De la grammatologie*.

69. Arkoun, *Pour une critique*, "Comment étudier la pensé islamique," 7–38.

70. Ibid., 15.

71. Ibid., 32.

72. Ibid.

73. Ibid., 169.

74. For a detailed, if somewhat polemical, discussion that contradicts the conclusions of Khomeini, see J. Eliash, "Misconceptions Regarding the Juridical Status of the Iranian 'Ulama,'" *International Journal of Middle East Studies*, 10, no. 1 (February 1979): 9–25.

75. Arkoun, *Pour une critique*, 181.

76. Ibid.

77. *Islam and Revolution, Writings and Declarations of Imam Khomeini*, tr. and annotated by Hamid Algar (Berkeley: Mizan Press, 1981), esp. pp. 40–125

5

1. *Les Frères Musulmans (1928–1982)*, présenté par Olivier Carré et Gérard Michaud, (Paris(?): Gallimard/Julliard, Collection Archives, 1983), 91–92, 227, n. 10; Ahmed M. Gomaa, "Islamic Fundamentalism in Egypt during the 1930's and 1970's: Comparative Notes," in *Islam, Nationalism and Radicalism in Egypt and the Sudan*, G. R. Warburg, and U. M. Kupferschmidt, eds. (New York: Praeger, 1983), 149; Yvonne Yazbeck Haddad, "Sayyid Qutb: Ideologue of Islamic Revival," in *Voices of Resurgent Islam*, J. L. Esposito, ed. (New York: Oxford University Press, 1983), 85, 89; Haddad, "The Qur'anic Justification for an Islamic Revolution: The View of Sayyid Qutb," *The Middle East Journal* 37, no. 1 (Winter 1983): 26–27.

2. Carré, *Les Frères Musulmans*, 99; Haddad, "The Qur'anic Justification," 26–27; Fouad Ajami, "In the Pharaoh's Shadow: Religion and Authority in Egypt," in *Islam in the Political Process*, James Piscatori, ed. (Cambridge: Cambridge University Press, 1983), 27.

3. Haddad, "Sayyid Qutb," 81.

4. Saad Eddin Ibrahim, "Anatomy of Egypt's Militant Islamic Groups: Methodological Note and Preliminary Findings," *International Journal of Middle East Studies* 12, no. 4 (December 1980): 423–53, includes a discussion of social origins.

5. Gomaa, "Islamic Fundamentalism, 155; Carré, "Les Frères Musulmans," 98–106.

6. Hanafi, "The Relevance of the Islamic Alternative," 60–61.

7. Gomaa, "Islamic Fundamentalism," 154.

8. Carré, "Les Frères Musulmans," 113, 122; Gomaa, "Islamic Fundamentalism," 155.

9. Saad Eddin Ibrahim, "Anatomy," 441f.

10. Gomaa, "Islamic Fundamentalism," 149.

11. ʿAbd al-Moneim Said Aly, and Manfred Wenner, "Modern Islamic Reform Movements: The Muslim Brotherhood in Contemporary Egypt," *The Middle East Journal* 36, no. 3 (Summer 1982): 336–61. *See also* Carré, "Les Frères Musulmans," 99.

12. Said Aly and Wenner, "Modern Islamic Reform Movements," 352.

13. Saad Eddin Ibrahim, "Anatomy," 435.

14. Said Aly and Wenner, "Modern Islamic Reform Movements," 350; Saad Eddin Ibrahim, "An Islamic Alternative in Egypt: The Muslim Brotherhood and Sadat," *Arab Studies Quarterly* 4, nos. 1 and 2 (Spring 1982): 81.

15. E.g., Muhammad al-Ghazzali, *Mi'ah Su'al ʿan al-Islam* (Cairo: Dar Thabit, 1983).

16. Saad Eddin Ibrahim, "Anatomy," 434f.; Nazih N. M. Ayubi, "The Political Revival of Islam: The Case of Egypt," *International Journal of Middle Eastern Studies* 12, no. 4 (December 1980): 491f.; Carré, *Les Frères Musulmans,* 114f.

17. Sayed Kotb, *Social Justice in Islam,* tr. John B. Hardie (Washington, D.C.: American Council of Learned Societies, 1953); *see* Hanafi, "The Relevance of the Islamic Alternative," 60.

18. Sayyid Qutb, *Ma'alim fi al-Tariq* (Beirut(?): Dar al-Shuruq, n.d.). *See* Haddad, "Sayyid Qutb," 94–95, nn. 1 and 3, and idem, *Contemporary Islam and the Challenge of History* (Albany: SUNY, 1982), 225 n. 1.

19. See above, note 4. On Mawdudi, see Charles J. Adams, "Mawdudi and the Islamic State," in Esposito, *Voices,* 99f. *See also* Khurshid Ahmad, and Zafar Ishaq Ansari, eds., *Islamic Perspectives* (London: Islamic Foundation, 1979); W. C. Smith, *Modern Islam in India: A Social Analysis* (London: Gollancz, 1946); and L. Binder, *Religion and Politics in Pakistan* (Berkeley: University of California Press, 1961), 78f.

20. Muhammad *ʿAbd al-Salam Faraj, Al-Farida al-Gha'iba,* reprinted in *al-Ahrar* (weekly newspaper), 14 December 1981.

21. Hanafi, "The Relevance of the Islamic Alternative," 60; and Carré, *Les Frères Musulmans,* 227, where he refers to another paper by Hanafi. Note also Ajami's criticism, "In the Pharaoh's Shadow," 28.

22. Abu al-ʿAla al-Mawdudi, *al-Hukuma al-Islamiyya,* tr. Ahmad Idris, al-Mukhtar al-Islami, Cairo, 2d ed. (1980?), 100–101.

23. On the concept "Hakimiyya," see Gomaa, "Islamic Fundamentalism," 150; and Haddad, "Sayyid Qutb," 89.

24. *Ma'alim,* 24.

25. Ibid., 8.

26. Ibid., 24–25.

27. Ibid., 149.

28. Ibid., 8.

29. Ibid., 107–8.

30. Ibid., 118.

31. Ibid., 136–40.

32. See Haddad, "Sayyid Qutb," 85, on Jahiliyya. *See also* Mahdi Fazlallah, *Maʿa Sayyid Qutb fi Fikrihi al-Siyasi w'al-Dini* (Beirut: Mu'assasat al-

Risalah, 1978), 129, where he argues that Qutb's use of the term is influenced by the work of Abu al-Hasan al-Nadwi. *See also* Gomaa, "Islamic Fundamentalism," 153.

33. *Ma'alim*, 5, 15, 37, 38, 61f., 84, 95, etc.

34. *Ibid.*, 50, 61, 100, 117, 118, etc.

35. Fazlallah, *Maʿa Sayyid Qutb*, p. 71f; Qutb, *Ma'alim*, 5, 40, 134, etc.

36. *Ma'alim*, pp. 18–19.

37. Ibid., 37.

38. Ibid., 47–48.

39. In his *Khasa'is al-Tasawwur al-Islami wa-Muqawwimatuhu*, Qutb explicitly attacks ancient Greek dualism and its influence upon Western thought as well as upon Islamic philosophy. He juxtaposes a nonmetaphysical Islamic monism (tawhid) to this "alien" dualism. Volume I, 1st edition, (n.p., Dar Ihya al-Kutub al-ʿArabiyya, 1962) pp. 12f.

40. *Ma'alim*, pp. 51, 113.

41. Ibid., 88, 93.

42. Mawdudi, *al-Hukuma*, discusses Jihad on pp. 32f.; Haddad, "Sayyid Qutb," 83; see also Mawdudi, *al-Jihad fi Sabil Allah*, tr. from Urdu to Arabic by Mas'ud al-Nadwi, published by Lajnat al-Shabab al-Muslim, printed in Cairo, n.d.

43. Mawdudi, *al-Hukuma*, 27; Qutb, *Ma'alim*, 91.

44. *Ma'alim*, 82.

45. Ibid., 81.

46. Ibid., 61.

47. Ahmad and Ansari, *Islamic Perspectives*, 374f.; *Ma'alim*, 86.

48. *Ma'alim*, 86.

49. Ibid., 117.

50. Ibid., 117–8.

51. *Al-Farida al-Gha'iba*.

52. Sura al-Ma'ida, verses 43, 44, 46.

53. Salim Ali al-Bahansawi, *al Hukm wa-Qadiyya Takfir al-Muslimin* (Cairo: Dar al-Ansar, 1977); Dr. Mustafa Hilmi, *al-Khawarij, al-Usul al-Tarikhiyya li-Mas'alat Takfir al-Muslim*, (Cairo: Dar al-Ansar, 1977.)

54. Binder, *Religion and Politics*, 259f.

55. Sayed Kotb, *Social Justice in Islam*, (Washington, D. C., American Council of Learned Societies, 1953) (Tr. John B. Hardie).

56. Ibid., 175.

57. Ibid., 177.

58. Ibid., 193.

59. Ibid., 235.

60. Ibid., 241.

61. Ibid., 139–40.

62. Ibid., 253.

63. Ibid., 256.

64. *Ibid.*, 251; *see also* Ahmad and Ansari, *Islamic Perspectives*, 374f., on Mawdudi's differentiation between Tajdid and Tajaddud.

65. *Ma'alim*, 10.

66. Sayyid Qutb, *al-Taswir al-Fanni fi al-Qur'an*, (Cairo: Dar al-Maʿarif, 1963); Fazlallah, *Maʿa Sayyid Qutb*, 57.

67. Ibid., 9.

68. Fazlallah, *Maʿa Sayyid Qutb*, 49–50. He visited the United States in 1949 and joined the Ikhwan in 1951.

69. Nadav Safran, *Egypt in Search of Political Community* (Cambridge, Mass.: Harvard University Press, 1961), 181f.

70. Fazlallah, *Maʿa Sayyid Qutb*, 49.

71. *See* Haddad, *Contemporary Islam*, 46f.

72. Safran, *Egypt in Search*, 153f.

73. Fazlallah, *Maʿa Sayyid Qutb*, 51, argues that, while in the United States, Qutb altered his earlier views regarding the relative independence of fine arts from religion, and that he abandoned literature (*al-adab*) completely after he joined the Ikhwan in 1951. Fazlallah also discusses Qutb's early involvement in a controversy over the miraculousness of the Qur'an in which he sided with his mentor al-ʿAqqad against Mustafa Sadiq al-Rafiʿi. Al-ʿAqqad denied this miraculousness. "It reached the point where Mahmud Muhammad Shakir entered the fray regarding the position of Sayyid [Qutb] saying, 'Sayyid's critique of Rafiʿi's literary position indicates his alienation from religion and piety and shame . . . ' But as for us, we are inclined to believe that for Sayyid Qutb it was not a question of religion or no religion, it was rather a question of the difference between two schools: 'the school of the intellect' represented by Rafiʿi and the 'school of the heart' represented by al-ʿAqqad" (pp. 47–48).

74. *Taswir*, 5.

75. Ibid., 8.

76. Ibid., 9–10.

77. Ibid., 32–33.

78. Ibid., 23.

79. M. Heidegger, *Nietzsche*, vol. 1, "The Will to Power as Art" (New York: Harper and Row, 1979), 108.

80. *Taswir*, 32.

81. Ibid., 26–32.

82. Haddad, *Contemporary Islam*, 226, n. 1, and following pages where she discusses some passages from Qutb's tafsir. Haddad's is the only work I know of that reflects study of this massive work, but it offers no evidence of a persistent aesthetic theme.

83. *Taswir*, 11f., 19. [The magic] cannot but be located in the essence of the Qur'anic system itself, and not alone in the subject discussed"; *Khasa'is*, 50 *et passim*.

84. Haddad, *Contemporary Islam*, 226.

85. See note 39.

86. *Taswir*, 34.

87. Ibid., 58.

88. Ibid., 195.

89. Ibid.

90. Alfred Schutz, *The Phenomenology of the Social World* (Evanston: Northwestern University Press, 1967), 45.

91. Heidegger, *Nietzsche*, 34, and esp. 19: ". . . Nietzsche says the following, 'Recapitulation: To stamp Becoming with the character of Being—that is the supreme will to power. This suggests that Becoming only *is* if it is grounded in Being as being.'"

92. Haddad, "Sayyid Qutb," 73–77 discusses the *Khasa'is*.

93. *Khasa'is*, 50.

94. Ibid., 15.

95. Ibid., 17.

96. Muhammad Iqbal, *The Reconstruction of Religious Thought in Islam*, Lahore, 1968.

97. *Khasa'is*, 15; *See* M. Foucault, *The Archaeology of Knowledge* (New York: Harper Torchbooks, 1972), 38, 120.

98. Heidegger, *Nietzsche*, 97–98: "But from the passage in *Twilight of the Idols* we gather that rapture is the basic aesthetic state without qualification . . . it can no longer be a matter simply of unraveling Nietzsche's doctrine of art from the opposition of the Apollonian and the Dionysian"; and page 105: ". . . it is questionable whether the essence of art is thereby defined in terms of art, or whether it isn't rather defined as a mode of the Being of beings."

99. *Ma'alim*, 97–99.

100. Ibid., 97ff., and esp. 100.

101. Edmund Husserl, *The Crisis of European Sciences and Transcendental Phenomenology*, trans. David Carr, (Evanston: Northwestern University Press, 1970), 103f.

102. *Ma'alim*, pp. 43–44. Compare Alfred North Whitehead, *Process and Reality* (New York: The Free Press, [copyright 1929] 1969), 243–44: "Concrescence is the name for the process in which the universe of many things acquires an individual unity. . . . An instance of concrescence is termed an 'actual entity'—or, equivalently, an 'actual occasion' . . . an actual occasion is a concrescence effected by a process of feelings." The similarity in usage is astonishing and justifies translating tajammuʿa as concrescence.

103. *Ma'alim*, 80. Here *manhaj* is probably best translated as process in Whitehead's terms. Haddad, "Sayyid Qutb," 90, suggests both method and process as alternatives. In other places, manhaj seems to stand for the moral action which follows from Islamic consciousness.

104. Translation of E. H. Palmer, *The Koran* (London: Oxford University Press, 1953; first published 1900), 522.

105. *Ma'alim*, pp. 173f.

106. Ibid., 181.

107. Ibid., 174.

108. Edward Said, *Orientalism*, (New York: Vintage Books, 1979), 268–72, discussing Massignon on al-Hallaj.

109. *Ma'alim*, 148.

110. E.g. ibid., 37, 41 *et passim*.

111. Ibid., 93f.

112. *Khasa'is*, 16.

113. *Ma'alim*, 93 and 183.

114. Ibid., 148.

115. Heidegger, *Nietzsche*, 161.

116. *Ma'alim*, 18. *See also* 181.

6

1. Maxime Rodinson, *Islam and Capitalism,* trans. Brian Pearce (Austin: University of Texas Press, 1978). Originally published in France as *Islam et le capitalisme* (Paris: Editions du Seuil, 1966).

2. Ibid., 5, 10, 211.

3. Ibid., 214.

4. Ibid., 136, 184.

5. Samir Amin, *The Arab Nation: Nationalism and Class Struggle,* trans. Michael Pallis, (London: Zed Press, 1978), 111.

6. Ibid., 67–68.

7. Peter Gran, *Islamic Roots of Capitalism: Egypt 1760–1840* (Austin: University of Texas Press, 1979). *See also* the exchange between Gran and F. de Jong, *International Journal of Middle East Studies* 14, no. 3 (August 1982): 381–400.

8. Amin, *The Arab Nation,* 19; Gran, "Political Economy as a Paradigm for the Study of Islamic History," *International Journal of Middle East Studies* 11, no. 4 (July 1980): 523.

9. Rodinson, *Islam and Capitalism,* 1.

10. Ibid., 222f.

11. Ibid., 136, 165.

12. Ibid., 121.

13. Ibid., 136–37.

14. Ibid.

15. Brian Turner, *Weber and Islam,* (London: Routledge & Kegan Paul, 1974); Idem, *Marxism and the End of Orientalism,* (London: George Allen and Unwin, 1978).

16. Edward W. Said, *Orientalism* (New York: Vintage Books, 1979), 326, 335, 350.

17. Amin, *The Arab Nation,* 87.

18. *See* Walter L. Adamson, *Hegemony and Revolution* (Berkeley: University of California Press, 1980) 169f.

19. Alfred Schutz, *The Phenomenology of the Social World* (Evanston: Northwestern University Press, 1967), chap. 1.

20. Ibid., 223–41.

21. Turner, *Weber and Islam,* 20.

22. Ibid.

23. Ibid., 137f.

24. Ibid., 54.

25. Turner, *Marxism and the End of Orientalism,* 67.

26. Amin, *The Arab Nation,* 114.

27. Gran, *Islamic Roots,* 33.

7

1. Tariq al-Bishri, *al-Harakah al-Siyasiyah fi Masr, 1945–1952* (Cairo: al-Haya al-Misriya lil-kitab, 1972); Idem, *al-Muslimun wal-Aqbat fi Itar al-Jamaʿa*

al-Wataniyya (Muslims and Copts in the framework of a national society) (Cairo: al-Haya al-Misriyya lil-kitab, 1980).

2. al-Bishri, *al-Muslimun wal-Aqbat*, 6.
3. Ibid., esp. his concluding sections, 685ff.
4. Al-Bishri, *al-Harakah*, 535.
5. Ibid., 9.
6. Ibid., 182.
7. Ibid., 30.
8. Ibid., 183.
9. Ibid., 185.
10. Ibid., 196.
11. Ibid., 223.
12. Ibid., 217, 219.
13. Ibid., 34.
14. Ibid., 35.
15. Ibid., 30.
16. Ibid., 33.
17. Ibid., 34.
18. Ibid., 39.
19. Ibid., 157, 217.
20. Ibid., 538, 553.
21. Ibid., 526
22. Ibid.: see p. 373 where al-Bishri appears to be fairly sympathetic.
23. Ibid., 45.
24. Ibid., 65–67, 373.
25. Ibid., 59, 61–63, 70–74, 367.
26. Ibid., 65.
27. Ibid., 52, 55.
28. Ibid., 53.
29. Ibid., 49, 61–62, 65.
30. Ibid., 48–49.
31. Ibid., 65–67.
32. Ibid., 69.
33. Ibid., 73.
34. Ibid., 72.
35. Ibid., 373.
36. Ibid., 378.
37. Ibid., 420.
38. Ibid., 420, 422, 424.
39. Ibid., 428.
40. Ibid., 434.
41. Ibid.
42. Ibid., 407.
43. Ibid., 454.
44. Ibid., 413.
45. Ibid., 415.
46. Ibid., 408–9.
47. Ibid., 410.
48. Ibid., 532–33.
49. Al-Bishri, *al-Muslimun wal-Aqbat*, 3.
50. Ibid., 4.
51. Ibid., 305f; *see also* Muhammad ʿImara, *al-Islam wa-usul al-hukm liʿAli ʿAbd al-Raziq* (Beirut, 1972).
52. Al-Bishri, *al-Muslimun wal-Aqbat*, 305–23.
53. Ibid., 5.
54. Ibid., 473.
55. Ibid., 517ff.
56. Ibid., 537.
57. Ibid., 534.
58. Ibid., 524.
59. Ibid.
60. Ibid., 532, 537–38, and 541.
61. Ibid., 502.
62. Ibid., 500.
63. Ibid., 506–7.
64. Ibid., 508.
65. Ibid., 507.
66. Ibid., 509, 515.
67. Ibid., 505–6.
68. Ibid., 675–77.
69. Ibid., 687.
70. Ibid., 688–89.
71. Ibid., 689.
72. Ibid., 692.
73. "Al-Fikr al-Siyasi al-Arabi wal-Fikr al-Siyasi al-Muʿasir, II" (Arab political thought and contemporary political thought) *al-Fikr al-ʿArabi* (Beirut) 3, no. 23 (November 1981).
74. Ibid., 442.

75. Ishkaliyya al-ʿUlum al-Ijtimaʿiyya fi al-Watan al-ʿArabi (National Center for Sociological and Criminological Research) Mimeo; al-Bishri's paper was titled "Nahnu . . . bayna al-Mawruth wal-Wafid," (We . . . between the tradition the imported), 390f. See also *al-Ahali* (7 June 1983): 7.

76. Ibid., 393.

77. Al-Bishri, *al-Muslimun wal-Aqbat*, 6, 702f.

78. Ibid., 692–93.

79. Ibid., 693–96.

80. Literally, the people of loosing and binding, i.e., the political elite.

81. Al-Bishri, *al-Muslimun wal-Aqbat*, 712.

82. W. C. Smith, *Modern Islam in India*, 2d ed. (London: 1946).

83. Al-Bishri, "Nahnu," Symposium paper, "Problematic Character . . ." p. 400.

8

1. The terminology is that of Martin Heidegger, *Being and Time* (New York, 1962).

2. Hans-Georg Gadamer, *Truth and Method* (New York: The Seabury Press, 1975), e.g., p. 333.

3. Quoted in Richard E. Palmer, *Hermeneutics, Interpretation Theory in Schleiermacher, Dilthey, Heidegger, and Gadamer* (Evanston: Northwestern University Press, 1969), 6.

4. Gadamer, *Truth and Method*, 476.

5. Ibid., 323–24.

6. Ibid., 329.

7. Zaki Najib Mahmud, *Tajdid al-Fikr al-ʿArabi* (Beirut: Dar al-Shuruq, 1971).

8. Ibid., 11–12.

9. Ibid., 43.

10. Ibid., 16–18.

11. Ibid., 19–20.

12. Ibid., 20–26.

13. Ibid., 118f.

14. Ibid., 145f.

15. Ibid., 241.

16. Ibid., 384.

17. Ibid., 328.

18. Ibid., 330–40.

19. Ibid., 76–77.

20. Ibid., 78–82.

21. Ibid., 173ff.

22. Ibid., 227.

23. Ibid., 238.

24. Ibid., 233.

25. Ibid., 218.

26. Ibid., 242–45.

27. Ibid., 247.

28. Ibid., 248.

29. Ibid., 249.

30. Ibid., 274.

31. Ibid., 278.

32. Ibid.

33. Ibid., 279.

34. Ibid., 282.

35. Ibid., 288.

36. Ibid., 302.

37. Ibid., 298.

38. Ibid., 303–17.

39. Ibid., 306.

40. Ibid., 316.

41. Ibid., 317.

42. Ibid., 318–21.

43. Ibid., 322.

44. Ibid., 344–45.

45. Ibid., 349.

46. Ibid., 380.

47. Ibid., 384.

48. Ibid.
49. Ibid., 385.
50. Tarif al-Khalidi, "Nahnu Thalath Qaba'il . . ." (We are three tribes: Islamic, Arab and Marxist; and every generation is equally distant from God in its worldliness) *al-Nahar al-ᶜArabi wal-Duwwali* (Beirut) 19 August 1978.
51. Tarif al-Khalidi, *Dirasat fi Tarikh al-Fikr al-ᶜArabi al-Islami* (Studies in Arab-Islamic intellectual history) 2d printing (Beirut: Dar al-Taliᶜa, 1979), 12.
52. Khalidi, *Dirasat*, 38–39.
53. Said, *Orientalism*, 297–98.
54. Abdallah Laroui, *The Crisis of the Arab Intellectual: Traditionalism or Historicism*, trans. Diarmid Cammel (Berkeley: University of California Press, 1976), 21.
55. Laroui, *The Crisis*, 24f., 61 note 18; Abdallah Laroui, *L'idéologie arabe contemporaine* (Paris: François Maspero, 1967), 95; H. A. R. Gibb, *Modern Trends in Islam*, (Chicago: University of Chicago, 1950), 126f.; Gustave E. von Grunebaum, *Modern Islam: The Search for Cultural Identity* (Berkeley: University of California, 1962), 108; Qustantin Zurayq, *Nahnu wal-Tarikh* (Beirut, 1959).
56. Laroui, *The Crisis*, 44–80.
57. Ibid., 79 n. 49
58. Ibid., 126.
59. Ibid., 125.
60. Ibid., 135.
61. Laroui, *L'idéologie arabe contemporaine: Essai critique* (Paris: Maspero 1967).
62. Ibid., 164.
63. Theodor W. Adorno, *The Jargon of Authenticity* (Evanston: Northwestern University Press, 1973).
64. Laroui, *l'idéologie*, 168.
65. Ibid., 9.
66. Ibid.
67. Ibid., 150f.
68. Ibid., 134 n. 19.
69. Nicos Poulantzas, *Political Power and Social Classes* (London: NLB 1975), 141.
70. Laroui, *l'idéologie*, 157.
71. Ibid., 140, 151–55.
72. Ibid., 169.
73. Ibid., 157.
74. Ibid., 158.
75. Ibid., 163.
76. Ibid., 167.
77. Ibid., 174.
78. Ibid., 181.
79. Ibid., "C'est en effet Salâma Mûsa qu'il décrit sous le nom de Adlî Karîm, le directeur de revue, courageux et solitaire, maître à penser de la jeunesse progressiste" (Ibid., 182).
80. Ibid., 186.
81. Ibid., 188.
82. Ibid., 194.
83. Ibid., 197.
84. Ibid., 198.
85. Ibid., 203.
86. Ibid., 205.
87. Ibid., 207.
88. Ibid., 209.

89. Ibid., 212.
90. Ibid., 214.

9

1. Bizhan Jazani, *Capitalism and Revolution in Iran* (London: Zed Press, 1980).

Name Index

Historical figures generally known by their first name only are indexed under that first name. Certain political figures are indexed under the most well known element of their name. All others are indexed by the equivalent of their last name. In Arabic names the letter *ʿain* is disregarded in indexing. In modern names the element following the article *al* is considered the last name for indexing purposes except for names beginning with *Abd*.

Subject Index